BASEBALL TEAM COLLECTIBLES

A WALLACE-HOMESTEAD PRICE GUIDE

Baseball Team Collectibles

DON BEVANS ■ RON MENCHINE

Wallace-Homestead Book Company

Radnor, Pennsylvania

Designed by Arlene Putterman
Manufactured in the United States of America

Library of Congress Cataloging in Publication Data
Bevans, Don.
Baseball team collectibles / Don Bevans, Ron Menchine.
p.   cm.
Includes index.
ISBN 0-87069-679-3
1. Baseball—Collectibles—Prices—United States.
2. Baseball teams—United States—History.
I. Menchine, Ron, 1934– .
II. Title.
GV875.2.B48   1994
796.357′0973—dc20
93-32118
CIP

1 2 3 4 5 6 7 8 9 0   3 2 1 0 9 8 7 6 5 4

We gratefully dedicate this book to
Pat Bevans and **Mildred Menchine.**
Their hard work, patience, and understanding
played a major role in the completion
of this work.

CONTENTS

PREFACE

In the field of baseball memorabilia, pricing is the biggest variable. For example, at the 1992 Atlantic City Atlantique antiques show, an advertising postcard for Masterpiece Jockey Club cigars featuring the 1908 Pittsburgh Pirates and its Hall of Fame shortstop Honus Wagner sold for $1200. A year later an identical postcard in similar excellent condition sold at auction for $191. Obviously, the true value of the postcard lies somewhere in between. Auction prices also can be very misleading whenever collectors get caught in the bidding frenzy and pay well above a realistic value for a particular item.

Collectors trying to complete a set may also pay an inflated price at auction, simply to fill in the missing piece. Decide beforehand the maximum you are willing to pay and do not exceed that figure. *Remember: No matter how rare a particular item is, there is nearly always more than one available.* You may feel euphoric when a long-awaited treasure becomes part of your collection, but the joy of obtaining it frequently dissipates if you wind up paying more than you were willing to spend and more than the item realistically is worth. It is imperative that you control your hobby and not let your hobby control you.

Those who collect baseball memorabilia or any other collectible should do so, ideally, for the pure enjoyment. If you collect only because you think values of your collectibles will increase, you will experience a rude awakening if values decrease. By collecting for the pure enjoyment, you will be happy no matter what happens in the marketplace. Should your collection increase in value, as happens in most cases, you will be that much better off.

Because of the immense popularity of baseball memorabilia, a proliferation of collector issues has flooded the market. Plates, statues, trinkets and baseball-related junk of every description is appearing in the marketplace. Some are quite well done but cannot be considered true baseball memorabilia and will not be included in this price guide. For example, an item related to a team or player must be manufactured during that team's or player's era. The only exceptions would be advertising items that recount past achievements of a team or player or items produced under the auspices of a particular team to commemorate that team or its players' past glory. Any item associated with Babe Ruth manufactured during his career or at the time of his death, for example, would be legitimate memorabilia. Something produced only for the collector market years after his death would not be considered legitimate. The same applies to manufactured collectibles for a particular player long after his career is over. Some items may be attractive, but they definitely are not authentic baseball memorabilia.

ACKNOWLEDGMENTS

In order to reach a consensus on the fair market value of items listed in this price guide, we have assembled an outstanding group of baseball memorabilia experts throughout the United States. All have been involved in collecting or dealing in baseball memorabilia for a minimum of 10 years, and some have been associated with the hobby for half a century. They include accountants, corporate executives, engineers, judges, lawyers, memorabilia dealers, military retirees, sportscasters, and sports writers, to mention only a few. All have generously shared their tremendous knowledge of baseball memorabilia to help make this price guide a reality. In order to protect the privacy of some individual collectors, we have listed only their names. Addresses are listed for those dealers and collectors who welcome any inquiries regarding the buying and selling of baseball memorabilia. We are extremely proud of this group of experts and thank them for their enormous contributions to this work.

Mel Bailey
2886 Sandberg St.
Riverside, CA 92506

Don Bevans
2920 E. Baltimore St.
Baltimore, MD 21224

G.R. Blank
22 Twix Hill Rd.
Ridgefield, CT 06877

Joe Bosley
The Old Ball Game
100 Old Westminster Pike
Reisterstown, MD 21136

Elias Dudash
Mt. Pocono, PA 18344

Patrick Flynn
MinneMemories
108 Warren St.
Mankato, MN 56001

Brian Gettings
8331 Queen Elizabeth Blvd.
Annandale, VA 22003

Ted Hake
P.O. Box 1444
York, PA 17405
717-848-1333

Paul Hass
Sports Books, Etc.
5224 Port Royal Rd.
Springfield, VA 22151
703-321-8660

Jerry Hermele

Paul Jarrell
1800 Crumbley Rd.
McDonough, GA 30253

Mike Jaspersen

Blair Jett
Cottage Antiques
8181 Main St.
Ellicott City, MD 21043
410-465-1412

Gordon Kramp

Ron Menchine
P.O. Box 1
Long Green, MD 21092
410-592-7152

Andy Moursund
Georgetown Book Shop
77770 Woodmont Ave.
Bethesda, MD 20814
301-907-6923

Frank Nagy

Roy Nelson

Don Ortolani

Ted Patterson
WPOC Radio
Rotunda Bldg.
Baltimore, MD 21211
410-366-3693

Pat Quinn
Sports Collectors Store
1040 S. LaGrange Rd.
LaGrange, IL 60525
708-354-7970

Harry L. Rinker
Rinker Enterprises, Inc.
5093 Vera Cruz Rd.
Emmaus, PA 18049
215-965-1122

Robert E. Schmierer
EPSCC
P.O. Box 3037
Maple Glen, PA 19002

John Sullivan
3748 N. Damen
Chicago, IL 60618

Russ White
Orlando Sentinel
Orlando, FL

Charles S. Winner

Phil Wood
P.O. Box 204
Reisterstown, MD 21136

In addition to our Board of Memorabilia Experts, the following have provided us with valuable information and advice which we greatly appreciate and acknowledge: Bob Brown & Rick Vaughn, Baltimore Orioles; Ed Budnick; Tim Meade, California Angels; Herb Carneal; Jim Small, Baseball Commissioner's Office; Paul Dickson; Jeff Eastland; Bob Fickus; Chuck Pool, Florida Marlins; Rob Geis; Ernie Harwell; Rick Haskins; Tyler Barnes & Rob Matwick, Houston Astros; Rex Bradley; Hillerich & Bradsby; Joshua Leland Evans & Michael Heffner; Lelands Auctions; Lew Lipset; Dan McKee; Bill Meade; Ray Medeiros; Larry Shenk, Philadelphia Phillies; Tom Slater, Political Gallery Auctions; Anne Rudy Schaefer; Dave Aust, Seattle Mariners; Don Steinbach.

Our special thanks to the following collectors who graciously allowed us to photograph items from their outstanding collections: Joe Bosley, Elias Dudash, Blair Jett, Gordon Kramp, Ted Patterson, Charles S. Winner, and Phil Wood.

Harry Rinker, Sr., of Rinker Enterprises, Inc., was instrumental in getting this project off the ground. We would like to thank him and Harry, Jr., for their excellent work in photographing the collectible items which appear in black-and-white in this book.

We would also like to thank the people at Chilton Book Company, whose help and guidance brought this project to fruition: Christopher Kuppig, general manager; Edna Jones, managing editor; Susan Clarey, aquisitions editor; Michael Campbell, director of sales and marketing; Troy Vozzella, developmental editor; and Tim Scott, copyeditor.

BASEBALL TEAM COLLECTIBLES

Introduction

Baseball Team Collectibles deals exclusively with team items. Player memorabilia will be covered in our next publication. Every city in North America that had a recognized major league team is listed in alphabetical order, along with a history of the team or teams of that city and related collectibles.

The 1869 Cincinnati Red Stockings were America's first all-professional team, and they played the entire 1869 season without losing a game. The first professional league was the National Association, which operated from 1871 through 1875.

In 1876 the National League began continuous operation. In 1882 the American Association was organized as direct competition to the National League, and often operated in the same cities. In 1892 the American Association's stronger teams merged into the expanded National League, which consisted of 12 teams. In 1901 the present American League came into being. Other leagues also attempted to compete on the major league level, beginning with the Union Association in 1884; the Players League in 1890; and the Federal League, which was organized in 1914 and lasted two full seasons. Both the Union Association and Players League folded after only one year.

Cities such as Altoona, Pennsylvania; Richmond, Virginia; St. Paul, Minnesota; and Wilmington, Delaware, fielded major league teams for only a few weeks, but they are listed herein. Obviously, any memorabilia from such short-lived franchises would be extremely rare. Although memorabilia for these teams probably exists, unless it has been documented, we have not affixed a price. A good rule of thumb would be to accord it approximately the same value for similar items from that era and add a 10 percent premium for scarcity.

DETERMINING PRICES

Another determining factor in pricing the memorabilia is how elaborate the item is. For example, take two scorecards from 1890. One containing numerous pages and player profiles would command considerably more than a sheet of folded cardboard. This axiom applies to everything. The more elaborate and attractive the item is, the higher the value.

Pricing is hardly an exact science because many factors are involved. What a dealer pays for an item he intends to resell is very much a determining factor. Location also plays a key role. For example, Atlanta Braves memorabilia would command a higher price in Atlanta than it would in another major league market or in a location thousands of miles away. This guide takes that into consideration, as well as placing the same value on similar items from the same era. A premium is placed on items from a particular team's inaugural and championship years. These items usually command a premium of at least 10 percent, and this guide reflects that premium.

All of the prices in this guide are predicated on the item being in excellent to mint condition. Prices on items in lesser condition should be reduced significantly, as much as 50 percent in some cases. In the case of books, those with dust jackets generally bring twice what those without do. Condition is paramount to an items value.

In determining prices for this guide, we have assembled a panel of experts among dealers, collectors, writers, and broadcasters throughout the United States, all of whom have been associated with baseball memorabilia a minimum of ten years. Every category covered in this guide has been bought, sold or traded by at least two of our experts and in most cases all.

SELLING BASEBALL MEMORABILIA

More and more collectors are using auctions to dispose of their collections or particular items from their collections. They run their own auctions in various sports publications or go to one of the larger sports auction houses. A word of caution: No matter how hard an auction house tries to operate legitimately, dual bidders can get together and run up prices to establish an inflated value for that item. They then split all fees and sell later at an even higher price. They can also work in concert with the item's owner to drive the price up and then drop out of the bidding after a particular figure is reached, leaving legitimate bidders to pay more for the item. The best way to approach an auction is to determine beforehand what you are willing to pay and stick to that figure. Although you may wind up disappointed in not obtaining a particular piece of memorabilia, you'll be a lot more disappointed if you overpay. Be careful, and bear in mind that in nearly every case more than one of a particular item exists.

When selling directly to a dealer, realize that his object is to resell that item. Hence, do not expect more than 50 percent of an item's value. Since the dealer has operating expenses, he must buy accordingly in order to make a profit. If you decide to sell to a dealer, have a price in mind that you expect to receive. This guide will help you establish an item's worth. Don't hesitate to shop around, but realize that a dealer has a legitimate right to charge you an appraisal fee if you don't sell to him. If you do your homework properly, you will know beforehand what to expect. Preparation is vitally important.

COLLECTING CATEGORIES

We have divided the memorabilia into nine main collecting categories: 1) Advertising Specialties; 2) Ballpark Giveaways; 3) Miscellaneous (including bobbin' head dolls, cups, glasses and plates, photographs, stock certificates, etc.); 4) Pennants; 5) Pins; 6) Postcards; 7) Publications; 8) Schedules; and 9) Special Events (including All-Star games, grand openings, post-season and World Series games, etc.). A description of each category follows.

Advertising Specialties

Advertising specialties are marketing items which promote a product or business through association with a particular team or player and are not encompassed by other categories in this book. For example, an advertising sign or poster would fall under this category, as would such diverse cloth items as Homer Hankies (which became popular in Minnesota during the 1986 and 1991 World Series). Items such as pins, glassware and schedules, even though bearing a sponsor's name, would not be included here since they are categorized separately. Even though many ballpark giveaways are advertising items, the fact that they are primarily intended to be given to fans attending specific games warrants a separate category.

Ballpark Giveaways

Although the St. Louis Browns have not been in the major leagues since 1953, they proved to be great innovators in the area of team ballpark giveaways. The Browns celebrated the raising of their only American League pennant on May 1, 1945, by distributing a pennant-shaped program for the game against Cleveland. The program contained player biographies and other pertinent information on the 1944 champions. (Souvenirs, mainly pins and programs, were given to fans earlier in conjunction with special days for such luminaries as Cy Young and Frank Chance, but these will be covered in detail in our next book.)

Bat Day, the first popular ballpark giveaway event of modern times, also had its origin with the St. Louis Browns. Back in 1952, Rudy Schaefer, longtime assistant to Bill Veeck both at Cleveland and St. Louis, learned that a bat manufacturer in the Midwest was going out of business. Schaefer sold Veeck on the idea of purchasing the stock of bats and giving them to youngsters attending an upcoming Browns game. In a game that normally would have attracted a corporal's guard, thousands of fans turned out for the event.

Hillerich & Bradsby, manufacturer of

Louisville Slugger bats, began participating in the event at ballparks throughout America. For many years Bat Day was the only ballpark giveaway event for the season. Teams realized such events would increase attendance dramatically and began adding other special days, such as Cap Day, Ball Day, and Camera Day, where fans were provided with an album and encouraged to take pictures of their favorite players before the game.

In the beginning the clubs footed the bill for these events themselves, but as the ballpark giveaways increased, clubs found willing sponsors to pick up the tab in exchange for having their logo attached to the giveaway item. Today some clubs have more than 40 ballpark giveaways a season.

Throughout the years barbeque aprons, baseball cards, batting helmets, beach towels, beer and coffee mugs, bike bags, briefcases, calendars, coolers, cushions, digital clocks and watches, floppy hats, gloves, halter tops, key chains, magnet schedules, notebooks, pens, pins, posters, radios, sports bags, sun visors, T-shirts, team and player pictures, tote bags, umbrellas, wallets, and yearbooks have been among the more popular giveaways. The list is endless. In the final years of the Washington Senators, pantyhose was an inducement to get more women to the park.

Ballpark giveaways have more significance and value if they are dated and contain the sponsor's logo. (Many clubs feature a star player on their giveaway items, and these will be addressed in our next book.)

Ballpark giveaways will be listed under each team and, where known, the sponsor's name will be included. Sponsors for the same item frequently change from year to year. However, in some cases the same sponsor had a long tenure with the same item, so unless it has a specific date, it's impossible to tell the exact year of some items.

A good rule of thumb to follow is that identical items for different teams, given away during the same era, have identical values. Also note that the 1985 Seattle Mariners yearbook, the only one issued in club history, was an April 27 ballpark giveaway sponsored by Boeing, Holland America, and Rainier Bank. It will be listed under both ballpark giveaways and yearbooks. In addition, ballpark giveaways associated with a particular player will be featured in our next book.

Ballpark giveaways have more significance and value if they are dated and contain the sponsor's logo. There is a sponsor for nearly all ballpark giveaways, and in most instances the giveaway item carries their name, logo or both. This price guide has included a $1 premium for an item containing the sponsor's name. We have listed the sponsor's name whenever it is known. If, however, that sponsor has underwritten the giveaway but did not include its name on the item, that item is worth less. Using a hypothetical example, a cap bearing a sponsor's name or logo has a value of $6 while that same cap without the sponsor's name and/or logo is worth $5. In addition, when a specific date is included on the item denoting when it was given away, we have allowed another $1 premium. Going back to our example, the cap with both the sponsor's name and date of the giveaway would have a value of $7 as opposed to a plain cap worth $5. If the giveaway was before 1980, add $2, prior to 1970, add $3. This allows for a substantial premium on the earliest ballpark giveaways. Many clubs feature a star player on their giveaway items: these will be addressed in our next book.

Miscellaneous

Our miscellaneous category is a catchall for baseball memorabilia that has not been produced on a regular basis. This category covers such diverse items as bobbin' head dolls (also called nodders), stock certificates, team photographs, cups, glasses and plates.

Some of the most attractive banks ever manufactured were produced by Stanford Pottery of Sebring, Ohio, in 1948. This was the year that the Cleveland Indians and Boston Braves met in the World Series, so they were the focal point of the initial run of banks. Stanford Pottery also made a bank featuring a Pittsburgh Pirate figure complete with a patch over one eye. Although the Boston Braves mascot logo was considerably different than that of the Cleveland mascot, Chief Wahoo, Stanford Pottery used the Wahoo face for both banks and changed only the uniform lettering. The banks became so popular in Cleveland at least three other Chief

Wahoo-style banks were made in future years and sold through the ball club and at Richman Brothers department stores.

In the 1950s and 1960s, bat banks for various teams were sold at ballparks. The early ones contained a cylindrical plastic case in the basic team color where the money was deposited and wooden miniature Louisville Slugger bats containing player names that fit into slots around the case. In the 1960s and beyond, the bats were made of plastic and featured logos of the various league teams.

The earliest well-known baseball banks were manufactured in the 1930s as advertising specialties by the Mobil Oil Company. These baseball-shaped glass banks rested on a screw-top base and contained Mobil's flying red horse logo as well as the ball club's logo. Since these were available wherever Mobil gasoline was sold, banks were also made for the minor league market.

BOBBIN' HEAD DOLLS

The original bobbin' head dolls were manufactured in Japan by Lego Company, a Swiss firm, beginning in 1960–1961. Made entirely of papier-mâché, the heads of these dolls are attached by a spring to the neck which enables them to bob up and down (thus accounting for the name). Being made of such fragile material, many have become broken or chipped over the years, which has resulted in high prices for those that remain in pristine condition. Those with original boxes command a premium, although condition is the most important factor in determining price. Sold originally at ballpark souvenir stands or by mail order from the clubs, they retailed for between $1 and $2.98. Today, many sell for hundreds of dollars.

The earliest dolls (manufactured in 1960–1961) are distinguishable by various colored square bases and are classified as Category I. Thirteen major league and four minor league dolls have been documented. From the foot of the square base to the top of the head they measure 9 inches.

Category II, made in 1961–1962, features 22 dolls with white square bases, the rarest being a doll for the Houston Colt 45s wearing a blue uniform and fetching in excess of $400. All other dolls have white uniforms.

During 1961–1962 miniature dolls 4½ inches tall (or half the size of the regular dolls) were marketed individually as well as in large boxes by leagues (ten American League and ten National League dolls). Each has a round white base and is referred to as Category III.

From 1962 to 1964 Lego used green round bases, and all 20 teams were represented. The doll for the Colt 45s has a pistol rather than a bat in his hands. These dolls are classified as Category IV. At the same time Lego produced a similar series with black players for all 20 teams, which command a higher price. The rarest of these are the dolls of the Kansas City A's, Minnesota Twins, Pittsburgh Pirates, and San Francisco Giants. Fewer of these are known to exist and hence they are more expensive. The black players on the green round bases are Category V.

The most common bobbin' heads and the last manufactured in Japan were produced from 1967 to 1972 and are referred to as Category VI. All of these are on gold round bases. The rarest is the Seattle Pilots doll, which was made only during 1969, the Pilots only major league season.

Collectors should note there is an Angels bobbin' head dated 1961 with an Anaheim decal. There is absolutely no possibility that this was manufactured in 1961 with the name Anaheim affixed because the Angels did not agree to have a stadium built there until March 10, 1964, when Anaheim Mayor Rex Coons and club owner Gene Autry shook hands on the deal. Prior to this several other southern California locations were seriously considered as the Angels new home. Angels Assistant Vice President and Media Relations Director Tim Mead verifies that the team did not change its name to the California Angels until after the 1965 season. This is when they began an extensive marketing campaign to promote their move to Anaheim and Anaheim Stadium, which opened on April 19, 1966. Prior to that they were always called the Los Angeles Angels because they played their games there. One possible explanation for Anaheim dolls with the 1961 date is that the concessionaire had dolls left over with the Los Angeles name and simply covered it with the Anaheim decal. This much you can be sure of: No dolls were manufactured in 1961 with the Anaheim name. The earliest date for manufacture could have been spring 1964, when the Angels agreed to play in Anaheim.

MinneMemories, 108 Warren Street, Mantako, Minnesota 56001 has compiled a checklist and price guide for these delightful collectibles. Their telephone number is (507) 387-6864.

OTHER MISCELLANEOUS COLLECTIBLES

When the 1889 champion New York Giants were honored on a plate showing cameos of 20 members of the pennant winners, it started a trend that continues to the present. A plate featuring the 1910 champion Philadelphia Athletics as cameos surrounding a huge elephant is another highly sought-after collectible. After the opening of Pittsburgh's Forbes Field in 1909, images of the beautiful ballpark also appeared on plates as well as saucers, pitchers and creamers.

Since the 1930s baseball glasses have been popular collectibles, and in more recent years plastic cups have been produced in abundance showing teams, baseball scenes and individual players. When purchasing a drink at the ballpark, fans generally opt to spend an additional 25¢ to 50¢ to have their beverage served in a plastic cup with a baseball image rather than have it dispensed in a plain paper or plastic cup. Long after a game ends, it's not unusual to see dozens of fans looking under seats or in trash cans to retrieve these colorful collectibles. For big events such as All-Star games, World Series, and stadium openings and closings, it's not unusual to find them numbered, increasing their collectibility.

Carte de visites (calling cards), popularly known as CDVs and cabinet cards, date to the earliest days of baseball and generally bring thousands of dollars. Panoramic views of teams, stadiums, or both also command top dollar. These items are included in the miscellaneous section because they never have been issued on a regular basis. Generally they depict a championship team, but this is not always the case. These views will be randomly listed under the team they represent with a description of the image as well as the size of the item.

Although it turns up with some frequency, one of the nicest panoramics is a Yard of the National Game, measuring 14 by 46 inches. It shows the 1907–1908 world champion Chicago Cubs in cameos around West Side Park, when it was filled to capacity during the three straight World Series in which the Cubs appeared. This piece often brings $1500, with condition being of paramount importance.

Pennants

Although pennants predate the twentieth century, their rise in popularity among collectors is relatively new. More and more people appreciate them because they are attractive, easy to display, and in many cases informative. Some of the more collectible pennants, particularly those from World Series and All-Star games, carry the starting lineup as well as the date. Picking out the stars of a particular team is as easy as reading the names on the pennant.

For the same reason, picture pennants are popular because they enable the collector to know the exact year the pennant was produced. The more elaborate a pennant is the more desirable it becomes. A pennant containing only the team's name would pale in comparison to one which shows the stadium or lists the players for that particular year.

Most collectors concentrate on one team only and then branch out to better specimens of other teams. Taking two pennants from the same era, the more colorful one will invariably sell more quickly. Other factors, such as a team's popularity, determine value. Pennants from defunct teams, particularly originals from the Brooklyn Dodgers, New York Giants, St. Louis Browns, and Washington Senators are highly sought after. But be extremely careful because pennants from all these clubs have been reproduced.

Although there may well be earlier examples, the earliest seen by the authors is a three-piece stitched felt pennant from the Baltimore Orioles of the 1890s, a team that won three consecutive National League pennants. Measuring 8 by 19 inches, it has the Orioles logo, crossed bats and the word "Baltimore" in block letters down the center. Whereas most pennants today have the lettering done horizontally, this particular one has vertical lettering from the widest point down to the tip.

Another early gem honors the 1905 world champion New York Giants and shows a giant uniformed figure towering over the skyline of New York City. Considerably larger than today's pennants, it conjures up memories of the only World Series in history where every game ended in a shutout; the Giants beat the Philadelphia Athletics four games to one with the immortal Christy Mathewson hurling three shutouts and fellow Hall of Famer Joe McGinnity the other. Philadelphia's Chief Bender, another Hall of Famer pitched a shutout for the Athletics' only victory.

Prior to the 1930s, pennants were issued sporadically with special attention given to championship teams. In the 1930s, however, nearly all teams had felt pennants for sale at ballparks. Designs were relatively simple, with little more than the team's name. In the 1940s and 1950s, multicolored artwork was added, including team logos, stadiums, and often names of the players. All of these factors add to an item's collectibility.

Felt was the principal material used in pennant manufacturing into the 1960s, when the changeover to polyester took place. Although they vary slightly, most pennants today measure 12 inches at the widest point and are approximately 30 inches long. Special event pennants such as those manufactured for stadium openings and closings, World Series and All-Star games are frequently numbered and limited in production.

Pins

When Celluloid, a see-through trademarked substance consisting mainly of pyroxylin and camphor, was invented in 1896, it opened the floodgates on a wave of Celluloid pinback buttons. A thin sheet of Celluloid was placed over a printed image on paper, which then was placed over metal. These three pieces were then stamped out and placed in a metal ring known as a collet and pressed into the back opening. This simple process enabled Celluloid pinback buttons to be mass produced. Because Celluloid is highly flammable, it was replaced by an acetate sheet in the 1940s.

Prior to 1896 baseball pinback buttons usually were made of solid brass or silver. The earliest known example is a brass pinback button for the Cincinnati Red Stockings of 1869, America's first professional baseball team. With each package of Cameo Pepsin Gum purchased in 1896, the manufacturer included a pin of baseball's top stars.

Baseball pinback buttons are an extremely popular collectible with designs for current major league teams and players available for sale at souvenir stands in the stadiums and by mail from the ball clubs themselves. Pinback buttons for defunct teams are highly collectible and consequently some reproductions have appeared on the market. Since some of these defunct teams such as the Boston Braves, Brooklyn Dodgers, New York Giants, Philadelphia Athletics, and St. Louis Browns have been gone from their original locations nearly 40 years, a pinback button bearing any of these logos which appears too new could be a reproduction. Unfortunately, unscrupulous individuals have been able to artificially age pins, thus adding to the confusion.

American Nut & Chocolate was the first company to issue a set of pins in the 1930s for each of the 16 major league teams. These 1⅛ inch lithographs feature different styles on each pin. These pins sell for approximately $15 each, with no premium for any one item.

In 1961 Crane Potato Chips of Decatur, Illinois, began marketing one free pin in each bag of their product. The object was to collect one pin from all 18 teams on a card and then exchange it for a regulation baseball or softball. Ironically, one pin today commands more than a baseball or softball would, and a complete set would cost $90. Crane continued marketing the pins in their packages through 1969. Then, after a lapse of 15 years, Crane started again in 1984 for only that one year.

Guy's Potato Chips adopted the idea in 1964 and issued team pins through the 1966 season.

The most highly desirable baseball team pinback buttons are ones issued prior to 1930 and featuring the entire team. In recent years corporations anxious to capitalize on a close association with baseball in general or a team in particular have issued pinback buttons featuring the company's name or logo. Because of limited circulation, these are much more rare than those featuring only the team's name. The more imaginative the design, the more popular they are.

With major league teams and their sales venues the best source for current baseball pinback buttons, sports collectible stores, antiques shops, flea markets and auctions are the best sources for the older items. Two auctions which deal primarily in pinback buttons are Hake's Americana & Collectibles, P.O. Box 1444, York, PA 17405; and Political Gallery, 1325 W. 86th St., Indianapolis, IN 46260.

Postcards

Picture postcards made their debut in the United States at the 1893 Columbian Exposition at Chicago, Illinois. Sets featuring the various buildings were sold on the grounds for mailing. Until 1907, when the back or address side of the postcard was divided, only the receiver's name and address could be written on the back. Any message from the sender was written on the front or picture side of the card.

The earliest known baseball postcard of major league players is a real photo showing Tommy Leach, Duff Cooley and Honus Wagner of the 1900 Pittsburgh Pirates. The earliest known team postcard features the 1903 New York Giants sitting on the grand staircase of the Waldorf Astoria Hotel. From that time to the present, hundreds of baseball team postcards have been issued by postcard publishers, businesses and the teams themselves.

Unless otherwise noted, all postcards are standard size—three-and-one-half by five-and-one-half inches. The four categories are real photos (all eras), pre-linen (PL) 1893–1930, linen (LN) 1930–1950, chrome (CH) 1950 to present. Year, type, serial number and publisher are all listed when available.

Publications

The publications category encompasses all forms of printed works such as books, media guides, programs, scorecards, and yearbooks, which are listed under each team in that order.

In some instances no club histories have been written in book form, although this information is readily available in the media guide. Periodicals usually appear after a particularly memorable season. All clubs issue programs or scorecards while yearbooks have been produced by various teams on a sporadic basis. Some teams have replaced a yearbook with an enlarged, fact-filled program which changes several times a year; others are venturing into videos to present the team to the public. The Baltimore Orioles abandoned their printed yearbook after the 1986 season for a video version, but went back to the printed yearbook in 1993. Although 1972 was the first season for the Texas Rangers, the team didn't publish a yearbook until 1976. The Seattle Mariners, organized since 1979, issued a yearbook only in 1985.

BOOKS

Hundreds of team histories have been written throughout the years beginning with George Wright's *Record of the Boston Baseball Club 1871–1874*, published by Rockwell and Churchill in 1874. This exceptionally rare book chronicles the Boston Red Stockings of the National Association of Professional Baseball Clubs, the first professional league. Wright and his brother Harry had left Cincinnati to become the backbone of the Boston Red Stockings who dominated the National Association, winning pennants from 1872 through the final season of 1875. The Philadelphia Athletics won the initial championship in 1871. Wright's book is divided into sections, each covering one season by use of newspaper accounts and box scores. As the first team history ever written, it would command many thousands of dollars if offered for sale or auction.

Incidentally, the total salary for the 1869 Red Stockings was only $9,300 with George Wright making the most ($1,400), while brother Harry was paid $1,200. Asa Brainard, the pitcher, made $1,100 while third baseman Fred Waterman made $1,000. Charles Seasy, second base; Charles Gould, first base; Douglas Allison, catcher; Andrew Leonard, left field; and Calvin McVey, right field, all made $800 a season while the lone substitute Richard Hurley was paid $600. This amazing team played the entire 1869 season without losing a game, 60 wins and no defeats. Obviously this remarkable feat will never be equalled.

It was more than 20 years before another team history was written, and Boston's team was again the focal point. George V. Tuohey authored *A History of the Boston Baseball Club* in 1897. This book covered professional baseball in

Boston from 1871 through the 1897 season when Frank Selee's team was the National League champion.

Another highly sought after and rare book is Harry Ellard's classic *Baseball in Cincinnati,* the first team history of the twentieth century, published by Johnson and Hardin in 1907 with a white cover and reissued in 1908 with a black cover. Ellard's father, George, owned the largest sporting goods establishment in the west and, as a wealthy man with contacts throughout the country, was able to sign the cream of the baseball crop to professional contracts. Charles Gould was the only native of Cincinnati to play for the Red Stockings.

The most popular team histories were issued by G. P. Putnam's from 1943 through 1955 and covered 17 different teams. Baseball book collectors search far and wide for the complete set with individual books costing in excess of $75.

Andy Moursund, owner of Georgetown Books, has specialized in baseball books since 1984 and says that the dust jacket can literally double the value of a book, particularly those in the Putnam Series. Prices in this guide reflect only those books in pristine condition *with the dust jacket.*

The market value is also determined by scarcity, popularity, uniqueness, and above all, demand. Most used books generally sell for half the original price and many are sold as remainders for even less. However, popular team histories such as those in the Putnam Series or those published by Coward-McCann in the late 1950s and early 1960s sell for many times the original price. A bullet preceding book titles denotes that the book is currently available.

Paul Haas, proprietor of Sports Books, etc. in Springfield, Virginia, has the largest selection of baseball books and videos in the U.S. His books sell at the current retail price except when they are remaindered. Remainders occur when the publisher has a supply of books left over after a certain period of time and decides to sell them at wholesale prices to make room for new stock.

Some collectors wait until a book is remaindered to make a purchase, but many popular baseball histories never are and eventually sell for more than when they were new.

The following dealers specialize in used baseball books:

Andy Moursand, Georgetown Books Shop, 7770 Woodmont Avenue, Bethesda, Maryland, 20814; 301-907-6923. Shop open seven days a week.

R. Paplinger Baseball Books, P.O. Box 1062, Ashland, Oregon, 97520; 503-488-1220. Catalog sales.

Two excellent sources for new baseball books are:

Sports Books, Etc., 5224 Port Royal Road, Springfield, Virginia, 22151; 703-321-8660. Shop open seven days a week plus mail order service.

A & R Books, P.O. Box 285, Tiverton, Rhode Island, 02878; 1-800-942-8123.

MEDIA GUIDES

The elaborate major league media guides we are familiar with today evolved from large sheets of white or colored paper in varying sizes that were folded in half or thirds and bore the title "roster." Documented samples date back to the St. Louis Cardinals in 1926, although there may be earlier examples. Several teams, notably the Chicago Cubs and New York Giants, issued multiple-page rosters containing photographs as early as 1927, while most of the other teams did not use that format until 1932. These publications were issued as spring training guides and contained the names of all players invited to training camp. They usually listed the team's scheduled exhibition games and were issued only to members of the press radio corps. Because of limited circulation these items are extremely rare. However, as collector items they also have limited appeal because they typically are visually unattractive and contain few photographs other than those used on the covers.

Public Relations Director Marsh Samuel issued what is generally considered the first authentic press, radio and TV guide for the Cleveland Indians in 1948. It is an elaborate 55-page guide that contained player biographies and other useful information on the eventual world champion Indians. In fairness to the Cincinnati Reds, they issued a comparable piece in 1934 entitled "Press Information, Cincinnati Reds." The inside front piece of the 32-page publication states, "Official Handbook of Information compiled by the Cincinnati Reds Baseball Company" and includes photos of the players as well as front office personnel and Crosley field, home of the Reds. By all standards, this publication would have to rank as the very first press radio guide, while the 1948 Indians' publication would be the first modern press radio and TV guide.

In recent years the title media guide has been affixed to publications now containing hundreds of pages and issued by the public relations offices of the various major league teams. Because these media guides are generally not available to the general public, they are increasing in popularity among publications collectors. Although some collectors attempt to get guides for every team in both leagues, the majority concentrate on obtaining only those of their favorite teams.

When you see today's multi-page media guide, bear in mind that it had its humble beginning as a single-page roster sheet no later than 1926. Although all major league clubs make their yearbooks available to the general public, some will sell their media guides as well, so it pays to write the clubs individually in regard to their availability. In addition, the following memorabilia dealers specialize in publications:

Jerry Blank, 22 Twixt Hill Road, Ridgefield, CT 06877

Jeffrey Miller, 249 Winchester Dr., Horsham, PA 19044

Jerry Smolin, P.O. Box 2234, Amherst, MA 01004

J. C. Sports Publications, P.O. Box 1903, Ft. Lee, NJ 07024

PROGRAMS AND SCORECARDS

Programs and scorecards date back to the earliest days of baseball and always have been popular collectibles. All things being equal, a multi-page program containing articles will always command more money than a folded cardboard scorecard from the same era. Another value factor is the attractiveness of the item. A plain black-and-white scorecard will pale by comparison to a scorecard featuring an attractive design, color or both. Historical significance is another consideration. Programs and scorecards from pennant-winning teams command higher prices, as do these items from a team's first year. There has always been added interest in programs from defunct teams. The Seattle Pilots lasted just one season (1969), so Pilots' programs command a premium over programs of other teams from 1969.

Most program collectors concentrate on programs of their favorite team. With the addition of the Colorado Rockies and Florida Marlins in 1993, there are now 28 major league teams. Since expansion first occurred in 1961, a total of 12 new teams have joined the major league ranks. If your favorite team happens to be an expansion club, you could readily collect one program from each season and confine your collection to one box. Collecting the California Angels, baseball's first expansion team, would require only 34 programs; other expansion clubs would require even less. Chicago Cubs collectors have a considerably more difficult task since there is an unbroken line of National League baseball in Chicago dating to 1876.

Because most teams issue more than one program during the course of the season, many collectors will want one of each from each year. Beginning collectors are wise to concentrate on obtaining one from each year before branching out into the variations. Most major league teams sell their programs by mail orders. Inquire about back issues since teams have just so much room for storage. They would much prefer selling the item to throwing it away due to lack of storage space.

Baseball scorecards and programs are extremely difficult to price because they vary so much in makeup. Some are simple cardboard fold-overs with few or no graphics. Others are cardboard fold-overs with elaborate lithography, while others are magnificent programs containing player sketches and other useful information. In order to properly evaluate an item, it first must be seen. Two programs or scorecards from the same year can be as different as night and day. Our policy is to only price items personally seen by our board of experts. This applies only to nineteenth-century items. Because twentieth-century items are more readily available, it is possible to determine their values with greater accuracy.

We do feel there should be a premium on a league's first season: 1871 for the National Association, 1876 for the National League, 1882 for the American Association, 1884 for the Union Association, 1890 for the Players League, 1901 for the American League, and 1914 for the Federal

League. There is often a premium when a prominent player, particularly a Hall of Famer, appears on the cover. In cases where Hall of Famers grace the cover instead of less prominent teammates, a 10 percent premium is fair.

YEARBOOKS
(Including Championship Souvenir Books)

Boston Braves Public Relations Director Billy Sullivan is generally accepted as the father of the modern baseball yearbook. He published the first one for the Braves in 1946. However, there were many previous attempts at yearbook-type publications, some issued as early as 1880, when F. E. Pollard chronicled the Worcester Ruby Legs' first season in the National League. Entitled *Ups and Downs of the Worcester Baseball Club*, the publication reviews the season and provides information on the players.

Because many championship souvenir booklets were issued by various publishers to commemorate pennant-winning seasons, these will be incorporated into this section of publications. The earliest known of these is the *Detroit Tribune's Epitome of Baseball*, published in 1887 to celebrate the Detroit Wolverines' championship season. When the Philadelphia Athletics won their first American League pennant in 1902, Standard Engraving Company of Philadelphia produced *Our Champions*, featuring photos and sketches of the 1902 team. Thereafter, yearbooks were issued (1905, 1910, 1911, and 1929) most seasons when the Athletics won a pennant. The Cincinnati Reds produced two different yearbook-type publications for their 1919 champions, and in 1934 the *Detroit Free Press* published a pictorial booklet featuring pictures, biographies and statistics of the 1934 American League champs.

The Chicago Cubs had a yearbook-type publication as early as 1934. Publication was continuous through 1942, and since they had photos and stats on the various players, they would certainly be classified as yearbooks. In 1941, the Brooklyn Dodgers came out with *The Dodgers, 1941, Today and Yesterday in Brooklyn Baseball*. After winning the 1941 National League pennant, they reissued it with additional information on the championship season, changed the cover, renamed it *Dodger Victory Book*, and sold it throughout the 1942 season.

In the late 1940s and early 1950s, most major league teams began issuing some type of yearbook. In 1952 Jay Publishing Company began producing Big League Books, which became the official yearbook for many of the teams. Several, including the New York Yankees and Cleveland Indians, continued issuing their own yearbook while allowing Jay to publish Big League Books yearbooks for both teams. When there are two for the same year, the official yearbook generally commands a slightly higher price.

Pat Quinn of Sports Collectors Store in LaGrange, Illinois, who has been dealing in and collecting yearbooks for more than 25 years, and long-time yearbook collectors Brian Gettings and Don Ortolani, rank the 1946 Cincinnati Reds and 1951 Philadelphia Phillies as the rarest of modern yearbooks. Both command in excess of $500, if and when they turn up. All of this and similar information will be listed under yearbooks in the publication section of each specific team. Since many teams did not issue yearbooks continuously, this information will be provided as well.

Schedules

Schedules come in every shape, size, and form, dating back to the earliest times. While most collectors associate schedules with the small multiplefolded colorful paper or cardboard items in abundance today, they have been issued in every conceivable form over the years. Pencils, rulers, metal discs, cups and glasses, and postcards are only a few of the unique forms schedules have taken.

Because they are given away by ball clubs, sponsors and other commercial enterprises, the modern schedules are relatively inexpensive. Most are extremely colorful with tremendous eye appeal. A brief letter and a self-addressed stamped envelope sent to any major league team requesting a current schedule would almost always receive a favorable response. Collector friends in other locales are excellent sources. Wherever you see a large supply, make sure you take some extras to trade with friends in other areas.

Always check the back of the schedule

to see if the ad is different. The front is frequently the same, but because different sponsors make them available, they will imprint their message on the back. Long-time "Skedder" Paul Jarrell of College Park, Georgia, discovered 550 variations of the 1950 Boston Red Sox schedule alone. Marty Falk, publisher of "The Sked Notebook," says a typical major league season may yield over 1000 variations.

Particular images on the front of the schedule add to its collectibility. For example, if a club decides to feature a star player, it will have more value than one with a generic image. Schedules featuring stadiums are especially popular, while those showing a new facility in its first year command a premium.

The most valuable modern schedules are those from the first year of a team. A true schedule collector will try and find at least one from each year his favorite team has operated. Other premiums are placed on schedules of pennant-winning and world championship teams.

Schedules of defunct teams are highly prized. Schedules from the Boston Braves, Brooklyn Dodgers, Kansas City Athletics, Milwaukee Braves, New York Giants, Philadelphia Athletics, St. Louis Browns, Seattle Pilots, and Washington Senators would generally be worth more than those from other teams that same year. Special attention also should be paid to a defunct team's final season.

With everything being relative among schedules of equal value, the most colorful ones with the greatest eye appeal will be selected first. Schedules fit well in protective sleeves, don't take up much space, make a marvelous display, and are among the fastest-growing baseball collectibles.

Keith Gadbury, publisher of "Right on Schedules," the nation's oldest schedule publication (since 1980) calls California sportswriter Jim McConnell "the Father of Schedule Collecting." McConnell amassed a huge collection starting in the late 1960s and early 1970s and sold the bulk of it a few years back. He was the original publisher of "Right On Schedules." Proof of schedule collecting's growing popularity is the fact that there are now four monthly publications available:

Right On Schedules, 204 N. Charro Ave., Thousand Oaks, CA 91320

The Skedhead Bulletin, P.O. Box 71692, Madison Heights, MI 48071

The Skedder News, 4857 Millbrook Drive, Dunwoody, GA 30338

The Sked Notebook, 8 Fillmore Place, Lawrenceville, NJ 08648

$2.00 plus SASE will get you a sample copy of all 4 publications.

In addition, Paul Jarrell is a collector-dealer who specializes in schedules. His address is 1800 Crumbley Road, McDonagh, GA 30253.

Special Events

Our special events category encompasses all memorabilia associated with All-Star games, ballpark openings and closings, League Championship Series, and Temple Cup and World Series games. Press pins, programs, and tickets are included. Items for special events such as All-Star games, grand openings, and post-season games are much more limited. Tickets to regular season games are worth very little, but special event tickets command much higher prices and are usually much larger and fancier in design. This has been especially true in recent years, when elaborate opening day tickets for a new ballpark or new team are not torn when the fan enters the stadium, thus providing an attractive mint souvenir of the event.

Programs from All-Star games and the League Championship Series are particularly popular, while interest in current World Series programs has diminished because they are now generic in nature, feature four teams instead of the two participants, and are easily obtainable through the mail and at newsstands. In a few cases, participating teams added a few supplemental pages to feature their players and season statistics, making them decidedly more collectible than their generic counterparts. The last year individual teams produced their own World Series programs was 1973.

POST-SEASON CHAMPIONSHIP EVENTS

Post-season programs were issued as far back as 1882, when the American Association champion Cincinnati Reds met the National League champion Chicago White Stockings in the first World Series, which was stopped by league officials after each team won one game. The two leagues met again in 1884 and every season thereafter through 1890 when the American Association's Louisville Colonels and National League's Brooklyn Trolley Dodgers played to a mutually agreed-upon six-game draw. The series was cut short by atrocious weather.

That ended post-season play until 1894. By this time the strongest American Association teams had merged into a 12-team National League (beginning in 1892). Pittsburgh Pirates owner William Temple donated a cup to be awarded to the winner of a post-season series between the first- and second-place teams. The 1894 champion Baltimore Orioles lost to the New York Giants, and as repeat champions in 1895 lost again to the second-place Cleveland Spiders. In 1896 the champion Orioles beat the Spiders; as second-place finishers in 1897 they defeated the champion Boston Beaneaters. Interest in the Temple Cup waned because the Orioles were in all four series and three times the second-place team defeated the league champions. After the 1897 Temple Cup series, the idea was dropped.

Items pertaining to any of these post-season games command top dollar and are highly desirable among collectors. Pennants, pins, programs, and ticket stubs from these events are known to exist.

WORLD SERIES

In 1901, the National League rival American League was organized as a major league. In August 1903 Barney Dreyfuss, owner of the Pittsburgh Pirates, challenged Boston Puritans owner Henry Killilea to a best-of-nine World Series championship when it became obvious both teams were going to win league pennants. The Puritans shocked the Pirates by winning five games to three as Bill Dinneen won three and baseball's all-time winningest pitcher, Cy Young, took two for Boston. Deacon Phillipe pitched all three Pirate victories. The Puritans repeated as American League champs in 1904, but owner John Brush and manager John McGraw of the National League champion New York Giants refused to play them for fear of an embarrassing loss similar to Pittsburgh's the year before.

Since 1905 the World Series has been played continuously. In 1969 division play

began in both leagues with the top teams of each division meeting in the League Championship Series. The winner represented its league in the World Series.

From a collecting point of view, programs from the League Championship Series are a lot more desirable than World Series programs of recent vintage because major league baseball began issuing generic programs for the World Series in 1974. In some cases competing teams added supplemental pages for games played in their home parks, but in many cases the ballpark edition was the same in both parks and also available at newsstands and through the mail. The League Championship Series programs prepared exclusively by the competing teams offer original designs and information pertinent to the specific event. The last time World Series programs were produced by the respective teams was 1973.

World Series ticket prices vary tremendously and are often determined by the event itself. For example, a ticket stub from the 1956 World Series would generally run $40. However, a stub from game 5 at Yankee Stadium, in which Don Larsen pitched the only perfect game in World Series history, commands $150.

ALL-STAR GAMES

Conceived by *Chicago Tribune* Sports Editor Arch Ward, the major league All-Star game was born at Comiskey Park on July 6, 1933, in conjunction with the Century of Progress Exposition. Ward reasoned that visitors from all over the nation and world would be attending and it would be a golden opportunity to showcase America's national pastime. The idea was to feature at least one player from every team in baseball, a rule still in effect today. The game was an immediate success, as a capacity crowd of 47,595 fans attended.

It was fitting that Babe Ruth, in the twilight of a brilliant career with the New York Yankees, won the game for the American League with a two-run homer to give his team a 4 to 2 victory.

Since that initial "midsummer classic," the game has been played every year since with the exception of 1945, when World War II travel restrictions cancelled the game. From 1959 to 1963, two All-Star games were played to raise money for the player's pension fund.

With the cream of baseball's crop performing over these years, there have been many highlights during the All-Star classic. Some highlights include:

1934 Giants lefthander Carl Hubbell strikes out five of baseball's most feared sluggers in succession—Babe Ruth, Lou Gehrig, Jimmy Foxx, Al Simmons and Joe Cronin—while hurling three scoreless innings. The American League eventually wins, 9 to 7.

• 1941 A dramatic three-run homer by the Red Sox's Ted Williams with two out in the ninth at Detroit's Briggs Stadium gives the American League a 7 to 5 victory. It offset a brilliant performance by Pittsburgh's Arky Vaughn, who had 2 two-run homers and a single in a losing cause.

• 1946 In the first game after the war, Bob Feller, Hal Newhouser and Jack Kramer limit the National League to only three singles. Two home runs by Ted Williams and one by Charley Keller highlight a 12 to 0 American League romp at Boston's Fenway Park.

• 1950 Back at Comiskey Park, the first All-Star extra-inning game ends when St. Louis' Red Schoendienst slams a fourteenth-inning homer for a 4 to 3 National League win.

• 1955 At Milwaukee County Stadium Stan Musial's homer in the twelfth inning gives the National League a 6 to 5 win. The capacity crowd of 45,314 is doubly happy as Braves righthander Gene Conley strikes out the side in the twelfth inning to get the win.

• 1959 The All-Star game becomes a double feature as two games are played to raise money for the player's pension fund. In the first game, on July 7 at Forbes Field in Pittsburgh, the National League wins 5 to 4 on Willie Mays' eighth-inning triple. On August 3 at Los Angeles' mammoth Coliseum, only 55,105 (nearly 40,000 under capacity) watch the American League win 5 to 3 with homers by Frank Malzone, Yogi Berra and Rocky Colavito leading the way.

• 1964 Back to a single game format, Stan Musial makes his record twenty-fourth All-Star appearance as the National League wins 5 to 3 before only 44,160 at Cleveland's huge lakefront stadium, which can handle more than 80,000 spectators. It begins a string of eight straight National League victories.

• 1971 The American League breaks its eight-game losing streak at Detroit as a record-tying six home runs by six different players highlight the event. Reggie Jackson, Frank Robinson and Harmon Killebrew homer for the American League while Johnny Bench, Hank Aaron, and Roberto Clemente homer for the Nationals.

• 1981 The American League loses its tenth in a row and eighteenth in nineteen games before a record crowd of 72,086. A two-run homer by Philadelphia's Mike Schmidt in the eighth inning is the game winner for the National League.

• 1983 The American League celebrates the All-Star game's fiftieth anniversary in style at Comiskey Park, site of the first game, by walloping the National League 13 to 3. A grand-slam homer by California's Fred Lynn leads the way in snapping the American League's 11-game losing streak.

• 1986 At Houston's Astrodome Fernando Valenzuela ties Carl Hubbel's record of five consecutive strikeouts. However, the American League wins 3 to 2 thanks to home runs by two second basemen, Detroit's Lou Whitaker and Walt Weiss of Oakland.

All-Star collectibles are extremely popular. Programs, press pins and ticket stubs are the most widely sought after, followed by game souvenirs such as pennants, pins, cups and glasses.

PRESS PINS

During the 1911 World Series between the Philadelphia Athletics and Chicago Cubs, some fans in the standing-room-only crowd took refuge in the press area in order to watch the game, depriving legitimate members of the press corps their rightful seats. It was obvious that some form of identification was necessary to distinguish authentic writers from overzealous fans. The Baseball Writers of America devised the press lapel pin or press badge, which was ready in time for the 1912 World Series between the Athletics and New York Giants. That first year only the Athletics produced one for use at Shibe Park.

The press pin has been and is a popular collectible, although in recent years, values have diminished greatly. While they initially were issued in the hundreds and limited to baseball writers actually covering the World Series, today they are issued in the thousands and given to friends and employees of the competing teams as well as the media. Because pennant races can sometimes go down to the wire and even necessitate playoffs before the championship series, every club still in contention entering September must be prepared to produce these colorful collectibles. Since the beginning of the League Championship Series in 1969, at least four teams have been required to manufacture them.

Since only two clubs participate in the World Series, two clubs have an abundance of pins left over. These are called "phantoms" and frequently command a higher price than the legitimate pins. For years teams were putting the date on the pin. However, since pins were useless if the team did not play in the World Series, the practice in recent years has been to produce a pin designating a team's appearance in the "Fall Classic" i.e., first, second, and so forth. This way teams can get some benefit out of the pins by using them if and when they actually participate. In the meantime pins are locked away in storage for that happy day. A limited number of these phantoms find their way onto the market, but for the most part they are very difficult to obtain. The biggest danger in paying a high price for a recent phantom is if that team plays in the World Series a few years later. The phantom may become the official press pin for that year, diminishing its value considerably. Of course, if many years elapse before a team participates, they may decide on a new design altogether.

All-Star press pins did not appear until the sixth All-Star game at Cincinnati's Crosley Field in 1938, when a celluloid badge was issued to the press radio corps. No pins were produced for the 1939 and 1940 All-Star games, but one was made for the 1941 game at Briggs Stadium in Detroit. No pin appeared in 1942, but one was produced in 1943 at Philadelphia's Shibe Park. None were manufactured in 1944, and there was no All-Star game in 1945 because of World War II. Since the 1946 game at Boston's Fenway Park, All-Star press pins have been issued on a regular basis.

UNIFORMS

Although uniforms have become a highly popular collectible in recent years, pricing is usually predicated on whether the uniform was worn in games and, even more important, who wore it. There is no way to accurately price uniforms in this guide because the team factor is relatively unimportant, although there is generally a premium on uniforms of defunct teams and uniforms that are more colorful.

However, the more famous the player, the higher the value. For example, an authentic jersey worn by Babe Ruth of the New York Yankees during the 1926 World Series brought $82,500 at Leland's Auction on January 15, 1992. In that same auction a jersey worn by Roger Maris during his record breaking 61 home run season went for $66,000. A Sotheby's auction six weeks later had another 1961 Maris jersey that sold for twice that amount. Another Yankee, Mickey Mantle, holds the record for price realized when his 1960 home uniform brought $111,100 in another Leland's auction. A road uniform worn by Lou Gehrig sold for a record $363,000 in a Wolfer's Auction.

Prices like this are well beyond the means of most collectors and are the exception rather than the rule. Some modern uniform jerseys sell for less than $100, but in the case of prominent players, the price will always be higher. Because people attach tremendous importance to whether a uniform is game used, some have been artificially aged and others doctored to make the uniform fit the specifications of a particular player during a particular year. Name tags have been changed and recently made patches aged and sewn on the jersey.

Flannel was the material of choice for uniforms until the Pittsburgh Pirates went to double-knit polyester in 1970. In 1971 the Cardinals and Orioles jumped on the polyester bandwagon and by 1973 every team in baseball wore uniforms of this material.

Because so many uniforms are not what they appear, be extremely careful before spending thousands of dollars on what could well be a phoney. Uniform expert Phil Wood, who with Gary Hong publishes *Diamond Duds*, a bi-monthly newsletter devoted to uniforms and equipment, points out that the Chicago Cubs experimented with nylon uniforms in 1940 but abandoned the idea because they were too hot. In 1956 the Cincinnati Reds, and in 1963 the Kansas City Athletics, tried nylon uniforms with the same results.

AUCTIONS

Auctions have played an increasingly important role in the hobby. Pat Quinn of Sports Collectors Store in LaGrange, Illinois, is in his twenty-seventh consecutive year without missing a monthly auction. Joshua Evans who in 1987 began his Leland's Auction in Allentown, Pennsylvania, moved his operation to New York several years ago to take advantage of the larger market. Quinn and Evans deal exclusively in sports memorabilia. Ted Hake of York, Pennsylvania, has had a bimonthly Americana auction since 1967 that has always had a strong emphasis on sports, particularly baseball buttons. Political Gallery emphasized political items in its auctions until 1992, when it began auctioning sports memorabilia separately. Superior Galleries of Beverly Hills, California, a division of Superior Stamp and Coin Company, did its first sports auction on October 14, 1991. Another West Coast auction house, Richard Wolfers of San Francisco, also began sports auctions in 1991. Interest in sports memorabilia auctions was so high that worldwide auction houses like Sotheby's (in 1991) and Christies (in 1992) began separate auctions for sports memorabilia. Below in alphabetical order are the major sports auctions which issue catalogs:

Robert Edward Auctions, P.O. Box 1923, Hoboken, New Jersey, 07030, (201) 792-9324

Christies, East, 219 E. 67 St., New York, New York, 10021, (212) 606-0400

Hake's Americana & Collectibles Auction, P.O. Box 1444, York, Pennsylvania, 17405, (717) 848-1333

Leland's, 245 Fifth Ave., Suite 902, New York, New York, 10016, (212) 545-0800, Fax 545-0713

Political Gallery, 1325 W. 86th St., Indianapolis, Indiana, 46260, (317) 257-0863, Fax 254-9167

Pat Quinn's Sport Collector's Store Auction, 1040 S. LaGrange Rd., LaGrange, Illinois, 60525, (708) 354-7970, Fax 354-7972

Sotheby's, 1334 York Ave., New York, New York, (212) 606-7000

Superior Galleries, 9478 W. Olympic Blvd., Beverly Hills, California, 90212, (213) 203-9855

OTHER RESOURCES

Baseball memorabilia collectors are fortunate in having excellent publications in which to acquire or sell memorabilia. All are available by subscription and at many newsstands and sports memorabilia stores. They contain articles, auctions, classified ads and pertinent hobby information. As a service to our readers they are listed below:

Beckett Publications, 15850 Dallas Parkway, Dallas, TX 75248

Sports Collectors Digest (SCD), 700 E. State St., Lola, WI 54945

Tuff Stuff, 2309 Hungary Rd., Richmond, VA 23228

Another excellent resource, especially for uniform collectors, is the bimonthly publication "Diamond Duds," which carries a $20 yearly subscription price. "Diamond Duds" is available from P.O. Box 10153, Silver Spring, MD 20904–0153.

ABBREVIATIONS

These abbreviations are used in the team histories.

AL	American League
ALCS	American League Championship Series
BA	batting average
ERA	earned run average
HR	home run
MVP	Most Valuable Player
NL	National League
NLCS	National League Championship Series
RBI	runs batted in

Altoona, Pennsylvania

ALTOONA MOUNTAIN CITIES

Union Association 1884

Altoona, Pennsylvania's tenure as a major league baseball city was brief. Altoona was a charter member of the Union Association, which operated as a third major league in 1884. The Altoona Mountain Cities were admitted to the league on March 2, 1884, and were managed by Edward R. Curtis, who recruited most of his players from central Pennsylvania.

The Mountain Cities' most prominent player was shortstop Germany Smith, who led them in batting with a .315 average in the 25 games they played before the club disbanded on May 31. Smith went on to play 15 seasons in the big leagues and wound up with a career batting average of .243.

In the home opener on April 30 against the ultimate champion St. Louis Maroons, the Mountain Cities drew 2000 fans, most of whom went away disappointed when Altoona lost 15 to 2. In early May attendance reached a peak when 2,500 watched the Mountain Cities beat Boston 9 to 4. However, the team was overmatched most of the time and lost 19 of the 25 games played before disbanding. At the end the team was drawing crowds of only 250.

The Mountain Cities franchise was shifted to Kansas City, but the only Altoona player to accompany the franchise was outfielder Frank Shaffer who, after batting .284 for the Mountain Cities, hit only .171 for the Unions. Kansas City had even less success than Altoona and won 16 against 64 losses. Altoona's Germany Smith jumped to Cleveland of the National League.

The guiding light behind the Union Association was wealthy St. Louis businessman Harry Lucas, who fought against the baseball reserve clause and signed many players who fell into this category. His star on the Maroons was second baseman Fred Dunlap, who led the league in batting with a .412 average and in home runs with 13. St. Louis easily dominated the league, winning 94 and losing only 19 games. In addition to Altoona and St. Louis, the other six original Union Association teams were the Baltimore Monuments, Boston Reds, Chicago Browns, Cincinnati Outlaw Reds, Washington Nationals and Philadelphia Keystones.

Obviously, any memorabilia from the Altoona Mountain Cities would be extremely rare. Collectors should be on the lookout for scorecards, club stationery, stock certificates, ticket stubs, and pennants, all of which may or may not exist. It gives collectors something to search for, and any materials discovered on the Mountain Cities would be real treasures. For further reading see *Baseball (1845–1891) from the Newspaper Accounts* by Preston D. Orem.

Anaheim, California

CALIFORNIA ANGELS

American League 1961 to Present

If California Angels owner Gene Autry had one wish, it would probably be to see the American League pennant flying over the Big A Stadium in Anaheim. Since acquiring an expansion franchise in 1961, the Angels have reached the playoffs three times, but always lost in the American League Championship Series.

Firmly established in Anaheim, they played in and were called the Los Angeles Angels during the first five years of their existence. The first year the Angels played their games in Wrigley Field, former home of the minor league Angels of the Pacific Coast League. Beginning in 1962 the Angels played in Dodger Stadium although they referred to it as Chavez Ravine in order to establish their own identity. When their own stadium—the Big A—opened in Orange County, the Angels at last had their own state-of-the-art facility.

Although he played only 11 games during their initial season, six-time All-Star shortstop Jim Fregosi, played with the Angels through the 1971 season and became one of the most popular Angels in history. He also managed them to their first division title in 1979. That year Don Baylor became the only Angel to win the American League Most Valuable Player by compiling a .296 batting average with 36 home runs and a league high 139 runs batted in. In the 1979 American League Championship Series the Angels lost to Baltimore.

The Angels reached the championship series again in 1982, sparked by Hall of Fame outfielder Reggie Jackson. He led the league with 39 home runs, still a club record. This time the Angels bowed to Milwaukee.

Hall of Famer Rod Carew also was an integral part of the first two Angels championship teams and enjoyed his finest sea-

son with the Angels in 1983, when he led the league with a .339 batting average—best in Angels history.

Outfielder-catcher Brian Downing and second baseman Bobby Grich are the only Angels to play on all three Western Division champions, and both rank among the best players the Angels have had throughout the years. Grich, a three-time All-Star selection, is the only Angel other than Fregosi to play 1000 games or more at one position.

In 1986 the Angels won the Western Division title a third time but lost in seven games to the Boston Red Sox, who rallied from a three to one series deficit to win the last three games. Although batting has been the Angels strong suit over the years, future Hall of Famer Nolan Ryan pitched with California from 1972 through 1979 and was inducted into the Angels Hall of Fame in 1993. He joined Fregosi, Grich, Baylor and Carew in that honor. Although Carew and Jackson are the only former Angels to be inducted at Cooperstown, Ryan is certain to join them, with Baylor, Grich and Fregosi outside possibilities.

Meanwhile, Gene Autry, who has enjoyed so much success in business and the entertainment world, is hoping that a long-awaited American League pennant will someday be his.

Advertising Specialties

California Angels (American League)

1981 El Cholo Restaurant, multi-color matchbook schedule, manufactured by Universal Match Co., 7/8" × 5" $5

Ballpark Giveaways

California Angels

1977 Jersey, Bike Bag, Bat $5
1978 Poster $10
1978 Cushion $5
1979 Shirt, Cap $5

1965–66 window sticker, 3", denotes name change from Los Angeles Angels to California Angels and their new stadium in Anaheim, $10.

1980 Opening Night Poster, Maxwell
     House Mug $10
1980 Foremost Card Services Cushion $7
1980 T-Shirt $5
1981 Opening Night Poster $9
1982 Portrait Album, Thermal Mug............$9
1982 Cushion $5
1983 Calendar, No-spill Mug....................$9
1983 American League Mini Pennant Set ..$10
1984 Smokey the Bear Player Cards $12
1984 Calendar $8
1984 Yearbook $6
1984 Cushion $5
1985 Home Plate Serving Tray, National
     Secretary's Day Cushion $6
1985 Smokey the Bear Player Cards $10
1986 Calendar, Book Lamp, Desk Clock
     Calendar, Team Pennant $7
1986 Picnic Bag, Portable Radio, New
     Logo Cap $5
1986 Smokey the Bear Player Cards...........$9
1987 Calendar $7
1987 Smokey the Bear Card Set................$8
1987 License Plate Frame, Helmet,
     Flashlight, Visor, Cap, Cushion $5

1988 Calendar, Lunch Box, Team Photo,
     Windshield shade, Notebook, Bike
     Bag $7

Miscellaneous

BOBBIN' HEAD DOLLS

Los Angeles Angels

Category #I, 1960, 1961, Blue Square
    Base, boy head $85
Category #II, 1960, 1961, White Square
    Base, boy head $145
Category #III, 1960, 1961, White Round
    Miniature, boy head $130
Category #IV, 1962, 1963, 1964, Green
    Round Base, boy head $70
Category #V, 1962, 1963, 1964, Green
    Round Base, black player $650

California Angels

Category #VI, 1967, 1968, 1969, 1970,
    1971, 1972, Gold Round Base, boy
    head $50

Pennants

Los Angeles Angels

1961 First Year $50
1962, 1963, 1964, 1965 Regular Pennants ..$30

California Angels

1966 First Year in Anaheim Stadium $40
1967 All-Star game $75
1967, 1968, 1969, 1970 Regular Pennants ..$30
1971 through 1979 Regular Pennants $20
1979 League Championship $50
1980 Regular Pennant $20
1981, 1982 Regular Pennants $5
1982 League Championship $10
1983, 1984, 1985, 1986 Regular Pennants $5
1986 League Championship $10
1987, 1988, 1989 Regular Pennants $5
1989 All-Star Game $15
1990, 1991, 1992, 1993 Regular Pennants $3

1961 pennant, Los Angeles Angels,
white on red felt, 11½"
× 29½", $50.

Pins

Los Angeles Angels

1961, 1962, 1963, 1964, 1965 Crane Potato Chips, ⅞″, Round $5
1964, 1965 Guy's Potato Chips, ⅞″,
Round $5

California Angels

1966 Guy's Potato Chips, ⅞″, Round $5
1967, 1968, 1969 Crane Potato Chips, ⅞″,
Round $5
1984 Crane Potato Chips, ⅞″, Round $5

Publications

BOOKS

Newhan, Ross. *Angels Soar: A Cele-
bration of the 1985 California An-
gels*. Chicago, Il.: Contemporary
Books, 1985. ....$10.00
Newhan, Ross. *The California Angels*.
Garden City, N.Y.: Doubleday,
1982. ....$10.00
Rothaus, James R. *California Angels*.
Mankato, Mn.: Creative Educa-
tion, 1987. ....$5.00

MEDIA GUIDES

Los Angeles Angels

1961 First Year $50
1962 ....$45
1963 ....$40
1964, 1965 ....$25

California Angels

1966, 1967, 1968 ....$20
1969, 1970, 1971 ....$15
1972, 1973, 1974 ....$10
1975, 1976, 1977, 1978 ....$8
1979 Division Champs...........................$10
1980, 1981 ....$6

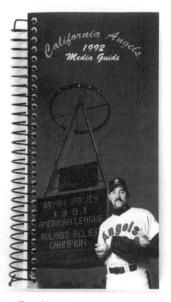

1992 media guide, 5″ × 9″, relief pitcher Bryan Harvey on cover, 352 pages, $4.

1982 Division Champs $8
1983, 1984, 1985 ....$4
1986 Division Champs $6
1987 through 1993 ....$4

PROGRAM AND SCORECARDS

Los Angeles Angels

1961 First Year $40
1962 ....$15
1963, 1964, 1965 ....$8

California Angels

1966, 1967, 1968 ....$7
1969, 1970, 1971 ....$6

1965–66 pins showing name
change from Los Angeles Angels
to California Angels, each
1¾″, $10 ea.

1972, 1973, 1974 ....$5
1975, 1976, 1977 ....$4
1978, 1979, 1980 ....$3
1981 through 1993 ....$2

YEARBOOKS

Los Angeles Angels

1962 First Yearbook............................$100
1963 ....$50
1964, 1965 ....$50
1966 First Yearbook in Anaheim $65
1967 ....$27
1968 through 1982 ....None Issued
1983, 1984, 1985 ....$7
1986 ....None Issued
1987 through 1993 ....$6

1988 schedule issued by Ticketron, 2½″ × 4″, $1.

1980 through 1985 ....$2
1986 through 1993 ....$1

Special Events

ALL-STAR PRESS PINS

1967 ....$150
1989 ....$85

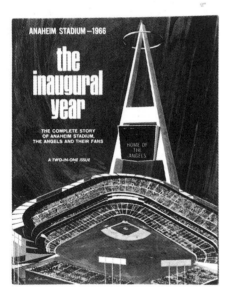

1966 yearbook, inaugural year, Anaheim, 8½″ × 11″,
64 pages, $65.

Schedules

Los Angeles Angels

1961 First Year $35
1962, 1963 ....$30
1964, 1965 ....$20

California Angels

1966 First Year in Anaheim Stadium $20
1967, 1968, 1969 ....$15
1970 through 1979 ....$10

1967 program, All-Star game, 8¼″ × 11″,
26 pages, $100.

1967 ticket (complete), All-Star
game, 2¾" × 8", $70.

ALL-STAR PROGRAMS

California Angels

1967 ....$100
1989 ....$10

ALL-STAR GAME TICKETS

1967 Complete Ticket $70
1967 Ticket Stub...................................$35
1989 Complete Ticket $30
1989 Ticket Stub...................................$15

LEAGUE CHAMPIONSHIP SERIES PROGRAMS

1979 ....$15
1982 ....$10
1986 ....$8

LEAGUE CHAMPIONSHIP SERIES TICKETS

1979 Complete Ticket $30
1979 Ticket Stub...................................$15
1982 Complete Ticket $30
1982 Ticket Stub...................................$15
1986 Complete Ticket $25
1986 Ticket Stub...................................$10

Arlington, Texas

TEXAS RANGERS

American League 1972 to Present

The Texas Rangers began operations in Arlington, Texas, when the Washington Senators franchise was moved to the Lone Star State following the 1971 season. Arlington Mayor Tom Vandergrift was the driving force behind the move by persuading owner Robert E. Short to abandon the nation's Capital with a huge radio and television contract. In 21 seasons since the move, the Rangers' best seasons were second-place finishes in the American League Western Division in 1974, 1977, 1978, 1981 and 1986. Five games is as close as they've ever come to the top spot.

The Rangers were hardly an instant success in Texas and drew only 662,974 fans their first season, only a slight improvement over their last season in Wash-

ington. In 1974 the Ranger's attendance exceeded one million fans; it wasn't until 1989 that more than two million fans passed through the turnstiles. The all-time attendance mark was reached in 1990, when the record-breaking performances of the ageless wonder Nolan Ryan lured 2,057,887 fans to attend games at Arlington Stadium. Ryan was largely responsible for drawing more than two million in 1989 as a sellout crowd in excess of 40,000 was on hand to cheer him on nearly every time he pitched. Ryan, the career strikeout leader in major league history, has been the prime reason the Rangers have become a successful franchise since he joined the club in 1989.

In 1974 outfielder Jeff Burroughs became the first and only Ranger player to win the American League's Most Valuable Player Award as he batted .301, hit 25 HR and knocked in 118 RBIs. In recent years outfielder Reuben Sierra (since traded to Oakland) emerged as one of baseball's top sluggers, hitting 30 HR in 1987 and setting a club record of 119 RBI in 1989. The club's single-season home run leader is catcher Lance Parrish, who hit 32 in 1987.

Only two former Rangers have been elected to Baseball's Hall of Fame, and both are former pitchers. Ferguson Jenkins, who set a Ranger's record with 25 victories in 1974, and Gaylord Perry, who won 48 of his 314 career victories with the Rangers, both were elected in 1991. Ryan still is pitching in 1993 and is almost certain to be elected five years after his playing career officially ends.

Ballpark Giveaways

Texas Rangers

1975 Cap, Bat, Ball, T-shirt, Wristband, Jacket $5
1975 Poster $10
1983 Bumper Sticker, Jacket, Tote Bag, Batting Glove, Wrist Band, Helmet, Equipment Bag, Uniform Shirt, Cap, Back Pack, T-shirt, Frisbee, Ball (with facsimile autographs, $15) $5
1984 Decal, Wrist Band, Equipment Bag, Visor, Umbrella, Tote Bag, Beach Towel, Batting Glove, Cap, T-shirt, Helmet, Jogging Shorts, Bumper Sticker, Pennant (if dated, $7)............$5
1984 Team Poster, Team Picture $10
1985 Calendar (first), Team Picture, Team Poster $10
1985 Decal, Wrist Band, Equipment Bag, Sun Visor, Pennant, Umbrella, Tote Bag, Beach Towel, Batting Glove,

Watch, Cap, Helmet Bank, Roll-up Cap, Shirt, Back Pack $5
1986 Jacket, Batting Glove, Wrist Band, Pennant, Roll-up Cap, Visor, Helmet, Glove, Tote Bag, Uniform Shirt, Cap, Bat, Watch, Equipment Bag, T-shirt $5
1986 Team Picture $10
1987 Calendar, Team Poster, Team Picture $8
1987 Beat the Yankees Hankee $6
1987 Blue Jacket, White Jacket, Visor, Home Uniform Shirt, Away Uniform Shirt, Ladies Tote Bag, Batting Glove, Wrist Band, Pennant, Helmet, Bat, Cap, Corduroy Cap, Equipment Bag, Watch $5
1988 Surf Baseball Card Book $15
1988 Calendar, Team Poster, Team Picture..$8
1988 White Jacket, Blue Jacket, Wrist Band, Cap, Batting Glove & Pennant, Home Shirt, Away Shirt, Glove Radio, T-shirt, Sun Visor, Equipment Bag, Watch, Notebook $5
1989 Windbreaker, Wrist Towel & Batting Glove, Watch, Home Uniform Shirt, Away Uniform Shirt, Painter's Cap, Glove, Car Shade, Bat, T-shirt, Equipment Bag, Warm-up Jersey, License Plate Frame, Men's Shaving Kit, Roll-up Cap, Back Pack..........$5
1989 Team Poster, Team Picture $7
1990 Miller Lite Magnet Schedule, State Fair Foods Wrist Towel & Batting Glove, Dr. Pepper Glove, Coca Cola/Kroger Bat, Affiliated Food Stores/Kool Aid Road Jersey, Dr. Pepper Squeeze Bottle, Affiliated/10 K Sunglasses, Coca Cola/Tom Thumb Home Jersey, Panine Stocker Album, Dr. Pepper/Minyard Equipment Bag, Gatorade Cap, HSE

1978 placemat, multi-colored plastic, from Polar Bear Ashburn's homemade style ice cream parlors, 11″ × 17″ (there are at least four different placemats, each featuring three players), each $6.

Sun Visor, Hills Brothers Coffee Warm-up Jersey, Coca-Cola Watch, Decker Foods Lunch Bag, Milk Duds Back Pack $6

1990 Mother's Cookie Poster, Tarrant Printing Team Picture, Decker's Food Calendar, Budweiser All-Star Poster $7

1991 Decker's Food Calendar, Tarrant Printing Team Picture $7

1991 Coca-Cola/Diamond Shamrock Baseball Cards.................................$8

1991 Mother's Cookies Baseball Cards.....$10

1991 Sunglasses, Notepad.........................$5

1991 Miller Lite Magnet Schedule, Coca-Cola/Tom Thumb Home Jersey State Fair Foods Wrist Towel & Batting Glove, Dr. Pepper/Skaggs Baseball Glove, HSE Helmet, Decker's Food Lunch Bag, Gatorade Cap, NCNB Roll-up Cap, Fina Warm-up Jersey, Coca-Cola/Minyard's Watch, Milk Duds Back Pack $6

1991 Donruss Card Book, Upper Deck Cards $7

1992 Decker's Calendar, Decker's Poster, Dr. Pepper/Tom Thumb Lunch Box, Tarrant Printing Team Picture $7

1992 Coca-Cola/7-11 Autograph Baseball ..$10

1992 Upper Deck Cards $7

1992 Mother's Cookies Baseball Cards......$10

1992 Miller/WBAP Magnet Schedule, Dr. Pepper Glove, Fina Warm-up Jersey, Gatorade Cap, Coca Cola/Minyard Watch, Dr. Pepper Road Jersey, Bizmart Roll-up Hat, Dr. Pepper Wrist Band, Jolly Rancher Helmet, Dr. Pepper/Minyard Sports Bag, Coca-Cola Belt Bag, Coca-Cola/Tom Thumb Home Jersey, Nation's Bank Back Pack..................$6

1992 Donruss Baseball Book $7

1992 Coca-Cola Food Lion Baseball Cards $8

1993 Decker Food Calendar, Memories of Arlington Stadium Cassette $7

1993 Dr. Pepper's Collector Pins 1, 2, 3, 4 ....ea. $8

1993 Upper Deck Cards, Donruss Card Book $7

1993 Coca-Cola Cap, Coca-Cola Cooler, Dr. Pepper Glove, Coca-Cola Beach Towel, Coca-Cola Bat, Fina Commemorative Cap, Gatorade Sports Bottle, Dr. Pepper Sports Bag, Coca-Cola Belt Bag $6

Miscellaneous

BOBBIN' HEAD DOLLS

Category #VI, 1972, Gold Round Base, Boy Head $55

Pennants

1972 First Year $30
1973 through 1980 ....$20
1981 through 1990 ....$5
1991, 1992, 1993 ....$3

Pins

1984 Crane Potato Chips, ⅞", Round $3

Publications

BOOKS

Keating, Bern. *An Illustrated History of the Texas Rangers.* Chicago: Rand McNally, 1976. ....$20.00
• Rogers, Phil. *Impossible Takes a Little Longer: The Texas Rangers from Pretenders to Contenders.* Dallas: Taylor Publishing Co., 1990. ....$16.95
Rothaus, James R. *Texas Rangers.* Mankato, Mn.: Creative Education, 1987. ....$5.00

MEDIA GUIDES

1972 First Year $18
1973 ....$15
1974, 1975 ....$10

Regulation size baseball in plastic ball holder, sponsored by Coca-Cola and 7-11 Stores, carries the logos of both companies and Texas Rangers. Red, white, and blue box measures 3¾" × 5". Manufactured by Sports Products Corporation, Cleveland, Ohio, $6.

1976, 1977	$8
1978, 1979	$7
1980, 1981	$6
1982, 1983	$5
1984 through 1993	$4

PROGRAMS AND SCORECARDS

1972 First Year	$20
1973	$5
1974 through 1983	$4
1984 through 1993	$3

YEARBOOKS

1976 First Yearbook	$30
1977	$20
1978	$15
1979	$12
1980	$10
1981, 1982	$8
1983	None Issued
1984, 1985	$5
1986, 1987, 1988, 1989	None Issued
1990, 1991, 1992, 1993	$5

Schedules

1972 First Year	$12
1973 through 1979	$10
1980 through 1985	$2
1986 through 1993	$1

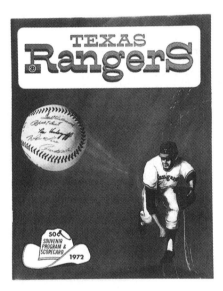

1972 program, Rangers first home game against the Kansas City Royals on April 6, 8½″ × 11″, 40 pages, $50.

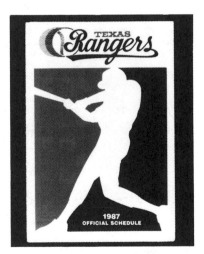

1987 schedule, Rangers, red, white, and blue, produced by Budweiser and KTVT, 2½″ × 4″, $1.

Atlanta, Georgia

ATLANTA BRAVES

National League 1966 to Present

The Atlanta Braves became the first major league team in the deep south when the Milwaukee Braves moved there in 1966. Faltering attendance in Milwaukee brought about the franchise shift; only 555,584 saw the Braves in action during their final season there in 1965. Attendance in Atlanta the first season was nearly three times better, as 1,539,801 fans passed through the turnstiles at Fulton County Stadium.

The Braves can trace their baseball lineage to the Boston Red Stockings, members of the original National League in 1876. After finishing fourth that season, the Red Stockings won two straight National League pennants under manager Harry Wright in 1877 and 1878, and again in 1883 with John Morrill at the helm. The team nickname became Beaneaters in 1891 and the team won three consecutive pennants under Frank Selee and two more in 1897 and 1898 with Selee as manager. It wasn't until 1914 that Boston won another pennant, and they went on to upset the Philadelphia Athletics in the World Series. The team went from last place in July to the championship under miracle man Frank Stallings. The franchise moved from Boston to Milwaukee in 1953, and the Braves won pennants in 1957 and 1958 and were world champs in 1957.

The Braves drew more than a million fans during their first six seasons in Atlanta, but attendance fell sharply as team success diminished. It was not until 1980, when a fourth-place finish under manager Bobby Cox, brought 1,048,411 fans to the ballpark. Under manager Joe Torre in 1983, a second-place finishh attracted 2,119,935 fans. That was the attendance high-water mark until the Braves won consecutive National League pennants in 1991 and 1992, drawing 2,140,217 and 3,077,400 respectively.

Even though the Braves finished fifth their first year in Atlanta, Braves fans had much to cheer about as future all-time home run king Hank Aaron let the league in home runs with 44 (his uniform number) and 127 RBI.

With the advent of divisional play in 1969, the Braves won the National League Western Division championship as knuckleballing Phil Niekro won 23 games and Hank Aaron hammered 44 homers and drove in 97. However, they lost to the miraculous New York Mets three games to none in the playoffs. Even though Rico Carty won the batting title with a .366 batting average and Hank Aaron hit 38 home runs and picked up his three-thousandth career hit, the Braves finished seventh in 1970.

On April 8, 1974, Hank Aaron broke Babe Ruth's all-time home run record by slamming number 715 against Al Downing of the Los Angeles Dodgers. Television magnate Ted Turner bought the team in 1976 and made news in 1977 when he took over as field manager during a 17-game losing streak. His tenure lasted only one game—a 2 to 1 loss to Pittsburgh—before Commissioner Bowie Kuhn ruled he could not manage the team.

In 1981 Hank Aaron was elected to the Baseball Hall of Fame, the first Atlanta player to earn that honor. In 1982 outfielder Dale Murphy became the National League MVP by hitting 36 HR and driving in 109 runs to lead the Braves to the Western Division title. However, they lost to the St. Louis Cardinals in the championship series. Murphy won the MVP crown again in 1982 as the Braves drew more than two million fans for the first time.

In 1991 everything fell into place for the Braves as they went from the worst record in the National League in 1990 to the World Series. Terry Pendleton, signed by new general manager John Schuerholz as a free agent during the off-season, won the National League batting title (.319) and was named league MVP. Lefthander Tom Glavine won the Cy Young award with a record of 21 and 11 and a 2.55 ERA, and Bobby Cox was named Manager of the Year. After defeating the Pittsburgh Pirates in the NLCS, the Braves lost the World Series to Minnesota four games to three; the Twins swept four games at home while the Braves won all three in Atlanta.

With the finest young pitching staff in baseball (Tom Glavine, Steve Avery and John Smoltz, with veteran Charley Liebrandt contributing 15 wins), the Braves reached the World Series again in 1992 only to lose to the Toronto Blue Jays four games to two. If Atlanta can keep its team intact, it figures to be a pennant contender into the twenty-first century.

In addition to Hank Aaron, other Atlanta Braves in the Hall of Fame are Eddie Mathews, who played only one season in Atlanta (1966); Gaylord Perry, another one-season Brave (1981); and Hoyt Wilhelm (1969–1971).

Ballpark Giveaways

Atlanta Braves

1971 Ball, Bat, Helmet	$5
1971 Ball with Facsimile Autographs	$25
1972 Helmet, T-shirt, Cap	$5

1973 Bat, Ball (with facsimile auto-
      graphs, $25) $5
1974 Helmet, Batting Glove, Bat, Jacket $5
1975 Poster $20
1976 Bat, Halter Top, Jacket, Cushion,
      Cap, Equipment Bag, Belt, Visor $5
1976 Photo Album (first one) $15
1977 Photo Album, Poster $13
1977 Jacket, Scarf, Jersey, Bat $5
1977 Pennant (with date, $12) $10
1978 English Leather Jacket $6
1978 Helmet, Bat, Batting Glove $5
1979 Cap, Jacket, Helmet, Jersey $5
1980 Jacket, Helmet, Cushion, Jersey,
      Cap $5
1981 Cap, Cushion, Equipment Bag $5
1982 Gulf Oil Road Jersey, U.S. Army
      Gym Bag, Treasure Drug Wrist
      Band, Treasure Drug Batting Glove,
      Treasure Drug Tube Socks................$6
1982 Maxwell House Coffee Mug $10
1983 Maxwell House Coffee Mug $10
1983 Seat Cushion, Ball (with facsimile
      autographs, $15) $5
1983 U.S. Army Mini Cooler.....................$6
1984 Day's Inn Braves Calendar (first
      one), Canon Team Photo, Canon
      Poster $10
1984 U.S. Army Painters Cap, Digital
      Sports Bag, Kinnett Jersey $6
1985 Canon Team Photo, Canon Poster $9
1985 Hostess Autographed Ball $12
1985 Treasure Drug Shirt, U.S. Army/
      Braves Beach Towel, Domino Pizza
      Cup, Domino Pizza Sports Bag $6
1986 Maxwell House Calendar, Bud-
      weiser Mug $9
1986 Kook Aid Watch, HFC Sunglasses,
      Kook Aid Cap, Butterfinger/Baby
      Ruth Helmet $6

1987 Oscar Mayer Calendar, Fuji Team
      Photo $8
1987 Surf Braves History Book $20
1987 Budweiser Umbrella, S.E. American
      Dairy Assn. Jersey $6
1987 U.S. Forestry Service Baseball
      Cards $7
1988 Fuji Team Photo $8
1988 Sony Sunglasses, Whoppers Base-
      ball Glove, Cap $6
1989 Good Cents Magnetic Calendar,
      Bounce Team Poster, Bud Light
      Stein $8
1989 Flav-o-Rich T-shirt, Hero's Painters
      Cap, Coca-Cola/Winn Dixie Cap,
      Irish Spring Helmet, Wheaties
      Glove, Coca-Cola Squeeze Bottle,
      U.S. Forestry Wallet $6
1989 Kraft Lunch Box, Gatorade Pouring
      Pitcher $8
1990 25th Anniversary Pin or Poster $10
1991 Nestle Coffee Mug, Dubuque Hot
      Dog Team Photo, Flav-o-Rich
      Lunch Box $7
1991 Dubuque Hot Dog Baseball Card
      Book $8
1991 Sony Sunglasses, Jolly Rancher Bat,
      Tony the Tiger Sports Bag.................$6
1991 Upper Deck Card Set.......................$7
1992 Nestle Tea Squeeze Bottle, Sony
      Sunglasses, Coca-Cola Wallet, Toy-
      ota Batting Glove, Kraft Kroger Bat-
      ting Helmet, Jolly Rancher Glove,
      Holiday Inn Cap, Olive Garden Pen-
      nant, Georgia Power Magnet,
      Colgate Bat, Kellog's Wrist Band,
      Colonial Bread Notebook $6
1992 Flav-o-Rich Thermos, Subway
      Team Funpack, Kids Cuisine
      Poster, Gatorade Commemorative
      Stein $7

Miscellaneous

BOBBIN' HEAD DOLLS

Category #VI, 1967 through 1972, Golf
      Round Base, Mascot $50

Pennants

1966 First Year $40
1967, 1968, 1969 Regular Pennants $30
1969 League Championship Series...........$75
1970, 1971, 1972 Regular Pennants $20
1972 All-Star Game $50
1973 through 1980 Regular Pennants $20
1981, 1982 Regular Pennants $5
1982 League Championship Series..........$15
1983 through 1990 ....$5
1991, 1992 Regular Pennants $5
1991, 1992 League Championship Series ..$10
1991, 1992 World Series $10
1993 Regular Pennant $5

1965 window sticker, 6", Braves logo and message
"This Year the Crackers/Next Year the Braves," sig-
nifying the minor league Atlanta Crackers would be
replaced by the Braves (who announced they were
moving from Milwaukee to Atlanta), $20.

1972 pennant, All-Star game, Braves logo and Atlanta stadium, 12″ × 30″, $50.

Pins

1966 Guy's Potato Chips, ⅞″, Round $5
1967, 1968, 1969 Crane Potato Chips, ⅞″,
    Round $5
1984 Crane Potato Chips, ⅞″, Round $3

1992 pin, 6″, National League champions limited edition (#20, 124 of 30,000), $8.

Postcards

1973 Atlanta Braves, CH 5258, Multiple
    Photos, Los Angeles, California $15

Publications

BOOKS

Bisher, Furman. *Miracle in Atlanta.*
    World Publishing Co., 1966. ....$15.00
•Blackburn-Tyson, Jackie, ed. *The Sil-
    ver Season, 25 Years of Braves
    Baseball in Atlanta.* Atlanta:
    Sports Printing, 1990. ....$6.95
Couch, J. Hudson, *The Braves First
    Fifteen Years in Atlanta.* Atlanta:
    The Other Alligator Creek Co.,
    1985. ....$10.00
Martin, Mollie. *Atlanta Braves.* Man-
    kato, Minnesota: Creative Educa-
    tion, 1982. ....$5.00
May, Frank. *The Amazing Braves:
    Story of the Braves 1982 Start.* At-
    lanta: Philmay Enterprises, Inc.,
    1983. ....$10.00
Onigman, Mark. *This Date in Atlanta
    Braves History.* New York: Stein &
    Day, 1982. ....$5.00

1973 postcard, Atlanta Braves, chrome color, 3½″ × 5½″, $15.

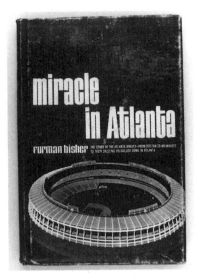

1966 *Miracle in Atlanta* by Furman Bisher (the story of how Atlanta acquired the Milwaukee Braves), 5¾″ × 8½″, 180 pages, $15.

• Rosenberg, J.J. *Miracle Season, The Inside Story of the 1991 Atlanta Braves: Race For Baseball Glory.* Atlanta: Turner, 1991. ....$19.95

MEDIA GUIDES

1966 First Year	$30
1967	$20
1968	$18
1969 Division Champs	$22
1970, 1971, 1972	$15
1973, 1974, 1975	$10
1976, 1977, 1978	$8
1979, 1980	$7
1981	$6
1982 Division Champs	$8
1983 through 1990	$5
1991, 1992 Division Champs	$6
1993	$4

PROGRAMS AND SCORECARDS

1966 First Year	$25
1967	$15
1968	$10
1969	$12
1970 through 1976	$5
1977 through 1984	$4
1985 through 1993	$3

YEARBOOKS

1966 First Year	$100
1966 Atlanta Braves Photo Album	$20
1967	$75
1968	$60

1969	$55
1970	$45
1971	$35
1972, 1973	$25
1974	$20
1975, 1976	$18
1977	$15
1978, 1979	$12
1980, 1981	$10
1982 Division Champs	$15
1983	$6
1984 through 1993	$5

Schedules

1966 First Year	$30
1967, 1968, 1969	$15
1970 through 1979	$10
1980 through 1985	$3
1986 through 1993	$1

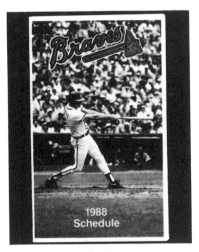

1988 folding schedule by Colony Square Hotel of Atlanta, 2½″ × 4″, Dale Murphy batting, $1.

Special Events

ALL-STAR GAME PRESS PIN

1972	$165

ALL-STAR GAME PROGRAMS

1972 Program	$35

ALL-STAR GAME TICKETS

1972 Complete Ticket	$55
1972 Ticket Stub	$15

LEAGUE CHAMPIONSHIP PROGRAMS

1969	$50
1982	$10

1966 ticket (complete), 2½″ × 5⅜″, first Major League game in Atlanta on April 12, $75.

1991, 1992 (Programs are very hard to find and command a premium)........$20

LEAGUE CHAMPIONSHIP SERIES TICKETS

1969 Complete Ticket $30
1969 Ticket Stub..................................$15
1982 Complete Ticket $15
1982 Ticket Stub $5
1991 Complete Ticket $10
1991 Ticket Stub $5
1992 Complete Ticket $10
1992 Ticket Stub $5

WORLD SERIES PRESS PINS

1991 ....$30
1992 ....$30

WORLD SERIES PROGRAMS

1991 ....$10
1992 ....$10

WORLD SERIES GAME TICKETS

1991 Complete Ticket $20
1991 Ticket Stub..................................$10
1992 Complete Ticket $20
1992 Ticket Stub..................................$10

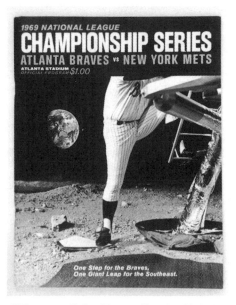

1969 program, National League Championship Series vs. N.Y. Mets, 8½″ × 11″, 80 pages, $50.

Baltimore, Maryland

BALTIMORE LORD BALTIMORES

National Association 1872 to 1874

Baltimore had a major league baseball team as early as 1872, when the Lord Baltimores (also called the Canaries) joined the National Association in its second sea-son. Bill Craver's team gave a good account of itself and finished third in the ten-team league with a record of 34 wins and 19 defeats, eight games back of the champion Boston Red Stockings. Right-hander Bobby Mathews, who pitched and won the first major league game in history for the Fort Wayne Kelciongas in 1871, was Baltimore's ace and finished with a record of 25 and 16. Mathews signed with the New York Mutuals in 1873, but Hall of Famer Candy Cummings, inventor of the curve ball and winner of 33 games with the Mutuals in 1872, promptly signed with Baltimore when Mathews joined the Mutuals. The Lord Baltimores finished third again as Cummings won 28 and lost 14, even better than Mathews' mark the previous year. However, in 1874 the financially troubled Lord Baltimores lost all their top players to other teams and finished last. Bankrupt, the Canaries dropped out of the majors.

BALTIMORE ORIOLES

American Association 1882–1891, National League 1892–1899, American League 1901–1902, 1954 to Present

Had the Canaries been more successful, another member of the bird kingdom, the Orioles, may never have been associated with Baltimore baseball. However, when Baltimore rejoined the major leagues as charter members of the American Association in 1882, they were called the Baltimore Orioles, a name synonymous with baseball success to this day.

The American Association was set up to compete as a second major league against the established National League. When the two leagues merged in 1892 to become the National League, the Orioles were part of the merger and soon became the most feared team in the game. They intimidated rivals not only with their magnificent skills on the diamond but also their rowdy tactics—which included flying fists and razor-sharp spikes that struck fear into the hearts of the opposition. No less than seven future Hall of Famers graced the Orioles lineup during the fabulous 1890s, when the Birds won three consecutive National League pennants (1894, 1895 and 1896) and two Temple Cup championships (1896 and 1897). Oriole stars Wee Willie Keeler, Joe Kelley and Hughie Jennings were sold to the Brooklyn Dodgers after the 1898 season and promptly led the Dodgers to two championships in 1899 and 1900. The Orioles lost their National League franchise

after the 1899 season, but when the American League was organized in 1901, the Orioles were again charter members. John McGraw, hero from the National League championship days, acted as player-manager and directed them to a fifth-place finish. However, in 1902 the Orioles finished last and McGraw took off for New York to manage the National League Giants in the middle of the season. After the dismal 1902 season, the franchise was sold to New York interests where it became the Highlanders and later the Yankees. Baltimore was relegated to minor league status until 1914, when a third major league known as the Federal League was established and the Terrapins carried the Baltimore banner. Huge financial losses doomed the Federal League after only two seasons and Baltimore once again was back in the minor leagues. That changed permanently in 1954 when Baltimore civic leaders, spearheaded by Clarence Miles and James Keelty, purchased the financially troubled St. Louis Browns and moved them to the shores of the Chespaeake Bay. Since then they have become one of baseball's most successful franchises, winning American League pennants in 1966, 1969, 1971, 1979 and 1983, and winning World Series championships in 1966, 1970 and 1983. Hall of Famers Brooks and Frank Robinson, Jim Palmer, George Kell, Hoyt Wilhelm and Luis Aparicio are only a few of the stars who have worn the orange and black of the modern Orioles as they carry on a rich century-old baseball tradition in Baltimore.

Baltimore was represented by the Monumentals in the Union Association in 1884 and the Terrapins in the Federal League in 1914 and 1915.

Hall of Famers who played major league baseball in Baltimore include: Luis Aparicio, Chief Bender, Roger Bresnahan, Hughie Jennings, "Wee Willie" Keeler, George Kell, Joe Kelley, Joe McGinnity, John McGraw, Jim Palmer, Robin Roberts, Brooks Robinson, Frank Robinson, Wilbert Robinson, and Hoyt Wilhelm.

For additional information on the Baltimore Orioles, see *The Home Team* by James Bready, Hawke, 1979; *The Baltimore Orioles* by Frederick G. Lieb, Putnam, 1955; and *100 Years of Baseball in Baltimore,* Maryland Historical Society, 1959.

Advertising Specialties

Baltimore Orioles (American Association)

1887 Kalamazoo Bats Team Card N690, 4½″ × 6½″, Cabinet Card issued by Charles Gross & Co. of Philadelphia as a promotion for its Kalamazoo Bats Cigarettes. The Baltimore Baseball Club features a team photo with the caption in a white box at the bottom of the photo **$2,000**

Baltimore (Federal League)

Publications

PROGRAMS AND SCORECARDS

1914 Program, Baltimore Federal League Team's initial season **$500**

1915 Program, Baltimore Federal League Team's final season **$450**

Advertising Specialties

Baltimore Orioles (National League)

1894 Orange, Black, and White Paper Pennant issued by Foster's German Army & Navy Cure measuring 4″ × 2″. Back says "Our Club takes the Pennant, Our Cure takes the Palm"...**$500**

Baltimore Orioles (American League)

1959 *The 1959 Baltimore Orioles Story* by Phillies Cigars.................................**$25**
1993 Multi-Color Budweiser Beer Tap Handle **$25**

Ballpark Giveaways

1972 T-shirt **$10**
1972 Cap, Helmet **$5**
1972 Ball with Facsimile Autographs **$25**

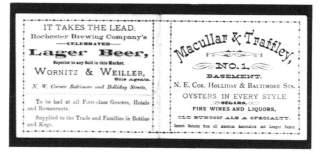

1884 schedule, pink cardboard, 3″ × 6⅞″, opened to reveal an ad by Macullar & Traffley oyster house on the front cover and Rochester Brewing Company's Lager Beer on the back. The schedule on the inside shows the home games on the left and road games on the right, $250.

1914, one share of preferred stock in The Federal Baseball Club of Baltimore, 9½″ × 11½″, $1,500.

1914, photo postcard of Federal League Terrapins taken during spring training by R. S. McConnell on March 16, at Southern Pines, North Carolina (believed to be the earliest postcard of a Federal League team), 3½" × 5½", $750.

1973 Cap, Golf Cap, Helmet $5
1973 Special T-shirt $10
1973 Ball with Facsimile Autographs $25
1974 Poster, Set of Trading Cards $20
1974 Helmet, Bat $5
1975 Crown Orioles Jacket, RPS Seat
        Cushion $10
1975 Cap, Team Shirt $5
1976 Crown Orioles Jersey.....................$10
1976 Jacket, Cap $5
1976 Coca-Cola Orioles Tankard (first
        one) $15
1977 Autographed Ball, Photo Album
        (first one) $20
1977 Jacket, Helmet $5
1977 Tankard $13
1978 Orioles Toyota Black Bat (first one) ..$10
1978 Orioles WJZ Photo Album $15
1978 English Leather Jacket, Hardee's
        Back Pack, Baltimore Federal Shirt $6
1978 Cap, Ski Cap $5
1979 Photo Album A.L. Champs $15
1979 Budweiser Orioles Tankard $14
1979 Crown Team Jersey, Larry Beck
        Stick Pin, Esskay Poncho..................$7
1979 Halter Top, Ski Cap.........................$5
1980 Orioles Championship Pennant $15

1980 Larry Beck Ladies Charm, Esskay
        Seat Cushion $6
1980 Cap, Halter Top $5
1981 Frito Lay Orioles Hall of Fame
        Poster, Busch Beer Tankard, Gulf
        Team Picture $13
1981 Gulf Team Picture, American Dairy
        Assn. Back to School Thermos $13
1981 Esskay Seat Cushion, Coca-Cola
        Jacket, Larry Beck Ladies Key
        Chain $6
1982 Busch Calendar (first one), Gulf
        Team Picture, Mid Atlantic Milk
        Assn. Thermos $13
1982 Carrier Jacket, Coca-Cola Cap, Ess-
        kay Team Jersey, Gulf Gym Bag,
        Larry Beck Key Chain $6
1982 Busch Orioles Hall of Fame Tan-
        kard $13
1982 Maxwell House Ski Cap $6
1983 Baltimore Sun Orioles Fanatic Sur-
        vival Kit, Anheiser Busch Tankard,
        Orioles Photo Album, Coca-Cola
        Hall of Fame Poster, WMAR/
        MAMMA Thermos (world champs) ...$15
1983 Burger King Bat, National Premium
        6 Pack Cooler, Yago Barbecue

1894 paper pennant, orange, black, and white, 2" × 4", issued by Foster's German Army & Navy Cure, states on the back, "Our club takes the pennant, Our cure takes the Palm," $500.

1966 plastic wall display, 9″ × 14″, National Brewing Company, color picture of the Baltimore Orioles who upset the Los Angeles Dodgers in four straight games in the World Series, $60.

Apron, Gulf Travel Bag, Super TV Jersey, Thom McAnn Socks, Esskay Women's Tote Bag, United Airlines Beach Towel, Hershey Park Helmet ...$6

1984 Championship Ring Replica $20

1984 Busch 30th Anniversary Tankard......$15

1984 30th Anniversary Poster, Sun Orioles Fanatic Survival Kit, World Championship Bats from Burger King $15

1984 Esskay Commemorative 30th Anniversary Cap, Coca-Cola World Championship Commemorative Bottle..$10

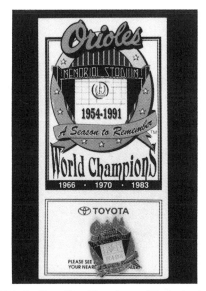

1991 pin, 1″, on 2″ × 5″ card, one of three pins by Toyota commemorating Orioles World Series championships in 1966, 1970, and 1983, $10 ea.

1984 Hershey Park Jacket, Gulf Oil Umbrella, Merritt S & L Jersey, Toyota Watch, Perdue Seat Cushion, Miller Visor, National Premium Cooler, Digital Equipment Sports Bag, Home Team Sports Beach Towel $6

1985 Burger King Calendar, Sunpapers Survival Kit, Budweiser Tankard $12

1985 Burger King Glove $6

1985 Umbrella, Cap, Picnic Cooler, Seat Cushions, Floppy Hat, Sunglasses, Kid's Jersey, Adult Jersey, Sports Bag, Sports Watch, Wallet $6

1986 Sunpapers Opening Day Kit, Chase Bank Calendar, Budweiser Tankard ..$10

1986 Coca-Cola Backpack, National Premium Cooler, Burger King Glove, Kay Jewelers Cosmetic Case, Esskay Seat Cushion, Baby Ruth/Butterfinger Cap, Miller Lite Floppy Hat, Kool-Aid Youth Jersey, WMAR-TV Umbrella, Toyota Travel Bag, Home Team Sports Visor, Chase Bank Sports Bag, Kool-Aid Shorts, Back to School Carrying Case $6

1987 WCBM Radio, Esskay Corduroy Cap, Coca-Cola Backpack, National Premium Cooler, Toyota Travel Bag, Miller Lite Floppy Hat, HTS Youth Jersey, Carefirst/WMAR-TV Umbrella, Chase Bank Sports Bag, Gatorade Sports Watch, MAMMA Back to School Binder, Kay Jewelers Table Clock $6

1987 Baltimore Sun Photo Album, Coors Orioles Hall of Fame Poster, Player-Team Photo Cards, Budweiser Tankard $10

1987 Youth Jacket, Travel Mug $5

1988 WBAL Calendar, Crown Commemorative Poster, Toyota Pins 1, 2, 3 (set $25), French Bray Photo Cards, Budweiser Thermal Pitcher, Lays Ruffles Mug $10

1988 Surf Baseball Card Book $15
1988 Kay Jewelers Desk Clock, Burger King Back Pack, Baltimore Sun Visor, Miller Lite Floppy Hat, Gatorade Bat, WMAR-TV/Carefirst Umbrella, HTS Rally Cap, MAMMA Jacket, Whoppers/Mild Duds Notebook...$6
1989 WBAL Calendar, French Bray Trading Cards, Kentucky Fried Chicken Team Picture, Crown Poster, Ruffles Travel Mug, Coors Tankard, Toyota Hall of Fame Poster $8
1989 Smokey the Bear Helmet, Esskay Cap, Miller Lite Cooler, Coca-Cola Jersey, Hero Cologne Painters Cap, Gatorade Bat, Jolly Rancher Candy Beach Towel, HTS Corduroy Cap, "The One Book" Sunglasses, Texaco Baseball, MAMMA/General Mills Gym Bag, Jello Gym Shorts, Burger King Frisbee, Baltimore Sun Squeeze Bottle $6
1990 WBAL Radio Calendar, Smokey the Bear Wallet, Toyota Picnic Cooler, Esskay Signature Cap, Miller Lite Floppy Hat, Breyer's Neon Cap, Texaco Squeeze Bottle, HTS Corduroy Hat, Crown Sunglasses, WMAR-TV Umbrella, MAMMA Relief Pitchers, Warner Brothers Sun Visor, Coors Lite Tankard, Kook-Aid Lunch Bag, French Bray Team Picture Poster, Coca-Cola Baseball Glove, Gatorade Bat $6
1990 Kenner Products Starting Line-Up, Donruss Baseball Card Book & Starter Set $10
1991 Kellog's Tony Tiger Cereal Bowl, Smokey the Bear Batting Helmet, HTS Orioles Replica Cap, Crown/Coca-Cola All-Time Orioles Card Set #1, Esskay Seat Cushion, Toyota Commerative Logo Pin, Miller Lite Floppy Hat, Diet Pepsi 1966 Replica Cap, Crown/Coca-Cola All-Time Orioles Card Set #2, Gatorade Squeeze Bottle, WMAR/Carefirst Umbrella, Donruss 1991 Orioles Baseball Card Book, Toyota Memorial Stadium Pin, One Book/French Bray Memorial Moments Poster Series 1, Texaco Sports Bag, Coors Lite Tankard, Crown/Coca-Cola All-Time Orioles Card Set #3, One Book Memorial Moments Poster Series II, Sports Illustrated For Kids Magazine, One Book Memorial Moments Poster Series III, Busch Lite Orioles 1992 Magnet Schedule..$6
1991 Kenner Starting Line-Up Collectible $10

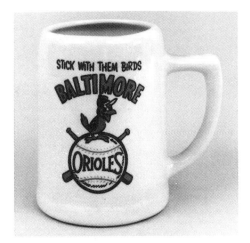

1954 white ceramic mug, 1954 Orioles logo and slogan "Stick with Them Birds" Mug is 4" × 5", handle extends 2", $150.

1992 Miller Lite Opening Night Flash Light, Hi Fi Player Decals, HTS/Texaco Replica Cap, C&P Telephone Picnic Coolers, The Baltimore Sun Donruss Card Book, USPS Collector's Stamps, Crown Orioles Action Stand-Ups #1, Smokey the Bear Waist Pack Miller Genuine Draft Orioles Zebra Cap, Major League Baseball, Maryland Marathon Baseball Day & Rookie League Magazine, Anheuser Busch Sports Bag, Crown Orioles Action Stand-Ups #II, Coca-Cola Beach Towel, WMAR/Carefirst Umbrella, French Bray Team Picture Poster, Coors Lite Tankard, Ryland Homes Pinstripe Cap, Gatorade Squeeze Bottle, SI Kids Magazine, MCI Baseball Glove, Cheerio's Cereal Bat.........$6

Miscellaneous

BOBBIN' HEAD DOLLS

Category #II, 1960, 1961, Green Diamond Base, (Lego on base) Mascot (Large) $175
Category #II, 1961, 1962, White Square Base, Mascot $265
Category #III, 1961, 1962, White Round Miniature, Mascot $285
Category #IV, 1962, 1963, 1964, Green Round Base, Mascot $115
Category #V, 1962, 1963, 1964, Green Round Base, Black Player $375

Category #VI, 1967 through 1972, Gold
Round Base, Mascot $70

Pennants

1894, 1895, 1896 3 Piece stitch felt pennant from the Baltimore Orioles,
1894, 1895, 1896, 8″ × 19″, containing the Orioles Logo, crossed bats
and the name Baltimore in block
letters down the center $2,000
1954 First Year $65
1955, 1956, 1957, 1958 Regular Pennants ..$50
1958 All-Star Game $125
1959, 1960 ....$50
1961 through 1966 Regular Pennants $30
1966 World Series...............................$75
1967, 1968, 1969 Regular Pennants $30
1969 League Championship Series...........$75
1969 World Series...............................$75
1970 Regular Pennant $30
1970 League Championship Series...........$75
1970 World Series...............................$75
1971 Regular Pennant $20
1971 League Championship Series...........$50
1971 World Series...............................$50
1972 through 1979 Regular Pennants $20
1979 League Championship Series...........$50
1979 World Series...............................$50
1980 Regular Pennant $20
1981, 1982, 1983 Regular Pennants $5
1983 League Championship Series...........$15
1983 World Series...............................$15
1984 through 1990 Regular Pennants $5
1991, 1992, 1993 Regular Pennants $3
1993 All-Star Game $12

Pins

1961 through 1965 Crane Potato Chips,
7/8″, Round $5
1967, 1968, 1969 Crane Potato Chips, 7/8″,
Round $5

1954 pin, 3½″, Baltimore in black block letters at top,
Orioles bird logo designed by Sunpapers artist
Jim Hartzel, $35.

1964, 1965, 1966 Guy's Potato Chips, 7/8″,
Round $5
1984 Crane Potato Chips, 7/8″, Round $3

Postcards

Baltimore Terrapins (Federal League),
Taken in Spring Training at Southern
Pines, N.C., 1914, RP, R.S. McConnel,
Southern Pines, N.C. $750
Baltimore Orioles, 1894, 1895, 1896
National League Champions, PL,
Bachrach Bros., Baltimore in 1907 .....$350
1956 RP, Baltimore Orioles $100

Publications

BOOKS

Bready, James. *The Home Team.*
1958. 1st Ed. $40.00

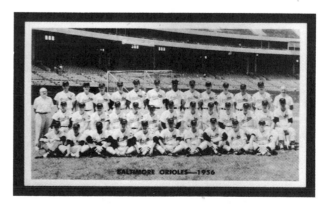

1956 postcard, black and white,
3¼″ × 5½″, Orioles, $100.

Hawkins, John C. *This Date in Baltimore Orioles/St. Louis Browns History.* New York: Stein & Day, 1982. ....$5.00
•Keplinger, Steve. *The Comeback Kids: A Fan Relives the Amazing Baltimore Orioles 1989 Season.* Salt Lake City: Publishers Press, 1989. .....$9.95
Lieb, Frederick. *The Baltimore Orioles.* G.P. Putnam's Sons, 1955. ......$100.00
Maryland Historical Society. *One Hundred Years of Baseball in Baltimore.* 1959. ....$35.00
•Miller, James E. *The Baseball Business: Pursuing Pennants and Profits in Baltimore.* Chapel Hill, N.C.: University of North Carolina Press, 1990. ....$24.95
Patterson, Ted. *Day By Day in Orioles History.* West Point, N.Y.: Leisure Press, 1984. ....$10.00
Rothaus, James R. *Baltimore Orioles.* Mankato, Mn.: Creative Education, 1987. ....$5.00

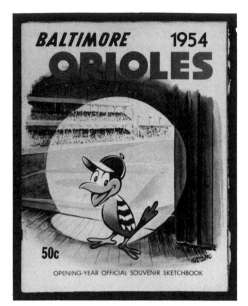

1954 yearbook, Orioles, 8¼″ × 10¾″, 48 pages, opening year, Jim Hartzel bird in spotlight, $200.

MEDIA GUIDES

1954 First Year $75
1955 ....$50
1956 ....$45
1957 ....$40
1958 ....$35
1959 ....$30
1960 through 1965 ....$20
1966 World Champs...............................$25
1967, 1968 ....$20
1969 League Champs $25
1970 World Champs..............................$25
1971 League Champs $20
1972 through 1975 ....$15
1976, 1977, 1978 ....$10
1979 League Champs $12
1980, 1981, 1982 ....$6
1983 World Champs $8
1984 through 1993 ....$4

PROGRAMS AND SCORECARDS

1954 First Year $75
1955 ....$65
1956 ....$55
1957, 1958, 1959 ....$20
1960, 1961 ....$15
1962, 1963, 1964, 1965 ....$10
1966 World Champions $12
1967, 1968 ....$7
1969 League Champs $10
1970 World Champions $10
1971 League Champs $10
1972, 1973, 1974 ....$6
1975, 1976, 1977, 1978 ....$5

1979 League Champs $6
1980, 1981, 1982 ....$4
1983 World Champions $6
1984 through 1993 ....$3

YEARBOOKS

1894 Pennant Souvenir of Baltimore by D.D. Guy...................................$2,500
1954 First Year $200
1955 ....$150
1956 ....$125
1957 ....$115
1958 ....$110
1959 ....$100
1960 ....$90
1961, 1962 ....$75
1963, 1964 ....$55
1965 ....$40
1966 World Champions $65
1967, 1968, 1969 ....$35
1970 World Champions $40
1971, 1972 ....$25
1973, 1974 ....$20
1975 ....$15
1976 through 1979 ....None Issued
1980 ....$10
1981, 1982 ....$8
1983 World Champions $15
1984, 1985, 1986 ....$7
1987 through 1992 ....None Issued
1993 ....$10

Schedules

1954 First Year $50
1955, 1956 .... $40
1957, 1958, 1959 .... $25
1960 through 1969 .... $15
1970 through 1979 .... $10
1980 through 1985 .... $3
1986 through 1993 .... $1

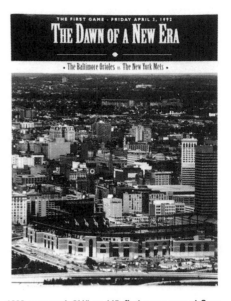

1954 Gunther Brewing Co. schedule, Orioles' first season, 2½″ × 3¾″, $50.

1992 scorecard, 8½″ × 11″, first game ever at Camden Yards, an exhibition between the Orioles and New
York Mets. Front has "The Dawn of a New Era" above
an aerial view of downtown Baltimore which shows a
closeup of the new ball park and Memorial Stadium,
the Orioles previous home, in the distance, $10.

Special Events

ALL-STAR GAME PRESS PINS

1958 All-Star Game $400
1993 First All-Star Game at Camden
    Yards $150

ALL-STAR PROGRAMS

1958 All-Star Game $200
1993 All-Star Game $12

ALL-STAR GAME TICKETS

1958 Complete Ticket $200
1958 Ticket Stub $100
1993 Complete Ticket (No Stub—Tickets
    were not torn) $40

LEAGUE CHAMPIONSHIP SERIES PROGRAMS

1969 .... $65
1970, 1971 .... $50
1973, 1974 .... $40

1993, complete ticket, All-Star game, Oriole Park at
Camden Yards, Baltimore, Md., 3″ × 7″, $40.

1979	$20	1979 (not dated)	$75
1983	$10	1983 (not dated)	$50

LEAGUE CHAMPIONSHIP SERIES TICKETS

WORLD SERIES PROGRAMS

1969 Complete Ticket	$50	1966 Orioles First World Series	$85
1969 Ticket Stub	$25	1969	$70
1970, 1971 Complete Ticket	$30	1970	$65
1970, 1971 Ticket Stub	$15	1971	$50
1973, 1974 Complete Ticket	$20	1979	$15
1973, 1974 Ticket Stub	$10	1983	$10
1979 Complete Ticket	$20		
1979 Ticket Stub	$7	**WORLD SERIES GAME TICKETS**	
1983 Complete Ticket	$15	1966 Complete Ticket	$100
1983 Ticket Stub	$5	1966 Ticket Stub	$40
		1969, 1970 Complete Ticket	$70
		1969, 1970 Ticket Stub	$25
WORLD SERIES PRESS PINS		1971 Complete Ticket	$50
		1971 Ticket Stub	$20
1966	$200	1979 Complete Ticket	$30
1969 (not dated)	$175	1979 Ticket Stub	$10
1970 (not dated)	$125	1983 Complete Ticket	$20
1971	$100	1983 Ticket Stub	$10

Boston, Massachusetts

BOSTON RED STOCKINGS

National Association 1871–1875

After the Boston Red Stockings dominated the National Association by winning four consecutive pennants, it was obvious that Harry Wright's team had the finest talent in baseball. Foremost among the National Association Red Stocking's stars was pitcher Al Spalding, who led the association in victories all five years of its existence.

This did not go unnoticed by wealthy Chicago businessman William A. Hulbert, who organized the National League in the winter of 1875–1876. As owner of the Chicago White Stockings, Hulbert signed Spalding not only as his premier attraction but also as manager. Spalding was able to entice the heart of the Boston team—second baseman Ross Barnes, catcher Cal McVey and outfielder Jim White—to join him in Chicago. The White Stockings easily won the National League's first pennant, with Spalding

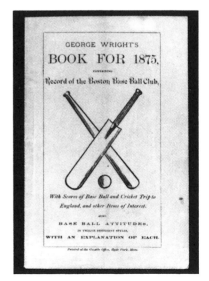

1875, the first baseball team history ever written, 30 pages, 4¾″ × 7¼″. Manager George Wright chronicles the history of the Boston Red Stockings, champions of the National Association from 1872 through the league's final season of 1875, $10,000.

leading the league with 46 wins and Barnes topping all league batters with a .429 BA. The decimated Red Stockings (now nicknamed the Red Caps) finished fourth. Thus began a series of nicknames for Boston's National League team which included Beaneaters (1883–1906), Doves (1907–1910), Rustlers (1911) and Braves (starting in 1912). The name "Braves" stuck, although from 1936 through 1940 the team became known as the Bees. Unfortunately, they didn't exhibit much sting and they reverted to Braves in 1941, a name they carried to Milwaukee when they left Boston following the 1952 season.

BOSTON BRAVES

National League 1876–1952

The organizational genius of Harry Wright became apparent when the revamped Red Caps won the National League pennant thanks to his acquisition of righthander Tommy Bond from Hartford. Bond lead the league with 40 wins two years in a row (1877 and 1878), and the Red Caps won two consecutive pennants. Harry's brother, George, a fellow Hall of Famer, anchored the defense while Deacon White led the league in batting in 1877 (.387). Jim O'Rourke, another Hall of Famer, finished close behind with a .382 average. Had it not been for Spalding and his teammates' defection from Boston following the 1875 season, Boston would have won seven consecutive pennants.

In 1883 Boston first baseman John Morrill replaced Jack Burdock as manager during the final third of the season, and the Beaneaters responded to his leadership by winning 32 of 41 games to win the pennant by four games over Chicago.

In 1891 the Beaneaters, now managed by Frank Selee and led by Hall of Fame pitchers John Clarkson (33–19) and Kid Nichols (30–17), were back on top of the National League. In addition, the Boston Reds American Association team featured many of the stars from the Boston Players League team, including Brouthers, who won the batting title with a .350 BA. Hall of Famer Hugh Duffy was second among league batters with a .336 BA. Boston's three championships in three different leagues in two years established "The

Hub" as the prominent baseball city in America. It didn't stop there. In 1892 and 1893 the Beaneaters won two more National League pennants. After the Baltimore Orioles reeled off three consecutive pennants, the Beaneaters were back atop the baseball world in 1897 and 1898. Hugh Duffy led the league with 11 homers in 1897 and was third in RBI with 129. Fellow Hall of Famer and third baseman Jimmy Collins was second with 132 RBI. Duffy batted .340, Collins .346, and Hall of Famer centerfielder Billy Hamilton batted .343. In 1898 Collins led the league with 15 homers and Hamilton was second in batting with a .369 BA. Kid Nichols topped all league pitchers with 32 wins. It hardly mattered that the Beaneaters lost in the Temple Cup series to Baltimore, who finished second during the regular season.

Boston had a Union Association team in 1884. In 1890 Boston entered the Players League with a team known as the Reds. Managed by Hall of Famer King Kelly, they won the only pennant in the league's one-year history. Kelly (.326 BA) and fellow Hall of Famers first baseman Dan Brouthers (.330 BA) and pitcher Old Hoss Radbourn (27–12) were among the league's top stars.

Since the formation of the National Association in 1871, Boston had won a total of 14 pennants in 27 seasons, an unparalleled record of success during that era.

Boston's National League team took a back seat to the Red Sox of the American League in the early part of this century. The Red Sox won American League pennants in 1903, 1904, 1912, 1915, 1916, and 1918 and were world champs in 1903, 1912, 1916, and 1918. The Red Sox' string of success forever won the hearts and minds of Boston fans.

The Braves did have two moments of glory. In 1914 the Braves were in last place on July 4 and went on to capture the pennant under Miracle Manager George Stallings. Only two Hall of Famers, Rabbit Maranville and Johnny Evers, graced the 1914 Miracle Braves; Maranville topped the team with 78 RBI and led league shortstops in putouts, assists and double plays. Pitcher Dick Rudolph bested the league with 27 wins, while teammate Bill James was right behind with 26.

To make the miracle complete, the

Braves stunned the Philadelphia Athletics in the 1914 World Series four games to none as Rudolph and James each won two. Hall of Famer second baseman Johnny Evers was series MVP with a .438 BA. The Braves moved into Braves Field, the largest ballpark in baseball, in 1915, and finished second to the Philadelphia Phillies. From then on the Braves began a steady decline and typically finished in the second division.

After World War II, the Braves began inching up the National League ladder under manager Billy Southworth. In 1946 righthander Johnny Sain was second in the league with 20 wins, while future Hall of Famer Warren Spahn won 8 games in his rookie season on the way to becoming the winningest lefthander in big league history (363 victories). In 1947 Spahn and Sain each won 21 games, prompting the expression "Spahn and Sain and Pray for Rain" as the Braves finished third. In 1948 they hit the jackpot and won their first pennant since 1914. Sain led the league with 24 wins while Spahn had 15, Bill Voiselle 13, and rookie Vern Bickford 11 victories. Second baseman Al Dark was Rookie of the Year and batted .322 to finish fourth in the league. Third baseman Bob Elliott had 23 homers and 100 RBI to supply most of the power. In the World Series, the Braves lost to the Cleveland Indians four games to two.

After this high-water mark, Braves attendance began to decline even though Rookie of the Year Sam Jethroe joined the team in 1950 and power hitter Eddie Ma-

thews hit 25 homers in 1952 on his way to a Hall of Fame career. After drawing only 281,278 fans in 1952, the Braves moved to Milwaukee in time for the 1953 season.

In addition to those players already mentioned, the following Hall of Famers played with the Boston National League franchise: Earl Averill, Dave Bancroft, Burleigh Grimes, Billy Herman, Rogers Hornsby, Joe Kelley, Ernie Lombardi, Al Lopez, Rube Marquard, Tom McCarthy, Bill McKechnie, Ducky Medwick, Babe Ruth, Al Simmons, George Sisler, Casey Stengel, Ed Walsh, Lloyd Waner, Paul Waner, and Cy Young.

For further reading on this fascinating franchise see *Baseball 1845–1891 from the Newspaper Accounts,* by Preston D. Orem.

Advertising Specialties

1887 Kalamazoo Bats Team Card N-690, 4½″ × 6½″, Cabinet Card issued by Charles Gross & Co. of Philadelphia as a promotion for its Kalamazoo Bats Cigarettes. The Boston Baseball Club features a team photo with the caption in a white box at the bottom of the photo **$2,700**

1887 Kalamazoo Bats Team Card N690-1, 4½″ × 6½″, Cabinet Card issued by Charles Gross & Co. of Philadelphia as a promotion for its Kalamazoo Bats Cigarettes. The Boston Baseball Club features a team photo with the caption in a white box at the bottom of the photo. They are related to the N-690 series and are extremely rare **$2,000**

1888 advertising poster, Boston Beaneaters players in ballpark, 20¾″ × 26½″, published by Boston Cigar Co., $2,500.

1888 Boston Baseball Club Joseph Hall
Cabinets Team Cards, 6½″ ×
4½″ $2,200
1913 Boston Nationals T200 Fatima
Team Card, 2⅝″ × 4¾″ $150

Miscellaneous

EXHIBIT CARDS

1948 Boston Braves Exhibit Supply Co.
Team Photo $14

Pennants

1936, 1937 Boston Bees Premium Pennant, 2½″ × 4½″, nickname of
team and Bee emblem (BF3-Type
5) $35
1900 through 1914 Regular $750
1914 World Series............................$1,500
1915 through 1920 Regular $750
1921 through 1930 Regular $500
1931 through 1936 Regular $200
1936 All-Star Game $400
1937 through 1940 Regular $200
1941 through 1948 Regular $100
1948 World Series $200
1949, 1950 Regular $100
1951, 1952 Regular $50

Pins

1930/1940s Boston Braves American Nut
and Chocolate Co., 1⅛″, Round $15

1940s pin, 1¼″, Blue Brave on white field (this style
has been reproduced), $10.

Postcards

1948 Boston Braves, LN Tichnor Bros.,
Boston, Mass................................$20

Publications

BOOKS

Hirshberg, Al. *The Braves, The Pick
and the Shovel.* Waverly House,
1948. ....$50.00
Kaese, Harold, *The Boston Braves.*
G.P. Putnam's Sons, 1948. ....$65.00
Onigman, Mark. *This Date in Braves
History.* New York: Stein & Day,
1982. ....$5.00
Tuohey, George V. *Boston Baseball
Club 1871–97.* M.F. Quinn,
1897. ....$1,000.00
Wright, George. *Record of the Boston
Baseball Club, 1871–74.* Rockwell
and Churchill, 1874. ....$10,000.00

Media Guides

1927 Roster Sheet $125
1928 through 1931 Roster Sheet $100
1932 through 1935 Roster Booklet $100
1936 through 1940 Roster Booklet $75
1941 through 1949 Roster Booklet $60
1950, 1951, 1952 Roster Booklet $50

1927 roster sheet and spring training schedule for
Braves, 9½″ × 6″, the forerunner of the elaborate
media guides used today, $125.

Programs and Scorecards

1900 through 1904 ....$400
1905 through 1909 ....$200

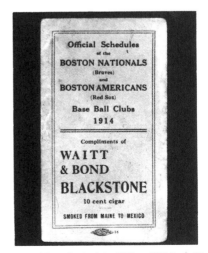

1876, Harry Wright's official scorecard for game between Boston and Hartford, first season of the National League, 6″ × 7″ unfolded, $1,500.

1946 *Boston Braves Sketch Book*, 8½″ × 11″, 48 pages, considered to be the first of the modern yearbooks, produced by William H. Sullivan (publicity director for the Braves), Manager Billy Southworth on the cover, $350.

1910 through 1913 ....$150
1914 World Champions.........................$200
1915 through 1920 ....$125
1921 through 1925 ....$75
1926 through 1930 ....$50
1931 through 1935 ....$40
1936 through 1940 Boston Bees $35
1941 Boston Braves and Bees Cover $25
1941 Bees Cover $35
1942 through 1945 ....$20
1946, 1947 ....$18
1948 National League Champs $25
1949, 1950, 1951 ....$17
1952 Final Season $20

Yearbooks

1874 George Wright's Record Book of
    the Boston Club 1871–1874 ....$10,000
1936 *Who's Who in Boston Major League*
    Baseball......................................$200
1946 First Year $350
1947 ....$225
1948, 1949 ....None Issued
1950, 1951 ....$150

Schedules

1900 through 1909 ....$150
1910 through 1919 ....$100
1920 through 1929 ....$75

1914 cardboard schedule, 2¾″ × 4¾″, issued by Waitt & Bond Blackstone cigars for the Braves and Red Sox (Braves were world champions in 1914), $100.

1930 through 1939 ....$45
1940 through 1949 ....$30
1950, 1951, 1952 ....$25

Special Events

ALL-STAR PRESS PINS

1936 ....None Issued

ALL-STAR PROGRAMS

1936 All-Star Game $1,000

1936 All-Star Program (one of the rarest), 6¾" × 10", 12 pages, $1,000.

ALL-STAR GAME TICKETS

1936 Complete Ticket $400
1936 Ticket Stub $200

WORLD SERIES PRESS PINS

1914 ....$5,000
1948 ....$300

WORLD SERIES PROGRAMS

1914 ....$2,000
1948 ....$175

WORLD SERIES GAME TICKETS

1914 Complete Ticket $1,600
1914 Ticket Stub $800

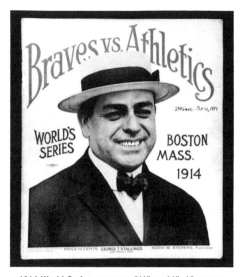

1914 World Series program, 9¼" × 11", 16 pages, Braves vs. Philadelphia Athletics. The Miracle Braves went from last place under Manager George Stallings (pictured on the cover) to win the National League pennant and then swept the Athletics in 4 straight games to become world champions, $2,000.

1948 Complete Ticket $200
1948 Ticket Stub $100

BOSTON RED SOX

American League 1901 to Present

The history of the Boston Red Sox could well be characterized as "feast or famine." As charter members of the American League in 1901, the Red Sox won their first pennant two years later and then amazed the baseball world by winning the first World Series in 1903. They stunned the Pittsburgh Pirates thanks to two wins by the immortal pitcher Cy Young. Initially known as the Puritans, the Boston squad wore red baseball socks. The name Red Sox was adopted in 1906 and remains the team's nickname. The Red Sox repeated as champs in 1904, but the New York Giants refused to play them in the World Series. Another pennant and World Series triumph followed in 1912 and the Red Sox were world champions in 1915, 1916, and 1918. In only 18 seasons of existence, the Red Sox captured six pennants and never lost a World Series.

Late in 1914 a young pitcher named Babe Ruth joined the team and promptly established himself as one of the game's best. He had records of 18 and 8 in 1915, 23 and 12 in 1916 (when his 1.75 ERA topped the American League), and 24 and 13 in 1917. Developing a reputation as a fearsome slugger, Ruth saw action in 95 games as an outfielder in 1918 but still managed to win 13 games while losing only 7 as a pitcher. He also won two World Series games in 1918 with a 1.07 ERA over 17 innings. Ruth and the Red Sox were on top of the baseball world.

Red Sox owner Harry Frazee was a broadway producer who needed money to sustain his many theatrical flops. After the 1919 season he unloaded many of his top stars—including Ruth—to the New York Yankees for a bundle of ready cash. Called the "Babe Ruth Curse," the Red Sox have never won another world championship. Ironically, a few years after Ruth and most of his stars were sold, Frazee produced the big Broadway hit "No, No Nannette," which earned him millions. He later admitted he never would have sold the players had his Broadway success come earlier. Undoubtedly, many championship pennants that adorned New York's Yankee Stadium would have flown from the flagpole at Fenway Park.

Beginning in 1922 the Red Sox finished last in eight of the next ten seasons with only a seventh place finish in 1924 and a sixth place finish in 1931 to prevent total futility. It was not until Tom Yawkey purchased the Red Sox in 1933 that the club's fortunes took a turn for the better. A fresh infusion of cash enabled the Red Sox to sign such future Hall of Famers as Lefty Grove, Jimmie Foxx, Joe Cronin, Bobby Doerr, and the incomparable Ted Williams to Boston contracts. With additions such as these, Boston climbed to second place in 1938 and 1939 and again in 1941 and 1942 but failed to win the pennant until 1946. They lost the 1946 World Series to the St. Louis Cardinals in seven games. When Williams, the last major league player to bat .400 (.406 in 1941) retired after 19 brilliant seasons in 1960, future superstar Carl Yastremski replaced him in left field starting in 1961.

In recent years the Red Sox have been led by third baseman Wade Boggs and flame-throwing righthander Roger Clemens. Although the Red Sox won additional pennants in 1967, 1975, 1986, 1988 and 1990, the "Babe Ruth Curse" continues to haunt them—they have lost every World Series they've appeared in since 1918.

In addition to those previously named, other Red Sox Hall of Famers who played much of their careers in Boston include Tris Speaker, Jimmy Collins, Herb Pennock, Red Ruffing, Harry Hooper, George Kell, Luis Aparicio, and Rick Ferrell, while Jesse Burkett, Lou Boudreau, Ferguson Jenkins, Heinie Manush, Al Simmons, Waite Hoyt, Tom Seaver, Juan Marichal and Jack Chesbro all played briefly with the Boston Red Sox. Ed Barrow and Tom Yawkey gained admission as Red Sox executives.

Advertising Specialties

1913 Boston Americans T200 Fatima Team Card, 2⅝″ × 4¼″ $100
1983 Adams Co-Operative Bank Schedule Matchbook, 1⅞″ × 5″, manufactured by Universal Match Co. $3

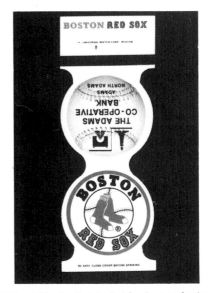

1983 matchbook schedule, Red Sox Logo on front and The Adams Co-Operative Bank of North Adams, Mass., on the back, 1⅞″ × 5″, manufactured by Universal Match Corp. of Boston, $3.

Felt round, white on red, Bazooka-Blony, 5", "My Favorite Team" and "Bazooka Blony" in white ring surrounding Red Sox logo, $35.

Miscellaneous

BOBBIN' HEAD DOLLS

Category #I, 1960, 1961, Green Square
Base, Boy Head $175
Category #II, 1961, 1962, White Square
Base, Boy Head $215
Category #III, 1961, 1962, White Round
Miniature, Boy Head $220
Category #IV, 1962, 1963, 1964, Green
Round Base, Boy Head $80
Category #V, 1962, 1963, 1964, Green
Round Base, Black Player $600
Category #VI, 1967 through 1972, Gold
Round Base, Boy Head $50

Ballpark Giveaways

1986 Baby Ruth/Butterfinger Cap, Kool-
Aid Glove, Chunky Painter Cap,
Budweiser Watch, Kool-Aid T-shirt,
Coca-Cola Flight Bag........................$6
1987 Budweiser Calendar (first one) $10
1987 Glove, Cracker Barrell Beach
Towel, Chunky Painter Hat $6
1988 Miller Beer Calendar, Tropicana
Tankard.......................................$10
1988 Gatorade Batting Helmet $6
1988 Surf Baseball Card Book $11
1989 Calendar $9
1990 Very Fine Helmet...........................$6
1991 Kellog's Cereal Dish, WRKO Visor $6
1991 Upper Deck Cards $7
1992 Donruss Baseball Card Book, Up-
per Deck Cards $7
1992 Thompson Painter Hat.....................$6
1992 Coca-Cola Calendar $8
1993 Upper Deck Cards $6

Pennants

1936, 1937 Boston Red Sox Premium
Pennant, 2½" × 4½", with a ball
and bat on pennant (BF3-Type 5) $35
1936, 1937 Boston Red Sox Premium
Pennant, 2½" × 4½", with a bat
only on pennant (BF3-Type 5)..........$35
1901 through 1920 ....$750
1921 through 1930 ....$300
1931 through 1940 ....$200
1941 through 1946 Regular....................$100
1946 All-Star Game $200
1946 World Series...............................$200
1947 through 1950 ....$100
1951 through 1960 ....$50
1961 Regular.....................................$30
1961 All-Star Game $75
1962 through 1967 Regular $30
1967 World Series $75
1968, 1969, 1970 Regular $30
1970 through 1975 Regular $20
1975 League Championship Series...........$50
1975 World Series...............................$50
1976 through 1980 ....$20
1981 through 1986 Regular $5
1986 League Championship Series..........$15
1986 World Series................................$15

1950s pennant, 28½" × 11½",
white lettering on blue field, aerial
view of Fenway Park, $50.

1960s plate, 7″, Fenway Park, $125.

1979 pin, 4″, Red Sox logo surrounded by cameos of nine prominent Red Sox players, $15.

1987 through 1990 Regular $5
1990 League Championship Series...........$15
1991, 1992, 1993 ....$3

Pins

1930/1940s American Nut and Chocolate
    Pin, 1⅛″, Round $15
1961 through 1969 (none in 1966) Crane
    Potato Chips, ⅞″, Round....................$5
1984 Crane Potato Chips, ⅞″, Round $3
1964, 1965, 1966 Guy's Potato Chips, ⅞″,
    Round $5

Postcards

1908 Boston Red Sox, PL, J.F. Furlong,
    Boston, Massachusetts. Mechanical
    Postcard featuring individual mem-

bers of team in accordian fold com-
ing out of baseball on front of the
Postcard which features ball park
and club executives $1,200
1966 RP Boston Red Sox $15

Publications

BOOKS

Berry, Henry, *Boston Red Sox.* New
    York: McMillan, 1975. ....$15.00
Berry, Henry. *The Boston Red Sox:
    The Complete Record of Red Sox
    Baseball.* New York: McMillan,
    1984. ....$10.00
Clark, Ellery H. *Boston Red Sox: 75th
    Anniversary History, 1901–1975.*
    New York: Exposition Press, 1975. ...$20.00

1908 mechanical postcard, 3½″ ×
5″, Huntington Avenue Grounds,
John Taylor, Hugh McBreen, and
large baseball which opens into an
accordion fold of the 1908 Red Sox
team (extremely rare), $1,200.

• Clark, Ellery H. *Red Sox Fever*. New York: Exposition Press, 1979. ....**$9.95**

• Clark, Ellery H. *Red Sox Forever*. New York: Exposition Press, 1977. ....**$7.50**

Cole, Milton. *Baseball's Greatest Dynasties: The Red Sox*. New York: Gallery Books, 1990. ....**$5.00**

Coleman, Ken. *The Impossible Dream Anthology: Boston Baseball*. Pittsfield, Ma.: Literations, 1983. ....**$10.00**

Coleman, Ken. *Impossible Dream Remembered: The 1967 Boston Red Sox*. Boston: Steven Greene Press, 1987. ....**$10.00**

• Crehan, Herbert F. *Lightening in a Bottle: The Sox of '67*. Brandon Pub. Co., 1992. ....**$19.95**

Frommer, Harvey. *Baseball's Greatest Rivalry: The New York Yankees vs. the Boston Red Sox*. New York: Athenium, 1984. ....**$10.00**

Gammons, Peter. *Beyond the Sixth Game*. Boston: Houghton-Mifflin, 1985. ....**$10.00**

Germano, Eddie. *Red Sox Drawing Board: 25 Years of Cartoons*. Lexington, Ma.: Stephen Green Press, 1989. ....**$10.00**

• Golenbock, Peter. *Fenway, An Unexpurgated History of the Boston Red Sox*. New York: G.P. Putnam, 1992. ....**$24.95**

Hirschberg, Al. *The Red Sox, the Bean and the Cod*. Waverly House, 1947. ....**$40.00**

• Higgings, George V. *The Progress of the Seasons: 40 Years of Baseball in Our Town*. New York: Henry Holt & Co., 1989. ....**$2.98**

Honig, Donald. *Boston Red Sox: An Illustrated History*. New York: Prentice-Hall, 1990. ....**$15.00**

Honig, Donald. *The Boston Red Sox: An Illustrated Tribute*. New York: St. Martin's Press, 1984. ....**$20.00**

Hough, John Jr. *A Player for the Moment: Notes from Fenway Park*. San Diego: Harcourt Brace Jovanovich, 1988. ....**$10.00**

Lieb, Frederick. *The Boston Red Sox*. G.P. Putnam's Sons, 1947. ....**$50.00**

Liss, Howard. *The Boston Red Sox*. New York: Simon & Schuster, 1982. ....**$10.00**

Martin, Mollie. *Boston Red Sox*. Mankato, Mn.: Creative Education, 1982. ....**$5.00**

Meany, Tom. *The Boston Red Sox*. A.S. Barnes & Co., 1956. ....**$25.00**

Mercurio, John A. *Chronology of Boston Red Sox Records*. New York: Harper & Row, 1989. ....**$5.00**

Remington-Urquhart Press. *The Red Sox Album*. Boston, 1912. ....**$500**

Riley, Dan. *30 Years of Musings on Baseball's Most Amusing Team*. Thousand Oaks, Ca.: Ventura Publications, 1987. ....**$10.00**

Rothaus, James R. *Boston Red Sox*. Mankato, Mn.: Creative Education, 1987. ....**$5.00**

Shaughnessy, Dan. *Curse of the Bambino*. New York: E.P. Dutton, 1990. ....**$10.00**

Sullivan, George. *The Picture History of the Boston Red Sox*. New York & Indianapolis: Bobbs-Merrill, 1979. ....**$15.00**

Valenti, Dan. *From Florida to Fenway*. Pittsfield, Ma.: Literation, 1982. ....**$10.00**

Valenti, Dan. *Red Sox: A Reckoning*. Wilkes Barre, Pa., 1979. ....**$15.00**

Walton, Edward H. *Red Sox Triumphs & Tragedies. A Second Volume of Boston Red Sox History*. New York: Stein & Day, 1980. ....**$10.00**

Walton, Edward H. *This Date in Red Sox History*. New York: Stein & Day, 1978. ....**$5.00**

MEDIA GUIDES

1927 Roster Sheet **$125**
1928 through 1933 Roster Sheet **$100**
1934 Roster Booklet First Year of the New Fenway Park on Cover **$150**
1935 Roster Booklet.............................**$100**
1936, 1937 Roster Booklet **$75**
1938, 1939, 1940 Roster Booklet **$65**
1941 through 1945 Roster Booklet **$60**
1946 World Champions **$70**
1947, 1948, 1949 Roster Booklet **$60**
1950 through 1955 ....**$50**
1956 through 1961 ....**$40**
1962, 1963, 1964 ....**$30**
1965, 1966 ....**$20**
1967, 1968 ....**$17**
1969, 1970 ....**$15**
1971, 1972 ....**$12**
1973, 1974 ....**$10**
1975 American League Champs **$10**
1976, 1977, 1978 ....**$7**
1979, 1980, 1981 ....**$6**
1982, 1983, 1984, 1985 ....**$5**
1986 American League Champs **$6**
1987 ....**$4**
1988 Division Champs **$6**
1989 ....**$4**
1990 Division Champs **$5**
1991, 1992, 1993 ....**$4**

PROGRAMS AND SCORECARDS

1901 First Year of the American League ..**$600**
1902, 1903, 1904 ....**$400**
1905 through 1909 ....**$200**
1910 through 1913 ....**$150**

1914 through 1920	$125
1921 through 1925	$75
1926 through 1930	$50
1931 through 1940	$35
1941 through 1949	$20
1950 through 1959	$15
1960 through 1969	$10
1970 through 1974	$6
1975 American League Champs	$8
1976 through 1979	$6
1980 through 1985	$4
1986 American League Champs	$6
1987	$4
1988 Division Champs	$5
1989	$4
1990 Division Champs	$4
1991, 1992, 1993	$3

YEARBOOKS

1912 *The Red Sox Album* by Brown & Leahy, Remington Urquhat Press (Photos & sketches of 1912 World Champions) $500
1936 *Who's Who in Boston Major League Baseball* $200
1946 *Boston Red Sox, American League Champions*, Boston Globe $200
1951 .... $200
1952 .... $175
1953, 1954 .... None Issued
1955 .... $165
1956 .... $150

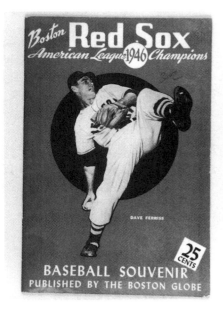

1946 souvenir published by the Boston Globe commemorating the 1946 American League champions, 6¾″ × 10″, 32 pages, $200.

1957	$130
1958	$120
1959	$100
1960	$75
1961, 1962	$65
1963, 1964	$55
1965, 1966	$45
1967 American League Champions	$50
1968, 1969	$30
1970, 1971	$25
1972, 1973, 1974	$20
1975 American League Champions	$25
1976, 1977, 1978	$15
1979, 1980, 1981	$12
1982, 1983	$10
1984 through 1993	$7

Schedules

1901 through 1909	$150
1910 through 1919	$100
1920 through 1929	$75
1930 through 1939	$45
1940 through 1949	$30
1950 through 1959	$25
1960 through 1969	$15
1970 through 1979	$10
1980 through 1985	$2
1986 through 1993	$1

Special Events

ALL-STAR GAME PRESS PINS

1946	$400
1961	$200

ALL-STAR GAME PROGRAMS

1946	$550
1961	$100

ALL-STAR GAME TICKETS

1946 Complete Ticket	$200
1946 Ticket Stub	$100
1961 Complete Ticket	$75
1961 Ticket Stub	$35

LEAGUE CHAMPIONSHIP SERIES PROGRAMS

1975	$15
1986	$6
1988	$6
1990	$5

LEAGUE CHAMPIONSHIP SERIES TICKETS

1975 Complete Ticket	$45
1975 Ticket Stub	$20
1986 Complete Ticket	$30
1986 Ticket Stub	$15
1988 Complete Ticket	$30

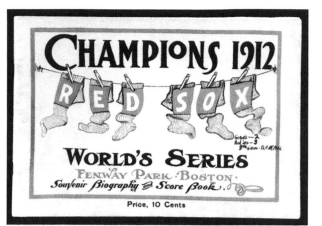

1912 World Series program at Fenway Park, 7″ × 10″, 32 pages, Red Sox vs. New York Giants, $2,000.

1988 Ticket Stub	$15
1990 Complete Ticket	$20
1990 Ticket Stub	$10

WORLD SERIES PRESS PINS

1903	None Issued
1912	$6,000

1946 program, All-Star game at Fenway Park, 6½″ × 12″, 12 pages, $550.

1915	$5,000
1916	$4,000
1918	$3,000
1946	$300
1967 (not dated)	$75
1975 (not dated)	$200
1986	$40

WORLD SERIES PROGRAMS

1903	$15,000
1912	$2,000
1915	$2,000
1916	$2,000
1918	$3,000
1946	$200
1967	$100
1975	$50
1986	$40

WORLD SERIES TICKETS

1903 Complete Ticket	$6,000
1903 Ticket Stub	$3,000
1915 Complete Ticket	$1,200
1915 Ticket Stub	$600
1916 Complete Ticket	$1,200
1916 Ticket Stub	$600
1918 Complete Ticket	$1,200
1918 Ticket Stub	$600
1946 Complete Ticket	$200
1946 Ticket Stub	$100
1967 Complete Ticket	$70
1967 Ticket Stub	$36
1975 Complete Ticket	$40
1975 Ticket Stub	$20
1986 Complete Ticket	$30
1986 Ticket Stub	$15

Brooklyn, New York

BROOKLYN ATLANTICS

National Association 1872–1875

Brooklyn's rich baseball history predates the professional game. The Brooklyn Atlantics were considered national champions in 1864 and 1866. The Atlantics were also the first team to defeat the Cincinnati Red Stockings, America's first professional team. The Red Stockings had gone through the entire 1869 season (65 games) without a loss. Cincinnati reeled off 27 more victories in 1870 until they were stopped by the Atlantics at the Capitoline Grounds in Brooklyn on June 14. Brooklyn won 8 to 7 in ten innings to end the Red Stockings' unbeaten streak at 92 games.

From 1872 to 1875 the Brooklyn Atlantics were members of the National Association, America's first professional league, and never finished higher than sixth place.

BROOKLYN DODGERS

American Association 1889–1890, National League 1890–1957

In 1884 major league baseball returned to Brooklyn when the Trolley Dodgers became members of the American Association. The team was named for Brooklyn residents who jumped out of the way of trolleys on the narrow Brooklyn streets. In the 12-team association, Brooklyn finished ninth with a record of 40 wins and 64 losses in their initial season. Not one Trolley Dodger batted .300, and although Adonis Terry won 20 games in his rookie season he also lost 35.

The Dodgers finished sixth in 1885, third in 1886, sixth in 1887, second in 1888, and finally struck paydirt in 1889 when they won the American Association pennant. In their pennant year the team became known as the Bridegrooms because six of the players were married during the season. The Bridegrooms won mainly on the strength of righthander Bob Caruthers, who led the league with 40 wins against 11 losses. Manager Bill McGunnigle directed the team to 93 wins and 44 losses and finished two games ahead of the St. Louis Browns. The Bridegrooms played their Sunday games at suburban Ridgewood Park and on May 5 attracted 12,614 fans for a game against Philadelphia. They used Washington Park in Brooklyn for their other games, which could hold 15,000 with standing room. For the season Brooklyn set an attendance record of 353,690. The Bridegrooms met the National League champion New York Giants in an 11-game world championship series and lost as the Giants won six games to three, taking the last five in a row.

In November, Brooklyn jumped from the American Association to the National League and repeated as champions in 1890. The Bridegrooms' excellent pitching staff was led by Tom Lovett (30–11), while Adonis Terry (26–16) and Bob Caruthers (23–11) contributed greatly. Darby O'Brien (.314), George Pinckney (.309) and Dan Fouts (.303) were the leading batters. After the season the Bridegrooms met the American Association champion Louisville Colonels in the World Series. Each team won three games and played to a tie in the other game. The remaining games were cancelled due to frigid October weather.

Brooklyn's 1890 Players League team, known as the Wonders, finished second to Boston under future Hall of Famer Monty Ward.

Future Hall of Famer Monty Ward became manager of the Brooklyn National League team in 1891 when Bill McGunnigle was fired after two consecutive pennants and the Bridegrooms declined to sixth place. They were third in 1892 as future Hall of Fame first baseman Dan Brouthers led the team and league with a .335 BA. Again known as the Trolley Dodgers, they placed sixth in 1893, fifth in 1894 and 1895, ninth in 1896, sixth in 1897, and tenth in 1898.

After Baltimore had won consecutive pennants in 1894, 1895 and 1896, attendance in Baltimore began to decline. Owner Harry Von de Horst retained his ownership in the Orioles and bought controlling interest in the Dodgers in 1899. He shipped many of his best players to Brooklyn, as well as manager Ned Hanlon. The result was a pennant for Brooklyn as former Orioles and future Hall of Famers Willie Keeler (.379 BA), Joe Kelley (.325 BA) and Hughie Jennings (.296 BA) played key roles. The Dodgers repeated as champions in 1900 with another ex-Oriole and future Hall of Famer Joe McGinnity leading the league with a 28 and 8 record. Because there was a popular vaudeville troupe known as Hanlon's Superbas (no relations to the Dodgers manager), the writers began referring to Brooklyn as the Superbas and the name caught on.

Although the Superbas finished third in 1901 and second in 1902, they began a steady decline into the second division and ended the 1905 season in last place. Future Hall of Famer Zach Wheat broke in with the Dodgers in 1909, and Cooperstown-bound Casey Stengel began in 1912, but even these superb outfielders could not get Brooklyn out of the second division. Beginning in 1911 the nickname Dodgers reappeared, and in 1913 a brand new concrete and steel ballpark named after owner Charley Ebbetts replaced outmoded Washington Park. In 1914 Hall of Famer Wilbert Robinson took over as manager and in his honor the team became known as the Robins. Called Uncle Robbie, the famous ex-catcher and captain of the champion Orioles of the 1890s had the Dodgers in third place in 1915.

Just two years after Robinson's arrival, the Robins won the 1916 National League pennant. First baseman Jake Daubert was second in the league with a .316 BA while future Hall of Famer Rube Marquard posted a 14–6 record and had the league's second-best ERA (1.58). Righthander Jeff Pfeffer led the Robins with 25 wins and only 11 defeats. They lost the World Series to the Boston Red Sox four games to one as Babe Ruth won one of the games for Boston and Jack Coombs got the only Robins' victory.

In 1920 the Robins were champs again. Burleigh Grimes led the way with a 23–11 record while Zach Wheat finished fourth among league batters with a .328 BA. In the World Series the Dodgers lost five games to two to the Cleveland Indians.

The Ward brothers of Brooklyn renovated Washington Park and their Brooklyn Federal League team, known as the Tip Tops, played there in 1914 and 1915 before the league folded.

For almost 20 years afterward the Dodgers languished in the second division, with a second-place finish in 1924 and fourth-place finishes in 1930 and 1931 (the final two years of Wilbert Robinson's reign) their best showing. Hall of Famer Max Carey managed for two years, finishing third in 1932 and sixth in 1933 before being replaced by fellow Hall of Famers Casey Stengel (who lasted three years) and Burleigh Grimes (who took the helm for two). Finally, when Leo Durocher became manager in 1939, Dodger fortunes rose. They finished third in 1939, second in 1940, and first in 1941. Kirby Higbe and Whitlow Wyatt led the league with 22 wins each and Pete Reiser was batting champ with a .343 BA. First baseman Dolph Camilli led the league with 34 HR and 120 RBI. There were an abundance of future Hall of Famers, including second baseman Billy Herman, shortstop Pee Wee Reese and left fielder Joe Medwick. Unfortunately, in the World Series the results were the same. The Dodgers lost to the New York Yankees four games to one, with Wyatt getting the only Dodgers' win. The Dodgers were champs again in 1947 as first baseman Jackie Robinson, became the first black since the Walker brothers in 1884 to play in the major leagues, won Rookie of the Year honors. By breaking the color line Robinson provided opportunities for the hundreds of black ballplayers who followed, including teammate and three-time Most Valuable Player Roy Campanella. Both Robinson and Campanella were named to the Baseball Hall of Fame. In the 1947 World Series the

Dodgers were edged by the Yankees four games to three.

The Dodgers won pennants in 1949, 1952, and 1953 but bowed to their arch-rival Yankees all three years. Finally, in 1955, the Dodgers took the pennant and turned the tables on the Yankees in the World Series by winning four games to three. The 1955 season will long be savored by Brooklyn Dodger fans since it was the only world championship won in Brooklyn. Future Hall of Famer Duke Snider led the league with 136 RBI and Campanella was league MVP. Right-hander Don Newcombe had the league's best winning percentage with a record of 20–5.

The Dodgers won another pennant in 1956 but lost again to the Yankees in the World Series. Despite drawing more than a million fans in 1957, owner Walter O'Malley moved the team after the season from Brooklyn to the greener pastures of Los Angeles. Although the Dodgers have prospered greatly in Los Angeles, Brooklyn fans will never forgive O'Malley for taking their beloved "Bums" away. But the wonderful memories of baseball in Brooklyn will live as part of the game's lore forever.

In addition to those players already mentioned, other Hall of Famers who played at least one season in Brooklyn include: Dave Bancroft, "Kiki" Cuyler, Don Drysdale, Waite Hoyt, George Kelly, Sandy Koufax, Tony Lazzeri, Fred Lindstrom, Ernie Lombardi, Al Lopez, Heinie Manush, Rabbit Maranville, Thomas McCarthy, Dazzy Vance, Arky Vaughn, Lloyd and Paul Waner, and Hack Wilson.

For further reading on baseball in Brooklyn see *Baseball 1845–1891 from the Newspaper Accounts*, by Preston D. Orem; and *The Brooklyn Dodgers, An Informal History* by Frank Graham.

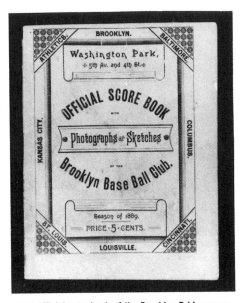

1889 official scorebook of the Brooklyn Bridegrooms, champions of the American Association, 5″ × 6¾″, 32 pages. This superb scorebook features player photographs and biographies of the players and is much like a yearbook. This particular game was against the Philadelphia Athletics who finished third. The inside front cover shows a standing-room-only crowd at Washington Park watching Brooklyn play St. Louis on Decoration Day, 1887, $2,500.

Advertising Specialties

Brooklyn Dodgers (National League)

1888 Brooklyn Baseball Club Joseph Hall
    Cabinets Team Cards, 6½″ ×
    4½″ $1,800
1956 Schaefer Beer Table Tent featuring
    1955 World Champions on one
    side, Schaefer Logo on the other, 4″
    × 6″ $50

1956 Schaefer Beer table tent, 4″ × 6″, 1955 world champion Dodgers, $50.

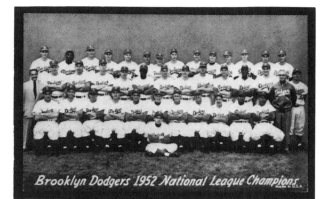

Brooklyn Dodgers 1952 National League Champions

Exhibit card of the 1952 Brooklyn National League champions, 3½″ × 5¼″, produced by the Exhibit Supply Co. of Chicago, $16.

Miscellaneous

EXHIBIT CARDS

1949 Exhibit Supply Co. $20
1952 Exhibit Supply Co. $16
1955 Exhibit Supply Co. $15
1956 Exhibit Supply Co. $14
1913 Brooklyn Nationals T200 Fatima
     Team Card, 2⅝″ × 4¾″ $100

Pennants

1936, 1937 Felt Pennants BF3, Type IV,
     Batter on pennant $35
1936, 1937 Felt Pennants BF3, Type IV,
     Fielder on pennant $35
1936, 1937 Felt Pennants BF3, Type V,
     Bat, Ball & Glove on pennant $35
1936, 1937 Felt Pennants BF3, Type V,
     Ball on pennant $35
1900 through 1920 ....$750
1921 through 1930 ....$500
1931 through 1940 ....$200
1941 Regular $100
1941 World Series $200
1942 through 1947 Regular...................$100
1947 World Series $200
1948 ....$100
1949 Regular $100

1949 All-Star.......................................$200
1949 World Series $200
1950, 1951, 1952 Regular $50
1952 World Series $125
1953 Regular..$50
1953 World Series $125
1954, 1955 Regular $50
1955 World Series $125
1956 Regular...$50
1956 World Series $125
1957 ....$50

Pins

1930/1940s American Nut and Chocolate
     Co., 1⅛″, Round $15

Publications

BOOKS

Barber, Walter (Red). *The Rhubarb
     Patch.* Simon & Schuster, 1954. ....$75.00
•Bjarkman, Peter C. *Baseball's Great
     Dynasties: The Dodgers.* New
     York: Gallery Brooks, 1990. ....$7.98
•Borst, Bill, *A Fan's Memoir: The
     Brooklyn Dodgers, 1953–1957.*
     Glyndon, Md.: Chapter & Cask,
     1982. ....$5.95

1940s–1950s generic pennant seen in most ballparks, 11″ × 28″, player sliding into base in a cloud of dust, team name in white on a blue felt background, $100.

1950s generic ballpark pin, 1¼", sold at all major league stadiums, crossed bats and a ball at top and Brooklyn Dodgers spelled in block letters between the seams of the baseball, $15.

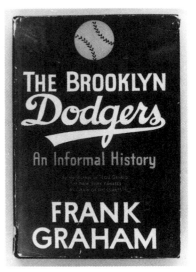

1948 updated 6th edition of *The Brooklyn Dodgers* by Frank Graham, published by Putnam in 1945. One of the most sought after in a 16-book series dealing with the history of the original 16 teams (books with dust jackets command twice the price of one without), $30.

•Cohen, Stanley, *Dodgers: The First 100 Years*. New York: Birch Lane Press, 1990. ....$3.98

Durant, John. *The Dodgers*. Hastings House, 1948. ....$50.00

Fitzgerald, Ed, ed. *The Story of the Brooklyn Dodgers*. Bantam Books, 1949. ....$5.00

Goldstein, Richard. *Superstars & Screwballs: 100 Years of Brooklyn Baseball*. New York: E.P. Dutton, 1991. ....$12.00

•Golenbock, Peter. *Bums: An Oral History of the Brooklyn Dodgers*. New York: G.P. Putnam, 1984. ....$4.95

Graham, Frank. *The Brooklyn Dodgers*. G.P. Putnam's Sons, 1945, 1948. ....$40.00

Holmes, Tommy. *Dodger Daze and Knights*. David McKay, Co., 1951. ....$40.00

Honig, Donald. *The Brooklyn Dodgers, An Illustrated History*. New York: St. Martin's Press, 1981. ....$20.00

Honig, Donald. *Dodgers: The Complete Record of Dodger Baseball*. New York: Collier-McMillan, 1986. ....$10.00

King, Arthur. *Dodger Fans of the World Unite*. William-Frederick Press, 1957. ....$40.00

Mann, Arthur. *Baseball Confidential*. David McKay Co., 1951. ....$25.00

Mann, Arthur. *Baseball Journey*. F.J. Law Co., 1951. ....$50.00

Meany, Tom. *The Artful Dodgers*. A.S. Barnes & Co., 1953, 1954, 1958. Grosset & Dunlap, 1963, 1966. ....$50.00

Rosenblum, Richard. *Brooklyn Dodger Days*. New York: Athenium, 1991. ....$10.00

Schoor, Gene. *The Complete Dodger Record Book*. New York: Facts on File, Inc., 1984. ....$10.00

Schoor, Gene. *A Pictorial History of the Dodgers, Brooklyn to Los Angeles*. West Point, N.Y.: Leisure Press, 1984. ....$15.00

•Sullivan, Neil. *The Dodgers Move West*. New York: Oxford University Press, 1987. ....$17.95

MEDIA GUIDES

1927 First Roster Sheet $125

1928 First Roster Booklet $150

1929 through 1935 Roster Booklet $100

1936 through 1940 Roster Booklet............$75

1941 National League Champs Roster Booklet $85

1942 through 1946 Roster Booket $65

1947 National League Champs Roster Booklet $70

1948 Roster Booklet $65

1949 National League Champs Roster Booklet $70

1950, 1951 ....$55

1952, 1953 National League Champs $60

1954 ....$50

1955 World Champions $60

1956 National League Champs $55

1957 Last Year in Brooklyn $55

PROGRAMS AND SCORECARDS

1900, 1901, 1902	$400
1903, 1904	$300
1905 through 1909	$200
1910 through 1914	$150
1915	$125
1916 League Champs	$135
1917, 1918, 1919	$125
1920 League Champs	$135
1921 through 1925	$75
1926 through 1930	$50
1931 through 1940	$35
1941 League Champs	$25
1942 through 1946	$20
1947 League Champs	$25
1948	$20
1949 League Champs	$25
1950, 1951	$15
1952, 1953 League Champs each year	$20
1954	$15
1955 World Champs	$30
1956 League Champs	$20
1957 Last Year in Brooklyn	$25

YEARBOOKS

1888 *Sketches of the New York & Brooklyn Baseball Clubs* by June Rankin (Sketch & Illustration of each player)	$2,500
1940 *The Brooklyn Dodgers* by Dispatch Press	$100
1941 *The Dodgers Today and Yesterday in Brooklyn Baseball* by Clinton Hoard & Charles Dexter	$400
1942 *Dodger Victory Book*	$450
1947 *Baseball's Beloved Bums* by Joe Hasel	$125
1947 League Champs	$300
1948	None Issued
1949 League Champs	$225
1950	$175
1951	$150
1952, 1953 League Champs	$175
1954	$125
1955 World Champions	$175
1956 League Champs	$125
1957 Last Year in Brooklyn	$150

Schedules

1900 through 1909	$150
1910 through 1919	$100
1920 through 1929	$75
1930 through 1939	$45
1940 through 1949	$30
1950 through 1954	$35
1955 World Champions	$45
1956, 1957	$35

Special Events

ALL-STAR GAME PRESS PINS

1949	$300

ALL-STAR PROGRAMS

1949	$450

ALL-STAR GAME TICKETS

1949 Complete Ticket	$170
1949 Ticket Stub	$85

WORLD SERIES PRESS PINS

1916	$4,000
1920	$2,500
1941	$450
1947	$400
1949	$375
1952	$225
1953 (not dated)	$300
1955 (not dated)	$500
1956 (not dated)	$500

1946 phantom world series program, 9″ × 12″, 38 pages, produced by Harry M. Stevens, Dodgers vs. the Boston Red Sox which never occurred since the Dodgers finished 2nd behind the St. Louis Cardinals. These phantoms are extremely rare and this one is most desirable because Dodger memorabilia is highly sought after, cover shows an aerial view of Ebbets Field, $1,000.

WORLD SERIES PROGRAMS

1916	....$2,000
1920	....$2,000
1941	....$525
1947	....$250
1949	....$200
1952	....$225
1953	....$225
1955	....$250
1956	....$250

WORLD SERIES GAME TICKETS

1916 Complete Ticket	........................$1,200
1916 Ticket Stub	..................................$600

1920 Complete Ticket	...........................$800
1920 Ticket Stub	..................................$400
1941 Complete Ticket	...........................$200
1941 Ticket Stub	..................................$100
1947 Complete Ticket	...........................$200
1947 Ticket Stub	..................................$100
1949 Complete Ticket	...........................$200
1949 Ticket Stub	..................................$100
1952 Complete Ticket	...........................$150
1952 Ticket Stub	...................................$75
1953 Complete Ticket	...........................$150
1953 Ticket Stub	...................................$75
1955 Complete Ticket	...........................$250
1955 Ticket Stub	..................................$125
1956 Complete Ticket	...........................$150
1956 Ticket Stub	...................................$75

Buffalo, New York

BUFFALO BISONS

National League 1879–1885; Players League 1890

Buffalo, New York enjoyed major league status in three different leagues, the National League (1879–1895), Players League (1890) and Federal League (1914–1915).

The Buffalo Bisons joined the National League in 1879 along with other upstate New York teams from Syracuse and Troy, all of which had played in the International Association in 1878. The Bisons were the most successful of the three and finished third in the eight-team league. Future Hall of Famer Pud Galvin won 37 games, fourth most in the league. Since not one Bison batted above .283, Galvin was largely responsible for the Bisons' success.

In 1880 Pud Galvin's record slipped to 19–35, and the Bisons fell to seventh place in league standings. Rookie Mike Moynahan came up late in the season and batted .330 in 27 games. No one else came close to .300. In 1881, the Bisons were back in third place as Galvin had 28 wins. Future Hall of Famer Dan Brouthers led the league in home runs with 8 and batted .319. Another Hall of Famer, Jim O'Rourke, managed and played third base

while batting .302. In 1882 the Bisons were fourth as Brouthers batted a league high .368 and Galvin again won 28 games. One of the crowd attractions for the 1882 Bisons was rookie pitcher Hugh Dailey, who won 15 and lost 14 despite having only one arm as a result of an accident years before. Known as "One Arm" Dailey, he pitched seven years in the big leagues and retired with a 73–89 record.

Brouthers won his second straight batting title in 1882 (hitting .374) and Galvin was second in the league with 46 wins. Still it was not enough to keep the Bisons from slipping into fifth place. Buffalo lost $199.60 during the 1883 season and rumors began circulating that Pittsburgh would replace the Bisons in 1884 (which turned out to be false).

In 1884 Brouthers batted .327 and Galvin won 46 games for the second straight year as the Bisons finished third. In 1885, the Bisons' last National League season, they finished seventh. Brouthers was second in the league with a .359 BA, but Galvin's record slipped to 13–19 as he wound up managing the team during the final part of the season. In a stock transfer on September 19, Buffalo's best players (Brouthers, Jack Rowe, Hardy Richardson, and Deacon White) went to Detroit while Detroit castoffs finished the season for Buffalo. By combining the best players of both teams into one, league officials hoped for one strong franchise and team. It worked well for Detroit: The Buffalo-bolstered Wolverines won the championship two years later. Unfortunately for Buffalo, they no longer had major league baseball. It returned briefly in 1890 when the Bisons joined the Players League, but they finished last and the league folded. Future Hall of Famer Connie Mack was the Bisons' catcher and batted .266.

BUFFALO BUFFEDS

Federal League 1914–1915

In 1914 Buffalo returned to the majors with a franchise in the Federal League. For want of a better name, they were called the Buffeds and finished fourth under manager Larry Schlafly. They featured righthander Russ Ford, who with 20 wins and only 6 losses had the best winning percentage (.769) among league pitchers. Center fielder Charley Hanford was among league leaders in home runs (13) and RBI (90) and batted .291. Shortstop Baldy Louden had the highest batting average among regulars.

The Buffeds anticipated an overflow crowd of 25,000 for the opener, but miserable weather held the crowd to 14,000. The team contended for the pennant most of the season and finished only seven games behind the champion Indianapolis Hoosiers.

In 1915 Ford suffered a complete turnabout and posted a record of 5–9. Offensively, not one batter hit .300. First baseman Hal Chase provided most of the offense and led the league with 17 home runs and finished third in RBI with 89. As a result the team now called the Blues finished sixth. When the Federal League folded, it signalled the end of major league baseball in Buffalo. In recent years Buffalo has operated a highly successful

Triple A International League franchise that consistently draws more than one million fans per season.

For further reading see *The Federal League of 1914–1915* by Marc Okkonon, *Baseball 1845–1891 from the Newspaper Accounts* by Preston D. Orem.

Publications

PROGRAMS AND SCORECARDS

1914 Program from Buffalo Federal
       League Teams initial season $500
1915 Program from Buffalo Federal
       League Teams second and final
       season $450

Schedules

1915 Buffalo schedule final year of the
       Federal League $125

1914 schedule, 2½″ × 4″, produced by The Buffalo News, Buffalo Buffeds on one side and Buffalo Bisons of the International League on the other, $150.

Chicago, Illinois

CHICAGO WHITE STOCKINGS

National Association 1871, 1874–1875, National League 1876–1900

The Chicago Cubs hold the distinction of being the only continuous member of the National League since its inception in 1876. In addition, the American League White Sox have operated continuously since that league was organized in 1901, which makes Chicago a very unique baseball town. To have teams operating continuously in both major leagues since their formation is a remarkable achievement.

Chicago's first National League team was known as the White Stockings. They went by other names (the Colts and Orphans) before they finally settled on Cubs in 1907, a moniker they have worn proudly ever since.

William A. Hulbert, first president of the White Stockings and a member of Baseball's Hall of Fame, was also the first president of the National League and was largely responsible for drawing up its constitution and by-laws in 1875.

Another Hall of Famer, Al Spalding, was not only the league's finest pitcher (with 46 victories in 1876) but also managed the White Stockings to the first pennant in National League history. So dominant was Chicago that year that four of the league's top five batters were White Stockings. Ross Barnes led the way with a .429 average, followed by Hall of Famer Cap Anson at .356 BA (for third place) and Johnny Peters at .351 and Cal McVey at .347. Catcher Deacon White led the league with 60 RBI, followed by Anson, Barnes, and Paul Hines with 59 and McVey with 58. The team batting average was .337.

Cap Anson took over as manager from Spalding in 1879, and the White Stockings won pennants in 1880, 1881, 1882, 1885 and 1886. Hall of Fame outfielder-catcher King Kelly was a key member of the champions from 1880 through 1886. Hall of Fame pitcher John Clarkson led the league with 58 wins for the 1885 champions; followed by 36 victories in the 1886 championship season, and led the league with 38 wins in 1887, when Chicago finished third behind Detroit and Philadelphia.

CHICAGO CUBS

National League 1901 to Present

Player-managers seemed to do particularly well in Chicago. First baseman Frank Chance became manager in 1905 and guided them to pennants in 1906, 1907, 1908 and 1910 and world championships in 1907 and 1908. The 1906 team still holds the record for most wins in a single season with 116, but was shocked in the World Series, four games to two, by the crosstown White Sox. They gained a measure of revenge by winning two more pennants in 1907 and 1908 along with World Series championships. Joining Chance in the Hall of Fame were fellow Cubs shortstop Joe Tinker, second baseman Johnny Evers, and pitcher Mordeci "Three Finger" Brown. Up to this point every manager of a championship Chicago team was also a player.

Joe Tinker ultimately left the Cubs to join the Cincinnati Reds in 1913, but he came back to manage the Chicago Whales of the Federal League in 1914. Tinker managed the Whales to a second-place finish in 1914 and a pennant in 1915, but the league folded.

Weeghman Park, home of the Whales, replaced West Side Park as the home of the Cubs after Whales owner Charles

Weeghman gained controlling interest in the Cubs in 1916.

Chewing gum magnate William Wrigley was among a group which purchased the club from Weeghman in 1919. Wrigley became majority stockholder in 1921, and the name of the ballpark was changed to Wrigley Field in his honor. The park has retained that name to this day.

Fred Mitchell, the first nonplaying Chicago manager to win a pennant, guided the Cubs to a league championship in 1918, but the Cubs lost to the Boston Red Sox four games to two in the World Series.

Hall of Famer Joe McCarthy managed the Cubs to their next championship in 1929. Second baseman Rogers Hornsby batted .380 and won the league MVP, center fielder Hack Wilson won the RBI crown (with 159), and left fielder Kiki Cuyler batted .360. All three were eventually elected to the Hall of Fame, but the Cubs lost in the World Series to the Philadelphia Athletics four games to one.

Although the Cubs finished second in 1930, Hack Wilson set two National League records that still stand: 56 HR and 190 RBI.

In 1932 they won another pennant but lost to the New York Yankees in the World Series four games to none. This was the series in which Babe Ruth pointed toward the bleachers before hitting a dramatic home run (although there is conjecture to this day whether the event actually took place). Righthander Lon Warneke led the league in wins with 22 and ERA with 2.37. First baseman Charley Grimm took over for player-manager Rogers Hornsby late in the season to direct the pennant drive; Grimm batted .307 with 80 RBI.

Although he played in only two games, Grimm was at the helm in 1935 for the Cubs' next pennant. Catcher Gabby Hartnett was named league MVP and batted .344 while driving in 91 runs. The World Series jinx held true as they lost to the Detroit Tigers four games to two.

In 1945 league MVP Phil Cavaretta (.355) led the Cubs to another pennant, but the Tigers won a thrilling World Series four games to three. Hank Wyse led the Cubs with 22 wins but Hank Borowy, who came from the New York Yankees in mid-season, won 11 and lost only 2.

Hall of Fame shortstop-first baseman Ernie Banks joined the Cubs in 1953 and played through the 1971 season. Although the Cubs never won a pennant during his time with the team, Banks was the first player from a losing team ever to win the league MVP (1958). In 1959 he became the first National League player to win the award in consecutive seasons. Another Hall of Fame Cub, Billy Williams, joined the Cubs in 1959. Although like Banks he never played on a pennant winner, he became the first National Leaguer to play in 1000 consecutive games and ran his string to 1,117 before it ended in 1970.

Hall of Fame righthander Fergie Jenkins, acquired from the Phillies in 1966, won 20 or more games in every season from 1967 through 1972 to trail only Charley Root and "Three Finger" Brown on the Cubs all-time win list.

Ryne Sandberg, a near-certain future Hall of Famer, joined the Cubs in 1982 and brought them as close as they have come to another pennant with an MVP season in 1984. In that year Sandberg batted .314, scored a league high 114 runs, and drove in 84. In the League Championship Series against San Diego, the Cubs won the first two games and then lost three straight to the Padres for the pennant. Sandberg, a ten-time All-Star, batted .368 in his first championship series. In 1984 righthander Rick Sutcliffe won the Cy Young award by capturing 16 of 17 decisions. Jim Frey was named Manager of the Year.

Chicago was represented by the Browns in the Union Association in 1884 and the Pirates in the Players League of 1890.

The Cubs won the National League Eastern Division again in 1989 but lost to the San Francisco Giants in the play-offs, once again thwarted in their quest for that elusive pennant. Don Zimmer was named Manager of the Year and the Cubs set an all-time attendance record of 2,491,942 during that season. Sandberg batted .400 in the play-offs against the Giants after leading the league in runs scored. During the regular season Sandberg batted .290, slammed 30 homes runs, and drove in 76 runs. In his first full season, first baseman Mark Grace batted .314 and drove in a club-high 79 runs. In the play-offs, Grace batted an astounding .647 and drove in eight runs in the five games.

The Cubs are hopeful that Sandberg and Grace will lead them to that long-awaited pennant in the near future. Cub fans, among the best in baseball, have been patiently waiting since 1945. In addition to those already named, the following former Cub players and managers have been elected to the Hall of Fame: Grover Cleveland Alexander, Roger Bresnahan, Lou Brock, Lou Boudreau, Dizzy Dean, Hugh Duffy, Jimmie Foxx, Frankie Frisch, Clark Griffith, Burleigh Grimes, Billy Herman, Monte Irvin, George Kelly, Ralph Kiner, Chuck Klein, Tony Lazzeri, Freddie Lindstrom, Rabbit Maranville, Robin Roberts, Rube Waddell, and Hoyt Wilhelm.

1930s tobacco tin for Chicago Cubs Chewing Tobacco, 6″ × 3½″, $175.

Advertising Specialties

1886 Chicago League Baseball Club Lorillard Team Card, 4″ × 5″ $1,500
1888 Chicago Baseball Club Joseph Hall Cabinets Team Cards, 6½″ × 4½″ $2,100
1913 Chicago Nationals T-200 Fatima Team Card, 2⅝″ × 4¾″ $100

Ballpark Giveaways

1977 Ladies Bonnett, Jacket, Sports Hat, Helmet, Pennant, Cap, Jacket, T-shirt $5

1979 Jacket, Helmet, Cap, T-shirt $5
1980 Jacket, Cap, Jersey $5
1983 Jersey, Jacket, Men's Hat, Lady's Hat, Sports Bag, Rag Ball, Batting Glove, Sun Visor, Home Uniform, Helmet, Cushion $5
1983 Calendar, Photo Mug $10
1984 Cubs Calendar, Thermos.................$10
1984 Surf Book $10
1984 Back Pack, Floppy Hat $5

1889 baseball money, 3½″ × 7″, good for 5% off the purchase price of $5 or more, President A.G. Spalding of the White Stockings and Manager Cap Anson on the front, 12 players from the 1889 team which finished 3rd in the National League on the back, $250.

1990 Homers Cookies box, 3½″ × 6¼″ × 2¼″, made expressly for the All-Star season, sold in stores in the Chicago area (logo from the 1990 All Star game played at Wrigley Field is in the upper righthand corner), $6.

1985 Sun Visor, Batting Helmet, Poncho, Briefcase, Floppy Hat, Tote Bag, Shaving Kit, Flight Bag, Beverage Carrier, Back Pack, Sports Equipment Bag, Wallet, T-shirt $5
1985 Watch $6
1985 Autographed Ball, Thermal Mug, Coffee Mug, Calendar $10
1986 Helmet, Poncho, Cap, Briefcase, Jersey, Sun Glasses, Back Pack, Beach Towel, Flight Bag, Sports Equipment Bag, Beverage Carrier, Wallet, Binder, Tote Bag, Scarf $5
1986 Autographed Ball $10
1986 Thermal Mug, Coffee Mug $8
1986 Budweiser Calendar, Budweiser Tankard Mug $9
1986 Budweiser Floppy Hat, Budweiser Sun Visor, AM Radio $6
1987 4 Color Calendar, Poster, Tankard Mug, Autograph Ball, Thermal Mug, Desk Clock, Helmet Bank $8
1987 Tote Bag, Cap, Umbrella, Floppy Hat, Beach Towel, Bat, Message Cub, Sports Equipment Bag, Ski Cap, Scarf, Notebook, Painter Cap, Wallet $5
1987 Digital Watch $6
1988 Magnet Schedule, Poster, Tankard Mug, Beverage Pitcher & Cups, Team Photo, Desk Set, Coffee Mug, Baseball Radio $7
1988 Digital Watch $6
1988 Cap, Lady's Broach, Umbrella, Floppy Hat, Vinyl Jacket, Painter Cap, Sunglasses, Glove, Bat, Sun Visor, Beach Towel, Helmet, Sports Socks, Key Chain $5
1990 Old Style Magnet Schedule, Headline Mug, Poster, Team Photo, Desk Set, Tankard Mug, Autograph Ball & Holder, Coffee Mug, Desk Clock $7

1990 Watch $6
1990 Neon Cap, Picnic Cooler, Squeeze Bottle, Blue Baseball Cap, Floppy Hat, Script Cap, Bat, Cubby Bear Cap, T-shirt, Beverage Pitcher, Key Chain, Neon Sunglasses, Beach Towel, Helmet, Sports Socks, Car Note Pad, Sports Equipment Bag, Lunch Bag, Knit Cap $5
1990 Lapel Pins ....ea. $7
1991 Old Style Magnet Schedule, Mug, Tankard Mug, Poster, Team Photo, Watch, Old Style Blue Cap, Autograph Ball & Holder, Special Export Light Hip Pack.................................$6
1991 Commemorative Coin $8
1991 Lapel Pins ....ea. $7
1991 Cubby Bear Cap, Neon Cap, Opening Night Cap, Pennant, Tote Bag, Floppy Hat, Script Cap, Squeeze Bottle, Key Chain, T-shirt, Sports Bag, Pinstripe Cap, Helmet, Cooler Bag, Pitcher, Travel Bag, Back Pack, Message Cube, Neon Cap, Holy Cow Cap $5
1992 Old Style Magnet Schedule, Old Style Tankard Mug, Autograph Ball & Holder, Poster, Beverage Mug, Coffee Mug, Beverage Pitcher, Poster, Cubs Cup Set $6
1992 Socks, Helmet, 2-Tone Cubs Cap, Pennant, Tote Bag, Cubs Blue Cap, Squeeze Bottle, Key Chain, Floppy Hat, Women's Sun Visor, Tank Top, Zebra Cap, Beach Towel, Pinstripe Cap, Mini Sports Bottle, Sports Bag, Wallet, Pen Set, Lunchbox $5
1993 Old Style Magnet Schedule, Commemorative Cup Set, Old Style Tankard Mug, Poster, 1945 N.L. Championship Cap, Autograph Ball & Holder, Travel Mug, Team Pen-

1976 certificate of attendance, given to fans who attended the first game of the second hundred years of Chicago National League baseball, $15.

nant, Old Style Commemorative
Cup..$6
1993 Opening Night Cap, Socks, Sports
Bottle, Key Chain, Bat, Sunglasses,
Pinstripe Cap, Sun Visor, Wallet,
Helmet $5
1993 1908 World Championship Pin..........$8

Miscellaneous

1908 14″ × 46″, Panoramic view Yard of
the National Game showing 1907–
1908 World Champion Cubs in
cameos around Westside Park filled
to capacity..................................$1,500

BOBBIN' HEAD DOLLS

Category #I, 1960, 1961, Light Blue
Square Base, Boy Head $200

1972 decal showing the entire Cubs team including
Hall of Famers Ernie Banks and Billy Williams,
8″ × 10″, $20.

Category #II, 1961, 1962, White Square
Base, Mascot $325
Category #III, 1961, 1962, White Round
Miniature, Mascot $325
Category #IV, 1962, 1963, 1964, Green
Round Base, Mascot $225
Category #V, 1962, 1963, 1964, Green
Round Base, Black Player $475
Category #VI, 1967 through 1972, Gold
Round Base, Mascot $50

Pennants

1900 through 1920 ....$750
1921 through 1930 ....$300
1931, 1932 Regular $200
1932 World Series $400
1933, 1934, 1935 Regular......................$200
1935 World Series $400
1936, 1937 Felt Pennants BF3, Type IV,
Batter on Pennant $35
1936, 1937 Felt Pennants BF3, Type V,
Cub on Pennant $35
1936, 1937 Felt Pennants BF3, Type V,
Cub's Head on Pennant $35
1936, 1937, 1938 Regular......................$200
1938 World Series $400
1939, 1940 Regular $200
1941 through 1945 Regular....................$100
1945 World Series $200
1946, 1947 Regular $100
1947 All-Star Game $200
1948, 1949, 1950 ....$100
1951 through 1960 ....$50
1961, 1962 Regular $30
1962 All-Star Game $50
1963 through 1970 ....$50
1971 through 1980 ....$20
1981 through 1984 Regular $5
1984 League Championship Series...........$15
1985 through 1989 Regular......................$5
1989 League Championship Series...........$15
1990 Regular $5
1990 All-Star Game $15
1991, 1992, 1993 ....$3

Pins

1930/1940s American Nut and Chocolate
Co., 1⅛″, Round $15

1950s Cubs pennant, cub standing
in Wrigley Field and Chicago Cubs
all in white on a blue field,
11½″ × 29″, $75.

1961 through 1965 Crane Potato Chips,
7/8", Round $5
1967, 1968, 1969 Crane Potato Chips, 7/8",
Round $5
1984 Crane Potato Chips, 7/8", Round $3
1964, 1965, 1966 Guy's Potato Chips, 7/8",
Round $5

Postcards

1906 RP 4" × 6", Fred H. Wagner, Chi-
cago, Il. $250
1906 PL Photo by Fred H. Wagner, Pub.
Suhling & Koehn, Chicago, Il..........$150
1906 PL Copyright George R. Lawrence,
Pub. V.O. Hammon, Chicago $150
1910 PL Entire team in individual ovals,
no Pub $150
1945 RP Grogan Photo Co., Danville, Il....$150
1946 RP Grogan Photo Co., Danville, Il. $75

Publications

BOOKS

Ahrens, Arthur and Eddie Gold. *The Complete Book of Chicago Cubs.* New York: Collier Books, 1986. ....$5.00
Ahrens, Arthur and Eddie Gold. *Day-by-Day in Chicago Cubs History.* Edited by Buck Peden. West Point, N.Y.: Leisure Press, 1982. ......$10.00
Aylesworth, Thomas. *Baseball's Great Dynasties: The Cubs.* New York: Gallery Books, 1986. ....$5.00
Brown, Warren. *The Chicago Cubs.* G.P. Putnam's Sons, 1946. ....$40.00
Chieger, Bob. *The Cubbies: Quotations on the Chicago Cubs.* New York: Athenium, 1987. ....$10.00
Enright, Jim. *The Chicago Cubs.* New York: McMillan, 1975. ....$15.00

Federal Writers' Project. *Baseball in Old Chicago.* A.C. McClurg and Co., 1939. ....$85.00
•Fulk, David, ed. *The Cubs Reader: The Best Writing Done on Baseball's Most Loveable Team.* Thousand Oaks, Ca.: Ventura Art, 1990. ....$9.95
Gifford, Barry. *The Neighborhood of Baseball: A Personal History of the Chicago Cubs.* New York: E.P. Dutton, 1981. ....$10.00
•Gold, Eddie & Arthur Ahrens. *The Goldern Era Cubs.* Chicago: Bonus Books, 1985. ....$12.95
•Gold, Eddie & Arthur Ahrens. *The New Era Chicago Cubs, 1941– 1985.* San Francisco: Donald S. Ellis, 1985. ....$14.95
•Gold, Eddie & Arthur Ahrens. *The Renewal Area Chicago Cubs, 1985– 1990.* San Francisco: Donald S. Ellis, 1990. ....$15.95
•Honig, Donald. *Chicago Cubs: An Illustrated History.* New York: Prentice-Hall, 1991. ....$24.95
Honig, Donald. *Cubs: A Complete Record of Chicago Cubs Baseball.* New York: McMillan, 1986. ....$10.00
Illinois State Historical Society. *Baseball in Illinois.* April 1961, vol. 14, no. 7. ....$30.00
•Langford, Jim. *The Cub Fan's Guide to Life: The Ultimate Self Help Book.* South Bend, Inc.: Diamond Communications, 1988. ....$4.95
•Langford, Jim. *The Game is Never Over: An Appreciative History of the Chicago Cubs.* South Bend, Indiana: Icarus Press, 1982. ....$7.95
Langford, Jim, ed. *Runs, Hits and Errors: A Treasury of Cubs History and Humor.* South Bend, Ind.: Diamond Communications, 1985. ....$10.00

1945 black-and-white postcard, Chicago Cubs, champions of the National League, 7" × 9", facsimile autographs of the team on the back (this was the Cubs last pennant winner), $150.

Logan, Bob. *Cubs Win.* Chicago: Contemporary Books, 1984. ....$10.00

Logan, Bob. *So You Think You're a Diehard Cub Fan.* Chicago: Contemporary Books, 1985. ....$10.00

Martin, Mollie. *The Chicago Cubs.* Mankato, Mn.: Creative Education, 1982. ....$5.00

Mitchell, Fred and Bob Langer. *Here Come the '86 Cubs.* Chicago: Bonus Books, 1985. ....$10.00

Moreland, George. *Fanfax of Cubs and Sox.* 1916. ....$500.00

•Names, Larry D. *Bury My Heart at Wrigley Field: The History of the Chicago Cubs.* Neshkoro, Wis.: Sportsbook Publishing Co., 1990. .....$18.95

Rothaus, James R. *Chicago Cubs.* Mankaton, Mn.: Creative Education, 1987. ....$5.00

Rothe, Emil. *Baseball in Chicago.* Cleveland: SABR, 1986. ....$5.00

Schwab, Rich. *Stuck on the Cubs.* Evanston, Il.: Sassefrass Press, 1977. ...$10.00

•Talley, Rich. *The Cubs of '69: Recollections of the Team That Should Have Been.* Chicago: Contemporary Books, 1989. ....$9.95

•Wheeler, Lonnie. *Bleachers: A Summer in Wrigley Field.* Chicago: Contemporary Books, 1988. ....$8.95

1927 spring training roster guide (one of the first to use cardboard covers), 3¾" × 9", $175.

1984 League Champs $6
1985 through 1988 ....$4
1989 League Champs $6
1990 through 1993 ....$4

MEDIA GUIDES

1927 Roster Booklet.............................$175
1928 Roster Booklet.............................$150
1929 National League Champs Roster Booklet..$150
1930, 1931 Roster Booklet $100
1932 National League Champs Roster Booklet..$125
1933, 1934 Roster Booklet $100
1935 National League Champs Roster Booklet..$115
1936, 1937 Roster Booklet $75
1938 National League Champs Roster Booklet $85
1939 through 1944 Roster Booklet $65
1945 National League Champs Roster Booklet $75
1946, 1947, 1948 Roster Booklet $65
1949, 1950, 1951 Roster Booklet $55
1952 through 1955 ....$45
1956 through 1961 ....$35
1962, 1963, 1964 ....$50
1965, 1966 ....$20
1967, 1968 ....$17
1969, 1970 ....$15
1971, 1972 ....$12
1973, 1974 ....$10
1975, 1976 ....$8
1977, 1978 ....$7
1979, 1980, 1981 ....$6
1982, 1983 ....$5

PROGRAMS AND SCORECARDS

1900, 1901, 1902 ....$400
1903, 1904 ....$300
1905 ....$200
1906 League Champs $200
1907, 1908 World Champs each year $225
1909 ....$200
1910 League Champs $160
1911 through 1914 ....$150
1915, 1916, 1917 ....$125
1918 League Champs $135
1919, 1920 ....$125
1921 through 1925 ....$75
1926 through 1928 ....$50
1929 League Champs $60
1930 ....$50
1931 ....$35
1932 League Champs $45
1933, 1934 ....$35
1935 League Champs $45
1936, 1937 ....$35
1938 League Champs $45
1939, 1940 ....$35
1941 through 1944 ....$20
1945 League Champs $25
1946 through 1949 ....$20
1950 through 1959 ....$15
1960 through 1969 ....$10
1970 through 1979 ....$6
1980 through 1983 ....$4
1984 League Champs $6

1942 roster and record book, 6″ × 9″, 32 pages, Bear Cub mascot dressed in a Chicago uniform, $200.

1886 official score book, 7″ × 10½″, 16 pages, Chicago White Stockings (later the Cubs) vs. the New York Giants, July 3. Chicago, under Manager Cap Anson, won the pennant by 2½ games over the Detroit Wolverines with a record of 90 wins and 34 losses (New York finished third), $1,500.

1985 through 1988 ....$4
1989 League Champs $6
1990 through 1993 ....$3

YEARBOOKS

1919 *Sketch Book & Complete Record of Our Sox and Cubs* $1,000
1934 *The Cubs of 1934* by Murray Book Corp.* $350
1935 *The Cubs of 1935* by Harold Speed Johnson*.......................................$350
1936 *Who's Who in Chicago Major League Baseball* by Harold Speed Johnson*.......................................$350
1937 *Who's Who in Chicago Major League Baseball* by Harold Speed Johnson*.......................................$350
1937 *Chicago Cubs Autograph Book Chicago National League Ball Club* $300
1938 *Who's Who in Chicago Major League Baseball* by Harold Speed Johnson*.......................................$300
1939 *Player's Records, Chicago National League Ball Club* by Neely Printing Co.* $300
1940 *Chicago Cubs Player's History & Record Book* by Neely Printing Co. ..$250
1941 *Chicago Cubs Player's History & Record Book* by Neely Printing Co. ..$250

1942 *Chicago Cubs Player Roster and Record Book* $200
1946 *Picture Parade of the Chicago Cubs* $200
1948 ....$150
1949 ....$125
1950 ....$100
1951, 1952 ....$90
1953, 1954 ....$80
1955, 1956 ....$75
1957 ....$100
1958 through 1984 ....None Issued
1985, 1986 ....$8
1987, 1988 ....$6
1989 League Champs $6
1990 through 1993 ....$5

Schedules

1900 through 1909 ....$150
1910 through 1919 ....$100
1920 through 1929 ....$75
1930 through 1959 ....$45
1940 through 1949 ....$30
1950 through 1959 ....$25
1960 through 1969 ....$15
1970 through 1979 ....$10
1980 through 1985 ....$2
1986 through 1993 ....$1

Special Events

ALL-STAR PRESS PINS

1947 ....$500
1962 ....$300
1990 ....$25

1990 program, All-Star game at Wrigley Field, 8″ × 11″, 96 pages, $10.

ALL-STAR PROGRAMS

1947	$200
1962	$100
1990	$10

ALL-STAR GAME TICKETS

1947 Complete Ticket	$200
1947 Ticket Stub	$100
1962 Complete Ticket	$70

1962 Ticket Stub	$35
1990 Complete Ticket	$20
1990 Ticket Stub	$10

LEAGUE CHAMPIONSHIP SERIES PROGRAMS

1984	$12
1989	$10

LEAGUE CHAMPIONSHIP SERIES TICKETS

1984 Complete Ticket	$35
1984 Ticket Stub	$15
1989 Complete Ticket	$30
1989 Ticket Stub	$15

WORLD SERIES PRESS PINS

1906, 1907, 1908, 1910, 1918	None issued
1929	$500
1932	$500
1935	$500
1938	$500
1945	$300

WORLD SERIES PROGRAMS

1906	$7,000
1907	$7,000
1908	$7,000
1910	$5,000
1918	$3,000
1929	$1,000
1932	$1,000
1935	$500
1938	$350
1945	$325

WORLD SERIES TICKETS

1906 Complete Ticket	$2,000
1906 Ticket Stub	$1,000

1910 World Series program, 7¾″ × 10¼″, 28 pages, Cubs vs. Philadelphia Athletics (Athletics defeated the Cubs 4 games to 1), bears surrounding a performing elephant, $5,000.

1907 Complete Ticket	$2,000
1907 Ticket Stub	$1,000
1908 Complete Ticket	$2,000
1908 Ticket Stub	$1,000
1910 Complete Ticket	$1,600
1910 Ticket Stub	$800
1918 Complete Ticket	$1,200
1918 Ticket Stub	$600
1929 Complete Ticket	$600
1929 Ticket Stub	$500
1932 Complete Ticket	$400
1932 Ticket Stub	$200
1935 Complete Ticket	$400
1935 Ticket Stub	$200
1938 Complete Ticket	$400
1938 Ticket Stub	$200
1945 Complete Ticket	$200
1945 Ticket Stub	$100

CHICAGO WHITE SOX

American League 1901 to Present

As charter members of the American League, the Chicago White Sox have enjoyed several great moments in baseball history. Unfortunately, they will be remembered most for the infamous Black Sox Scandal, when eight members of the team took gamblers' money to throw the 1919 World Series.

Charles A. Comiskey, a fine major league first baseman prior to the turn of the century, acquired a Chicago franchise in the fledgling American League in 1901. With future Hall of Famer Clark Griffith as manager and star pitcher (24–7), the White Sox won the pennant that initial season. However, since there was much bad blood between the new American League and established National League, no World Series was played to determine the best team in baseball.

When the White Sox won their next pennant in 1906, they were heavy underdogs to the cross-town National League champions Chicago Cubs, when they met in the World Series. The Cubs had won their pennant by 20 games over the defending world champion New York Giants by posting 116 wins, a record that still stands. Miraculously, the White Sox, known as the "Hitless Wonders," took the series four games to two.

Second baseman Frank Isbell's .279 BA was the team's highest. Shortstop George Davis was the RBI leader with 80. But it was the pitching that carried the White Sox to the pennant and stymied the Cubs in the World Series. Nick Altrock, later famous as a baseball clown, led the staff with 21 wins, followed closely by Ed Walsh and Frank Owen with 19 apiece and Doc White with 18. In the World Series Walsh won two games while Altrock and White each won one and lost one. Walsh ultimately was elected to Baseball's Hall of Fame, the only member of the 1906 world champions to be so honored.

Comiskey Park, known as the Baseball Palace of the World, opened on July 1, 1910, and immediately drew raves as the finest park in baseball. With seating capacity of approximately 30,000, it was three times larger than the wooden South End Grounds it replaced. In 1917 the Sox won their third American League pennant thanks largely to the pitching of 28-game-winner Eddie Cicotte, who led the league in victories, and the hitting of Happy Felsch (.308 BA and 102 RBI) and Shoeless Joe Jackson (.301 BA and 75 RBI). Ironically, these three stars were among the eight banned from baseball for life in 1920 for throwing the 1919 World Series to the Cincinnati Reds. But in the World Series of 1917 the White Sox disposed of the New York Giants four games to two, with Red Faber winning three games and Cicotte one.

Despite the success of the team, owner Comiskey paid notoriously low salaries, and when gamblers offered money to eight stars of the pennant-winning 1919 team to lose the World Series, they jumped at the opportunity. Forever after known as the Black Sox were Cicotte, Jackson, and Felsch plus Buck Weaver; Swede Risberg; Lefty Williams; Fred McMullin; and Chick Gandil, who engineered the fix with his teammates.

During the regular season Cicotte again led the league in wins with 29. Williams was third in the league with 23 wins, while Jackson led the Sox with a .351 BA and 96 RBI. In the World Series Lefty Williams lost three games and Cicotte two as they bowed to the Reds five games to three. Lefthander Dickie Kerr became the Sox's pitching hero by winning his two starts, but it wasn't enough given the circumstances.

When news of the fix broke in 1920, a trial was held and all eight players were acquitted. However, much damning evidence not allowed at the trial was considered sufficient by Commissioner Kenesaw Mountain Landis to ban the eight for life.

Had they not been banned for life, Cicotte, who won 207 games and Jackson, who had a .356 lifetime BA, third best in major league history, would undoubtedly have been elected to the Hall of Fame. Regardless, untainted teammates second baseman Eddie Collins, catcher Ray Schalk, and pitcher Red Faber ultimately joined the baseball immortals.

Future Hall of Fame pitcher Ted Lyons joined the White Sox in 1923 fresh from the campus of Baylor University. Another White Sox great and Hall of Famer, shortstop Luke Appling, began his 20-year career with the club in 1930. But the team could never climb higher than third until the 1959 Go Go Sox won the pennant.

Led by the American League MVP and second baseman Nellie Fox; future Hall of Fame shortstop Luis Aparicio, who topped the league with 56 stolen bases; and Cy Young Award winner righthander Early Wynn, whose 22 wins was the league's best; the White Sox relied on speed and defense to win their first pennant in 40 years. However, they bowed to the Los Angeles Dodgers four games to two in the World Series.

Al Lopez, who managed the 1959 champs almost won another pennant in 1964, but the Sox finished one game back of the New York Yankees. In 1972, thanks largely to an MVP season by Dick Allen, they finished second again. In 1983, with Cy Young winner Lamar Hoyt winning 24 games and outfielder Ron Kittle driving in 100 runs, Tony LaRussa managed the team to a division title. The White Sox lost to the eventual world champion Baltimore Orioles in the American League championship series.

In 1991 the White Sox moved into a brand new Comiskey Park across the street from the old one and drew an all-time record attendance of 2,934,154. At old Comiskey Park, the White Sox attracted more than two million fans three times in 1983, 1984, and the venerable park's final season of 1990.

The current White Sox have an excellent pitching nucleus for the future in six-foot five-inch righthander Jack McDowell, a 20-game winner for the first time in 1992 and Cy Young Award winner in 1993. Their infield of shortstop Ozzie Guillen, first baseman Frank Thomas, and

third baseman Robin Ventura figure to keep the White Sox among the pennant contenders for many years to come.

In addition to the White Sox Hall of Famers already named, Harry Hooper and Hoyt Wilhelm played more than five seasons in Chicago, while Johnny Evers, Al Simmons, Chief Bender, Eddie Rousch, Red Ruffing, Jocko Conlan, George Kell and Tom Seaver all played at least one game with the "Pale Hose." Nellie Fox is a good bet to achieve Hall of Fame status in the future. Once the career of ageless catcher Carlton Fisk finally ends, he, too, is likely to be honored.

Advertising Specialties

1913 Chicago Americans T200 Fatima
    Team Card, 2⅝″ × 4¾″ $100
1970s Popcorn Megaphone, 3½″ × 10½″...$15

1972 matchbook schedule, 2″ × 5″, Drovers National Bank of Chicago, $5.

Ballpark Giveaways

1971 Photo Mug, Poster $15
1971 Cushion, Scarf $8
1971 Decals (6 different), Complete Set $45

1971 T-shirt, Batting Glove, Helmet $5
1972 Photo Mug, Poster $8
1972 Cushion $15
1973 Bat, Helmet $5
1973 Poster, Photo Mug $15
1973 Beer Mug, Cushion $8
1978 Pin, 2¼″ Green on yellow for
   Lithunian Day, June 17, 1978 ....$10
1981 Seat Cushion, Pennant.....................$5
1981 Photo Mug, Color Team Picture $10
1983 All-Star Ring $20
1983 Calendar, All-Star Patch, All-Star
   Poster, Sox Team Poster, All-Star
   Pennant, Sox Team Picture, All-Star
   Tankard $10
1983 All-Star Gym Bag, All-Star Helmet,
   All-Star Jacket, Coffee Mug $8
1983 Cushion, Cap, Bat, Jersey, Ladies
   Tote Bag, Cowboy Hat, Beach
   Towel, Notebook, Ski Cap $5
1984 Calendar, Budweiser Photo Mug,
   Team Photo, Team Poster $10
1984 Wrist Watch, Coffee Mug $6
1984 Painter Cap, Roll-up Hat, Cap,
   Beach Towel, Cooler, Ladies Neck
   Scarf, Wallet, Ladies Tote Bag, Jer-
   sey, Bat, Brief Case, Batting Glove......$5
1985 Calendar, Coca-Cola Sox Cloth Cal-
   endar, Busch 75th Anniversary
   Commemorative Mug, Clarklift
   Thermal Mug, Color Team Photo,
   Chrysler/Plymouth Poster $10
1985 K-Mart Seat Cushion, Rustoleum
   Wrist Watch, Windex Necklace,
   Taco Bell Mitt, Yago Fisherman's
   Hat, Consort Hairspray Sunglasses,
   Clorox Beach Towel, Eckrich Jer-
   sey, Lee Jeans Tote Bag, Chernin's
   Beach Sandals, United Airlines
   Winter Scarf, McDonald's Cap, Be-
   atrice Umbrella, WMAQ Radio,
   Baby Ruth/Butterfinger Helmet,
   North Oak Chrysler/Plymouth Key
   Chain $6
1985 Backpack $5
1986 Calendar, Kool-Aid Mug, Color
   Team Photo, Busch Beer Mug...........$9
1986 Kitty Litter Musical Headband, K-
   Mart Cushion, Coca-Cola Bat Rack,
   Baby Ruth/Butterfinger Helmet,
   North Oak Chrysler/Plymouth Li-
   cense Plate Frame, Mr. Turkey
   Apron, Illinois State Lottery Beach
   Towel, Jovan Sunglasses, Henry K
   Jewelers Radio Watch, Gatorade
   Wrist Watch, Chernin's Shoes
   Beach Sandals, Kool-Aid Mitt, Mr.
   Foster Travel Message Cube,
   WMAQ Transistor Radio, United
   Airlines Ski Cap, WMAQ Umbrella $6
1986 Gym Bag, Jersey $5
1989 Magnet Schedule, New Comisky
   Park Car Shade, Bat, Painter Cap,
   1933 All-Star Game Youth Jacket,
   Sunglasses, Baseball Cap, South

Side Hit Mens Seat Cushion, White
   Sox Baseball Card Set, Sport Shorts,
   1959 A.L. Champion Tankard, Old
   Style Umbrella................................$5
1989 Old Style Tank Top $6
1989 Collectable Pictures 1, 2, 3, 4, 5 ....ea. $6
1989 Collectable Pins 1, 2, 3, 4, 5, 6 ......ea. $6
1990 Calendar, Chicago Tribune/Sports
   Channel Magnetic Schedule, Coca-
   Cola Card Set, WMAQ Commemorative Comiskey Park Baseball, CTA
   Poster, Miller Tankard, Kodak
   Collectible #6 Comiskey Park (all
   others are players) $7
1990 Coca-Cola 5 Pin Set ....ea. $7
1990 Donruss Card Book $7
1990 Old Style Neon Hats, Looney Tunes
   Visor, Miller Beach Bag, Miller
   Beach Towel, Old Style Key Chain,
   Gatorade Hip Pack, Miller Neon
   Sunglasses $6
1991 Calendar, Gatorade Magnetic
   Schedule, '76 Comiskey Park Pin,
   Miller Poster, United Airlines
   Comiskey Park Patch, Ski Power
   Tools Old Comiskey Poster, CTA
   Poster...$7
1991 Scott Peterson Pins 1, 2, 3, 4 ($7.00
   each), Complete Set........................$25
1991 WMAQ Sun Shield, Coca-Cola Gym
   Bag, Hallberg Insurance Neon Cap,
   Miller Lite Can Wrap, Coca-Cola
   Batting Gloves, Coca-Cola Batting
   Helmets, Coca-Cola T-shirts,
   Kemper Cap, Miller Lite Cap $6
1991 Donruss Card Book, Kodak Base-
   ball Cards $7
1992 Coca-Cola Magnetic Schedule, Cal-
   endar, Scott Peterson Pins 1, 2, 3, 4,
   Kodak Top Drafts Collectible, Mil-
   ler Beer Tankard, Ski Tools
   Comiskey Park Poster, Chicago Tri-
   bune Team Picture, CTA Comiskey
   Park Poster, "76" Exploding Score-
   board Pin, WMAQ Travel Mug, Chicago Tribune Team Picture $7
1992 Chicago Americans Cap, Cola-Cola
   Sunglasses, Miller Beach Towel,
   Coca-Cola Batting Practice Tops,
   Gatorade Squeeze Bottle, Iron Kids
   Bread Notebooks, United Airlines
   Patch, Coca-Cola Backpack,
   Kemper Cap $6
1993 Coca-Cola Magnet Schedule, Cal-
   endar, Coca-Cola Lunch Box, Chi-
   cago Tribune Team Picture, United
   Airlines Patch, Kodak White Sox
   All-Star Poster, Upper Deck Heros
   of Baseball $7
1993 Target Umbrella, Coca-Cola Kids
   Cap, American Giants Cap, Miller
   "Winning Ugly" Hats, Gatorade
   Wrist Band, Miller Sports Bag,
   Coca-Cola Ski Cap, Insure One
   Cap, Chicago Tribune Bat $6

1970s popcorn megaphone, 3½″ × 10½″, White Sox logo, $15.

Miscellaneous

BOBBIN' HEAD DOLLS

Category #II, 1961, 1962, White Square
Base, Boy Head $185
Category #III, 1961, 1962, White Round
Miniature, Boy Head $165
Category #IV, 1962, 1963, 1964, Green
Round Base, Boy Head $55
Category #V, 1962, 1963, 1964, Green
Round Base, Black Player $300
Category #VI, 1967 through 1972, Gold
Round Base, Boy Head $38

Pennants

1901 through 1920 ....$750
1921 through 1930 ....$300
1931, 1932, 1933 Regular......................$200
1933 All-Star Game $400
1934 through 1940 ....$200
1936, 1937 Felt Pennant BF3, Type IV,
Batter on Pennant $35
1936, 1937 Felt Pennant BF3, Type IV,
Catcher on Pennant $35
1936, 1937 Felt Pennant BF3, Type IV,
Pitcher on Pennant $35
1941 through 1950 Regular...................$100
1950 All-Star Game $200
1951 through 1959 ....$50
1959 World Series $100
1960 ....$50
1961 through 1970 ....$30
1971 through 1980 ....$20
1981, 1982, 1983 Regular $5
1983 All-Star Game $15
1983 Division Champs..........................$15
1984 through 1990 ....$5
1991, 1992, 1993 ....$5

Pins

1930s/1940s American Nut & Chocolate
Co., 1⅛″, Round $15
1961 through 1965 Crane Potato Chips,
⅞″, Round $5
1967, 1968, 1969 Crane Potato Chips, ⅞″,
Round $5
1984 Crane Potato Chips, ⅞″, Round $3
1964, 1965, 1966 Guy's Potato Chips, ⅞″,
Round $5

Postcards

1906 RP 4″ × 6″, Fred H. Wagner, Chi-
cago, Il. $250
1906 Copyright F.P. Burke, Pub. Suhling
& Koehn, Chicago, Il. $150

1906 black-and-white postcard, 3½″ × 5½″, manufactured by F.P. Burke, the White Sox amazed the world by beating the heavily favored Chicago Cubs 4 games to 2 in the 1906 World Series, $150.

1907 PL. George W. Hull, Chicago, Il., 15
Players appearing in circular head
shots within White Sox hanging on
clothes line with full length player
view in righthand corner $125

Publications

BOOKS

Asinov, Eliot. *Eight Men Out.*
Winston, 1963 (1st ed. $60) Ace
Books, 1970, reissue $20.00
Berke, Art & Paul Schmitt. *This Date
in Chicago White Sox History.*
New York: Stein & Day, 1982. ....$5.00
Brown, Warren. *The Chicago White
Sox.* G.P. Putnam's Sons, 1952. ......$40.00
Condon, Dave. *The Go-Go White Sox.*
Coward-McCann, 1960. ....$30.00
Lindberg, Richard. *Sox: The Com-
plete Record of Chicago White Sox
Baseball.* New York: McMillan,
1984. ....$15.00
Lindberg, Richard. *Stuck on the Sox.*
Evanston, Il.: Sassafrass Press,
1978. ....$15.00
Lindberg, Richard. *Who's on Third?
The Chicago White Sox Story.*
South Bend, Ind.: Icarus Press,
1982. ....$15.00
Logan, Bob. *The Miracle on 35th
Street: Winnin' Ugly with the 1983*

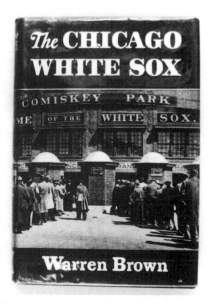

1952, *The Chicago White Sox* by Warren Brown, G.P.
Putnam, New York, complete history of the Chicago
White Sox from 1901 through 1951, 5¾" × 8½",
248 pages, $40.

White Sox. South Bend, Ind.:
Icarus Press, 1984. ....$15.00
Luhrs, Victor. *The Great Baseball
Mystery.* A.S. Barnes & Co., 1966. ....$40.00
Moreland, George. *Fanfax of Cubs
and Sox.* 1916. ....$100.00
Paige, David & Richard Whittingham.
*The Chicago White Sox: A Picto-
rial History.* Chicago: Contempo-
rary Books, 1982. ....$15.00
Rothaus, James R. *Chicago White
Sox.* Mankato, Mn.: Creative Edu-
cation, 1982. ....$5.00
Rothe, Emil. *Baseball in Chicago.*
Cleveland, Oh.: SABR, 1986. ....$7.00
Shaw, Bill. *Chicago White Sox.* Man-
kato, Mn.: Creative Education,
1982. ....$5.00
Ward, Arch. *The New Chicago White
Sox.* Henry Regnery Co., 1951. ......$50.00
Whittingham, Richard. *The White
Sox: A Pictorial History.* Chicago:
Contemporary Books, 1983. ....$15.00

MEDIA GUIDES

1927 Roster Sheet	$125
1928 through 1933 Roster Sheet	$100
1934, 1935 Roster Booklet	$100
1936 through 1940 Roster Booklet	$75
1941 through 1949 Roster Booklet	$60
1950 through 1958	$50
1959 American League Champs	$60
1960, 1961	$40
1962, 1963, 1964	$30
1965, 1966	$20
1967, 1968	$17
1969, 1970	$15
1971, 1972	$12
1973, 1974	$10
1975, 1976	$8
1977, 1978	$7
1979, 1980, 1981, 1982	$6
1983 Division Champs	$8
1984, 1985	$5
1986 through 1993	$4

PROGRAMS AND SCORECARDS

1901 American League Champs	$600
1902, 1903, 1904	$400
1905 through 1909	$200
1910 through 1913	$150
1914 through 1920	$125
1921 through 1925	$75
1926 through 1930	$50
1931 through 1940	$35
1941 through 1949	$20
1950 through 1959	$15
1960 through 1969	$10
1970 through 1979	$6
1980, 1981, 1982	$4
1983 Division Champs	$6
1984 through 1989	$4
1990, 1991, 1992, 1993	$3

YEARBOOKS

1947	$275
1948	$225
1949	$175
1950, 1951	$150
1952, 1953	$90
1954	$75
1955, 1956, 1957	$70
1958	$60
1959 American League Champs	$70
1960	$50
1961, 1962	$40
1963, 1964	$30
1965	$25
1966, 1967, 1968, 1969	$20
1970	$18
1971 through 1981	None Issued
1982	$7
1983 Division Champs	$8
1984	$6
1985 through 1989	None Issued
1990, 1991, 1992, 1993	$5

Schedules

1901 through 1909	$150
1910 through 1919	$100
1920 through 1929	$75
1930 through 1939	$45
1940 through 1949	$30
1950 through 1959	$25
1960 through 1969	$15
1970 through 1979	$10
1980 through 1985	$2
1986 through 1993	$1

Special Events

ALL-STAR GAME PRESS PINS

1933	None Issued
1950	$200
1983	$50

1983 gold press pin celebrating 50th anniversary of 1933 All-Star game, 1¼", $40.

ALL-STAR PROGRAMS

1933	$1,300
1950	$250
1983	$15

1933 scorecard, 6¼" × 9", the first All-Star game played at Comiskey Park on July 6. Regular season scorecard was used with printed line-ups of American and National League (All-Star won by the American League 4 to 2 on Babe Ruth's two run homer), $1,300.

ALL-STAR GAME TICKETS

1933 Complete Ticket	$400
1933 Ticket Stub	$200
1950 Complete Ticket	$150
1950 Ticket Stub	$75
1983 Complete Ticket	$30
1983 Ticket Stub	$15

LEAGUE CHAMPIONSHIP SERIES PROGRAMS

1983	$10

LEAGUE CHAMPIONSHIP SERIES TICKETS

1983 Complete Ticket	$15
1983 Ticket Stub	$5

WORLD SERIES PRESS PINS

1906	None Issued
1917 (not dated)	$4,000
1919 Black Sox Scandal (not dated)	$5,000
1959	$200

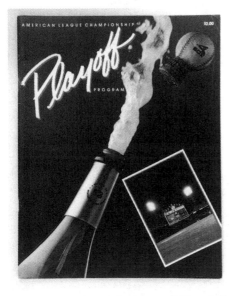

1983 program, 8½″ × 11″, 84 pages, ALCS vs. Baltimore, champagne bottle popping its cork and inset of the exploding scoreboard at Comiskey Park, $10.

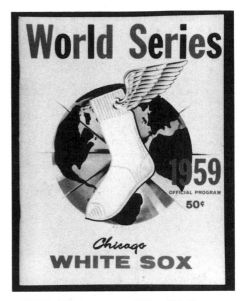

1959 World Series program, 8½″ × 11″, 72 pages, White Sox vs. Los Angeles Dodgers, winged White Sox covering a map of the world, $100.

WORLD SERIES PROGRAMS

1906	$7,000
1917	$5,000
1919 Black Sox Scandal	$5,000
1959	$100

WORLD SERIES GAME TICKETS

1906 Complete Ticket	$2,000
1906 Ticket Stub	$1,000

1917 Complete Ticket	$1,200
1917 Ticket Stub	$600
1919 Complete Ticket (Black Sox Scandal)	$3,000
1919 Ticket Stub	$1,500
1959 Complete Ticket	$150
1959 Ticket Stub	$75

Cincinnati, Ohio

CINCINNATI REDS

National League 1876–1880, 1890 to Present; American Association 1882–1889, 1891

Cincinnati is the cradle of professional baseball in America, as the 1869 Cincinnati Red Stockings were America's first professional team. Moreover, they played the first entire season, taking on all comers in their national tour, and did not lose a single game. A Newport, Kentucky, jeweler named Harry Wright organized the first team. The Red Stockings' star player was Harry's brother, George. Both had played cricket in their native England and adapted well to America's pastime.

When the National League was organized in 1876, the Reds were charter members, but they dropped out in 1881 because they were not allowed to sell beer in the Cincinnati ballpark. The American Association had no such rule and gladly welcomed the Reds, who played in the rival league until 1890 when they rejoined the National League and have remained since.

There were few bright spots for the Reds in their return to the National League. Their best records were third-place finishes in 1896, 1904 and 1918. However, in 1905 Reds outfielder Cy Seymour won the batting title with a .377 batting average. It still stands as the highest average in Reds history.

In 1919 the Reds finally won a pennant. Edd Roush's .321 batting average led the National League and his 71 RBI ranked third. Slim Salee had 21 wins, Hod Eller posted 20 victories and Dutch Ruether chipped in with 19. Despite these impressive stats, the Reds were heavy underdogs against the American League champion White Sox in the World Series. Miraculously the Reds won five games to three, although it was later learned that eight Chicago players took gamblers' money to throw the World Series to the Reds. Hod Eller won two games while Salee, Ruether, and Jimmy Ring each captured one. Greasy Neale, who later coached the NFL's Philadelphia Eagles to a world championship, led Reds regulars with a .357 BA. Ironically, Shoeless Joe Jackson, one of the tainted eight who eventually was banned from baseball for life, posted a .375 BA to lead all series regulars.

Cincinnati's pitching in the World Series was so good that even had there been no fix, the Reds might still have won. Because of the circumstances, however, it's something we'll never know.

It was 30 years before the Reds won another championship, but in 1939, after many dismal last-place finishes in 1931–1934 and 1937, they were back on top of the National League. first baseman Frank McCormick led the Reds with a .322 BA and 128 RBI, best in the National League. Future Hall of Fame catcher Ernie Lombardi contributed mightily with a team high 20 HR and 85 RBIs. Bucky Walters added 27 wins and Paul Derringer 25, making them the league's leading pitchers. Walters was named National League MVP. The Reds were no match for the New York Yankees in the World Series, however, and lost four games to none.

In 1940 manager Bill McKechnie's Reds repeated as champs and won the World Series by beating Detroit four games to three. McCormick had another banner year, batting .309 with 19 HR and 127 RBI to capture the MVP award. Walters again led the league with 22 wins while Derringer was right behind with 20.

Several highlights occurred prior to the championship seasons. On May 24, 1935, dynamic General Manager Larry MacPhail initiated night baseball in the major leagues, a move that forever changed the game. Then on June 11 and June 15, 1938, fireballing lefthander Johnny Vandermeer hurled back-to-back no hitters to become the first and only pitcher to accomplish the feat. Led by National League MVP Frank Robinson, who batted .323 with 37 HR and 124 RBI, the Reds won another pennant in 1961. League leader Joey Jay (21–10) and Jim O'Toole (19–9) contributed excellent pitching. Jay got the only World Series win for Cincinnati as the Reds lost four games to one to the Yankees.

Cincinnati was represented in the Union Association of 1884.

In 1970 the Reds moved into Riverfront Stadium, won the National League Western Division, and went on to beat the Pittsburgh Pirates in the NLCS. With Manager Sparky Anderson at the helm, the "Big Red Machine" dominated baseball in the 1970s by winning six National League Western Division titles (1970, 1972, 1973, 1975, 1976, and 1979) four pennants (1970, 1972, 1975, 1976) and world championships in 1975 and 1976. Catcher Johnny Bench, outfielders Pete Rose and George Foster, first baseman Tony Perez, and second baseman Joe Morgan were the heart of the team. Among them the Reds' superstars won the National League MVP award six times in eight years (Bench in 1970 and 1972; Rose in 1973; Morgan in 1975 and 1976; and Foster in 1977, when he set a club record with 52 HR and 149 RBI). Of that group Bench was inducted into the Hall of Fame in 1989 and Morgan entered in 1990. Rose, who had more hits than any player in history, was a certainty to be elected but because of gambling activities is ineligible for enshrinement at this time.

Although hitting predominated for Cincinnati during the 1970s, Jim Merritt had a 20–12 record in 1970 and Hall of

Famer Tom Seaver posted a 21–6 record in 1977. Although the Reds had four consecutive second-place finishes from 1985 through 1988 under Pete Rose, it was not until 1990, when Lou Pinella became manager, that the Reds were back on top of the baseball world. They became the first National League club in history to lead the league from the first day to the last. Third baseman Chris Sabo (25 HR) and Eric Davis (85 RBI) supplied most the power. Fifteen-game-winner Tom Browning and 14-game-winner Jose Rijo were backed up by outstanding relief pitchers Norm Charlton and Rob Dibble. They amazed the baseball world by sweeping the highly favored Oakland Athletics in the World Series to cap a perfect season. The Reds have drawn exceptionally well due their success in recent years, exceeding two million fans 11 times. The club record for attendance is 2,629,708 in 1976.

Advertising Specialties

1888 Cincinnati Ball Club, American Association, Joseph Hall Cabinets Team Cards, 6½″ × 4½″ $1,800
1913 Cincinnati Nationals T200 Fatima Team Card, 2⅝″ × 4¾″ $100
1950 Multi-Color Felt Round $35
1975 Multi-Color Commemorative Beer Can issued by Hudepohl..................$15

1975 Hudepohl Beer can, 2¼″ × 4¾″, 1975 world champion Reds with a montage of events from the dramatic seven game victory over the Boston Red Sox, $15.

1984 Multi-Color Matchbook Schedule manufactured by Universal Match Co. $5

Ballpark Giveaways

1984 Painter Cap $5
1985 Team Picture Mug, Calendar $10
1985 Autographed Ball $15
1986 Color Team Picture, LA Big Mug......$10
1986 Kool-Aid Bat, Kool-Aid Watch, Borden Back Pack, Klosterman Bakery Umbrella, HFC Sunglasses......$6
1987 Snapper Power Equipment Calendar, Maxwell House Team Picture $8
1987 Borden Dairy Mug, Klosterman Bakery Umbrella, Kinney Shoes Sports Socks, Hudepohl Beer Relief Pitcher $7
1987 Sealtest Beverage Cooler, Gatorade Watch, Haircuts Inc. Cup $6
1987 Kahn's Baseball Cards $7
1988 Frisch's Refillable Travel Mug, Maxwell House Coffee Team Poster ...$7
1988 Borden's 3 Ring Binder, Gatorade Watch, Hudepohl/Schoenling Painter Cap $6
1988 Kahn's Baseball Cards $7
1989 Frisch's Travel Mug, Maxwell House Team Picture $7
1989 Donruss Baseball Book, Kahn's Baseball Cards.................................$7
1989 Drumstick Batting Helmet, Fifth/Third Cap, Borden Pencil Pouch, Gatorade Baseball Watch $6
1990 Haircuts Inc. Magnet Schedule, Kahn's Baseball Cards $7
1990 Drumstick Helmet, Sports Channel Sports Bag, Pepsi Cap, Gatorade Watch $6
1991 Video Towne Calendar, Klosterman Magnet Schedule, Mezty Bone Poster, MCI Sports Bag, Sports Chanel Cap, Cap'N Crunch Watch, All America Raisin Batting Helmet, Ortho Thermos $7
1991 Super Pretzel Team Picture $6
1991 Gatorade Replica World Series Ring $15
1991 Donruss Card Book, Kahn's Baseball Cards $7
1991 Glove $5
1992 Klosterman Magnet, Nationwide Calendar, Sports Channel Umbrella, MCI Sports Bag, Gatorade Cap, Super Pretzel Team Picture, Bob Evans Hat $6

Miscellaneous

BOBBIN' HEAD DOLLS

Category #I, 1960, 1961, Red Square Base, Boy Head $200
Category #II, 1961, 1962, White Square Base, Mascot $375

Category #III, 1961, 1962, White Round
 Miniature, Mascot $285
Category #IV, 1962, 1963, 1964, Green
 Round Base, Mascot $135
Category #V, 1962, 1963, 1964, Green
 Round Base, Black Player $550
Category #VI, 1967 through 1972, Gold
 Round Base, Mascot $80

Pennants

1900 through 1920 ....$750
1921 through 1930 ....$300
1931 through 1939 ....$200
1936, 1937 Felt Pennant BF3, Type IV,
 Batter on Pennant $35
1936, 1937 Felt Pennant BF3, Type IV,
 Pitcher on Pennant $35
1936, 1937 Felt Pennant BF3, Type V,
 Ball on Pennant $35
1939 World Series $400
1940 Regular $200
1940 World Series $400
1941 through 1950 ....$100
1951, 1952, 1953 ....$50
1953 All-Star Game $125
1954 through 1960 ....$50
1961 Regular $30
1961 World Series $75
1962 through 1970 Regular $30
1970 All-Star Game $75
1970 League Championship $75
1970 World Series $75
1971, 1972 Regular $20
1972 League Championship $50
1972 World Series $50
1973 Regular $20
1973 League Championship $50
1974, 1975 Regular $20
1975 League Championship $50
1975 World Series $50
1976 Regular $20
1976 League Championship $50
1976 World Series $50

1950s–1960s pin, 2¼″, logo for the Red Legs but Cincinnati Reds in block letters surrounding it. From 1953 to 1958 the team was called the Red Legs rather than Reds to avoid any linkage with a synonym for communists (starting in 1959, the name Reds was used once again), $15.

1977, 1978, 1979 Regular $20
1979 League Championship $50
1980 ....$20
1981 through 1990 Regular $5
1990 League Championship $15
1990 World Series $15
1991, 1992, 1993 ....$3

Pins

1930s/1940s American Nut & Chocolate
 Co., 1⅛″, Round $15
1961 through 1965 Crane Potato Chips,
 ⅞″, Round $5
1967, 1968, 1969 Crane Potato Chips, ⅞″,
 Round $5
1984 Crane Potato Chips, ⅞″, Round $3
1964, 1965, 1966 Guy's Potato Chips, ⅞″,
 Round $5

1939 postcard, 3½″ × 5″, individual cameos of the National League champions, published by Orcajo Photo Studio of Dayton, Ohio, $150.

Publications

BOOKS

Alexis, Pete. *The Royal Reds: Baseball's New Dynasty.* Shelbyville, Ky., 1977. ....$15.00

Allen, Lee. *The Cincinnati Reds.* G.P. Putnam's Sons, 1948. ....$85.00

Bjarkman, Peter C. *Baseball's Great Dynasties: The Reds.* New York: Gallery Books, 1991. ....$5.00

Brannon, Jody. *Cincinnati Reds.* Mankato, Mn.: Creative Education, 1982. ....$5.00

Collett, Ritter. *The Cincinnati Reds: A Pictorial History of Professional Baseball's Oldest Team.* Virginia Beach, Va.: Jordan Powers, 1976. ....$20.00

Collett, Ritter. *Men of the Reds Machine: An Inside Look at the Baseball Team of the 1970's.* Dayton, OH.: Landfill Press, 1977. ....$15.00

Conner, Floyd & John Snyder. *Day-By-Day in Cincinnati Reds History.* West Point, N.Y.: Leisure Press, 1984. ....$10.00

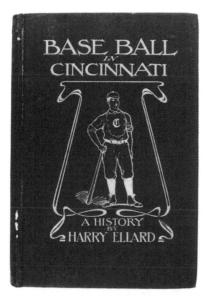

1907, *Baseball in Cincinnati* by Harry Ellard, 6¼″ × 9¼″, 277 pages, original Red Stocking in red on the blue cover, one of the rarer team histories. This is the 2nd edition published by the author a year after his original was published by Johnson and Hardin in 1906. It chronicles the history of baseball in Cincinnati starting with the 1869 Red Stockings, America's first professional team that played the entire season without losing a game, $750.

Ellard, Harry. *Baseball In Cincinnati.* Press of Johnson and Hardin, 1907. ....$750.00

Hertzel, Bob. *The Big Red Machine.* Englewood Cliffs, N.J.: Prentice-Hall, 1976. ....$15.00

•Honig, Donald. *The Cincinnati Reds: An Illustrated History.* New York: Prentice-Hall, 1992. ....$27.50

Rathgeber, Bob. *Cincinnati Reds Scrapbook.* Virginia Beach, Va.: J.C.P. Corp., 1982. ....$25.00

Rothaus, James R. *Cincinnati Reds.* Mankato, Mn.: Creative Education, 1987. ....$5.00

•Walker, Robert H. *Cincinnati and the Big Red Machine.* Bloomington, Ind.: Indiana University Press, 1988. ....$8.95

Wheeler, Lonnie & John Baskin. *The Cincinnati Game.* Wilmington, Oh.: Orange Frazer Press, 1988. ......$15.00

MEDIA GUIDES

1927 Roster Sheet	$125
1928 through 1931 Roster Sheet	$100
1932 through 1935 Roster Booklet	$100
1936 through 1938 Roster Booklet	$75
1939 National League Champs	$85
1940 World Champs	$85
1941 through 1949	$60
1950 through 1955	$50
1956 through 1960	$40
1961 National League Champs	$45
1962, 1963, 1964	$50
1965, 1966	$20
1967, 1968, 1969	$17
1970 National League Champs	$20
1971	$12
1972 National League Champs	$15
1973 Division Champs	$15
1974	$10
1975, 1976 World Champs each Year	$12
1977, 1978	$7
1979 Division Champs	$9
1980, 1981, 1982	$6
1983, 1984, 1985	$5
1986 through 1989	$4
1990 World Champs	$6
1991, 1992, 1993	$3

PROGRAMS AND SCORECARDS

1900, 1901, 1902	$400
1903, 1904	$300
1905 through 1909	$200
1910 through 1914	$150
1915 through 1918	$125
1919 World Champs	$130
1920	$125
1921 through 1925	$75
1926 through 1930	$50
1931 through 1938	$35
1939 League Champions	$45
1940 World Champs	$45

1941 through 1949 ....$20
1950 through 1959 ....$15
1960 ....$10
1961 League Champions $15
1962 through 1969 ....$10
1970 League Champions $10
1971 ....$6
1972 National League Champs $10
1973 Division Champs...........................$10
1974 ....$6
1975, 1976 World Champs each Year $10
1977, 1978 ....$6
1979 Division Champs...........................$10
1980 through 1989 ....$4
1990 World Champs $8
1991, 1992, 1993 ....$3

YEARBOOKS

1919 *Official Players Souvenir, The Reds
    of 1919*, Cincinnati Reds $2,500
1919 *Souvenir Record Book, World's
    Championship Series, Chicago vs.
    Cincinnati* by A. Prusank $2,500
1930 *Reds* by Cino Publishing Co...........$250
1947 ....$300
1948 ....$175
1949 ....$150
1950 ....None Issued
1951, 1952 ....$125
1953 ....$100
1954, 1955 ....$90
1956, 1957, 1958 ....$75
1959, 1960 ....$60
1961 League Champs $65
1962, 1963 ....$45
1964, 1965 ....$35
1966, 1967, 1968 ....$30
1969 ....$25
1970 League Champs $30
1971 ....$20
1972 League Champs $25
1973, 1974 ....$15
1975, 1976 World Champs each Year $18
1977, 1978 ....$12
1979 ....$10
1980, 1981 ....$8
1982, 1983 ....$6
1984, 1985 ....$5
1986 ....None Issued

1987, 1988, 1989 ....$5
1990 World Champs $7
1991, 1992, 1993 ....$5

Schedules

1900 through 1909 ....$150
1910 through 1919 ....$100
1920 through 1929 ....$75
1930 through 1939 ....$45
1940 through 1949 ....$30
1950 through 1959 ....$25
1960 through 1969 ....$15
1970 through 1979 ....$10
1980 through 1985 ....$2
1986 through 1993 ....$1

Special Events

ALL-STAR GAME PRESS PINS

1938 ....$500
1953 ....$200
1970 ....$100
1988 ....$45

ALL-STAR PROGRAMS

1938 ....$650
1953 ....$175
1970 ....$75
1988 ....$10

ALL-STAR GAME TICKETS

1938 Complete Ticket $400
1938 Ticket Stub $200
1953 Complete Ticket $150
1953 Ticket Stub...................................$75
1970 Complete Ticket $40
1970 Ticket Stub...................................$20
1988 Complete Ticket $30
1988 Ticket Stub...................................$15

LEAGUE CHAMPIONSHIP SERIES PROGRAMS

1970 ....$50
1972 ....$25
1973 ....$20
1975, 1976 ....$15

1988 Frisch's Big Boy schedule, 4″
× 9″ unfolded, Frisch Big Boy
holding a tray with the Reds logo
and a schematic of Riverfront Stadium (home of the Reds), $1.

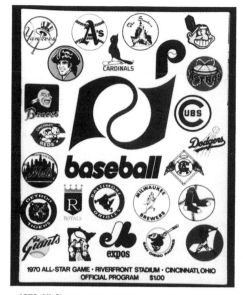

1970 All-Star program, 8½″ × 11″, 56 pages, $75.

1940	$350
1961	$100
1970	$75
1972	$50
1975	$50
1976	$30
1990	$12

WORLD SERIES GAME TICKETS

1919 Complete Ticket	$2,000
1919 Ticket Stub	$1,000
1959 Complete Ticket	$400
1939 Ticket Stub	$200
1940 Complete Ticket	$200
1940 Ticket Stub	$100
1961 Complete Ticket	$70
1961 Ticket Stub	$35
1970 Complete Ticket	$40
1970 Ticket Stub	$20
1975 Complete Ticket	$40
1975 Ticket Stub	$20
1976 Complete Ticket	$40
1976 Ticket Stub	$20
1990 Complete Ticket	$20
1990 Ticket Stub	$10

1979	$12
1990	$5

LEAGUE CHAMPIONSHIP SERIES TICKETS

1970 Complete Ticket	$35
1970 Ticket Stub	$18
1972 Complete Ticket	$35
1972 Ticket Stub	$18
1973 Complete Ticket	$35
1973 Ticket Stub	$18
1975 Complete Ticket	$35
1975 Ticket Stub	$18
1976 Complete Ticket	$35
1976 Ticket Stub	$18
1979 Complete Ticket	$35
1979 Ticket Stub	$18
1990 Complete Ticket	$18
1990 Ticket Stub	$10

WORLD SERIES PRESS PINS

1919	$4,000
1939	$300
1940	$300
1961	$200
1970 (not dated)	$150
1972 (not dated)	$125
1975 (not dated)	$125
1976 (not dated)	$125
1990	$30

WORLD SERIES PROGRAMS

1919	$2,500
1939	$350

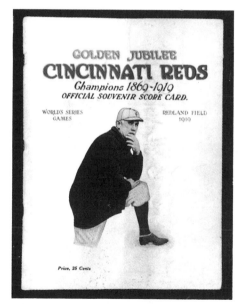

1919 official souvenir score book, 9″ × 12″, 48 pages, World Series against the Chicago White Sox at Redland Field. After Cincinnati defeated the White Sox it was learned that eight members of the Chicago team conspired with gamblers to purposely lose the Series. The eight players were banned from baseball for life and were thereafter known as the Black Sox. Reds manager Pat Moran adorns the cover of this rare collectible, $2,500.

Cleveland, Ohio

CLEVELAND FOREST CITIES

National Association 1871–1872

Cleveland's illustrious baseball history dates to the earliest times and has been marked by triumph and tragedy. A team known as the Forest Cities participated in the first game of professional baseball's first league, the National Association, when on May 4, 1871, they were shut out 2–0 by the Kekiongas at Fort Wayne, Indiana.

During that initial major league season, the Forest Cities finished seventh in the nine-team league with 10 wins and 19 losses. After winning only six and losing 15 during the 1872 season, the Forest Cities disbanded in late August.

CLEVELAND BLUES

National League 1879–1884, American Association 1887–1888

Cleveland was without major league ball until 1879, when the Blues joined the National League and finished sixth with a record of 27 wins and 55 defeats. In 1880 the Blues improved to 47 wins and 37 losses to finish third in the eight-team league. Jim McCormick led the league with 45 wins to account for all but two of the Blues' victories. He was also the team's manager.

The Blues tumbled to seventh in 1881 as McCormick's record plummeted to 26 and 30 despite a 2.45 ERA. In 1882 McCormick again led the league in victories (36) and the Blues finished fifth with 42 wins and 40 losses. The Blues were fourth in 1883 as McCormick won 28 and led the league with a 1.84 ERA. Midway in the 1884 season, McCormick jumped to Cincinnati of the Union Association, where he posted a 21–3 record and led the league with a 1.54 ERA. Without their ace pitcher

the Blues faltered to seventh and dropped out of the National League after the season.

The Blues resurfaced in the American Association in 1887 and finished last, with 39 wins and 92 defeats. In 1888 they improved to sixth place, winning 50 and losing 82.

CLEVELAND SPIDERS

National League 1889–1899

In 1889 Cleveland was back in the National League as the Spiders. The name change made little difference; the team was sixth again. In 1890 Cleveland finished seventh in both the National League and the new Players League.

Cy Young, the winningest pitcher in major league history, joined the Spiders during the 1890 season and ended with nine wins and six losses. He went on to record 509 victories over 22 seasons. Meanwhile, the Players League team called the Infants featured Pete Browning, who won the batting title with a .373 BA. The Players League folded after one season.

Young became a 27-game winner in 1891 as the Spiders moved up to fifth. In 1892 Young won 36 as the Spiders finished second. In future Hall of Famer Jesse Burkett's first full season with the Spiders, he batted .275 and led the team with six home runs. Burkett played 16 years in the majors and had a lifetime .338 BA. In 1893 he batted .348 and Young won 36 as the Spiders were third. In 1894 the Spiders dropped to sixth but rebounded to finish second to Baltimore in 1894 and stun the champion Orioles in the Temple Cup. Young led the league with 35 wins while Burkett's .409 BA won the batting title.

The Spiders were second to the Orioles in 1896, but the Orioles gained revenge in the Temple Cup. Burkett led the league in

80

batting again with a .410 BA and Young finished with 28 wins. In 1897 the Spiders were fifth; Burkett finished third with a .383 average and Young won 21 games. Third baseman Bobby Wallace, another future Hall of Famer, played his first full season and batted .335. A second consecutive fifth-place finish in 1898 was highlighted by Young's 25 wins and Burkett's .341 average. In 1899 the roof caved in on the Spiders. Team owner and Trolley magnate Frank Robinson (who also owned the St. Louis National League franchise) took Cleveland's best players and put them in St. Louis. The result was a record of 20 wins and 134 losses, the worst in major league history. Not one Spider batted .300, and the winningest Spider pitcher, Jim Hughey, had four victories and a league-high 30 defeats. That dismal season ended Cleveland's tenure in the National League.

CLEVELAND INDIANS

American League 1901 to Present

In 1901 Cleveland became a charter member of the new American League. The Cleveland Blues (as they were called that season) finished seventh, with outfielder Jack McCarthy leading the team with a .321 BA. In 1902 the Blues became the Broncos and moved up to fifth place as future Hall of Famer Addie Joss led with 17 wins and Hall of Famer Napoleon Lajoie led the league in batting for the second straight season. Lajoie played for the Philadelphia Athletics in 1901 and came to Cleveland in 1902 by court order: He could not play ball in Philadelphia since he had jumped contract with the National League Phillies in order to join the Athletics.

A newspaper contest to name the team ended with "Naps" in honor of their star second baseman. Lajoie became manager in 1905; his best record came in 1908 when the Naps finished one game behind Detroit. Lajoie's batting average declined to .289 with the added pressure of managing, so he gave up that job in 1909 and rebounded with a .324 average. He lost the 1910 batting title to Detroit's Ty Cobb by a mere fraction—.385 to .384.

In the twilight of his brilliant career, the immortal Cy Young, came back to Cleveland in 1909 to lead the Naps with 19 wins. Hall of Fame outfielder Elmer Flick, who came with Cleveland in 1902, finished his 13-year major league career with a .313 lifetime average. Lajoie was released after the 1915 season, and another newspaper contest gave Cleveland its current nickname of Indians in honor of Louis Sockalexis. Baseball's first well-known Native American player, Sockalexis played three seasons with the Spiders in the 1890s.

Hall of Famer Tris Speaker joined the Indians in 1916 and led them to their first pennant and world championship as player-manager in 1920. However, this championship season was marred by the death of shortstop Ray Chapman, who was hit in the head by a pitch thrown by New York's Carl Mays on August 16. The Indians beat Brooklyn in the 1920 World Series five games to two as Hall of Famer Stan Covaleski added three World Series victories to his 24 regular season triumphs. Jim Bagby's 31 wins during the 1920 season remains a club record, and he notched another victory in the World Series. Other highlights of the series were second baseman Bill Wambsganns' unassisted triple play and Elmer Smith's grand slam home run, the first in Series history. Rookie Joe Sewell replaced Chapman at shortstop and was ultimately elected to the Hall of Fame.

Although the Tribe contended for the pennant in 1921 and 1926, they didn't win another title until 1948 when player-manager Lou Boudreau led them to the world championship. The Indians had a plethora of Hall of Fame stars join the team in the 1920s and 1930s, including outfielder Earl Averill (1929), "Rapid" Robert Feller (1936), and Boudreau (1938). A player revolt against manager Oscar Vitt, forever known as the "Crybaby Rebellion," occurred in 1940 and cost Vitt his job. Boudreau was elevated to player-manager.

Bill Veeck, one of the greatest promoters in baseball history, bought the team in June 1946 and attendance reached new heights. A club record 2,620,627 fans passed through the gates during the 1948 championship season. In 1947 Veeck signed Larry Doby, the American League's first African-American player. He played a key role in the 1948 championship as did Satchel Paige, who joined the Tribe from the Kansas City Monarchs and promptly won six and lost one during the later part of the 1948 pennant race.

Boudreau, who won the batting title in 1944 (.327), was second to Boston's Ted Williams in 1948 with a career-high .355 BA and was league MVP. Second baseman Joe Gordon led the Tribe with 124 RBI. The "Big Three" pitching staff of Bob Lemon (20), Gene Bearden (20) and Bob Feller (19) trailed only Detroit's Hal Newhouser (21) in victories. In the World Series the Indians beat the Boston Braves four games to two, with Lemon contributing three victories.

In 1954 the Indians repeated as American League champions with a league record 111 wins as Hall of Famers Lemon and Early Wynn tied for the league lead with 23 wins and Mike Garcia chipped in with 19. Tribe batters also dominated the league. Second baseman Bobby Avila won the batting title (.341) while Doby was home run (32) and runs batted in (126) champion. The World Series was a disaster: The heavily favored Indians lost to the New York Giants in four straight games.

Cleveland had a Players League team nicknamed the Infants in 1890.

Although the Indians finished second in 1955, 1956 and 1959, they have not finished higher than third since. The club appeared to be on the upswing, but tragedy struck again during spring training in 1993 when pitchers Steve Olin and Tim Crews were killed in a boating accident.

The Indians have assembled some of baseball's young players, including second baseman Carlos Baerga and power-hitting outfielder Albert Belle, one of the most feared home run hitters in baseball. With the move to a brand-new ballpark at Gateway Center in 1994, after more than 60 years at Municipal Stadium, the Indians hope to recapture the glory days of Speaker and Boudreau when the Tribe was the finest team in baseball.

Advertising Specialties

1888 Cleveland Baseball Club Joseph
Hall Cabinets Team Cards, 6½″ ×
4½″ $1,800

1913 Cleveland Americans T200 Fatima
Team Card, 2⅝″ × 4¾″ $100

Ballpark Giveaways

1976 Helmet, Jacket, Jersey, Bat (if items contain sponsors name or logo, add $1) $5
1977 Helmet, Jacket, Jersey, Bat, Equipment Bag $5
1977 Dailey's Poster, Beer Cup $10
1978 Cushion, Jersey, Helmet, Bat, Ladies Tote Bag, Cap $5
1978 Ball with Facsimile Autographs $10
1978 Dailey's Poster $10
1979 Jacket, Jersey, Bat, Helmet $5
1980 Frito Lay Batting Glove, Burger King Bat $6
1980 Jacket, Jersey, Helmet $5
1981 Anheiser Busch Seat Cushion, Burger King Bat, Mr. Coffee All-Star Mug $6
1981 Shell Helmet $6
1981 Wishbone Autograph Ball, Mr. Coffee All-Star Mug, Team Picture $10
1981 Back Pack, Hat $5
1982 Seat Cushion, Plastic Cup, Jacket, Cap, Helmet, Sport Travel Bag..........$5
1982 Poster, Team Picture $8
1985 Wrist Watch, Mug, Calendar, Team Picture, Yankee Hankies $7
1985 Seat Cushion, Backpack, Cap, Sun Visor, Helmet, Notebook $5
1987 Tribe Lapel Pin, Calendar, Team Photo, Thermos, Autograph Ball, Radio $7
1987 Beach Ball, Floppy Hat, Beach Towel, White Cap, Snack Bag, Scarf ...$5
1988 Calendar, Cap & Lapel Pin, Team Photo, Musical Key Chain, Coffee

1974 leather case and key chain, 2¼″ × 3½″, presented to all fans on August 24, when the Indians drew more than a million fans, gold inscription on brown leather reads, "Thanks a Million", $15.

Rows 1 and 2: Complete set of 8 American League pins, 1 1/8" d, issued by American Nut & Chocolate, c. 1930s, $15 each, $125 for set (complete set of 16 pins, $250). Row 3, press pins: 1913 New York Giants World Series, $5,000; 1972 Oakland A's World Series, $200; 1985 Minnesota Twins All-Star game, $50; 1983 Chicago White Sox All-Star game, $40. Row 4, press pins: 1931 St. Louis Cardinals World Series, $500; 1969 New York Mets World Series, $200; 1984 Baltimore Orioles Japan tour, $200; 1962 Chicago Cubs All-Star game, $300; 1929 Philadelphia Athletics World Series, $1,500. Center: Los Angeles Dodgers stadium pin, c. 1958, $20. Rows 5 and 6: Complete set of 8 National League pins, 1 1/8" d, issued by American Nut & Chocolate, c. 1930s, $15 each, $125 for set (complete set of 16 pins, $250).

Clockwise from top: 1982 Chicago White Sox team picture, 8 1/2" x 11", ballpark giveaway, $10; 6 felt rounds, 5", advertising specialties, $35 each; c. 1960, Pittsburgh Pirates Iron City Beer coaster, 3 1/2", $10; 1992 Seattle Mariners wrist band, ballpark giveaway, $6; Budweiser beer tap handle, $20; 16 Fleer cloth patches, $5 each; 1993 Colorado Rockies bumper sticker, ballpark giveaway, $10; 1985 Chicago Cubs Camera Day ballpark giveaway, $6. Center: 1982 St. Louis Cardinals placemat, 11 1/4" x 17 1/4", $6.

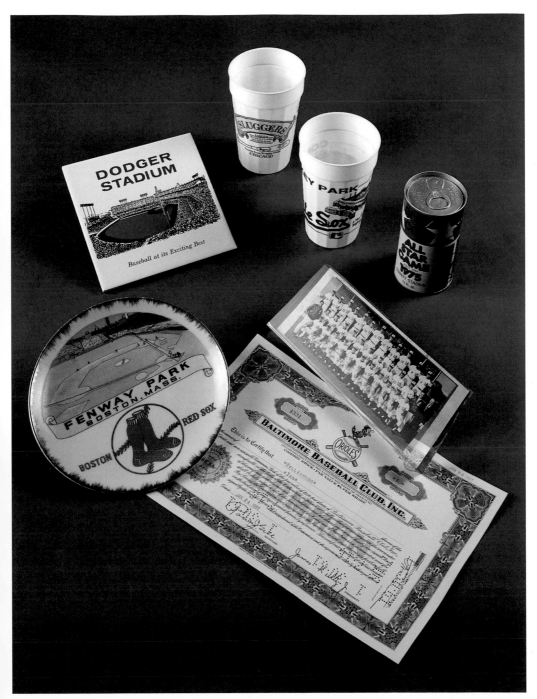

Clockwise from top: Plastic cup, Sluggers restaurant, $5; plastic cup, Comiskey Park, $10; soda can issued exclusively for 1975 All-Star game at Milwaukee, $15; paperweight showing 1969 Montreal Expos inaugural team, $50; 1954 stock certificate from Baltimore Orioles, $100; plate showing Fenway Park and Boston Red Sox logo, c. 1965, $125; ceramic tile coaster showing Dodger Stadium, Los Angeles, $25.

Top: Cardboard supplement to May 3, 1896 Philadelphia Press with diecut figures (bottom) of Philadelphia and Boston teams and Philadelphia ballpark, $1,500. Center: paper pennant issued by Foster's Skin Cream celebrating Baltimore Orioles 1894 national league championship, $500. Bottom: Die cut figures representing teams are St. Louis, New York (red stripes), Baltimore, Detroit, Philadelphia, Pittsburgh, Indianapolis (top), and Brooklyn (bottom), $400 each.

Row 1: 1969 ALCS program, Minnesota Twins vs. Baltimore Orioles, $35; 1993 Inaugural Series program, New York Mets vs. Florida Marlins, $10; complete ticket, 1970 dedication and inaugural game at Three Rivers Stadium, $100; 1993 All-Star program, $10. Row 2: 1986 ALCS program, California Angels vs. Boston Red Sox, $8; 1971 program from opening of Veterans Stadium, $100; 1937 All-Star program, Washington, D.C., $600. Row 3: 1982 All-Star program, Montreal, $25; 1960 All-Star program, New York, $75; 1934 World Series program, Detroit Tigers vs. St. Louis Cardinals, $550. Row 4: 1969 NLCS program, New York Mets vs. Atlanta Braves, $100; 1958 All-Star program, $200; 1978 NLCS program, Los Angeles Dodgers vs. Philadelphia Phillies, $15.

Pennants: 1983 Baltimore Orioles, World Series, with facsimile autographs, $15; 1969 All-Star game, $75; c. 1983 Philadelphia Phillies, $15; 1959 Milwaukee Braves, $125; 1990 generic World Series, $10.

Clockwise from top: 1969 Oakland A's yearbook, $90; 1963 Los Angeles Angels yearbook, $50; 1969 Seattle Pilots yearbook, $200; 1962 Houston Colt .45s yearbook, $200; Cleveland Indians photo album, $120; 1961 Minnesota Twins cartoon book, $100; 1960 Baltimore Orioles yearbook, $90; 1993 Toronto Blue Jays media guide, $4. Center: Postcard, interior view of Newark Federal League ballpark, $500.

Brochures and schedules, clockwise from top: 1981 Detroit Tigers, $2; 1979 Baltimore Orioles, $10; 1986 Texas Rangers, $1; 1970 Oakland A's, $20; 1990 Chicago Cubs, $1; 1953 St. Louis Browns, $30; 1977 Chicago White Sox, $10; 1987 Atlanta Braves, $1; 1986 Cincinnati Reds, $1; 1987 Los Angeles Dodgers, $1; 1988 Pittsburgh Pirates, $1. Center: 1969 Montreal Expos ticket brochure and schedule (first year), $25.

Mug, Autograph Notebook, Card
Collectors Book $7
1988 Cup, Vinyl Briefcase, Sunglasses,
Backpack $5
1989 Team Calendar, Autographed Ball $7
1989 Hero Cologne Umbrella, Milk
Duds/Jolly Rancher Beach Towel,
Gatorade Replica Jersey, Burger
King Sports Bottle, Growth Poster $6
1989 Sports Bag, Bat, Glove, Knit Cap,
Corduroy Cap $5
1990 Sports Channel Calendar, Oscar
Mayer Team Photo, Autographed
Ball $7
1990 Pay Day Corduroy Cap, Gatorade
Jacket, Sunoco Beach Towel, Coca-
Cola Bat, Yankee Hankie $6
1990 Jersey, Pitcher, Glove, Cap, Sports
Bag $5
1991 Calendar, Donruss Baseball Book,
Upper Deck Poster $7
1991 Sunoco Pins (complete set of 4) $24
1991 Sunoco Pins 1, 2, 3, 4; Coca-Cola
Bat..ea. $7
1991 Pay Day Neon Cap, Gatorade Belt
Bag, Slider Fun Book, Coca-Cola
Bat, Gatorade Squeeze Bottle, Mug $6
1992 Miller Genuine Draft Calendar, Gatorade Sports Mug, Donruss Baseball Card Book, Kahn's Playing
Cards, Tribe Mug............................$6
1992 Sunoco 1954, 1975, 1932 Lapel Pins
(complete set) $15
1992 1954 Cap, Wrist Band, Pay Day
Neon Cap, Lunch Box, Wahoo
Wave Towel, Batting Glove, Note
Pad, T-shirt, Back Pack Sack $5

Miscellaneous

BOBBIN' HEAD DOLLS

Category #II, 1961, 1962, White Square
Base, Mascot $285
Category #III, 1961, 1962, White Round
Miniature, Mascot $285

1948 Chief Wahoo bank, 8″, by Standord Pottery of Sebring, Ohio, manufacturer of Boston Braves and Pittsburgh Pirates banks, $175.

Category #IV, 1962, 1963, 1964, Green
Round Base, Mascot $120
Category #V, 1962, 1963, 1964, Green
Round Base, Black Player $530
Category #VI, 1967 through 1972, Gold
Round Base, Mascot $80

EXHIBIT CARDS

1948 Cleveland Exhibit Supply Co. $14
1954 Cleveland Exhibit Supply Co. $12

Pennants

1901 through 1920 ....$750
1921 through 1930 ....$300
1931 through 1935 Regular...................$200
1935 All-Star Game $400

1948 exhibit card of the world champions, 3½″ × 5″, $14.

1948 pennant, 8″ × 24½″, with white lettering, Chief Wahoo batting, Cleveland Indians in block letters, "American League Champions—World Series 1948," $200.

1936 through 1940 ....$200
1936, 1937 Felt Pennant BF3, Type V, Indian on Pennant.............................$35
1936, 1937 Felt Pennant BF3, Type V, Indian's Head $35
1936, 1937 Felt Pennant BF3, Type V, Indian's Head with Hat $35
1941 through 1948 Regular....................$100
1948 World Series $200
1950 ....$100
1951 through 1954 Regular $50
1954 All-Star Game $125
1954 World Series $125
1955 through 1960 ....$50
1961, 1962, 1963 ....$30
1963 All-Star Game $75
1964 through 1970 ....$50
1971 through 1980 ....$20
1981 Regular $5
1981 All-Star Game $15
1982 through 1990 ....$5
1991, 1992, 1993 ....$5

Pins

1930/1940s American Nut & Chocolate Co., 1⅛″, Round $15
1961 through 1965 Crane Potato Chips, ⅞″, Round $5
1967 through 1969 Crane Potato Chips, ⅞″, Round $5

1980s Indians logo pin, 1½″, produced for all Major League teams, $2.

1984 Crane Potato Chips, ⅞″, Round $3
1964, 1965, 1966 Guys' Potato Chips, ⅞″, Round $5

Postcards

1905 Cleveland Naps, Cleveland Naps Individual Players featured in Ovals, Souvenir Postcard Shop, Cleveland, OH. $400

1907 postcard, 3½″ × 5½″, Cleveland Naps (named after their star second baseman and manager Napoleon Lajoie). The Naps finished 4th in the American League, $250.

Publications

BOOKS

•Hetrick, J. Thomas. *Misfits, The Cleveland Spiders of 1899–A Day-By-Day Narrative of Baseball Futility.* Jefferson, N.C.: McFarland & Co., 1991. ....$25.95
Phillips, Jack. *The 1895 Cleveland Spiders.* Cabin John, Md.: Capital Publishing Co., 1990. ....$6.00
Phillips, Jack. *Chief Sockalexis and the 1897 Cleveland Indians.* Cabin John, Md.: Capital Publishing Co., 1990. ....$6.00
Brannon, Jody. *Cleveland Indians.* Mankato, Mn.: Creative Education, 1982. ....$5.00
Eckhouse, Morris. *Day-By-Day in Cleveland Indians History.* West Point, N.Y.: Leisure Press, 1983. ......$10.00
Lewis, Franklin. *The Cleveland Indians.* G.P. Putnam's Sons, 1949. .....$45.00
Phillips, John. *Bill Hinchman's Boner and the 1908 Naps.* Cabin John, Md.: Capital Publishing Co., 1990. .....$6.00
Phillips, John. *A Cleveland Baseball Notebook.* Cabin John, Md.: Capital Publishing Co., 1990. ....$6.00
Phillips, John. *Cleveland Baseball Winners.* Cabin John, Md.: Capital Publishing Co., 1987. ....$6.00
Phillips, John. *Cleveland Blues, 1901.* Cabin John, Md.: Capital Publishing Co., 1988. ....$6.00
Phillips, John. *The Crybaby Indians of 1940.* Cabin John, Md.: Capital Publishing Co., 1990. ....$6.00
Phillips, John. *96 Years of Hope.* Cabin John, Md.: Capital Publishing Co., 1987. ....$6.00
Phillips, John. *When Lajoie Came to Town: The 1902 Cleveland Indians.* Cabin John, Md.: Capital Publishing Co., 1988. ....$6.00
Rothaus, James R. *Cleveland Indians.* Mankato, Mn.: Creative Education, 1987. ....$6.00

MEDIA GUIDES

1927 Roster Sheet $125
1928 through 1931 Roster Sheet $100
1932 through 1935 Roster Booklet $100
1936 through 1940 Roster Booklet $75
1941 through 1947 Roster Booklet $60
1948 World Champs (first modern media guide) $150
1949 ....$60
1950 through 1953 ....$50
1954 American League Champs $60
1955 through 1961 ....$40

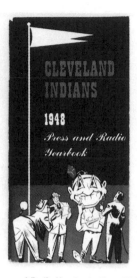

1948, *Press and Radio Yearbook,* 4″ × 8″, 55 pages, edited by Publicity Director Marsh Samual (considered the first of the modern media guides as previously most had only a few pages), $150.

1962, 1963, 1964 ....$30
1965, 1966 ....$20
1967, 1968 ....$17
1969, 1970 ....$15
1971, 1972 ....$12
1973, 1974 ....$10
1975, 1976 ....$8
1977, 1978 ....$7
1979, 1980, 1981 ....$6
1982, 1983, 1984 ....$5
1985 through 1993 ....$4

PROGRAMS AND SCORECARDS

1901 ....$600
1902 ....$400
1903, 1904 ....$300
1905 through 1909 ....$200
1910 through 1914 ....$150
1915 through 1919 ....$125
1920 World Champs $135
1921 through 1925 ....$75
1926 through 1930 ....$50
1931 through 1940 ....$35
1941 through 1947 ....$20
1948 World Champs...............................$30
1949 ....$20
1950 through 1953 ....$15
1954 American League Champs $20
1955 through 1959 ....$15
1960 through 1969 ....$10
1970 through 1979 ....$6
1980 through 1989 ....$4
1990, 1991, 1992, 1993 ....$3

1932 souvenir scorecard, 6¾″ × 10¾″, 20 pages, the first baseball game in the history of Municipal Stadium on July 31, between the Indians and Philadelphia Athletics who won the game 1-0 with Lefty Grove outdueling Mel Harder, $300.

YEARBOOKS

1948 World Champs	$150
1949	$100
1950, 1951	$75
1952, 1953	$65
1954 American League Champs	$95
1955 (very scarce)	$200
1956, 1957	$60
1958 (very scarce)	$180
1959	$55
1960, 1961, 1962, 1963	$50
1964, 1965, 1966, 1967	$45
1968	$40
1969	$35
1970	$30
1971, 1972	$25
1973 through 1983	None Issued
1984	$6
1985 through 1988	None Issued
1989 through 1993	$5

Schedules

1901 through 1909	$150
1910 through 1919	$100
1920 through 1929	$75
1930 through 1939	$35
1940 through 1949	$30
1950 through 1959	$25
1960 through 1969	$15
1970 through 1979	$10
1980 through 1985	$2
1986 through 1993	$1

Special Events

ALL-STAR GAME PRESS PINS

1935	None Issued
1954	$200
1963	$120
1981	$25

1954 gold press pin, 1¼″ × 1⅛″, manufactured by Balfour, smiling Chief Wahoo encircled by 10 stars above Municipal Stadium, $200.

ALL-STAR GAME PROGRAMS

1935	$500
1954	$175
1963	$100
1981	$15

ALL-STAR GAME TICKETS

1935 Complete Ticket	$400
1935 Ticket Stub	$200
1954 Complete Ticket	$150
1954 Ticket Stub	$75
1963 Complete Ticket	$70
1963 Ticket Stub	$35
1981 Complete Ticket	$30
1981 Ticket Stub	$15

WORLD SERIES PRESS PINS

1920	$2,500
1948	$250
1954	$200

WORLD SERIES PROGRAMS

1920 (same as regular season score-
　　card) $3,000
1948 (fairly easy to obtain) $150
1954 ....$200

WORLD SERIES GAME TICKETS

1920 Complete Ticket $800
1920 Ticket Stub $400
1948 Complete Ticket $200
1948 Ticket Stub $100
1954 Complete Ticket $150
1954 Ticket Stub $75

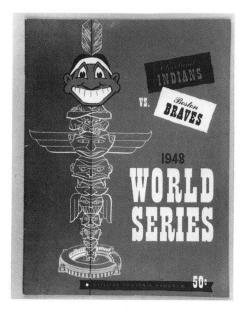

1948 World Series program, 9″ × 12″, 32 pages, smiling Chief Wahoo atop a totem pole ascending from
Municipal Stadium. (Cleveland won the Series in 6
games, as Hall of Fame pitcher Bob Lemon won 2
games.), $150.

Columbus, Ohio

COLUMBUS BUCKEYES

American Association 1883–1884, 1889–1891

Columbus, Ohio's first venture into the major leagues was in 1883, when Horace Phillips put together an American Association team from scratch. Ohio's capital city team was appropriately named the Buckeyes, after the state flower.

Working with a limited budget, Phillips, also the Buckeyes manager, assembled a lineup which consisted mainly of major league cast-offs and minor leaguers. Shortstop John Richmond was the Buckeyes' best player both offensively and defensively. He led the team with a .283 BA and was the American Association's best fielding shortstop with 304 assists and a .877 fielding percentage. Rookie right-fielder Tom Brown, a native of Liverpool, England, led the Buckeyes with five home runs, fourth best in the Association. Brown went on to enjoy a 16-year

career in the majors and compile a .264 lifetime BA.

Righthander Frank Mountain was the workhorse of the pitching staff, winning 26 games but losing 33, more losses than any Association pitcher. The team finished sixth with 32 wins and 66 losses. More importantly, they enjoyed enough fan support to break even on the season, assuring the Buckeyes' return to the American Association in 1884.

1884 was a banner year on the field. New manager Gus Schmelz led the rejuvenated Buckeyes to a second-place finish with 69 wins and only 39 losses. Surprisingly, the Buckeyes batting was no better than the previous year and they had no .300 hitters. Brown batted .273, center fielder Fred Mann .276, and rookie catcher Fred Carroll led the Buckeyes with a .278 BA. The pitching, however, was superb. Mountain won 23 games and lost 17 while rookie Ed "Cannonball" Morris burst on the major league scene with a spectacular record of 34 wins and only 13 defeats. In the entire American Association, Morris was second with a 2.18 ERA, second in winning percentage (.723), fifth in wins, and topped the league in fewest hits per nine innings (seven).

Unfortunately, the Buckeyes success on the field was not matched at the gate. Following the season, when the American Association went from a 12- to an 8-team league, Columbus was not included. The Buckeyes' best players went to Pittsburgh to form the nucleus of the Alleghenys, who finished third in the revamped Association in 1885. Ironically, Horace Phillips, who managed the first Buckeyes team in 1883, was the Allegheny manager in 1885.

Five years later the Buckeyes were back in the major leagues with another American Association team. In many respects the results were similar to Columbus' first venture into the majors as the team finished sixth and had the league's losingest pitcher in Mark Baldwin. Baldwin, a righthander, won 27 games for the Buckeyes but lost 34 times. First baseman Dave Orr led Buckeye batters with a .327 BA (fourth best in the Association) and topped the Buckeyes with 87 RBI. Orr, a hitting machine, never batted below .302 in eight major league seasons and compiled a .342 lifetime batting average. Rookie manager Al Buckenberger's team won 60 games and lost 78. Attendance in 1889 was quite respectable, with a season-high 5900 turning out for an August 31 game against St. Louis.

In 1890 a third major league called the Brotherhood or Players League came into being. Many of the game's top stars, including Orr, elected to join. Talent in both the American Association and National League diminished greatly, but the Buckeyes enjoyed a fine year and finished second to the Louisville Colonels. Righthander Hank Gastright, who won 10 games as a rookie for the Buckeyes in 1889, became one of the Association's premier pitchers by winning 30 games and

losing 14. Gastright was third in the Association in wins and winning percentage. Schmelz replaced Buckenberger as manager during the final third of the season and spurred the Buckeyes to 37 wins in 50 games, but they couldn't overcome Louisville's huge lead finished ten games back of the champions. Leftfielder Spud Johnson led Buckeye batters with a .346 BA and catcher Jack O'Connor, who enjoyed a 21-year major league career, batted .324.

The year 1891 marked the American Association's final season and the final major league fling for the Buckeyes. Allan Thurman, the Buckeyes stockholder largely responsible for bringing peace among the American Association, National League, and Players League became president of the American Association. Columbus' home opener drew a record 7,303 as fans anticipated a pennant after their fine showing in 1890. It was not to be, however, as attendance dropped dramatically after opening day and the Buckeyes finished sixth. Gastright, the pitching sensation of 1890, won only 12 games while losing 19. With a 28–27 record, lefthander Phil Knell became the ace of the staff. Only left fielder Charley Duffe batted above .300 (.301); he also led the Buckeyes with 90 RBI. When the season ended the Buckeyes agreed to be bought out for $12,000 as the stronger clubs in the American Association—Baltimore, Louisville, St. Louis and Washington—joined the National League to form a 12-team circuit. This marked the end of major league baseball in Columbus. During the Buckeyes' five-year tenure in the American Association, they finished second twice. Columbus memorabilia of any type would be rare, with program-scorecards most likely to surface. Although several Buckeyes, notably Morris, Orr and Gastright, enjoyed excellent short-term success, no Columbus players were ever enshrined in the Baseball Hall of Fame.

Denver, Colorado

COLORADO ROCKIES

National League 1993 to Present

Denver, Colorado, for many years a highly successful minor league franchise, achieved its ultimate goal when it was one of two cities selected for expansion franchises in the National League. On June 10, 1991, Baseball Commissioner Fay Vincent announced that Denver would join South Florida as the twenty-seventh and twenty-eighth major league teams. On July 5 it was announced that the team's official name would be the Colorado Rockies. John McHale, Jr., a guiding member of the commission to bring major league baseball to Colorado, was named Executive vice president of baseball operations in concert with Bob Gebhard, who became senior vice president and general manager.

By April 22, 1992, nearly a year before the start of the 1993 inaugural season, the Rockies had sold 24,168 season tickets, fourth best in baseball. In the major league baseball free agent draft on June 1, 1992, the Rockies selected Colorado native and University of Florida star pitcher John Burke as their top pick. On October 27, Don Baylor was chosen as the Rockies' first manager. On November 17 pitcher David Nied was the team's first selection in the expansion draft. Prior to that, on November 9, pitcher Travis Buckley was obtained from the Montreal Expos in the first trade in Rockies history. Another milestone occurred November 16, when free agent first baseman Andres Gallarraga was signed to a one-year contract. Gallarraga twice hit over .300 for the Montreal Expos and carried a .267 lifetime batting average into the inaugural season.

The Rockies opener on April 9 against the Montreal Expos was a spectacular success. The largest opening day crowd in major league history, 80,227 fans saw the Rockies defeat the Expos 11 to 4 at Mile High Stadium. This mammoth ballpark will serve as the Rockies' home for two seasons while Coors Stadium, a modern 43,800 seat facility in downtown Denver, is being built. Attendance there is not likely to exceed the record 4,483,350 fans who attended games during the Rockies' inaugural season. Despite a record of 67 wins and 95 losses, the Rockies averaged more fans per game than the new ballpark will seat.

Ballpark Giveaways

1993 Rocky Mountain News Ticket Holder, Magnetic Schedule, Donruss Baseball Card Holder, U.S. Home Key Chain, U.S. West Cellular Sunglasses, Bank One Kid's Cap, Invesco Funds Adult Cap, Kool 105/King Soopers Ladies Tote Bag,

1993 bumper sticker, 2¾″ × 6¾″, blue, purple, and yellow, "I Was There! Opening Day April 9, 1993," provided by Radio Station KOSI, $10.

1993 inaugural season photo pin, 6″, $10.

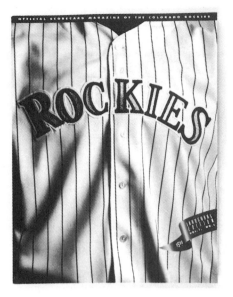

1993 program, Rockies first game, April 9th, against Montreal at Mile High Stadium (program was reprinted several times, reducing scarcity), 8½″ × 11″, 104 pages, $10.

Six Pack Cooler, Pace Kid's Squeeze Bottle, Bank One Sun Shades, Colorado Lottery BBQ Apron, Bank One Kid's Batting Glove, Beer Mug, Coca-Cola Kid's Batting Helmet, Rocky Mountain News Fanny Pack, Bank One Kid's T-shirt, Adult Cap, Hostess/Wonder Lunch Bag, Brother's Coffee Mug, Bank One Kid's Wallet, Vail Ski Cap, Colorado Lottery 1994 Schedule Holder $6

1993 media guide, 4½″ × 8¾″, 164 pages, $10.

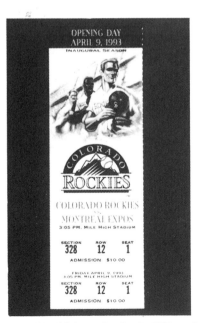

1993 complete ticket, opening day, April 9th, against Montreal, 2½″ × 7″, $50.

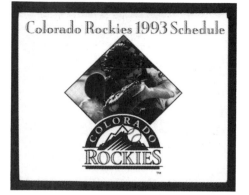

1993 schedule, 3″ × 3½″, issued by Colorado Rockies, 8 fold, $1.

1993 Coca-Cola Lapel Pin #1, 2, 3, 4, 5, 6, 7, 8, 9, 10, 11, 12, 13 ....ea. $8
1993 Colorado Rockies Calendar, King Soopers Kid's Autographed Baseball, Team Picture $10

Pennants

1993 First Year $10

Publications

PROGRAMS AND SCORECARDS

1993 First Year....................................$5

YEARBOOKS

1993 First Year $10

Detroit, Michigan

DETROIT TIGERS

National League 1881–1888, American League 1901 to Present

The Detroit Tigers are a team of numerous distinctions, including membership in the American League since its inception in 1901 and a ballpark located on the same site for every year of their existence. Their proudest boast is that Ty Cobb, the greatest batter in baseball history, played most of his career in Detroit.

Cobb joined the Tigers in 1905 and played with them through 1926, when he joined the Philadelphia Athletics for his final two seasons. Cobb also served as the Tigers' player-manager from 1921 through 1926, with a second-place finish in 1923 his best record. The "Georgia Peach" had no equal as a batter as his .367 lifetime average attests.

When 1890s Baltimore Orioles star Hughie Jennings became manager in 1907, the Tigers immediately won three consecutive pennants. Cobb won the first of eight consecutive batting championships in Jennings' first year at the helm. After finishing second to Cleveland's Tris Speaker in 1916 (.386 to .371), Cobb won three more titles in a row.

During Detroit's first three championship seasons, Cobb played beside another future Hall of Famer, center fielder Sam Crawford. With a 25 and 4 record, Wild Bill Donovan led a superb pitching staff that featured two other 20-game winners in Ed Killian (25–13) and George Mullin (20–20). In a disappointing World Series performance, the Tigers lost to the Chicago Cubs four games to none.

The Tigers won again in 1908 as Cobb and Crawford again hit over .300 and righthander Ed Summers led the pitchers with a 24 and 12 record. Again they lost to the Cubs in the World Series four games to one.

In 1909 Cobb won the Triple Crown by leading the league in batting (.377), home runs (9), and RBI (107). Crawford was second to Cobb with 97 RBI and a .314 average. George Mullin's 29 and 9 record was the league's best and Ed Willett won 22 and lost 9. Unfortunately, the World Series results were the same. Hall of Famer Honus Wagner clearly outplayed Cobb, and the Pittsburgh Pirates went on to win four games to three.

Although Cobb was joined in the Tigers outfield by future Hall of Famers Harry Heilmann in 1914 and Heinie Manush in 1923, the Tigers next pennant did not come until 1934, when player-manager Mickey Cochrane took charge. First baseman Hank Greenberg supplied most of the power with 26 home runs and 139 RBI while second baseman Charley Gehringer had 11 homers and 127 RBI. Left fielder Goose Goslin added 13 home runs and 100 RBI. Cochrane, Greenberg, Gehringer and Goslin all eventually made the Hall of Fame. Righthanders Schoolboy Rowe (24-8) and Tommy Bridges (22-11) led a dazzling pitching staff. The World Series jinx continued as they lost four games to three to the St. Louis Cardinals and the Dean brothers, Dizzy and Paul, each of whom won two games.

They repeated as champs in 1935 and finally got the World Series monkey off their back by beating the Cubs four games to two. Greenberg led the league with 36 home runs and 170 RBI, Goslin had 109 RBI, and Gehringer had 108 RBI and led Tigers batters with a .330 average. Bridges (21 wins) and Rowe (19 wins) again led the pitchers. Bridges had two World Series wins, including the seventh and deciding game, while Rowe and General Crowder got the other series victories.

The Tigers were American League champs again in 1940. Their power-packed lineup featured Hank Greenberg (41 HR and 150 RBI to lead the league) and first baseman Rudy York (33 HR and 134 RBI). Righthander Bobo Newsome led the pitchers with a 21-5 mark while Rowe (16-3) and Bridges (12-9) were still quite effective. In the World Series they lost to the Cincinnati Reds four games to three.

Fortunately for the Tigers World War II ended in 1945 and Hank Greenberg returned in mid-season from military service to lead them to another championship. In only half a season Greenberg had 13 homers and 60 runs batted in. Hall of Fame lefthander Prince Hal Newhouser was the league's top pitcher with a 25 and 9 record and the league's Most Valuable Player Award. Newhouser added two more wins in the World Series as the Tigers beat the Cubs four games to three.

Twenty-three years elapsed before the Tigers won another pennant, and it was the remarkable pitching of righthander Denny McLain that was mainly responsible. With an amazing 31 and 6 record, McLain was so dominant that he was a unanimous choice as the league's Cy Young award and was named MVP as well. Future Hall of Fame outfielder Al Kaline, in the twilight of a brilliant career, led Tiger batters with a .287 average. Although completely overshadowed by McLain's monumental season despite a fine 17 and 9 record, lefthander Mickey Lolich was the World Series pitching hero. Lolich contributed three wins while McLain won one to give Detroit another world championship. Unfortunately, McLain's image became tarnished when he was found guilty of cavorting with gamblers and suspended for a year in 1970.

Divisional play began in both leagues in 1969 and the Tigers won American League Eastern Division titles in 1972, 1984 and 1987. In 1972 and 1987 the Tigers lost the League Championship Series to Oakland and Minnesota respectively but captured the pennant in 1984 by beating Kansas City. Then they beat the San Diego Padres in the World Series in five games. Righthander Jack Morris led the 1984 Tigers with 19 wins (and won two more in the World Series) while Alan Trammell led batters with a .314 average and Lance Parrish supplied much of the power with 33 HR. Relief pitcher Willie Hernandez, who appeared in 80 games for the Tigers, was named the league's MVP.

A new slugging sensation burst on the scene for the tigers in 1990. Found wanting by the Toronto Blue Jays and after a year in Japan, Cecil Fielder joined the Tigers as a free agent and led the league with 51 homers and 132 RBI in 1990 and had 44 HR and 133 RBI to lead the league again in both categories in 1991.

Tiger Stadium, located at Michigan and Trumbull Avenues has been home to the Tigers since their inception and seats 52,466. Originally Bennett Park, it became Navin Field in 1912, Briggs Stadium in 1938, and Tiger Stadium in 1961. The Tigers best single-season attendance was 2,704,794 in 1984, but they have exceeded two million customers in 1968, 1985, 1987, and 1988.

In addition to those already named these former Tiger players, managers and executives have been admitted to the Hall of Fame: Earl Averill, Ed Barrow, Billy Evans, Rick Ferrell, Bucky Harris, Waite

Hoyt, George Kell, Eddie Mathews and Al Simmons. Dan Brouthers and Sam Thompson who played for the National League's Detroit Wolverines in the 1880's are also members.

Advertising Specialties

Detroit Wolverines (National League)

1886 Detroit League Baseball Club Lorillard Team Card, 4″ × 5″..............$1,500

1887 Kalamazoo Bats Team Card N690-1, 4½″ × 6½″, Cabinet Card issued by Charles Gross & Co. of Philadelphia as a promotion for its Kalamazoo Bats Cigarettes. The Detroit Baseball Club features a team photo with the caption in a white box at the bottom of the photo $2,000

1888 Detroit Baseball Club, Joseph Hall Cabinet, 6½″ × 4½″...................$2,100

Detroit Tigers (American League)

1913 Detroit Americans T200 Fatima Team Card, 2⅝″ × 4¾″ $150

Ballpark Giveaways

1975 Recognition Day honoring long-time stars Mickey Stanley, Gates Brown, Mickey Lolich, Willie Hor-

1950s, felt round, multicolored, 5″, $35.

ton and Bill Freehan. 5 × 7 picture of these players on Dugout steps given to fans $25

1989 Calendar, Lunch Box, Travel Mug, Hall of Fame Poster, Umbrella, Helmet, Visor, Tankard Mug, Thermo Bottle, Picnic Bag, Sports Equipment Bag, Cap, Sunglasses, Desk Clock, Wrist Band, Batting Glove, Beverage Carrier, Watch, Back Pack, Tote Bag, Banner, Notebook Binder $6

1989 Autograph Ball..............................$10

1987 bumper sticker, 3″ × 11¾″, WJR-Buddy's Pizza, station logo and a sleeping tiger (back of the sticker features discounts on Buddy's pizza and a chance to win free tigers tickets from WJR by displaying sticker), $5.

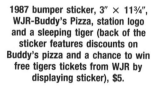

1975 picture of Tigers stars given to fans on Recogition Day honoring their accomplishments with the Tigers, 5″ × 7″, $20.

1990 Calendar, Tankard Mug, Travel
     Mug, Thermo Bottle $6
1990 Floppy Hat, Squeeze Bottle, Relief
     Pitcher, Batting Glove, Umbrella,
     Bat, Cap, Watch, Wallet, Wrist
     Band, Baseball Radio $5
1990 Autograph Baseball $10
1990 Baseball Card Set............................$7
1992 Coca-Cola/Kroger Team Poster,
     Budweiser Calendar, 1935 World
     Champions Pin, 1945 World Cham-
     pions Pin, 1968 World Champions
     Pin (complete set $20) $7
1992 Gatorade Relief Pitcher, Coca-Cola/
     Kroger Helmet, Coca-Cola/Kroger
     Batting Glove, Budweiser Wool
     Cap, Jolly Rancher T-shirt, Coca-
     Cola/Kroger Pennant, WJR Baseball
     Radio, American Dairy Assn. Fun
     Book, WDIV Bat $6
1992 Upper Deck Cards, Coca-Cola/
     Kroger Player Cards, Donruss Base-
     ball Card Book $7
1992 Autograph Baseball $10
1992 Sports Equipment Bag, Back Pack $5

Miscellaneous

BOBBIN' HEAD DOLLS

Category #I, 1960, 1961, Green Square
     Base, Mascot $200
Category #II, 1961, 1962, White Square
     Base, Mascot $175
Category #III, 1961, 1962, White Round
     Miniature, Mascot $300
Category #IV, 1962, 1963, 1964, Green
     Round Base, Mascot $135
Category #V, 1962, 1963, 1964, Green
     Round Base, Black Player $550
Category #VI, 1967 through 1974, Gold
     Round Base, Mascot $90

Pennants

1901 through 1920 ....$750
1921 through 1930 ....$300
1931 through 1934 Regular..................$200

Bobbin head doll with tiger head, green round base, 9", $135.

1934 World Series $400
1935 Regular $200
1935 World Series $400
1936 through 1940 Regular...................$200
1936, 1937 Felt Pennant BF3, Type V,
     Cap on Pennant $35
1936, 1937 Felt Pennant BF3, Type V, Ti-
     ger on Pennant $35
1940 World Series $400
1941 Regular $100
1941 All-Star Game $200
1942 through 1945 Regular...................$100
1945 World Series $200
1946 through 1950 ....$100
1951 Regular....................................$50
1951 All-Star Game $125
1952 through 1960 ....$50
1961 through 1968 Regular $30
1968 World Series................................$75
1969, 1970 ....$30
1971 Regular....................................$20
1971 All-Star Game $50

1950s pennant, 12" × 29½", sitting tiger cradling Briggs Stadium, $50.

1972 Regular $20
1972 League Champions $50
1973 through 1980 ....$20
1981 through 1984 Regular $5
1984 League Champions $15
1984 World Champions $15
1985, 1986, 1987 Regular $5
1987 League Champions $15
1988, 1989, 1990 ....$5
1991, 1992, 1993 ....$3

Pins

1930/1940s American Nut & Chocolate
   Co., 1⅛", Round $15
1961 through 1965 Crane Potato Chips,
   ⅞", Round $5
1967, 1968, 1969 Crane Potato Chips, ⅞",
   Round $5
1984 Crane Potato Chips, ⅞", Round $3
1964, 1965, 1966 Guy's Potato Chips, ⅞",
   Round $5

1940s–1950s laughing tigers pin, 1½", "Briggs Stadium" (the Tigers home ball park) written at the bottom, $15.

Postcards

1907 RP, American League Champions,
   Pub. unknown $150
1907 PL, American League Champions,
   Pub. by H. M. Taylor, Detroit, Michigan. Identical view of RP $150
1907 PL, American League Champions,
   Pub. by Heimer, Address un-
   known...$200
1935 Smooth finish, World Champs, Pub.
   unknown $150
1935 Smooth finish, World Champs, Pub.
   by Chrysler Corp. $250
1935 Smooth finish, World Champs, Pub.
   by Greenfield's Cafeteria (comes in
   both green and brown).................$250

Publications

BOOKS

Anderson, George "Sparky" with Dan
   Ewald. *Bless You Boys: Diary of
   the Detroit Tigers' 1981 Season.*
   Chicago: Contemporary Books,
   1985. ....$15.00
• Anderson, William M. *The Detroit Ti-
   gers: A Pictorial Celebration of the
   Greatest 1991 Players and Mo-
   ments in Tigers' History.* South
   Bend, Ind.: Diamond Communica-
   tions, 1991; 1992. ....$39.95
• Aston, Gerald. *Detroit Tigers, An Il-
   lustrated History.* New York:
   Walker, 1989. ....$12.95
• Bak, Richard. *Cobb Would Have
   Caught It: The Golden Age of
   Baseball in Detroit.* Detroit:
   Wayne State University Press,
   1991. ....$24.95
Craig, Roger, with Bern Plagennoef.
   *Inside Pitch: Roger Craig's '84 Ti-
   ger Journal.* Grand Rapids: L Wil-

1907 photo postcard, 3½" × 5½", American League champions starring Hall of Famer Ty Cobb who compiled a .367 lifetime BA, highest in baseball history (the Tigers lost the 1907 World Series to the Chicago Cubs as well as the next two to Chicago and Pittsburgh), $150.

liam B. Eardman's Publishing Co.,
1984. ....$10.00
Detroit Baseball Co. *Detroit in Base-
ball.* 1939. ....$75.00
Detroit Free Press. *Iffy's Book of Ti-
ger Tales.* 1935. ....$100.00
Evans, W. B. (Billy). *Tiger Feats.*
1948. ....$20.00
Falls, Joe. *Detroit Tigers.* New York:
McMillan, 1975. ....$15.00
Falls, Joe. *So You Think You're a Die-
hard Tiger Fan.* Chicago: Con-
temporary Books, 1986 (Paper-
back $5) $10.00
Green, Jerry. *Year of the Tiger: The
Diary of Detroit's World Cham-
pions.* New York: Coward-
McCann, 1969. ....$15.00
Hawkins, John C. *This Date in De-
troit Tigers History.* New York:
Stein & Day, 1981. ....$5.00
Lieb, Frederick. *Detroit Tigers.* G.P.
Putnam's Sons, 1946. ....$40.00
Martin, Mollie. *Detroit Tigers.* Man-
kato, Mn.: Creative Education,
1982. ....$5.00
Moreland, George. *Fanfax.* Fanfax
Publishing Co., 1930. ....$30.00
Phillies Cigars. *Detroit Tigers' Hall of
Fame.* 1959. ....$15.00
Rothaus, James R. *Detroit Tigers.*
Mankato, Mn.: Creative Educa-
tion, 1987. ....$5.00
Shine, N. & B. McGraw. *The Roar of
'84. The Tigers Championship Sea-
son.* Detroit: The Detroit Free
Press, 1984. ....$10.00
Smith, Fred T. *Fifty Years with the Ti-
gers.* Lothrup Village, Mi., 1984. ......$10.00
Smith, Fred T. *Tiger Records.* 1949,
1950. ....$10.00
Smith, Fred T. *Facts.* Lothrup Village,
Mi.: Russ Entwisle & John Duffy,
1986. ....$10.00
•Smith, Fred T. *Tiger Tales & Trivia.*
Lothrup Village, Mi.: Russ Ent-
wisle & John Duffy, 1988. ....$9.95
•Smith, Fred T. *Tiger S.T.A.T.S.* $12.95

MEDIA GUIDES

1927 Roster Sheet $125
1928 through 1931 Roster Sheet $100
1932, 1933 Roster Booklet $100
1934 American League Champs Roster
      Booklet.....................................$110
1935 World Champs Roster Booklet $115
1936 through 1939 ....$75
1940 League Champs $85
1941 through 1944 ....$60
1945 World Champs $70
1946 through 1949 ....$60
1950 through 1955 ....$50
1956 through 1961 ....$40

1962, 1963, 1964 ....$30
1965, 1966, 1967 ....$20
1968 World Champs.............................$25
1969, 1970, 1971 ....$15
1972 Division Champs..........................$17
1973, 1974 ....$10
1975, 1976 ....$8
1977, 1978 ....$7
1979, 1980, 1981 ....$6
1982, 1983 ....$5
1984 World Champs $6
1985, 1986 ....$4
1987 Division Champs $6
1988 through 1993 ....$4

PROGRAMS AND SCORECARDS

1901 ....$600
1902 ....$400
1903, 1904 ....$300
1905 ....$200
1906, 1907, 1908 American League
      Champs Each Year.......................$225
1909 ....$200
1910 through 1914 ....$150
1915 through 1920 ....$125
1921 through 1925 ....$75
1926 through 1930 ....$50
1931, 1932, 1933 ....$35
1934 American League Champs $40
1935 World Champs.............................$45
1936 through 1939 ....$35
1940 American League Champs $40
1941 through 1944 ....$20
1945 World Champs.............................$25
1946 through 1949 ....$20
1950 through 1959 ....$15
1960 through 1967 ....$10
1968 World Champs.............................$15
1969 ....$10
1970 through 1979 ....$6
1980 through 1983 ....$4
1984 World Champs $7
1985, 1986 ....$4
1987 Division Champs $6
1988, 1989 ....$4
1990, 1991, 1992, 1993 ....$3

YEARBOOKS

1887 *The Detroit Tribune's Epitome of
      Baseball* (Sketches on 1887 Detroit
      Wolverines, N.L. Champions).......$1,500
1912 *Word's Baseball Album &
      Sketchbook, Detroit Tigers* by An-
      drew H. Word $750
1934 *Detroit Tigers in Pictures* by Detroit
      Free Press $400
1935 *Following the Tigers* by Al Nagler,
      Detroit play-by-play announcer $30
1951 *Tiger Facts* by Fred T. Smith
      (Sketches & records of 1951 Tigers)..$25
1955 ....$275
1956 ....None Issued

1934 yearbook, 6″ × 9″, 20 pages, published by the Detroit Free Press, commemorating the 1934 American League championship season with sketches of the players, $400.

1957	$175
1958	$150
1959	$125
1960	$100
1961, 1962	$80
1963	$75
1964, 1965	$60
1966	$50
1967	$45
1968 World Champs	$60
1969, 1970	$40
1971	$35
1972 Division Champs	$30
1973	$25
1974, 1975	$20
1976	$15
1977	$10
1978, 1979, 1980	$8
1981, 1982, 1983	$7
1984 World Champs	$12
1985, 1986	$5
1987 Division Champs	$7
1988 through 1993	$5

Schedules

1901 through 1909	$150
1910 through 1919	$100
1920 through 1929	$75
1930 through 1939	$45
1940 through 1949	$30

1950 through 1959	$25
1960 through 1969	$15
1970 through 1979	$10
1980 through 1985	$2
1986 through 1993	$1

Special Events

ALL-STAR GAME PRESS PINS

1941	$500
1951	$275
1971	$150

ALL-STAR PROGRAMS

1941	$500
1951	$150
1971	$100

ALL-STAR GAME TICKETS

1941 Complete Ticket	$200
1941 Ticket Stub	$100
1951 Complete Ticket	$150
1951 Ticket Stub	$75
1971 Complete Ticket	$40
1971 Ticket Stub	$20

LEAGUE CHAMPIONSHIP SERIES PROGRAMS

1972	$25
1984	$8
1987	$6

1941 All-Star program, 7½″ × 10½″, 28 pages, $500.

LEAGUE CHAMPIONSHIP GAME TICKETS

1972 Complete Ticket $38
1972 Ticket Stub..................................$18
1984 Complete Ticket $28
1984 Ticket Stub..................................$15
1987 Complete Ticket $28
1987 Ticket Stub..................................$15

WORLD SERIES PRESS PINS

1908, 1909 ....None Issued
1934 ....$300
1935 ....$300
1940 ....$300
1945 ....$300
1968 (not dated) $100
1984 (not dated) $50

WORLD SERIES PROGRAMS

1934 ....$550
1935 ....$500

1940 ....$325
1945 ....$325
1968 ....$125
1984 ....$15

WORLD SERIES GAME TICKETS

1908 Complete Ticket $2,000
1908 Ticket Stub.............................$1,000
1909 Complete Ticket $2,000
1909 Ticket Stub.............................$1,000
1934 Complete Ticket $400
1934 Ticket Stub $200
1935 Complete Ticket $400
1935 Ticket Stub $200
1940 Complete Ticket $200
1940 Ticket Stub $100
1945 Complete Ticket $200
1945 Ticket Stub $100
1968 Complete Ticket $70
1968 Ticket Stub $35
1984 Complete Ticket $30
1984 Ticket Stub..................................$15

Elizabeth, New Jersey

ELIZABETH RESOLUTES

National Association 1873

The Elizabeth Resolutes joined the National Association in 1873, but lasted less than a season as a major league baseball team. In those days anyone willing to post the $10 entry fee could join the league.

The Resolutes' ballpark was actually outside the city limits of Elizabeth, in nearby Waverly. The most prominent player was catcher Doug Allison, who was a member of the undefeated Cincinnati Red Stockings in 1869. Allison batted .275 for Elizabeth before joining the New York Mutuals after the team folded 23 games into the season. The Resolutes had only two victories to show for their efforts, both of which were recorded by 16-game-loser Hugh Campbell. Hugh's brother, Mike,

played first base and batted only .146 during his 21-game major league career.

By mid-June the Resolutes had abandoned Waverly to play their games in Brooklyn. Brooklyn had suddenly become a three-team town, with the Mutuals and Atlantics also playing their home games there. Elizabeth announced it was disbanding but decided to play a July 4 doubleheader at Boston before doing so. The large crowd helped replenish the Resolutes' treasury and they even won the morning game by a score of 11 to 2. Things reverted to form in the afternoon game as the Red Stockings hammered hapless Elizabeth 32 to 3 in the Resolutes' swan song as a major league team.

During their brief tenure as a major league team, the Resolutes had no players elected to the Hall of Fame. Memorabilia of any description would be extremely rare.

Fort Lauderdale, Florida

FLORIDA MARLINS

National League 1993 to Present

Wayne Huizenga, chairman of Blockbuster Video, became the guiding light behind the Florida Marlins when he purchased a 50 percent interest in Joe Robbie Stadium in March 1990 and set his sights on obtaining a National League franchise to play there. His perseverance paid off when he was awarded one of two National League expansion teams on June 10, 1991.

Huizenga, a self-made millionaire and long-time sport fisherman, named the new team the Marlins because the fish is "a fierce fighter and an adversary that tests your mettle." In fact, the name had historical baseball significance because several Miami minor league teams carried the Marlins name.

On July 8, 1991, Pittsburgh Pirates President Carl Barger was named Marlins president. On September 18, 1991, Montreal Expos General Manager Dave Bombrowski was named executive vice president and general manager of the Marlins.

Clemente Nunex, a 16-year-old right-handed pitcher from the Dominican Republic, was signed to the first Marlins contract and assigned to the Gulf Coast League. On June 1, 1992, the Marlins selected catcher Charles Johnson from the University of Miami as their first-round pick in the amateur draft. On October 23, 1992, Rene Lachemann signed a three-year contract to manage the team.

The expansion draft took place on November 17, 1992, with outfielder Nigel Wilson becoming their first selection. On December 8 the Marlins signed their first two free agents, infielder Dave Magadan (for two years) and knuckleball pitcher Charley Hough (for one). Tragedy struck the next day when Marlins President Carl Barger suffered a heart attack and died at the winter meetings. On December 16 the Marlins signed four-time All-Star free agent catcher Benito Santiago to a two-year contract.

Baseball was an instant success in South Florida as the Marlins won their home opener at Joe Robbie Stadium before a sell-out crowd of 42,334. Charley Hough defeated the Los Angeles Dodgers 6 to 3. Despite winning only 64 games

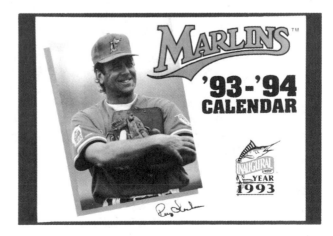

1993–1994 Florida Marlins calendar, 8½" × 11", given at the first Marlins game ever on April 4, 1993, 22 pages, $20.

while losing 98, the Marlins drew near-capacity crowds throughout the season and averaged better than 38,311 per game on the way to a total first year home attendance of 3,064,847.

Ballpark Giveaways

1993 Value Rent-A-Car Magnet Schedule, Cellular One Garmet Bag, Ryder Commuter Mug, Gatorade Wrist Band, Donruss Baseball Card Book, Burdines Batting Helmet, Blockbuster Video Cotton Cap, Holsum Growth Chart, Coca-Cola Beach Towel, Gatorade Squeeze Bottle, Blockbuster Video Kid's Jersey, Sunshine Network Sun Shade, SDS Florida Executive Pen, Miami Herald Kid's Back Pack, Winn-Dixie Lunch Box, Value Rent-A-Car Magnet Schedule $6

1993 pin, 3″, $5.

1993 photo pin, 6″, $8.

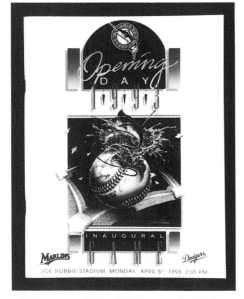

1993 program, 8½″ × 11″, 88 pages, first Marlins game against the Los Angeles Dodgers, $20.

1993 media guide, 5″ × 9″, 228 pages, $10.

1993 Bumble Seafoods Commemorative
Pin #1, Winn-Dixie Commemora-
tive Pin #2, 3, 4, 5.......................ea. $8
1993 Winn-Dixie Opening Day Calendar,
Tropicana Pennant, Winn-Dixie
Team Poster $10

Pennants

1993 First Year $10

Publications

PROGRAMS AND SCORECARDS

1993 First Year.......................................$5

YEARBOOKS

1993 First Year $10

Fort Wayne, Indiana

FORT WAYNE KEKIONGAS

National Association 1871

Fort Wayne, Indiana, has a very unique distinction. The city played host to the first major league baseball game ever played. On May 4, 1871, the Fort Wayne Kekiongas, one of nine charter members of the National Association of Professional Baseball clubs, entertained the Forest Cities of Cleveland and defeated them 2 to 0. Because of threatening weather, a crowd limited to 500 spectators saw righthander Bobby Mathews hurl major league baseball's first shutout as he limited Cleveland to only five hits. Fort Wayne got only four hits off Cleveland's Al Pratt, but Bill Lennon doubled to left field and ultimately scored on Joe McDermott's infield single. The Kekionga's second run scored in the fifth when Bill Kelley singled, advanced to third on two passed balls, and scored on an infield out. The game took two hours to play and ended in a torrential downpour before the Kekiongas got their final at bat.

The Kekiongas were put together quickly by club secretary George Mayer, who was in New York as late as April searching for players. Although the Kekiongas won their first game thanks to the brilliant pitching of Mathews, they won only six more all season and finished with a record of 7 wins and 21 defeats before disbanding in August. Even 120 years ago Fort Wayne was simply too small a market to sustain major league baseball. But the city's niche as site of the first game in major league history remains forever.

Of all the Fort Wayne players, Bobby Mathews, only 19 years old when he signed, went on to a distinguished career. He won 42 games with the New York Mutuals in 1874. When the National Association disbanded after the 1875 season, Mathews pitched ten more seasons in the National League and American Association and won 166 games, including 30 games for three consecutive years with the Philadelphia Athletics. Although Mathews warrants consideration for the Hall of Fame, no member of the Fort Wayne Kekiongas has been honored thus far.

A scorecard from the first game, if one exists, would be a priceless piece of memorabilia and would command thousands of dollars. Anything pertaining to the Kekiongas during their short-lived tenure as a major league baseball city would be rare indeed.

Hartford, Connecticut

HARTFORD CHARTER OAKS/DARK BLUES

National Association 1874–1875; National League 1876–1877

Although Hartford, Connecticut, was a major league baseball city for only four years (two years in the National Association and two in the National League), two members of the organization are enshrined in the Baseball Hall of Fame. Hartford's teams were known as the Charter Oaks and Dark Blues.

Hartford's president was Morgan Bulkely, who helped organize the National League in 1876 and became its first president. Bulkely left baseball to pursue a business and political career. He became president of Aetna Life Insurance Company in 1879, mayor of Hartford in 1883, governor of Connecticut in 1888, and U.S. senator in 1905. Throughout his life he maintained a deep interest in baseball and was elected to the Hall of Fame in 1937.

Candy Cummings was a star pitcher in the early days of baseball who was the first to develop the curve ball. Standing only five-feet nine-inches and weighing 120 pounds, Cummings pitched for the Charter Oaks in 1875 and posted a 35–12 record for a team that finished third in the 13-team National Association. When the Charter Oaks became members of the National League in 1876, Cummings continued to shine. He won 16 and lost 8, although teammate Tommy Bond was the pitching star with a 31 and 13 record. The Charter Oaks finished third in the National League's initial season. Manager Bob Ferguson batted .265 as the teams's third baseman and directed them to 47 wins and 21 losses. However, after the season, the franchise was shifted to Brooklyn, New York.

During Hartford's first season of 1874, the Charter Oaks finished seventh with a record of 17 wins and 37 losses. Manager Lip Pike batted .346 while playing center field. Third baseman Bill Boyd led Hartford with a .382 average while catcher Scott Hastings batted .371.

But in 1875, with Candy Cummings winning 35 games, the team's fortunes turned around and they won 54 games and lost 28 to finish third. Placing two members of the organization in baseball's Hall of Fame in only four major league seasons is something Hartford can always be proud of.

Houston, Texas

HOUSTON ASTROS

National League 1962 to Present

The Houston Astros have the distinction of being the first major league team to play in a domed stadium after moving into the Astrodome at the start of the 1965 season. Dubbed the eighth wonder of the world when it opened, the Astrodome received a $60 million facelift in 1989—an expenditure nearly four times the $16 million the multi-purpose stadium originally cost.

Initially called the Houston Colt 45s

when founded as a National League expansion team in 1962, the team played three years in Colt 45 Stadium while Harris County Domed Stadium, the Astrodome's official name, was being built. The Colt 45s drew 924,456 fans to their uncovered temporary home in 1962 and just over 700,000 each of the next two years.

However, in 1965, 2,151,470 fans poured through the turnstiles to see the fabulous Astrodome first hand. It was the best attendance mark for the Astros until 1980, when home attendance reached 2,278,217. These are the only two times the Astros have exceeded two million spectators, due largely to a lack of success on the playing field. Only twice, in 1980 and 1986, did the Astros win divisional titles, but they were defeated in the National League Championship Series each time, losing to Philadelphia and New York respectively. During the strike shortened season of 1981, they won the Western Division's second half race but bowed to the Los Angeles Dodgers in the Western Division play-offs.

Although never winning a National League championship, the Astros have had their share of stars over the years, particularly among the pitchers. The most famous of these is all-time strikeout king Nolan Ryan, who pitched for the Astros from 1980 through 1988 and as expected leads the team in career strikeouts. Joe Niekro pitched for the Astros from 1975 through 1985 and is the leader in victories with 144, followed closely by Larry Dierker with 137. Niekro set the single-season record with 21 wins in 1979 and followed with 20 victories in 1980. Other 20-game winners include Dierker in 1969; J. R. Richard in 1976; and Mike Scott, who is third in career victories and won 20 games in 1989. Reliever Dave Smith is by far the best reliever, with 199 over 11 seasons.

Part of the reason that pitching has been a dominant Astros feature over the years is because the Astrodome is the most difficult park in the major leagues in which to hit home runs. Jimmy Wynn set the club record of 37 back in 1967 while Rusty Staub established the single-season batting mark of .333 that same year. Bob Watson's 110 RBIs in 1977 is the club record. Second baseman Joe Morgan is the first product of the Houston organization elected to the Hall of Fame (1990) while

Hall of Famers infielder Eddie Mathews (1967) and pitcher Robin Roberts (1965 and 1966) played briefly with the Astros. Nolan Ryan, still pitching effectively in 1993 with Texas, is certain to be elected to the Hall of Fame five years after his fabulous career ends.

Ballpark Giveaways

1967	Helmet	$5
1969	Bat, Helmet	$5
1977	Astros Photo Album (first one)	$10
1978	Astros Photo Album	$10
1978	Gym Bag	$5
1979	Astros Photo Album	$10
1979	Cap, Bat, Ball, T-shirt	$5
1983	Orange Cap, Blue Cap	$5
1983	Finger Furniture Jacket, Coca-Cola T-shirt	$6
1986	25th Anniversary Calendar, All-Star Wrist Watch	$10
1986	Thermos	$9
1986	T-shirt, Travel Kit, Jacket, Helmet, Bat	$5
1987	Mother's Cookies Trading Cards	$6
1987	Calendar, Team Photo	$8
1987	Cap, Radio, Jacket, Wrist Band, Helmet, Bat, Batting Glove, Sun Visor, Notebook	$5
1988	Surf Book	$9
1988	Mother's Cookies Trading Cards	$6
1988	Calendar, Mug, Team Photo	$8
1988	Autograph Ball	$10
1988	Jacket, Bat, Baseball Mitt, Beach Towel, Cap, Scarf, Sports Bag, Bicycle Cap	$5

1969 cloth patch, issued by Fleer's Gum Co., Astros logo, 2½″ × 3¼″, $5.

1988 Colt 45 Cap, Relief Pitcher $6
1989 1980 Champs Pin, 1986 Champs
     Pin, Calendar, Team Photo, 1989
     Astros Pin $7
1989 Magnet Schedule (first one), Colt
     45 Cap, Relief Pitcher $6
1989 Mitt, Jacket, Bat, Orange Cap,
     Notebook $5
1990 Looney Tunes Visor, HSE Blue Cap,
     Kroger Coca-Cola Sports Bag, Fin-
     ger Furniture Jacket, Bud Light
     Colt 45 Cap, Kudos Batting Helmet,
     Coca-Cola Back Pack, Gatorade
     Pitcher $6
1990 Kroger Autograph Baseball $10
1990 Donruss Card Book $6
1991 Kellog's Cereal Bowl, HSE Astros
     Cap, Kroger Sports Bag, KPRC Um-
     brella $6
1991 Kroger Autograph Baseball $10
1991 Donruss Card Book, Upper Deck
     Cards $6
1992 Coca-Cola, KPRC Radio Facts &
     Record Book....................................$7
1992 Kroger Autograph Baseball $10
1992 HSE Blue Astros Cap, Kroger/Coca-
     Cola Sports Bag, Coca-Cola Neon
     Cap, Kroger Back Pack, KPRC Um-
     brella $6
1992 Mother's Cookies Trading Cards,
     Upper Deck Cards $6
1993 Chevron Ball, Coca-Cola Wall Cal-
     endar $7
1993 Gatorade Squeeze Bottle, J.C.
     Penney Sports Bottle, Exxon Batting
     Helmet, Randall's T-shirt, Kroger/
     Coca-Cola Sportsbag, HSE Blue
     Cap, Exxon Beach Towel, KPRC
     Flight Bag $6
1993 Exxon Notebook, Kroger Back
     Pack, Chevron Jacket $6

Miscellaneous

BOBBIN' HEAD DOLLS

Houston Colt 45's

Category #II, 1962, White Square Base,
     Boy Head $165
Category #II, 1962, White Square Base
     (blue uniform), Boy Head $450
Category #III, 1962, White Round
     Miniature, Boy Head $215
Category #IV, 1962, 1963, 1964, Green
     Round Base, Boy Head $200
Category #V, 1962, 1963, 1964, Green
     Round Base, Black Player $850

Houston Astros

Category #VI, 1967 through 1972, Gold
     Round Base, Boy Head $60

Pennants

1962 Colt 45's.....................................$50
1963 Colt 45's.....................................$40
1964 Colt 45's.....................................$35
1965 Astros $35
1966, 1967, 1968 Regular $30
1968 All-Star Game $75
1969, 1970 ....$30
1971 through 1980 ....$20
1981 Regular $5
1981 League Championship $15
1982 through 1986 Regular $5
1986 All-Star Game $15
1986 League Champs $15
1987 through 1990 ....$5
1991, 1992, 1993 ....$3

Pins

1963, 1964, 1965 Colt 45's, Crane Potato
     Chips, 7/8", Round $5
1964, 1965 Colt 45's, Guy's Potato Chips,
     7/8", Round $5
1966 Astros, Guy's Potato Chips, 7/8",
     Round $5
1967, 1968, 1969 Astros, Crane Potato
     Chips, 7/8", Round $5
1984 Astros, Crane Potato Chips, 7/8",
     Round $3

1964 pin, 7/8", issued by Guys Potato Chips, $5.

Publications

BOOKS

Hinz, Bob. *Houston Astros.* Mankato,
     Mn.: Creative Education, 1982. ....$5.00
Houston Sports Association. *The As-
     tros First Year in the Astrodome.*
     Houston, 1965. ....$25.00
McLemore, I. *An Astronomical Expe-
     rience: A Running Account of the*

1965 postcard, Astros, 6″ × 7¾″, first team to play in the Astrodome, $30.

1986 Astros Season. Houston: Priv. Printing, 1986. ....$10.00
Rothaus, James R. *Houston Astros.* Mankato, Mn.: Creative Education, 1987. ....$5.00

MEDIA GUIDES

1962 Colt 45's..	$35
1963, 1964 Colt 45's	$30
1965, 1966 Astros..................................	$20
1967, 1968 Astros..................................	$17
1969, 1970	$15
1971, 1972	$12
1973, 1974	$10
1975, 1976	$8
1977, 1978	$7
1979, 1980, 1981	$6
1982, 1983, 1984	$5
1985	$4
1986 Division Champs	$6
1987 through 1993	$4

PROGRAMS AND SCORECARDS

1962 First Year Colt 45's	$35
1963, 1964 Colt 45's	$20
1965 Astros	$12
1966 through 1969 Astros	$10
1970 through 1979	$6
1980 through 1985	$4
1986 Division Champs	$6
1987, 1988, 1989	$4
1990, 1991, 1992, 1993	$3

YEARBOOKS

1962 First Year Colt 45's	$200
1963 Colt 45's	$175
1964 Colt 45's	$150
1965 Astros	$100

1966 through 1976 ....None Issued
1977, 1978, 1979 Astros Photo Album........$10
1980, 1981 ....None Issued
1982 ....$20
1983 through 1993 ....None Issued

Schedules

1962 Colt 45's.......................................	$50
1963 Colt 45's.......................................	$40
1964 Colt 45's.......................................	$35

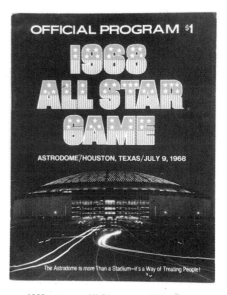

1968 program, All-Star game, 8½″ × 11″, 60 pages, $75.

1965 Astros $20
1966 through 1969 Astros $15
1970 through 1979 ....$10
1980 through 1985 ....$2
1986 through 1993 ....$1

Special Events

ALL-STAR GAME PRESS PINS

1968 ....$100
1986 ....$30

ALL-STAR PROGRAMS

1968 ....$75
1986 ....$12

ALL-STAR GAME TICKETS

1968 Complete Ticket $70
1968 Ticket Stub...................................$35
1986 Complete Ticket $30
1986 Ticket Stub...................................$15

LEAGUE CHAMPIONSHIP SERIES PROGRAMS

1981 Division Play-Offs (very hard to
       find) $50
1981 ....$35
1986 ....$20

LEAGUE CHAMPIONSHIP GAME TICKETS

1981, 1986 Complete Ticket $28
1981, 1986 Ticket Stub $15

1965 program, first series in the Astrodome as the Astros played exhibition games against the New York Yankees and Baltimore Orioles April 9th, 10th and 11th, 6¾″ × 10″, 52 pages, $50.

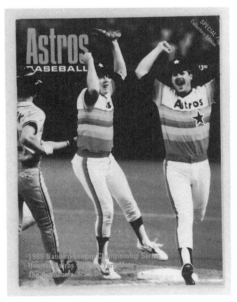

1986 program, 8½″ × 11″, 76 pages, League Championship Series against N.Y. Mets, $20.

Indianapolis, Indiana

INDIANAPOLIS HOOSIERS

National League 1878, 1887–1889; American Association 1884; Federal League 1914

Indianapolis, Indiana, had a major league franchise in the National League as early as 1878. Known as the Hoosiers, they finished fifth in the six-team league with a record of 24 wins and 36 losses under manager John Clapp. George "Orator" Shaffer led the Hoosiers with a .338 BA. Two rookies, third baseman Ned Williamson and catcher Silver Flint, batted .232 and .222 on the way to 13- and 12-year major league careers. Another rookie, pitcher Edward Sylvester "The Only" Nolan, won 13 and lost 22 and was fourth in the league with 125 strikeouts.

Indianapolis was out of the majors from 1879 until 1884, when a team also called Hoosiers joined the American Association. The result was a dismal 29 and 78 record in which no player batted over .298 (Jerry Dorgan) and pitcher Larry McKeon led the league with 41 losses as the Hoosiers finished twelfth in the 13-team circuit.

The Hoosiers gave major league baseball another try when they joined the National League for a second time in 1887 and played three seasons before folding. In 1887 they were last with a record of 37 wins and 89 defeats. Third baseman Jerry Denny was the Hoosier's batting star with a .324 average, 11 home runs and 97 runs batted in. Shortstop Jack Glasscock, who had an outstanding 17-year major league career, hit .294. First baseman Otto Shomberg had a fine season batting .308 with 5 homers and 83 RBI. Not surprisingly, righthander "Egyptian" Healy was the league's losingest pitcher with 29, and Henry Boyle lost 24.

The Hoosiers climbed to seventh place

in 1888 but had 85 losses and only 50 wins to stay out of the cellar (occupied by Washington) by a game and a half. Denny's average dipped to .261, but he was among the league leaders in homers with 12 and RBI with 63. Healy lost 24 games, as did Lev Shreve, while Henry Boyle lost 22.

The year 1889 was the last hurrah for National League baseball in Indiana, and the Hoosiers again finished ahead of Washington in seventh place. Glasscock was second in the league in batting with a .352 average, drove in 85 runs and fielded superbly to lead league shortstops in putouts, assists, and double plays. Denny again supplied most of the power with 18 HR and 112 RBI. Boyle won 21 games but lost 23 as pitching problems continued to plague the Hoosiers. Glasscock replaced Frank Bancroft as manager at midseason and had a winning record (34–33), but when the season ended so did Indianapolis' venture in the National League. No former Hoosiers grace the Hall of Fame, although Glasscock's .290 average over 17 seasons certainly earned him consideration.

Indianapolis' final fling in the majors was by far their most successful. When the Federal League declared major league status in 1914, the Hoosiers won the pennant by two games over Chicago. Bill Phillips directed the Hoosiers to 88 wins and 65 losses. Future Hall of Fame outfielder Edd Roush batted a solid .325 in this first full major league season. The team and league's outstanding star, however, was right fielder Benny Kauff. Kauff led the league in batting (.370), hits (211), stolen bases (75), doubles (44), runs scored (120), and total bases (305). Second baseman Frank LaPorte batted .311 and was the league's RBI champ with 107. Bill McKechnie, who gained his Hall of Fame status as a manager, led Federal League third basemen in assists and double plays while batting .304. Cy Falkenberg led a solid Hoosier pitching staff with 25 wins.

Although 15,000 fans turned out for the season opener at Hoosier Park, attendance declined during the course of the season. When the Federal League decided to put another team in the New York market, the original plan was to move Kansas City. But Packer backers threatened a lawsuit, so oil millionaire Harry Sinclair bought the Hoosiers and moved them to Newark, New Jersey, just outside New York City, to end Indianapolis' tenure in the major leagues.

Advertising Specialties

1888 Joseph Hall Cabinet Team Card,
    6½″ × 4½″ $2,100

Publications

PROGRAMS AND SCORECARDS

1914 Program from Indianapolis Federal League team's initial season (league champions) $550

1880s multi-color die cut figure, 2¼″ × 1½″, unidentified player in home uniform (ten different specimens, in varying sizes, of players from both the American Association and National League have been seen), $400.

Kansas City, Missouri

KANSAS CITY UNIONS

Union Association 1884

Kansas City's status as a major league city spans two centuries and five different leagues. Starting in 1884 with the Unions of the Union Association, Kansas City had franchises in the National League (1886), American Association (1888–1889), Federal League (1914–1915), American League (1955–1967) and American League (1969 to present).

Kansas City became a member of the Union Association after the Altoona Mountain Cities disbanded. The Unions played their first major league game at home on June 7, 1884, and lost to Chicago 6 to 5 before 1500 fans. The Unions set an attendance record in late August when 7500 turned out for a game against Cincinnati. Despite winning only 16 games

while losing 63 under manager Ted Sullivan, the team made a $6000 profit, proving Kansas City was a fine baseball town even then. First baseman Jeremiah Sweeney led the Unions in batting with a .264 average in his only major league season.

KANSAS CITY COWBOYS

National League 1886, American Association 1888–1889

In 1886 the Kansas City Cowboys were members of the National League and suffered through a season of 30 wins and 91 defeats under manager Dave Rowe. Pitcher Stump Weidman topped the league with 36 losses and wound up a 9-year major league career with 102 wins and 156 setbacks. Second baseman Al

Myers was the Cowboys' leading batter with a .277 mark.

After a one-year hiatus, the Cowboys returned with an entirely new lineup (but the same manager, Dave Rowe) as members of the American Association. The results, however, were much the same: 43 wins and 89 losses. Rowe was replaced as manager by Sam Barkley and later Bill Watkins, but no one could keep the Cowboys out of last place. This time Henry Porter had the dubious distinction of leading league pitchers in losses with 37. Jim McTamany's .246 BA was the highest on the team. Future Hall of Famer Billy Hamilton made his major league debut with the Cowboys, appearing in 35 games as a reserve outfielder and batting .264.

The next season (1889) Hamilton batted .301, for Kansas City, the first of 12 consecutive seasons in which he batted .300 or better on his way to a .344 lifetime average. Centerfielder Jim Burns led Cowboy batters with a .304 BA. The Cowboys improved to seventh place but still won only 55 games while losing 82. This was Kansas City's last season in the majors until they joined the Federal League in 1914.

KANSAS CITY PACKERS

Federal League 1914–1915

The Packers, managed by George Stovall, finished sixth with a 67 and 84 record. Second baseman Duke Kenworthy led the league with 15 HR and was fifth overall with 91 RBI. Ted Easterley led the Packers with a .335 average to finish third in the league.

The Packers climbed to fourth place in 1915 by winning 81 and losing 72 games. Nick Cullop (with 22 wins) and Gene Packard (with 20 following his 21 victories in 1914) were among the league's best pitchers. Kenworthy's .298 BA was highest on the team.

KANSAS CITY ATHLETICS

American League 1955–1967

The Federal League folded after the 1915 season. Kansas City was without major league baseball until the American League's Philadelphia Athletics moved there in 1955. Because of declining attendance in Philadelphia, the Mack family sold the franchise to Arnold Johnson, who moved the team to his hometown. The team finished a surprising sixth under manager Lou Boudreau and had four players bat above .300. They were led by Elmer Valo's .364 average and futue Hall of Famer Enos Slaughter contributed mightily with a .322 average. First baseman Vic Power batted .319 and led American League first basemen in every defensive category. Gus Zernial's 30 home runs was second only to Yankee Mickey Mantle's 37. Former President Harry S. Truman was among the 32,844 who turned out for the opening game at Municipal Stadium. Before the season was over, 1,393,054 passed through the turnstiles—exceeding Philadelphia's 1954 attendance by more than a million. It was all downhill from that point: The Athletics never finished higher than seventh over the next 12 seasons. Charley Finley, who had purchased the franchise from the Johnson estate in 1960, moved the franchise to Oakland, California, following the 1967 season. The nucleus for Oakland pennant winners was built in Kansas City, where Finley signed future Hall of Fame pitcher Jim "Catfish" Hunter, who was 8 and 8 during his initial major league season of 1965. Second baseman Dick Green, shortstop Bert Campaneris, and pitcher Blue Moon Odom, all key players in Oakland, got their start in Kansas City. However, the best was yet to come. The expansion Kansas City Royals joined the American League in 1969 and developed into one of baseball's strongest franchises.

KANSAS CITY ROYALS

American League 1969 to Present

The names Kansas City Royals and George Brett are virtually synonymous. Although the Royals' superstar did not join the team until 1973, five years after the American League expansion franchise was founded by Ewing Kauffman, Brett figures prominently in every great moment in club history.

Brett is the only player in major league history to win batting titles in three different decades: (.333 in 1976, .390 in 1980, and .329 in 1990). He was Major League Player of the Year in 1979 and 1980 and American League MVP in 1976 and 1980. When the Royals won their only world championship in 1985, Brett had 10 hits in 27 at bats for a .370 BA. Even though the Royals lost to the Phillies in their only other World Series appearance (in 1980), Brett batted a lusty .375. Despite numerous injuries during his career, Brett became only the eighteenth player in history to get more than 3,000 career hits (in 1992).

The Royals were a surprise from the outset. In 1969 they finished fourth under the direction of manager Joe Gordon. In 1971, with Hall of Famer Bob Lemon at the helm, the Royals surprised everyone by finishing second in the American League Western Division. Cookie Rojas, named the American League's best second baseman, along with center fielder Amos Otis and and shortstop Fred Patek were the club's sparkplugs. Otis batted .301 to match the average set in 1970 by the Royals' first .300 hitter, Lou Pinella. The Royals have had ten different .300 hitters during their 24-year history. Brett reached that plateau 11 times, including his .390 average in 1980, which was the highest mark in the majors since Ted Williams batted .406 with the Boston Red Sox in 1941. Hal McRae, the Royals current manager, was a .300 hitter six times while Willie Wilson reached the mark five times.

Strong pitching has been a Royals trademark over the years. Two-time Cy Young winner Bret Saberhagen (1985 and 1989) holds the club record with 23 wins in 1989. Royals 20-game winners (in order of victories) are: Steve Busby (22 in 1974); Dennis Leonard (21 in 1979 and 20 in 1977 and 1980); Paul Splittorf (20 in 1973); Saberhagen (20 in 1985); and Mark Gubicza (20 in 1988). The Royals all-time saves leader is Dan Quisenberry with 238. He was Fireman of the Year five times (1980, 1982, 1983, 1984, and 1985).

The Royals won American League Western Division titles in 1976, 1977 and 1978 and lost to the New York Yankees in the ALCS each time. They finally beat the Yankees in 1980—only to bow to the Philadelphia Phillies in the World Series. In 1984 they lost to the Tigers in the ALCS. In 1985, after an exciting seven-game ALCS victory over the Toronto Blue Jays, manager Dick Howser guided the Royals, with Saberhagen winning two complete games, over the St. Louis Cardinals in seven to become world champions at last.

Despite having the smallest market in baseball, the Royals have drawn exceptionally well. Since moving into their Royals Stadium showcase in 1973, Kansas City has drawn over two million fans 12 times, with a record 2,477,700 in 1989. If Yankee Stadium in New York is known as the House that Ruth Built, Royals Stadium could well be called the Stadium Brett Filled to honor the Royals' preeminent star who has thrilled Kansas City fans since 1973.

Ballpark Giveaways

Kansas City Royals

1970	T-shirt, Helmet, Bat (if dated $10) $5
1971	Cushion, Bat, Cap, Ball (with facsimile autographs $20) $5
1972	Cushion, Bat, Cap, Ball (with facsimile autographs $20) $5
1972	Team Picture................................$15
1977	English Leather Jacket $6
1977	Shirt...$5
1981	A.L. Champs Cup $8
1981	Cools Poster, Coca-Cola Wrist Band, Guy's Sun Visor, Photo Album, Skelley's Jacket $6
1982	Yago Poster Schedule, Jones Shoe Team Picture $10
1982	Coca-Cola Tube Socks, Coors Foam Dome, Guy's Helmet, Skelley's Jacket $6
1982	Batting Glove, Halter Top $5
1983	Getty Poster Schedule.......................$9

1959 patch, 5″, felt round, red outer ring reads "My Favorite Team/Bazooka-Blony", team's elephant logo in center, $35.

1969 cloth patch by Fleer's Gum Co., 2½″ × 3¼″, Royals logo (initial season), $10.

1983 Coca-Cola Wallet, Coors Seat Cushion $6
1984 Getty Poster Schedule $7
1984 Ortega Tote Bag, Coca-Cola Sports Bag, Hostess Cap, Coors Cooler, Guy's School Notebook, Getty Ski Cap $6
1985 Royals Sportstime Calendar, Getty Poster Schedule $8
1985 Coca-Cola Sports Watch, Coors Brief Case, Hostess Back Pack $6
1986 Royals Baseball Cards $7
1986 Miller Lite Beer Calendar, Coors Lite Umbrella, WDAF TV Baseball & Batting Glove, Food Travel Bag, McDonald's/Coca-Cola Glove, Lee's Jeans Seat Cushion, Guy's Jacket $6
1987 Miller Lite Calendar, Coca-Cola Watch, Dairy Council Growth Poster, Lee's Jeans Sports Bag, Coors Lite Tankard, WDAF TV Notebook $6
1988 Surf Book $9
1988 Miller Lite Calendar, Coca-Cola Jersey, WDAF TV Sports Bag, Lee's Jeans Royals Baseball with Holder, Gatorade Helmet, Smokey the Bear Card Set $6
1989 Western Auto Pins 1, 2, 3 ....ea. $7
1989 Miller Lite Calendar, WDAF Jacket, Zarda Pennant & Fan Kit, Lee's Sports Bag, Gatorade Watch, Smokey the Bear Helmet, Phillips 66 Seat Cushion, Miller Lite Tank Top, Missouri Lottery Umbrella, Guy's School Notebook $6
1990 Phillips 66 Pins 1, 2; Donruss Card Book ....ea. $7

1990 Smokey the Bear Wallet, WDAF Sports Bag, Coca-Cola Beach Towel, Missouri Lottery Visor, Miller Lite Cap, Lee's Baseball & Holder, Gatorade Watch $6
1991 Kansas City Life Baseball Card Set, Donruss Card Album, Upper Deck Heros of Baseball $7
1991 Phillips 66 Pins 1, 2 ....ea. $7
1991 Kelloggs Helmet, WDAF TV Jersey, Pizza Hut Sports Bag, Kraft/Oscar Mayer Lunch Box, Missouri Lottery Cooler Bag, Gatorade Neon Cap........$6
1992 Kodak Stadium Panoramic Poster.......$8
1992 Kansas City Life Baseball Card Set, Upper Deck Heros of Baseball $7
1992 Phillips 66 Pins 1, 2 ....ea. $7
1992 Gatorade Sports Bag, Smokey the Bear Sports Watch, WDAF TV Sports Pouch $6
1993 Kansas City Life Card Set, Upper Deck Cards, Donruss Card Album $7
1993 Phillips 66 Royals Pins 1, 2; Kemper Commemorative Coin......................$8
1993 Jolly Rancher Sports Bag $6
1993 Gatorade 25th Anniversary Ring.......$10

Miscellaneous

BOBBIN' HEAD DOLLS

Kansas City Athletics

Category #II, 1961, 1962, White Square Base, Boy Head $275
Category #III, 1961, 1962, White Round Miniature, Boy Head $230
Category #IV, 1962, 1963, 1964, Green Round Base, Boy Head $215
Category #V, 1962, 1963, 1964, Green Round Base, Black Player $1,550

Kansas City Royals

Category #IV, 1969 through 1972, Gold Round Base, Boy Head $60

Pennants

1955 through 1960 Kansas City A's Regular..$50
1960 Kansas City A's All-Star Game $125
1961 through 1967 Kansas City A's $30
1969, 1970 Kansas City Royals $50
1971, 1972, 1973 Regular $20
1973 All-Star Game $50
1974, 1975 ....$20
1976, 1977, 1978 Division Champs each Year $50
1979, 1980 Regular $20
1980 League Champs $50
1980 World Series.................................$50
1981 through 1985 Regular $5
1985 League Champs $15

1950s pennant, 11½″ × 30″, green with white lettering and gold trim, $50.

1985 World Series $15
1986 through 1990 ....$5
1991, 1992, 1993 ....$3

Pins

1961 through 1965 Kansas City A's,
Crane Potato Chips, ⅞″, Round $5
1967 Kansas City A's, Crane Potato
Chips, ⅞″, Round $5
1964, 1965, 1966 Kansas City A's, Guy's
Potato Chips, ⅞″, Round....................$5
1969 K. C. Royals, Crane Potato Chips,
⅞″, Round $5
1984 K. C. Royals, Crane Potato Chips,
⅞″, Round $3

1980s pin, 1¾″, Royals team logo, $3.

Publications

BOOKS

Bordman, Sid. *Expansion to Excel-
lence.* Marceline, Mo.: Walsworth
Publishing Co., 1981. ....$15.00
Cameron, Steve. *Moments, Memories,
Miracles: A Quarter Century with
the Kansas City Royals.* Taylor
Publishing Co., 1992. ....$15.00

Eskew, Alan. *A Royal Finish: A Cele-
bration of the 1985 Kansas City
Royals.* Chicago: Contemporary
Books, 1985. ....$10.00
Martin, Mollie. *Kansas City Royals.*
Mankato, Mn.: Creative Educa-
tion, 1982. ....$5.00
Rosthaus, James R. *Kansas City
Royals.* Mankato, Mn.: Creative
Education, 1987. ....$5.00

MEDIA GUIDES

1955 Kansas City A's First Year $65
1956 through 1961 Kansas City A's $40
1962, 1963, 1964 Kansas City A's $30
1965, 1966, 1967 Kansas City A's $20
1969, 1970 Kansas City Royals $30
1971, 1972 ....$12
1973, 1974 ....$10
1975 ....$8

1993 media guide, 4¼″ × 9″, $4.

1976, 1977, 1978 Division Champs each
    Year $10
1979 ....$6
1980 American League Champs $8
1981 through 1984 ....$5
1985 World Champs $8
1986 through 1993 ....$4

PROGRAMS AND SCORECARDS

1955 Kansas City A's First Year $25
1956 through 1959 Kansas City A's $15
1960 through 1967 Kansas City A's $10
1969 Kansas City Royals First Year $25
1970 through 1975 ....$6
1976, 1977, 1978 Division Champs each
    Year $8
1979 ....$6
1980 American League Champs $8
1981 through 1984 ....$4
1985 World Champs $6
1986 through 1989 ....$4
1990, 1991, 1992, 1993 ....$3

1955 program, 6¾″ × 10¼″, Athletics first year in Kansas City, $30.

YEARBOOKS

1955 Kansas City A's............................$200
1956 Kansas City A's............................$150
1957 Kansas City A's............................$100
1958 Kansas City A's $90
1959, 1960 Kansas City A's $80
1961, 1962 Kansas City A's $125
1963, 1964 Kansas City A's $45

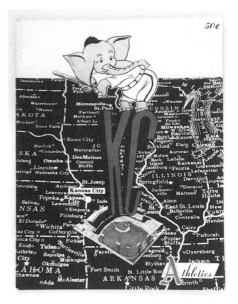

1955 yearbook, 8½″ × 11″, 52 pages, A's first season in Kansas City, $200.

1965 Kansas City A's $40
1966 Kansas City A's $45
1967 Kansas City A's $50
1969 Kansas City Royals $45
1970 ....$40
1971 ....$35
1972 ....$30
1973 ....$25
1974 ....$20
1975 ....$18
1976 through 1982 ....None Issued
1983, 1984 ....$7
1985 World Champs...............................$12
1986 through 1993 ....$5

Schedules

1955 Kansas City A's $40
1956, 1957 Kansas City A's $30
1958, 1959 Kansas City A's $25
1960 through 1967 Kansas City A's $15
1969 Kansas City Royals $20
1970 through 1979 ....$10
1980 through 1985 ....$2
1986 through 1993 ....$1

Special Events

ALL-STAR GAME PRESS PINS

1960 Kansas City A's............................$300
1973 Kansas City Royals.......................$200

ALL-STAR PROGRAMS

1960 Kansas City A's.............................$150
1973 Kansas City Royals $75

ALL-STAR GAME TICKETS

1960 Kansas City A's, Complete Ticket $70
1960 Kansas City A's, Ticket Stub.............$35
1973 K.C. Royals, Complete Ticket $40
1973 K.C. Royals, Ticket Stub $20

LEAGUE CHAMPIONSHIP SERIES PROGRAMS

1976 ....$15
1977 ....$15
1978 ....$12
1980 ....$12
1981 Western Division Play-Offs $50
1984, 1985 ....$10

LEAGUE CHAMPIONSHIP GAME TICKETS

1976 Complete Ticket $38
1976 Ticket Stub..................................$18
1977 Complete Ticket $38
1977 Ticket Stub..................................$18
1978 Complete Ticket $38
1978 Ticket Stub..................................$18
1980 Complete Ticket $28
1980 Ticket Stub..................................$15

1973 All-Star program, 8½″ × 11″, 56 pages, Royals Stadium, $75.

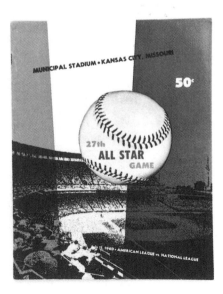

1960 All-Star program, 8½″ × 11″, Municipal Stadium, $150.

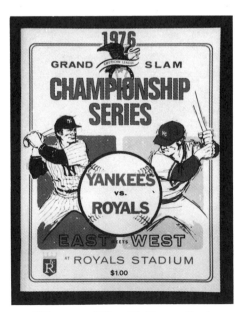

1976 program, 8½″ × 11″, 46 pages, Royals Stadium, $15.

1981 Complete Ticket, Western Division
Play-Off..$28
1981 Ticket Stub.....................................$15
1984, 1985 Complete Ticket $28
1984, 1985 Ticket Stub $15

WORLD SERIES PRESS PINS

1980 (not dated) $50
1985 (not dated) $50

WORLD SERIES PROGRAMS

1980 ....$30
1985 ....$15

WORLD SERIES GAME TICKETS

1980 Complete Ticket $30
1980 Ticket Stub..................................$15
1985 Complete Ticket $30
1985 Ticket Stub..................................$15

Keokuk, Iowa

KEOKUK WESTERNS

National Association 1875

Keokuk, Iowa, had a one-year fling as a major league baseball city when the Westerns were members of the National Association in 1875. This was the final year of the National Association and Keokuk was one of 13 members. Unfortunately, they did not finish the season and wound up with a record of one win and 12 losses.

The Westerns elected to go with National Association players of the past and signed Jimmy Hallinan and Joe Quinn, who played with the Fort Wayne Kekiongas in 1871. Unfortunately, their batting credentials left much to be desired as Quinn was a .190 hitter and Hallinan batted only .200 with the Kekiongas. With Keokuk, Hallinan raised his batting average to .240, while Quinn batted .298 in the 11 games he played with Keokuk. Joe Simmons, who batted .230 for the Cleveland Forest Cities in 1872, wound up hitting only .161 with the Westerns.

Catcher Billy Barnie is probably the most well-known of the Westerns, but his fame came primarily as a manager long after his career with Keokuk. Barnie managed 14 seasons in the major leagues, but a third-place finish with the Baltimore Orioles in the American Association in 1887 was his best record. Overall Barnie's teams won 578 games while losing 768.

Keokuk's largest crowd came on May 5 when 1,500 turned out to see the Westerns lose 15 to 1 to the Chicago White Stockings. Attendance declined steadily in Keokuk; in early June only 300 spectators turned out for a game with the Boston Red Stockings. Boston's share of the gate receipts was only $13, so they refused to play there the next day. Finally, on June 16, the Keokuk Westerns disbanded. It was the end of major league baseball in Keokuk. Any memorabilia pertaining to the 1875 Keokuk Westerns would be extremely rare. If any still remains, it would most likely be scorecards or photographs.

Los Angeles, California

LOS ANGELES DODGERS

National League 1958 to Present
(See also Anaheim, California)

Although many Dodger fans will never forgive the move from Brooklyn to Los Angeles in time for the 1958 season, the franchise has enjoyed enormous success in the City of Angels. Owner Walter O'Malley made the move strictly for business reasons since the Dodgers drew more than a million fans during their final season in Flatbush. However, there was no way to expand Ebbetts Field, which had a seating capacity of just over 32,000.

Playing temporarily in the mammoth Memorial Coliseum, the Dodgers drew 1,845,556 their first season in Los Angeles, 800,000 more than they drew the previous year in Brooklyn. When the Los Angeles Dodgers won their first pennant in 1959, attendance was 2,071,045. The Dodgers defeated the Chicago White Sox in the World Series four games to two. In the fifth game attendance reached a World Series record of 92,706, a mark that will never be exceeded.

When Dodger Stadium opened for the 1962 season, 2,755,184 poured through the turnstiles. Since then attendance has exceeded three million nine times. Through the 1993 season more than 90 million fans have seen the Dodgers at home since they moved to the West Coast. Since the move west, the Dodgers have been baseball's most successful franchise.

Many great players have worn Dodger blue, including three Hall of Famers pitchers Don Drysdale and Sandy Koufax and outfielder Duke Snider, who played with the first team in Los Angeles. During the pennant-winning 1959 season, Snider led the team in batting (.308) and RBI (88). Drysdale posted the best record (17–13) while Johnny Podres was next at 14–9. In the World Series victory over the White Sox, Drysdale and Podres won one game each while righthander Larry Sherry, who was 7–2 during the season, won the other two games.

The 1959 pennant and World Series championship was just the beginning of Dodger success in Los Angeles. They were world champs again in 1963, 1965, 1981 and 1988. In addition, they won National League pennants in 1966, 1974, 1977 and 1978.

Four Los Angeles Dodgers have received the National League MVP award: Maury Wills in 1962, Sandy Koufax in 1963, Steve Garvey in 1974 and Kirk Gibson in 1988. Since pitching has been the Dodgers strong suit, Cy Young Award winners have included Don Drysdale (1961), Sandy Koufax (1963, 1965, 1966), Mike Marshall (1974), Fernando Valenzuela (1981) and Orel Hershiser (1988).

In addition to those Dodgers already mentioned for Hall of Fame honors, pitchers Juan Marichal (1975) and Hoyt Wilhelm (1971, 1972), who played briefly in Los Angeles, are also members. Walter Alston coached or managed the Dodgers from 1954 through 1976 and is also a Hall of Fame member. Undoubtedly, others who played for baseball's most successful franchise over the last 35 years will someday be honored.

Advertising Specialties

1958 Plastic Change Purse with Schedule on one side and place for sponsor's message on the other $20

Ballpark Giveaways

1970 Pennant $8
1970 Cap, Helmet, Bat, Ball $5
1970 Pennant (if dated) $10
1970 Ball (if containing facsimile autographs) $25
1971 Pennant, Cap, Helmet, Ball $5
1971 Ball (if containing facsimile autographs) $25
1972 Cap, Ball, Helmet $5

116

1958 5", felt round, white on blue, "My Favorite Team/
Bazooka-Blony" surrounding Dodgers logo, $35.

1972 Ball (if containing facsimile auto-
      graphs) $20
1973 Batting Glove, Cap, Helmet, Ball $5
1973 Ball (if containing facsimile
      autographs) $20
1974 Dodger Poster (National League
      champs) $15
1974 Ball (if containing facsimile auto-
      graphs) $25
1974 Batting Glove, Helmet, Ball $5
1975 Opening Night Pennant $10
1975 Batting Glove, Cap, Helmet, Ball $5
1975 Ball (if containing facsimile auto-
      graphs) $20
1976 Jacket, Batting Glove, Cap, T-shirt,
      Helmet, Ball $5
1976 Dodger Photo Album, Ball (with
      facsimile autographs) $15
1977 Dodger Photo Album N.L. Champs ...$17
1977 Jacket, Helmet, Cap, Batting Glove,
      Ball $5

1977 Ball (with facsimile autographs)
      N.L. Champs $25
1978 Dodger Photo Album N.L. Champs ...$15
1978 Pennant (if dated) $10
1978 Plain Ball, Generic Pennant..............$5
1978 Ball (with facsimile autographs)
      N.L. Champs $25
1979 Poster, Photo Album $12
1979 Wrist Band, Batting Glove, Ball
      (with facsimile autographs $15) $5
1980 Dodgers Baseball Cards, Poster,
      Photo Album $10
1981 Poster, Photo Album, Team Photo
      (world champs)...............................$10
1982 Poster, Team Photo, Baseball Cards ..$10
1983 Calendar, Team Photo $7

1958 change purse, white plastic, 2" × 2½", sponsor's
message on front and schedule of Dodgers games for
their first season in Los Angeles on back, $20.

1989 calendar, 8½" × 11", ten
pages, given away March 30 for
an exhibition game against the
California Angels. Cover shows
world championship trophy from
1988 superimposed over color picture of Dodger Stadium. Sponsors
of this giveaway were the four
Dodger broadcasting stations
KABC, KWKW, KTTV and
Z Channel, $6.

1983 Poster, Jacket, Baseball Cards, Ball,
     Helmet, Batting Gloves, Wrist Band,
     T-shirt, Sports Socks $5
1984 Calendar, Poster, Team Photo $10
1985 Calendar, Team Photo $10
1985 Pen, Ball, Batting Glove, Visor $5
1985 Ball (with facsimile autographs) $15
1986 Calendar, Team Photo, Poster $10
1986 Glove, Visor, Wrist Band, T-shirt,
     Sports Socks, Pen $5
1987 Calendar, Dodger All-Stars of 25
     Years Cards, Team Photo, Poster $9
1987 Unocal Pins 1, 2, 3, 4, 5, 6 ....ea. $8
1987 Watch, Visor, Back Pack, Cap,
     Glove $5
1987 Ball (with facsimile autographs) $15

Miscellaneous

BOBBIN' HEAD DOLLS

Category #I, 1961, 1962, Blue Square
     Base, Boy Head $90
Category #II, 1961, 1962, White Square
     Base, Boy Head $130
Category #III, 1961, 1962, White Round
     Miniature, Boy Head $130
Category #IV, 1962, 1963, 1964, Green
     Round Base, Boy Head $50
Category #V, 1962, 1963, 1964, Green
     Round Base, Black Player $275
Category #VI, 1967 through 1972, Gold
     Round Base, Boy Head $40

Pennants

1958, 1959 Regular $50
1959 World Series $125
1959 All-Star Game $125
1960, 1961, 1962, 1963 Regular $30
1963 World Series................................$75
1964, 1965 Regular $30
1965 World Series................................$75
1966 Regular......................................$30
1966 World Series................................$75
1967 through 1970 ....$30
1971, 1972, 1973, 1974 Regular $20
1974 League Champs $50
1974 World Series $50
1975, 1976, 1977 Regular $20
1977 League Champs $50
1977 World Series $50
1978 Regular......................................$20
1978 League Champs $50
1979, 1980 Regular $20
1980 All-Star Game $50
1981 Regular $5
1981 World Series $15
1982 through 1987 Regular $5
1988 League Champs $15
1988 World Series $15
1989, 1990 ....$5
1991, 1992, 1993 ....$3

1962 pennant, 11½″ × 29″, red, white, and blue, grand opening of Dodger Stadium April 9 (a large number were discovered in recent years, decreasing the value), $35.

Pins

1961 through 1965 Crane Potato Chips,
     ⅞″, Round $5
1967, 1968, 1969 Crane Potato Chips, ⅞″,
     Round $5
1984 Crane Potato Chips, ⅞″, Round $3
1964, 1965, 1966 Guy's Potato Chips, ⅞″,
     Round $5

1950s–1960s pin, 3″, red, white, and blue, $10.

1963 Dodgers postcard, 3½" × 5½", world champions, CHP 55773, Colourpicture Publishers, Inc., Boston, MA, $20.

Postcards

1971 CH 7480 D, 5½" × 7", Pub. Dexter Press, Inc., West Nyack, N.Y. $20
1974 CH KV6432, 5½" × 7", Pub. Mitock & Sons, Los Angeles, CA. $20

Publications

BOOKS

Allen, Lee. *The Giants and the Dodgers.* G.P. Putnam's Sons, 1964. ....$35.00
Bartruff, Jim & Toby Zwjiebel. *The Los Angeles Dodgers: The Championship Year.* Los Angeles: Rosebud Books, 1981. ....$10.00
Bjarkman, Peter C. *Baseball's Dynasties: The Dodgers.* New York: Gallery Books, 1990. ....$5.00
Brannon, Jody. *Los Angeles Dodgers.* Mankato, Mn.: Creative Education, 1982. ....$5.00
Claire, Fred. *The Dodgers All-Time Greats: A Pictorial History.* Los Angeles Dodgers, 1972. ....$10.00
Cohen, Stanley. *Dodgers: The First 100 Years.* New York: Birch Lane Press, 1990. ....$15.00
Finch, Frank. *The Los Angeles Dodgers: The First 25 Years.* Virginia Beach, Va.: Jordan-Powers, 1977. ....$20.00
Honig, Donald. *Dodgers: The Complete Record of Dodger Baseball.* New York: Collier-McMillan, 1986. ....$15.00
Honig, Donald. *The Los Angeles Dodgers: The First Quarter Century.* New York: St. Martin's Press, 1983. ....$15.00
Kahn, Roger. *The Boys of Summer.* Harper & Row, 1971. ....$15.00

Paige, David & Richard Whittingham. *The Los Angeles Dodgers: An Illustrated History.* New York: Harper & Row, 1982. ....$15.00
Rothaus, James. *Los Angeles Dodgers.* Mankato, Mn.: Creative Education, 1987. ....$5.00
Sahadi, Lou. *The Los Angeles Dodgers, The World Champions of Baseball.* New York: Quill, 1982. ......$10.00
Schoor, Gene. *The Complete Dodger Record Book.* New York: Facts on File, 1984. ....$10.00
Schoor, Gene. *Official Los Angeles Dodgers Pictorial History.* West Point, N.Y.: Leisure Press, 1982. ......$10.00
Schoor, Gene. *A Pictorial History of the Dodgers: Brooklyn to Los Angeles.* West Point, N.Y.: Leisure Press, 1984. ....$10.00
Sullivan, Neil. *The Dodgers Move West.* New York: Oxford University Press, 1987. ....$15.00
Talley, Rick. *Out of the Blue: A Celebration of the 1985 Los Angeles Dodgers.* Contemporary Books, 1985. ....$10.00
Thompson, Fresco L. & Cy Rice. *Inside the Dodgers.* Holloway House, 1966. ....$15.00
Zimmerman, Paul. *The Los Angeles Dodgers.* New York: Coward-McCann, 1960. ....$25.00
Zimmerman, Tom. *A Day in the Season of the Los Angeles Dodgers.* New York: Shaplosky, 1990. ....$10.00
Zimmerman, Tom. *Working at the Stadium.* Los Angeles: Pac Tides Press, 1989. ....$10.00

MEDIA GUIDES

1958 First Year $100
1959 World Champs.............................$50

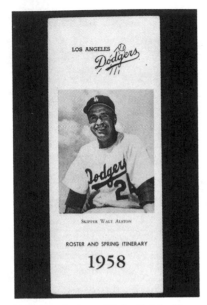

1958 Dodgers Roster and Spring Training Itinerary, 3½″ × 8″, first season in Los Angeles, $100.

1961 ....$40
1962 ....$30
1963 World Champs...............................$35
1964 ....$30
1965 World Champs...............................$25
1966 League Champs $20
1967, 1968 ....$17
1969, 1970 ....$15
1971, 1972 ....$12
1973 ....$10
1974 National League Champs $12
1975, 1976 ....$8
1977, 1978 National League Champs
    each Year $9
1979, 1980 ....$6
1981 World Champs $8
1982 ....$5
1983 Division Champs $7
1984 ....$5
1985 Division Champs $7
1986, 1987 ....$4
1988 World Champs $7
1989 through 1993 ....$4

PROGRAMS AND SCORECARDS

1958 ....$25
1959 World Champs...............................$20
1960, 1961, 1962 ....$10
1963 World Champs...............................$12
1964 ....$10
1965 World Champs...............................$12

1966 League Champs $12
1967, 1968, 1969 ....$10
1970, 1971, 1972, 1973 ....$6
1974 League Champs $8
1975, 1976 ....$6
1977, 1978 League Champs each Year.......$8
1979, 1980 ....$6
1981 World Champs $8
1982 ....$4
1983 Division Champs $6
1984 ....$4
1985 Division Champs $6
1986, 1987 ....$4
1988 World Champs $6
1989 ....$4
1990, 1991, 1992, 1993 ....$3

YEARBOOKS

1958 First Year $150
1959 World Champs.............................$130
1960 ....$100
1961 ....$75
1962 ....$60
1963 World Champs...............................$65
1964 ....$45
1965 World Champs...............................$50
1966 League Champs $35
1967, 1968 ....$25
1969, 1970 ....$20
1971 ....$18
1972, 1973 ....$15
1974 National League Champs $18
1975, 1976 ....$12
1977, 1978 National League Champs
    each Year $12
1979, 1980 ....$10
1981 World Champs...............................$10
1982 ....$8
1983 Division Champs $10
1984 ....$7
1985 Division Champs $9
1986, 1987 ....$7
1988 World Champs $9
1989 through 1993 ....$6

Schedules

1958 ....$30
1959 ....$25
1960 through 1969 ....$15
1970 through 1979 ....$10
1980 through 1985 ....$2
1986 through 1993 ....$1

Special Events

ALL-STAR GAME PRESS PINS

1959 ....$75
1980 ....$50

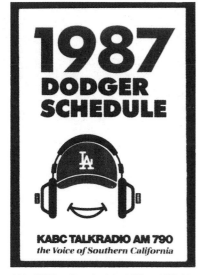

1987 KABC radio schedule, 2⅜″ × 3½″, $1.

ALL-STAR PROGRAMS

1959 ....$75
1980 ....$25

ALL-STAR GAME TICKETS

1959 Complete Ticket $150
1959 Ticket Stub....................................$75
1980 Complete Ticket $30
1980 Ticket Stub....................................$15

LEAGUE CHAMPIONSHIP SERIES PROGRAMS

1974 (this program is very hard to come
       by)..$150
1977 ....$20
1978 ....$15
1981 Regular..$10
1981 Western Division Play-Off $35
1983 ....$10
1985 ....$8
1988 ....$6

LEAGUE CHAMPIONSHIP GAME TICKETS

1974 Complete Ticket $38
1974 Ticket Stub....................................$18
1977 Complete Ticket $38
1977 Ticket Stub....................................$18
1978 Complete Ticket $38
1978 Ticket Stub....................................$18
1981 Complete Ticket $28
1981 Ticket Stub....................................$15
1983 Complete Ticket $28
1983 Ticket Stub....................................$15

1985 Complete Ticket $28
1985 Ticket Stub....................................$15
1988 Complete Ticket $28
1988 Ticket Stub....................................$15

WORLD SERIES PRESS PINS

1959 (not dated) $200
1963 (not dated) $200
1965 (not dated) $200
1966 ....$200
1974 (not dated) $200
1977 (not dated) $100
1978 (not dated) $100
1981 (not dated) $50
1988 ....$30

WORLD SERIES PROGRAMS

1959 ....$75
1963 ....$75
1965 ....$40
1966 ....$40
1974 ....$35
1977 ....$25
1978 ....$20
1981 ....$18
1988 ....$12

WORLD SERIES GAME TICKETS

1959 Complete Ticket $150
1959 Ticket Stub....................................$75

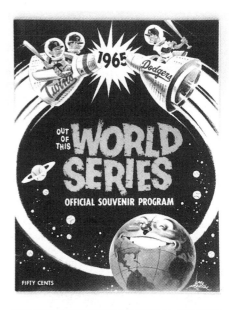

1965 World Series program, Dodgers vs. Minnesota Twins (Dodgers won the series 4 games to 3), 8½″ × 11″, 64 pages, $40.

1963 Complete Ticket	$70	1977 Complete Ticket	$40
1963 Ticket Stub	$35	1977 Ticket Stub	$20
1965 Complete Ticket	$70	1978 Complete Ticket	$40
1965 Ticket Stub	$35	1978 Ticket Stub	$20
1966 Complete Ticket	$70	1981 Complete Ticket	$30
1966 Ticket Stub	$35	1981 Ticket Stub	$15
1974 Complete Ticket	$40	1988 Complete Ticket	$30
1974 Ticket Stub	$20	1988 Ticket Stub	$15

Louisville, Kentucky

LOUISVILLE GRAYS

National League 1876–1877

Louisville, Kentucky, most famous for horse racing and bourbon whiskey, was an original member of the National League in 1876 and had teams in major league baseball as late as 1899. In that year, owner Barney Dreyfuss moved the franchise, including future Hall of Famers Honus Wagner and Fred Clarke, to Pittsburgh.

Although Colonels is the name most frequently associated with Louisville baseball, the team was nicknamed the Grays in the National league's initial season of 1876. With a capital investment of $20,000, Grays' President W. H. Haldemen of the *Louisville Courier Journal* made this the first newspaper-owned team in major league history. Righthander Jim Devlin, later banned for life for purposely losing games, won 30 but led the league in losses with 35. The Grays finished fifth in the eight-team league with a record of 30 wins and 36 losses. Devlin, with a .315 BA, was the only player on the team to bat above .300.

In 1877 Louisville was in first place much of the season when they began to perform badly. On August 31 Grays Director Charles E. Chase received an anonymous telegram from Hoboken, New Jersey, that read: "something is wrong with the Louisville players as the gamblers were betting on the Hartfords and to watch your men." Due to errors by Al Nichols, Bill Craver, and George Hall,

Louisville was beaten 6 to 3. The next day a similar telegram arrived that stated they would lose again. They did—on errors by Nichols, Hall and Devlin. The team returned from its long road trip with one two wins and a string of losses that knocked them out of first place. When confronted by the board of directors, the players confessed they purposely lost and were expelled from baseball. Ironically, Jim Devlin was a 35-game winner for the Grays but again led the league in losses with 25. Thus ended the careers of Devlin, Nichols, Hall and Craver, who repeatedly applied for readmission but were never allowed back. Louisville dropped out of the National League that year. It was the first betting scandal in baseball history.

LOUISVILLE ECLIPSE

American Association 1882–1884

Louisville again emerged as a major league city when the Eclipse joined the American Association in 1882 as a charter member. J. H. Pank, who along with J. W. Reccius was a principle stockholder in the Eclipse, was selected vice president of the Association. Second baseman Pete Browning led the Eclipse and Association in batting during that initial season with a .378 average while Tony Mullane was second among Association pitchers with 30 wins. The team finished third in the six-team league with a 42–38 record. In 1883

Browning had another banner year and finished second in batting with a .338 average as the team finished fifth in the now eight-team circuit.

Browning, a native of Louisville, was the most colorful player in the Association. He acquired such nicknames as "Gladiator," "Inspector of Red Lights" and "The Prince of Bourbon" for obvious reasons. Despite his off-field activities, he played 12 seasons in the major leagues with a lifetime batting average of .341. In 1884 the American Association increased to 12 teams and the Eclipse finished third (as did Browning among Association batters with a .336 average).

LOUISVILLE COLONELS

American Association 1885–1891, National League 1892–1899

In 1885 the team became known as the Colonels. With hopes high for a pennant, more than 8000 fans turned out to see the opener against Cincinnati. The 4 to 1 loss to the Red Stockings was a portent of things to come as the Colonels were a disappointing eighth in the ten-team league. Browning had another marvelous year and led the league with a .362 BA. In 1886 the Colonels finished fourth as Guy Hecker not only won 26 games but also led the league in batting by edging out teammate Browning .341 to .340. In 1887 the team was fourth again. Browning batted .402 but finished second to Tip O'Neill of St. Louis, who batted .435. Louisville fell to ninth place in 1888 while Browning was third in the league in batting with a .313 average. Browning had his worst year in 1889; his average dropped to .256 and the club finished last. In 1990 Browning jumped to Cleveland of the Players League, where he led the league in batting with a .373 average. The Colonels prospered without him, winning the American Association pennant under Jack Champman (who had managed the Grays in 1877). Louisville native Chicken Wolf, a team member since 1882, won the Association batting title with a .363 BA. Some newspapers began calling the Colonels the Cyclones as they wreaked havoc on

other Association members with their outstanding play. Disillusioned Louisville fans of past years came back in droves and on the Fourth of July, 13,500 fans turned out for a morning and afternoon doubleheader. When the season ended in October, Louisville was the only team to show a profit due to strong attendance all season. After the season the Cyclones met the Brooklyn National League champions in the World Series. Each team won three games and one ended in a tie before the Series was called off by mutual consent because of the frigid October weather.

Things started out well for the defending champions in 1891. A crowd of 4,277 enjoyed the pennant-raising ceremonies and a ninth-inning rally in which the Colonels scored five runs to beat Columbus 7 to 6. It was literally the high point of the season, the club finished seventh. After this season the American Association merged with the National League for 1892. The Colonels finished ninth in the 12-team league.

Pete Browning returned to the Colonels in 1893, and although he batted .355 the team finished eleventh. In 1894 the team finished last as future Hall of Famer Fred Clarke made his major league debut and batted .268 in half a season. Despite Clarke's .347 BA in 1895, the Colonels were last again. In 1896 the Colonels finished last a third consecutive year while Clarke batted .325. Clarke batted a career high .390 in 1897, but the Colonels moved up only a notch to finish eleventh while Clarke took over as manager. It also marked the major league debut of Hall of Famer Honus Wagner, who batted .338. The year 1898 saw the Colonels climb to ninth place; in 1899 they finished there again although their record improved to 75 and 77. Another future Hall of Famer, pitcher Rube Waddell, won 7 and lost 2. It was obvious that Louisville was a team of rising stars, but fate would step in and years of glory were achieved elsewhere. The National League had been trying to cut down from the unwieldy 12 teams, and Louisville, as one of the smaller markets, was deemed expendable. When the Colonels ballpark burned down in the fall, it was the perfect excuse to drop Louisville from the roster of major league cities. Owner Barney Dreyfuss was allowed to buy the Pittsburgh franchise and take his best Louisville players along. Two years later, with Clarke and Wagner leading the way, the Pirates won their first of three consecutive National League pennants. For further reading on Louisville's rich history in the major leagues see *Baseball 1845–1891 from the Newspapers Accounts* by Preston D. Orem and *The Pittsburgh Pirates* by Frederick G. Lieb.

Miscellaneous

1888 Joseph Hall Cabinet Team Cards, 4¼" × 6½" **$1,800**

Middletown, Connecticut

MIDDLETOWN MANSFIELDS

National Association 1872

Middletown, Connecticut, once enjoyed status as a major league baseball city. Known as the Mansfields, the team was a member of the National Association in 1872.

Although they finished ninth in the ten-team league, the Mansfields spawned the careers of several outstanding players, including future Hall of Famer James H. "Orator Jim" O'Rourke. A product of Yale Law School, O'Rourke batted .287 in his first major league season with Middletown and continued his career as a regular until 1893. Although primarily an outfielder, O'Rourke played all positions, including pitcher. His active career finally concluded after a lapse of 11 seasons when he appeared in one game with the 1904 New York Giants. In 19 National League seasons his career batting average was a lofty .310.

Other notable Mansfields include first baseman Tim Murnane, who batted .296 and later managed Boston in the Union Association in 1884. Murnane eventually became president of the New England League and a famous baseball writer. Catcher John Clapp led the team with a .306 BA.

Not only did the Mansfields draw poorly at home, but the crowds were generally quite small when they went on the road. As a result of being unable to meet expenses, the club disbanded in August after posting a record of 5–19. Any material on the Mansfields would be extremely rare and command high prices. Most likely to exist are scorecards with tintypes or cabinet photographs of players or the team.

Milwaukee, Wisconsin

MILWAUKEE CREAM CITIES

National League 1878, Union Association 1884

Milwaukee, Wisconsin, had its first major league team as early as 1878, when the Cream Cities were members of the National League. The Cream Cities were a young team headed by outfielder Abner Dalrymple, who finished second in the league with a .354 BA, his highest mark in 12 major league seasons. Another Cream Cities rookie was Charley Bennett. Considered one of the nineteenth century's premier defensive catchers, Bennett compiled a .256 BA in 15 seasons. This inexperienced team found competition too tough and finished last with only 15 wins and 45 losses. Milwaukee gave up its franchise to Troy, New York, following the dismal season.

A team also nicknamed the Cream Cities surfaced in the Union Association in 1884. After compiling a record of 46 wins and 30 losses in the Northwestern League, they joined the Union Association when Pittsburgh disbanded on September 19. They promptly won 8 of 12 games played and drew large crowds when they played in Milwaukee. Al Myers batted .326 in the 12 games while lefthander Ed Cushman had a perfect 4 and 0 record before the Union Association disbanded following the season.

MILWAUKEE BRAVES

National League 1953–1965

The Milwaukee Braves had a highly successful although relatively brief history, which lasted from 1953 until they moved to Atlanta in 1966. Originally the Boston Braves, the Perini brothers moved the franchise to Milwaukee while the club was in spring training just prior to the 1953 season. After drawing less than 300,000 fans in Boston in 1952, the Braves were an instant success in Milwaukee. Playing in brand new County Stadium, they drew a league record 1,826,397 fans, more than six times the number they attracted during their final season in Boston. It was even better in 1954 as the Braves became the first National League team to draw more than two million fans (2,131,388). By 1957, when they won their first pennant in Milwaukee, Braves attendance had exceeded two million fans four consecutive years.

Propelled by sluggers Hank Aaron and Eddie Mathews with a pitching staff anchored by Warren Spahn, all future Hall of Famers, the Braves not only won the 1957 pennant but also defeated the New York Yankees in an exciting seven-game World Series. Aaron led the league with 44 home runs and 132 runs batted in while Mathews hit 34 homers and drove in 94 runs. Spahn, who ultimately became the winningest lefthander in major league history, led the National League with 21 wins against 11 losses. Righthanders Bob Buhl (18–9) and Lew Burdette (17–9) compli-

mented Spahn exceptionally well. In the World Series victory over the Yankees, Burdette was the star, winning three games while Spahn gained the other victory.

It was deja vu in 1958 as the Braves won their second straight pennant. Mathews led the team with 31 home runs while Aaron contributed 30 and led the club with 95 RBI. Spahn again led the league with 22 wins while Burdette was right behind with 20. After leading the Yankees three games to one in the World Series, Milwaukee faltered and New York won the final three to become world champs. Of the three Milwaukee victories, Spahn posted two wins and Burdette the other.

Attendance declined rapidly after the 1958 season and the Perini brothers sold the club. By the 1960s attendance dwindled to less than a million and by 1965 hit an all-time low of 555,584. The next season the Braves moved to Atlanta.

It was a wild, wonderful ride while it lasted, as the Braves and their fans were the best in baseball. Fittingly, major league baseball returned in 1970 as the Seattle Pilots ironically moved to Milwaukee during spring training to become the Brewers, a successful American League franchise to this day. In another twist of irony, another team called the Brewers was a charter member of the American League in 1901, but moved to St. Louis after finishing last. The current team appears set for a long stay.

Miscellaneous

BOBBIN' HEAD DOLLS

Category #II, 1961, 1962, White Square
  Base, Mascot $215
Category #III, 1961, 1962, White Round
  Miniature, Mascot $285
Category #IV, 1962, 1963, 1964, Green
  Round Base, Mascot $160
Category #V, 1962, 1963, 1964, Green
  Round Base, Black Player $650

Pennants

1953 through 1955 Regular $50
1955 All-Star Game $125
1956, 1957 Regular $50
1957 World Series $150
1958 Regular......................................$50
1958 World Series $150

1958 pennant, 11½″ × 28½″, National League champion Milwaukee Braves, scroll with players' names, brave dancing on a baseball, white lettering on a blue field, $125.

1959, 1960 ....$50
1961 through 1965 ....$30

Pins

1961 through 1965 Crane Potato Chips,
   ⅞″, Round $5
1964, 1965 Guy's Potato Chips, ⅞″,
   Round $5

1950s Milwaukee Braves Boosters pin, 1¼″, baseball with smiling face and feathers on a yellow field, $25.

Publications

BOOKS

Allen, Robert. *The Fabulous Milwau-
   kee Braves.* 1959, 1960. ....$20.00
•Buege, Bob. *The Milwaukee Braves: A
   Baseball Eulogy.* Milwaukee:
   Douglas American Sports Publica-
   tions, 1988. (Paperback $12.95) $19.95
Kaese, Harold & R. G. Lynch. *The
   Milwaukee Braves.* G. P. Putnam's
   Sons, 1954. ....$85.00
Meany, Tom. *Milwaukee's Miracle
   Braves.* A. S. Barnes & Co., 1954. .....$30.00
Onigman, Mark. *This Date in Mil-
   waukee Braves History.* New York:
   Stein & Day, 1982. ....$5.00

MEDIA GUIDES

1953 First Year $55
1954, 1955 ....$50
1956 ....$40
1957 World Champs...............................$45
1958 League Champs $45
1959, 1960, 1961 ....$40
1962, 1963, 1964 ....$40
1965 ....$30

PROGRAMS AND SCORECARDS

1953 First Year $75
1954 through 1956 ....$15
1957 World Champs...............................$20
1958 League Champs $20
1959 ....$15
1960 through 1965 ....$10

YEARBOOKS

1953 ....$150
1954 ....$75
1955 ....$100
1956 ....$75
1957 World Champs $100
1958 League Champs $75
1959, 1960 ....$65
1961 ....$55
1962 ....$45
1963 ....$40
1964 ....$35
1965 Last Year (highly sought after).........$75

Schedules

1953 ....$30
1954 through 1959 ....$25
1960 through 1965 ....$15

Special Events

ALL-STAR GAME PRESS PINS

1955 ....$200

ALL-STAR GAME TICKETS

1955 Complete Ticket $150
1955 Ticket Stub $75

1954 yearbook, second for Milwaukee Braves,
8½″ × 11″, $75.

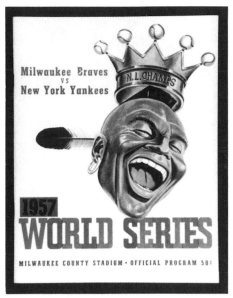

1957 World Series program, County Stadium, Braves
vs. New York Yankees, 8½″ × 11″, 40 pages, $175.

WORLD SERIES PRESS PINS

1957 ....$200
1958 ....$200

WORLD SERIES PROGRAMS

1958 ....$175

WORLD SERIES GAME TICKETS

1957 Complete Ticket...........................$150
1957 Ticket Stub..................................$75
1958 Complete Ticket...........................$150
1958 Ticket Stub..................................$75

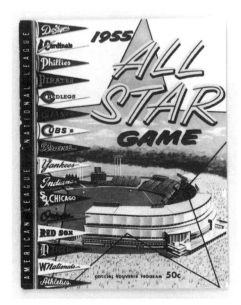

1955 All-Star program, 8½″ × 11″, 36 pages, pennants of all 16 Major League teams surrounding
County Stadium, $150.

1958 ticket stub, 7th game of the World Series at
County Stadium (won by the New York Yankees 6-2),
4¼″ × 2⅜″, $75.

MILWAUKEE BREWERS

American Association 1891;
American League 1901,
1970 to Present

In 1891 the Brewers joined the American Association during the last two months of its final season. With many teams having financial difficulties, Milwaukee agreed to assume all debts of the Cincinnati Kellys, named after their manager and star "King" Kelly, and paid $6,000 in cash plus $6,000 in notes. The Kellys gave Milwaukee first option on all the Cincinnati players except Kelly, who was free to make his own deal and joined the National League Boston Beaneaters. The Brewers did well financially and on September 13 drew 20,000 fans for a home game against Philadelphia and followed that up with a crowd of 12,000 for a game against Boston. When the Association merged with the National League following the 1891 season, Milwaukee was left out in the cold and they once again returned to the minor leagues. During their short tenure in the American Association, the Brewers won 21 and lost 15. Abner Dalrymple, who broke into the majors with the Cream Cities in 1878, finished his 12-year major league career with the Brewers and was the team's leading hitter with .311 batting average.

When the American League became a second major league in 1901, the Brewers were charter members. Managed by future Hall of Famer center fielder Hugh Duffy, the Brewers finished last with 48 wins and 89 losses. John Anderson led the team with a .330 BA and 99 RBI. At .302, Duffy was the Brewers' only other .300 hitter. When the season ended the Brewers franchise was shifted to St. Louis and they became the Browns. That was the end of big league ball in Milwaukee until the Boston Braves moved there in 1953.

Like the Milwaukee Braves nearly two decades earlier, the Milwaukee Brewers (again) became a major league franchise when an existing team (Seattle Pilots) moved there during spring training of 1970. Milwaukee Brewers Inc., headed by Allan "Bud" Selig and Edmund Fitzgerald, had been working more than two years to bring major league baseball back to Mil-

waukee and succeeded when they acquired the Pilots on April 1, 1970. The Brewers name was chosen because of the city's long affinity with the brewing industry and the long association of the name with baseball. The original American League franchise of 1901 had been called the Brewers and the minor league team bore the same nickname.

Second baseman Tommy Harper led the first-year Brewers in nearly every offensive category: batting (.296), runs (104), hits (179), home runs (31), RBI (82), and stolen bases (38). He was the lone Brewer on the American League All-Star team.

Even though there was little time to market the team, nearly a million fans (933,690) supported a woeful team that finished with a record of 65 wins and 97 losses—only one game better than the Pilots' record in 1969. Milwaukee attendance, however, exceeded Seattle's by nearly 300,000.

Although the club finished last in 1971, the Brewers pitching was outstanding. With 7 wins and 31 saves, Ken Sanders was named "Fireman of the Year" by *The Sporting News;* starters Marty Pattin, Skip Lockwood, and Jim Slaton hurled a combined 23 shutouts.

When the Washington Senators moved to Texas following the 1971 season, the Brewers moved to the American League Eastern Division, but the club had difficulty vacating last place and finished there again in 1972. In 1973 attendance cracked a million for the first time (1,092,158). In 1974 future Hall of Famer Robin Yount joined the team as shortstop. In 1975 baseball's all-time home run king, Hank Aaron, returned to Milwaukee to finish his career. First baseman George "Boomer" Scott took a page from Aaron's book by hitting 36 HR to tie Reggie Jackson for the league lead. Scott led the league in RBI with 109.

Following a disappointing 1977 season, Harry Dalton became general manager. One of his first moves was to appoint Orioles pitching coach George Bamberger as manager. Pitcher Jim Slaton was traded to Detroit for Ben Oglivie, who added punch to the lineup and became an integral part of Bambi's Bombers, who amazed everyone with the fourth-best record in baseball in 1978. It's also the year the Paul Molitor, who became an instant Brewers star, was named Rookie of the Year by *The Sporting News.* Don Caldwell won 22 games (highest total in Brewers history) and was named Comeback Player of the Year. Oglivie led the team with a .303 BA while Larry Hisle paced the Brewers in HR (34) and RBI (115). Third baseman Don Money became the first Brewer ever voted to the American League All-Star team by the fans. Following the season Yount, Hisle and Molitor were named to post-season All-Star teams. Harry Dalton and George Bamberger walked off with General Manager and Manager of the Year Awards.

In 1979 the Brewers improved their record to 95 and 66 (best in club history) as Gorman Thomas fronted the league with 45 HR (still a Brewers record).

The Brewers of 1982 finally won the American League pennant after Harvey Kuenn took over as manager from Buck Rogers on June 2. Known as Harvey's Wallbangers, the Brewers had punch at every position. Yount led with a .331 BA, Thomas was tops with 39 HR, Cecil Cooper was team RBI leader with 121, and Molitor scored a club record 136 runs and led the Brewers in stolen bases with 41. Relief pitcher Rollie Fingers, who was named American League MVP in 1981, was brilliant again as he saved 29 games. Yount was American League MVP while Bill Vukovich won the Cy Young Award with an 18 and 6 record. In the World Series the Brewers lost in seven games to the St. Louis Cardinals.

In 1983 the Brewers set an all-time attendance record of 2,397,131 fans but finished a disappointing fifth in the American League Eastern Division. This was followed by seventh- and sixth-place finishes in 1984, 1985 and 1986. In 1987 pitcher Juan Nieves became the first Brewer and first Puerto Rican-born pitcher to hurl a no-hitter, while Paul Molitor batted .353—the highest mark in Brewers' history. The team won an impressive 91 games to finish third.

In 1992 Robin Yount became only the seventeenth player in major league history to record 3,000 hits when he singled off Cleveland's Jose Mesa on September 9. At 37 Yount was the third-youngest player (behind Ty Cobb and Hank Aaron) to reach the milestone. Pat Listach was named American League Rookie of the Year as he batted .290 and stole 54 bases.

The 1993 Brewers fell off badly after losing long-time star Paul Molitor to free agency. However, a new stadium is planned and, with Listach and pitcher Paul Eldrid as the nucleus, the Brewers hope to rebound into contention in the near future. Hank Aaron and Rollie Fingers are two former Brewers in the Hall of Fame while Molitor and Yount are almost certain to be named when their careers are over.

Advertising Specialties

1984 Shoey's Brown Jug Matchbook
Schedule $5

Ballpark Giveaways

1974 Cap, Jacket, T-shirt, Cushion............$5
1974 Maxwell House Photo Mug $15
1974 McDonald's Ball (if autographed
$20) $6

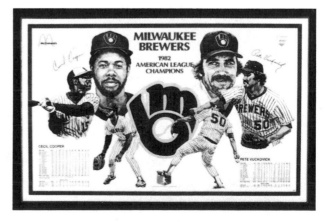

1983 McDonald's placemat, 11″ × 17″, 1982 American League champions (there were 6 placemats in the set), $6 ea.

1989 Brewers tankard, 20th anniversary, by Miller Lite and WKTI, 3½″ × 6¼″, blue and gold Brewers colors, $8.

1975 Maxwell House Photo Mug $15
1975 McDonald's Ball $6
1975 McDonald's Ball (with facsimile autographs) $15
1975 Cushion.......................................$5
1976 Cushion, Road Cap, Helmet, Jacket, Back Pack $5
1976 Maxwell House Mug.......................$13
1977 Maxwell House Mug.......................$13
1977 Red Bat $7
1977 Jacket, Helmet, Back Pack $5
1978 Wisconsin Master Charge Seat Cushion $7
1978 Maxwell House Coffee Mug $13
1978 Jacket, Sports Shorts, Coca-Cola Gym Bag...$5
1980 Pappy's Pizza Jacket, Marine Bank Helmet, Pepsi Sports Bag, Foremost Card Service Cushion, Kinney Shoes Sports Socks $7
1980 Maxwell House Coffee Mug $12
1981 Marine Bank Helmet, Foremost Card Service Cushion $6
1981 Maxwell House Coffee Mug $12
1982 Pepsi Sports Bag, Foremost Card Service Cushion, Wyler Cap $6
1982 Mountain Dew Green Bat (American League champs) $7
1983 Elan Seat Cushion, Wishbone/Lipton Visor..$6
1983 Wonder Bread Poster, Milwaukee Police Dept. Cards $12
1984 Burger King Calendar (first one) $13
1984 Pepsi Road Cap...............................$6
1984 Baseball Cards $10
1985 Milwaukee Journal Baseball Cards ...$10

1985 McDonald's Cap, Elan Cushion..........$6
1986 Roundy's/Pepsi Glove, Kool-Aid Helmet, Kool-Aid Digital Watch, Elan Cushion, Miller Lite Cooler........$6
1986 Full Set Brewers Player Cards $9
1987 Kinney Shoes Baseball Cards.............$9
1987 Kool-Aid Digital Watch, Pepsi Glove, Elan Travel Kit, Henri's Hardee's Pencil Bag, H.H. West Swingline Binder, Miller Lite 12 Pack Cooler $6
1987 Maxwell House Thermos Bottle, Miller Lite Tankard $9
1987 Team Sportraits $8
1988 Stadia Athletic Shoe Jacket, Miller Lite Cooler, Haircuts Helmet, Elan Seat Cushion $6
1988 Brewers Full Set Players Cards $8
1988 WTMJ Team Sportraits.....................$9
1988 Surf Book $10
1989 Henn's Jacket, Herrs Painter Cap, Scott Paper Glove, Pepsi/Pick 'N Save Bat, Haircuts Helmet, Elan Seat Cushion $6
1990 Henn's Jacket, Mastercard Seat Cushion, Scott Paper Glove, Looney Tunes Visor, Haircuts Helmet, Sher-Mare Sunglasses, Maxwell House Travel Mug $6
1991 Pabst Panoramic Poster $7
1991 Police Baseball Card $8
1991 Haircuts Helmet, Sher-Make Beach Towel, Miller Lite Card Book $6
1992 Milwaukee Journal/Sentinal Donruss Card Book $7
1992 Haircuts Helmet, Fuji/WTMJ Poster, Sher-Make Glove $6

1975 Graf's Cola can, 2½″ × 5″, produced for the All-Star Game at County Stadium, $10.

1993 Sher-Make Police Baseball Cards, Donruss Baseball Card Book, Sentry Foods Commemorative Baseball Cards, Pick 'N Save/Snickers Bar Cap, Sher-Make Sports Bag $5

Miscellaneous

BOBBIN' HEAD DOLLS

Category #VI, 1970, 1971, 1972, Gold Round Base, Boy Head $32

Pennants

1970 First Year $35
1971 through 1975 Regular $20
1975 All-Star Game $50
1976, 1977 Regular $20
1977 All-Star Game $50
1978, 1979, 1980 ....$20
1981, 1982 Regular $5
1982 League Champs $15
1982 World Series................................$15
1983 through 1990 ....$5
1991, 1992, 1993 ....$3

Pins

1984 Crane Potato Chips, ⅞", Round $3

Publications

BOOKS

•Everson, Jeff. *This Date in Milwaukee Brewers History.* Appleton, Wis.: Everson House, 1987. ....$7.95
Martin, Millie. *Milwaukee Brewers.* Mankato, Mn.: Creative Education, 1982. ....$5.00
Okrent, Daniel. *Nine Innings.* New York: Ticknor & Fields, 1985. Out of Print $10.00
•Olson, Don. *Bambi's Bombers: The First Time Around.* Milwaukee, Wis.: Noslo Publishing Co., 1985. ......$5.95
Rothaus, James R. *Milwaukee Brewers.* Mankato, Mn.: Creative Education, 1987. ....$5.00

MEDIA GUIDES

1970 First Year $20
1971, 1972 ....$12
1973, 1974 ....$10
1975, 1976 ....$8
1977, 1978 ....$7
1979, 1980, 1981 ....$6
1982 League Champs $8
1983, 1984 ....$5
1985 through 1993 ....$4

PROGRAMS AND SCORECARDS

1970 First Year $25
1971 through 1979 ....$6
1980, 1981 ....$4
1982 League Champs $6
1983 through 1989 ....$4
1990, 1991, 1992, 1993 ....$3

YEARBOOKS

1970 ....$50
1971 ....$10
1972 ....$8
1973 ....$6
1974 ....$5
1975 through 1981 ....$4
1982 League Champs $6
1983 through 1993 ....$3

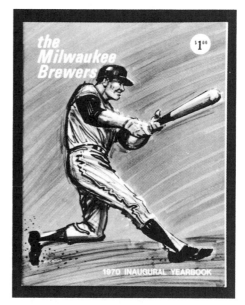

1970 Brewers inaugural yearbook, 8½" × 11", 36 pages, $50.

Schedules

1970 ....$15
1971 through 1979 ....$10
1980 through 1985 ....$2
1986 through 1993 ....$1

Special Events

ALL-STAR GAME PRESS PINS

1975 ....$100

1970 Brewers schedule, 3 fold, 2⅛″ × 3⅜″, blue and gold logo, $15.

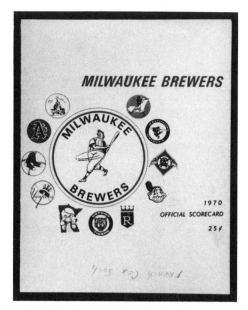

1970 Brewers scorecard, 8½″ × 11″, first game played on April 7, against the California Angels (Brewers lost to Andy Messersmith and the California Angels 12-0), $50.

ALL-STAR PROGRAMS

1975 ....$40

ALL-STAR GAME TICKETS

1975 Complete Ticket $45
1975 Ticket Stub..................................$20

LEAGUE CHAMPIONSHIP SERIES PROGRAMS

1981 Eastern Division Play-Offs (this
    program is very hard to find) $50
1982 ....$75

LEAGUE CHAMPIONSHIP SERIES GAME TICKETS

1982 Complete Ticket $28
1982 Ticket Stub..................................$15

WORLD SERIES PRESS PINS

1982 ....$75

WORLD SERIES PROGRAMS

1982 ....$15

WORLD SERIES GAME TICKETS

1982 Complete Ticket $30
1982 Ticket Stub..................................$15

Minneapolis, Minnesota

MINNESOTA TWINS

American League 1961 to Present

The Minnesota Twins were born in 1961 when the Washington Senators moved to Minnesota to represent the twin cities of Minneapolis and St. Paul. Meantime, an expansion club was awarded to Washington and retained the name Senators. The Senators had not won a American League pennant since 1933, but it took the Twins only five years to win the league championship. In 1965 the Twins, managed by Sam Mele, won 102 games, still a club record, and finished seven games in front of second-place Chicago. The Twins had a formidable offense, led by shortstop Zoilo Versalles, the American League's Most Valuable Player; league batting champion Tony Oliva (.321); and slugging third baseman Harmon Killebrew, who hit 25 home runs and drove in 75 runs despite an elbow injury that kept him out of more than 40 games. Jim "Mudcat" Grant was the American League's leading pitcher with 21 wins and only 7 losses, and he won 2 more games in the World Series against the Los Angeles Dodgers. However, the Dodgers won the exciting World Series four games to three.

The Twins won division titles in 1969 and 1970 but lost to the Baltimore Orioles both years in the American League Championship Series. In 1969 future Hall of Famer Killebrew won both the home run title (with 49) and the RBI title (with 140). Jim Perry and Dave Boswell each won 20 games for the Twins in 1969 while Perry tied for the league lead with 24 wins in 1970.

When the Twins moved to Minnesota in 1961 they played at Metropolitan Stadium in Bloomington, a suburb of Minneapolis and St. Paul approximately midway between the twin cities. During their first ten years at the Met, the Twins drew the largest total attendance in the American League (13,264,656).

However, as team success declined, attendance fell dramatically to an all-time low of 469,090 during the strike-shortened 1981 season. The Twins moved into the Metrodome, an indoor facility in downtown Minneapolis, in 1982, and attendance began to rise. The Twins were league champions in 1987 and a club record 2,081,976 watched the home games. That record fell the next season when more than three million fans passed through the gates. During the 1987 championship season, lefthander Frank Viola led the team in wins (17), earned run average (2.90), and strikeouts (197). He won one American League championship game against Detroit and then won two World Series games to defeat the St. Louis Cardinals four games to three. Offensively, the Twins were led by center fielder Kirby Puckett, who had a .332 batting average, slammed 28 home runs, and drove in 99 runs. Puckett led the Twins again in 1991 when the Twins shocked baseball by going from last in 1990 to first

and then defeated another last to first team, the Atlanta Braves, in the World Series.

Ballpark Giveaways

1968 through 1973 Bat (if any bats are dated, those prior to 1970 would be $15 and those from 1970 through 1973 $10) $5
1974 Ball (with facsimile autographs $25) $5
1975 Bat, Ball, Jacket (with facsimile autographs $25) $5
1975 Mug $20
1976 Bat, Ball, Jacket (with facsimile autographs $25) $5
1976 Mug $20
1977 Jacket, Jersey, Helmet $5
1978 Jacket, Jersey, Helmet, Halter Top $5
1979 Jacket, Helmet, Halter Top, Jogging Shorts...$5
1980 Dairy Queen Jacket, Coca-Cola Shirt, Burger King Helmet.................$6
1980 Stocking Cap $5
1981 Gillette Gift Pack, Gulf Visor.............$6
1981 Jacket, Helmet $5
1982 Brown Photo & Fuji Film Helmet, Dairy Queen Jacket, Dayton's Visor, Totino's Gym Bag $6
1982 Cap...$5
1989 McDonald's/Coca-Cola Helmet, Dairy Queen Cap, Schmidt's Beach Towel, Wheaties Glove, Berkeley Tackle Box, Scott Paper Jersey,

1989 "Relief Pitcher," 7½" × 9¼", red and blue lettering on white with a red top, sponsored by the American Dairy Association, $7.

Kinney Shoes Sports Socks, Henri's
Back Pack $6
1989 American Dairy Assn. Relief Pitcher ...$7
1991 Super American Magnet Schedule,
Bud Lite Gym Bag, Wheaties Bat,
Kinney's Socks, Dairy Queen Cap $6
1991 Special Export Light 30th Anniver-
sary Poster $10
1991 Special Export Light Mug $8
1991 Donruss Card Book $7
1992 Pepsi Magnet Schedule, Dairy
Queen Cap, Budweiser Gym Bag,
American Dairy Assn. BBQ Apron,
Target/Berkeley/Plano Tackle Box,
St. Paul Book & Stationary 3 Ring
Binder, Michelob Ski Cap..................$6
1992 Upper Deck Cards, Donruss Card
Book $7
1992 Special Export Commemorative
Poster, Special Export Tankard $7
1992 Josten's Championship Ring $10
1993 Pepsi Magnet Schedule, Dairy
Queen Cap, Cost Cutters Bat, Ga-
torade Batting Glove & Wrist Band,
American Dairy Assn. Spatula, Su-
per America Book Cover, Michelob
Sports Bag $6
1993 Upper Deck Cards, Special Export
Tankard $7
1993 Chevrolet Autograph Ball $10

Miscellaneous

BOBBIN' HEAD DOLLS

Category #I, 1961, Blue Square Base, Boy
Head $32
Category #II, 1961, 1962, White Square
Base, Boy Head $285
Category #III, 1961, 1962, White Round
Miniature, Boy Head $180
Category #IV, 1962, 1963, 1964, Green
Round Base, Boy Head $50
Category #V, 1962, 1963, 1964, Green
Round Base, Black Player $1,550
Category #VI, 1967 through 1972, Gold
Round Base, Boy Head $60

Pennants

1961 First Year $40
1962 through 1965 Regular $30

1965 All-Star Game $75
1965 League Champs $75
1965 World Series................................$75
1966, 1967, 1968, 1969 Regular $30
1969 League Champs $75
1970 Regular $30
1970 League Champs $75
1971 through 1980 ....$20
1981 through 1985 Regular $5
1985 All-Star Game $15
1986, 1987 Regular $5
1987 World Champs $15
1988, 1989, 1990 ....$5
1991 Regular $3
1991 League Champs $10
1991 World Champs $10
1992, 1993 ....$3

Pins

1961 through 1965 Crane Potato Chips,
⅞", Round $5
1967, 1968, 1969 Crane Potato Chips, ⅞",
Round $5
1984 Crane Potato Chips, ⅞", Round $3
1964, 1965, 1966 Guy's Potato Chips, ⅞",
Round $5

1991 pin, 6", No. 9765 of 30,000, 1991 American
League champs (the Twins became world champions
by defeating the Atlanta Braves 4 games to 3), $8.

1962, pennant, 4¾" × 14½",
Bazooka Gum, $35.

Postcards

1983 CH, Minnesota Twins (part of team
    Picture Pack) $5
1986 CH, Minnesota Twins (part of team
    Picture Pack) $5

Publications

BOOKS

Hall, Halsey. *Minnesota Twins Base-*
ball Fun. Station WCCO, 1967. ....$10.00
Mona, Dave & Jarzyna, Dave. *25 Sea-*
sons: The First Quarter Century
Century of the Minnesota Twins.
Minneapolis: Mona, 1986. ....$10.00
Morlock, Bill & Rick Little. *Split Dou-*
bleheader: An Unauthorized His-
tory of the Minnesota Twins.
Brooklyn Center, Mn., 1979. ....$15.00

MEDIA GUIDES

1961 First Year $50
1962, 1963, 1964 ....$30
1965 League Champs $32
1966 ....$20
1967, 1968 ....$17
1969, 1970 Division Champs $20
1971, 1972 ....$12
1973, 1974 ....$10
1975, 1976 ....$8
1977, 1978 ....$7
1979, 1980, 1981 ....$6
1982, 1983, 1984 ....$5

1993 media guide, 4¼″ × 9″, 320 pages, star outfielder Kirby Puckett on the cover, $4.

1985, 1986 ....$4
1987 World Champs $6
1988, 1989, 1990 ....$4
1991 World Champs $6
1992, 1993 ....$4

PROGRAMS AND SCORECARDS

1961 First Year $35
1962 ....$15
1963, 1964 ....$10
1965 League Champs $12
1966, 1967, 1968 ....$7
1969 Division Champs $10
1970 Division Champs $10
1971, 1972, 1973 ....$6
1974, 1975, 1976 ....$5
1977 through 1986 ....$4
1987 World Champs $6
1988, 1989, 1990 ....$4
1991 World Champs $6
1992, 1993 ....$3

YEARBOOKS

1961 First Year $185
1962 ....$95
1963 ....$85
1964 ....$75
1965 League Champs $80
1966, 1967 ....$60
1968 ....$50
1969 Division Champs $55
1970 Division Champs $50
1971, 1972 ....$30
1973 ....$25
1974 ....$20
1975, 1976 ....$15
1977, 1978 ....$12
1979, 1980 ....$10
1981, 1982 ....$8
1983, 1984 ....None Issued
1985, 1986 ....$6
1987 World Champs $7
1988, 1989, 1990 ....$5
1991 World Champs $6
1992 ....$5
1993 ....$10

Schedules

1961 First Year $20
1962 through 1969 ....$15
1970 through 1979 ....$10
1980 through 1985 ....$2
1986 through 1993 ....$1

Special Events

ALL-STAR GAME PRESS PINS

1965 ....$200
1985 ....$75

1970 Twins schedule, 2¾″ × 5″, $15.

1985 program, 8½″ × 11¼″, 50 pages, All-Star game at Metropolitan Stadium in Bloomington, $15.

ALL-STAR PROGRAMS

1965 ....$75
1985 ....$15

ALL-STAR GAME TICKETS

1965 Complete Ticket $70
1965 Ticket Stub...................................$35
1985 Complete Ticket $30
1985 Ticket Stub...................................$15

LEAGUE CHAMPIONSHIP SERIES PROGRAMS

1969 ....$35
1970 ....$30
1987 ....$6
1991 ....$5

LEAGUE CHAMPIONSHIP GAME TICKETS

1969 Complete Ticket $65
1969 Ticket Stub...................................$30
1970 Complete Ticket $35
1970 Ticket Stub...................................$15
1987 Complete Ticket $35
1987 Ticket Stub...................................$15
1991 Complete Ticket $18
1991 Ticket Stub...................................$10

WORLD SERIES PRESS PINS

1965 ....$200
1987 ....$40
1991 ....$30

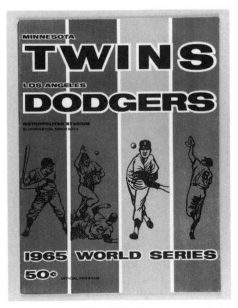

1965 program, 8¼″ × 11¼″, 48 pages, Twins first World Series (they lost to the Los Angeles Dodgers 4 games to 3), $75.

WORLD SERIES PROGRAMS

1965	$75
1987	$12
1991	$10

WORLD SERIES GAME TICKETS

1965 Complete Ticket	$100
1965 Ticket Stub	$50

1987 Complete Ticket	$30
1987 Ticket Stub	$15
1991 Complete Ticket	$20
1991 Ticket Stub	$10

Montreal, Quebec, Canada

MONTREAL EXPOS

National League 1969 to Present

The Montreal Expos, founded in 1969 as a National League expansion team, have the distinction of being Canada's first major league baseball club. Original owners Charles Bronfman, Huch Hallward and Lorne Webster saw the team finish last its first two years and languish in the second division most of its first ten years. Then in 1979 the Expos finished second in the National League Eastern Division under manager Dick Williams and wound up second again in 1980. In the strike-shortened 1981 season, the Expos finished first during the second half of the season but bowed to the Philadelphia Phillies in the division play-offs. Those three consecutive years as Eastern Division contenders proved to be the high-water mark in franchise history. In 1991 the original owners sold the Expos to a limited partnership of 13 Canadian investors.

Although a National League pennant has proved elusive through the 1992 season, the Expos have had their share of stars. The first was Rusty Staub, nicknamed "Le Grande Orange", because of this flaming red hair. Staub was Montreal's lone All-Star during their first three seasons. Catcher Gary Carter came along in 1975 and immediately established himself as one of the game's best, participating in All-Star games in 1975, 1979, and 1980 through 1984. Outfielder Tim Raines, who played with the Expos from 1979 through 1980, was like Carter a seven-time All-Star; outfielder Andre Dawson was a three-time All-Star; and former third baseman Tim Wallach was a five-time National League All-Star.

The most successful pitcher in Expos history is righthander five-time All-Star Steve Rodgers, who won 158 games (nearly twice the 81 victories of runner-up Bryn Smith. Ross Grimsley is the Expos' only 20-game winner, notching 20 victories in 1978. With 152 saves Jeff Reardon is the team's most successful relief pitcher and a two-time All-Star; Dennis Martinez, a three-time All-Star and the first major leaguer in history born in Nicaragua, hurled the team's only perfect game against the Los Angeles Dodgers on July 28, 1991.

Olympic Stadium, erected for the 1976 Olympic Games, has been home to the Expos since the start of the 1977 season. Prior to that the Expos performed in Jarry Park, which seated less than 30,000 fans. The largest crowd in Expos history is 59,282, which turned out for a doubleheader against the St. Louis Cardinals on September 16, 1979. The all-time season attendance mark is 2,320,651 in 1983.

Thus far no Hall of Famer has graced the Expos lineup. Some of the Expos' stars previously mentioned could receive Hall of Fame recognition in the future.

Miscellaneous

BOBBIN' HEAD DOLLS

Category #VI, 1969 through 1972, Gold Round Base, Boy Head $27

Pennants

1969 First Year $35
1970 ....$30
1971 through 1980 ....$20
1981, 1982 ....$5
1982 All-Star Game $15
1983 through 1990 ....$5
1991, 1992, 1993 ....$3

Pins

1969 Crane Potato Chips, ⅞″, Round $5
1984 Crane Potato Chips, ⅞″, Round $5

1969 pin, 1¾″, Expos first season, red, white, and
blue logo on a white field, $10.

Publications

BOOKS

Connor, Floyd. *Day-By-Day In Mon-
treal Expos History.* West Point,
N.Y.: Leisure Press, 1984. ....$5.00
Humber, William. *Cheering for the
Home Team: The Story of Baseball
in Canada.* Erin, Ont.: Boston
Mills Press, 1983. ....$20.00
Rothaus, James R. *Montreal Expos.*
Mankato, Mn.: Creative Educa-
tion, 1987. ....$5.00
Snyder, Bob. *The Year the Expos
Almost Won the Pennant.* Toronto:
Virgo, 1979. ....$10.00

MEDIA GUIDES

1969 First Year $50
1970 ....$15
1971, 1972 ....$12
1973, 1974 ....$10
1975, 1976 ....$8
1977, 1978 ....$7
1979, 1980, 1981 ....$6

1993 media guide, 4½″ × 9″, 298 pages, $4.

1982, 1983, 1984 ....$5
1985 through 1993 ....$4

PROGRAMS AND SCORECARDS

1969 First Year $30
1970 through 1979 ....$6
1980 through 1989 ....$4
1990, 1991, 1992, 1993 ....$3

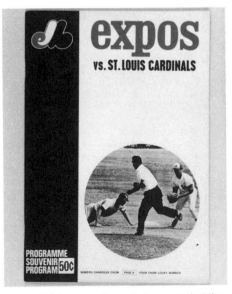

1969 official program, Expos first game against the
St. Louis Cardinals on April 14, 62 pages,
6¾″ × 10″, $50.

1969 full ticket, Expos first game on April 14, against St. Louis, 2½" × 7½", $100.

YEARBOOKS

1969 First Year $100
1970 ....$70
1971 ....$50
1972 ....$50
1973 through 1981 ....None Issued
1982 ....$8
1983 ....$7
1984, 1985, 1986 ....$6
1987 through 1993 ....None Issued

Schedules

1969 First Year $25
1970 through 1979 ....$10
1980 through 1985 ....$2
1986 through 1993 ....$1

Special Events

ALL-STAR GAME PRESS PINS

1982 ....$50

ALL-STAR GAME TICKETS

1982 Complete Ticket $30
1982 Ticket Stub..................................$15

LEAGUE CHAMPIONSHIP SERIES PROGRAMS

1981 National League Division Play-Off $75

LEAGUE CHAMPIONSHIP GAME TICKETS

1981 Complete Ticket $28
1981 Ticket Stub..................................$15

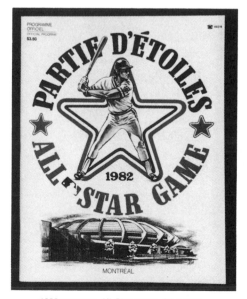

1982 program, All-Star game, 84 pages, 8½" × 11", $25.

1981 program, 8¼" × 11", 46 pages, $75.

Newark, New Jersey

NEWARK PEPPERS

Federal League 1915

Newark, New Jersey's one-season fling as a major league city was brought about when the Federal League, anxious for another team in the New York City area, moved the 1914 champion Indianapolis Hoosiers to the New Jersey metropolis. Oklahoma oil millionaire Harry Sinclair purchased the Indianapolis franchise, which despite winning the pennant, was not a financial success.

Sinclair hastily constructed a ballpark in the Newark suburb of Harrison for slightly more than $100,000 and renamed the team the Newark Peppers. Although the Peppers inherited most of the players from the Indianapolis champions, there was one glaring exception. Benny Kauff, called the Ty Cobb of the Federal League, went to Brooklyn to bolster the franchise there. Kauff had led the league and the Hoosiers with a .366 BA and was sorely missed in Newark.

Although they were in the thick of the pennant race right up to the final weeks of the season, the Peppers finished fifth, five and one-half games behind the champion Chicago Whales.

Future Hall of Famer Edd Roush, in only his third season of a brilliant 18-year career in the majors, batted .298 to lead the Peppers. Ed Reulbach, former National League champion Chicago Cubs pitching hero in 1906 through 1908 and 1910, was the Peppers leader with a 21 and 10 record.

Third baseman Bill McKechnie replaced Bill Phillips as manager after 53 games and began what turned out to be a 25-year big league managerial career which culminated with election to the Hall of Fame in 1962.

Although the roof at Peppers Park was not yet complete when it opened on April 16, an enormous crowd of approximately 30,000 fans was on hand for Newark's first major league game. One unique feature of the park was a bicycle track which surrounded the playing field, as bicycle races were an added inducement to attract more customers.

The 1915 season was the last for the Federal League, and with its demise went Newark's status as a major league baseball city.

Postcards

1915 3½″ × 5½″, Color Pre-Linen (PL) Postcard, PL by M. Seidl, Newark, N.J., showing interior of Newark Federal League grounds taken from right centerfield toward home plate $500

Publications

PROGRAMS AND SCORECARDS

1915 Program from Newark Peppers Federal League Team's initial season $450

New Haven, Connecticut

NEW HAVEN ELM CITIES

National Association 1875

New Haven, Connecticut, was represented in the National Association by the Elm Cities in 1875. Managed by Charley Gould of the famous Cincinnati Red Stockings of 1869, New Haven recorded only 7 wins and 40 losses to finish ninth out of 13 teams in the National Association's final season. Manager Gould also played first base and batted .252. Outfielder Johnny Ryan, who had played previously with Philadelphia and Baltimore, batted only .150 while center fielder Jim Tipper had even less success with a .147 BA. It was obvious from the start that the Elm Cities were overmatched in most of their games.

Eight hundred fans came out for the first championship game in New Haven history on a cold and windy April 21, and Boston defeated the Elm Cities 14 to 3. Righthander Tricky Nichols took the loss for New Haven, one of 28 he would sustain that season along with four wins. Nichols did manage to pitch five seasons in the National League and American Association, but his best record was 18 and 23 with St. Louis in 1877.

In early June the Elm Cities signed George Latham to bolster their feeble attack, but the former Boston player only batted .183 for New Haven. To add to the club's woes, Latham, along with teammates Billy Geer and Henry Luff, were expelled from the team for detrimental conduct. Latham, whose nickname was "Juice," had a drinking problem while the others were arrested in Syracuse during an exhibition contest for stealing a suit of clothes and gold watch from a guest at the hotel where the team was staying. Because of financial problems the team was unable to make a western swing late in the season.

This was New Haven's first and only season in the major leagues. The National Association disbanded after the 1875 season and the stronger teams formed the nucleus of the National League in 1876.

New Haven memorabilia for their lone major league season would be extremely rare. Collectors seeking this material should focus on scorecards and photographs.

New York, New York

NEW YORK GIANTS

National League 1883–1957, Players League 1890

Although the New York Giants moved to San Francisco following the 1957 season, they enjoyed exceptional success during their long tenure in New York. The small-town Troy franchise was moved from up-state New York following the 1882 season to take advantage of America's largest city.

Even the presence of four future Hall of Famers, first baseman Roger Connor, pitcher-outfielder Monty Ward, pitcher Mickey Welch, and catcher Buck Ewing couldn't elevate them higher than sixth place in the eight-team league. Throughout history, no franchise has provided the

Baseball Hall of Fame with more members than the Giants.

Originally called the Gothams, they became known as the Giants in 1885 when they had a preponderance of big burly players and the nickname stuck. Under manager Jim Mutrie, the Giants won back-to-back championships in 1888 and 1889. By now Hall of Famers pitcher Tim Keefe and outfielder Jim O'Rourke had joined Connor, Ward, Welch and Ewing to boost the Giants to the top.

The Giants floundered for a number of years thereafter until the sparkplug of the mighty Baltimore Orioles of the 1890s, John McGraw, became manager of the Giants in midseason of 1902. He jumped from Baltimore, where he was managing the American League Orioles, and brought Hall of Fame pitcher Joe McGinnity along with him.

Although he played a few games each season with the Giants through 1906, it was as their innovative manager that McGraw made his biggest impact. Christy Mathewson, who had been with the Giants since 1900, really blossomed under the tutelage of McGraw and pitching coach Wilbert Robinson, another ex-Oriole Hall of Famer. In 1904 Mathewson became the National League's premier pitcher by winning 34 games and giving McGraw his first championship in New York. McGinnity won 33 games as the Giants recorded 106 victories and finished 13 games in front of second-place Chicago. Giants owner John Brush and McGraw refused to play the defending world champion Boston Puritans in the World Series, so their championship was somewhat tainted. They made amends in 1905 when they repeated as National League champs and demolished the Philadelphia Athletics in the World Series as Mathewson pitched three shutouts and McGinnity one. Chief Bender pitched a shutout for Philadelphia's only win, the first and only time in World Series history that every game ended in a shutout. During the 1905 season Mathewson again led the league with 32 victories while Red Ames won 22 and McGinnity 21. Catcher Roger Bresnahan, another Hall of Famer, was the lone Giant to hit above .300 and ended the season at .302.

Great players would come and go, but McGraw always had the knack of getting the maximum out of his teams. It was six years before the Giants won another pennant, but starting in 1911 they won three in a row. By this time McGinnity was gone but another Hall of Famer, Rube Marquard, took his place and paced the Giants with 25 wins while Mathewson chipped in with 24. In the 1911 World Series, Philadelphia avenged 1905 by winning four games to two. The 1912 and 1913 Giants also lost in the World Series, bowing to Boston in seven games and Philadelphia in five respectively. In 1912 Marquard led the league with 27 wins while Mathewson won 23; in 1913 Mathewson won 25, Marquard 24 and Jeff Tesreau 22. Pitching was always the strong suit of the Giants under McGraw, particularly in the early years.

However, in 1921, 1922 and 1923, when the Giants were again National League champs, it was hitting that dominated as future Hall of Famers Frankie Frisch, Dave Bancroft, George Kelly, Casey Stengel and Ross Youngs propelled the Giants. During those three championship seasons, only Art Nehf was a 20-game winner (1921). Making victory even sweeter, in 1921 and 1922 the Giants beat the Yankees and Babe Ruth in the World Series.

By this time the home run-slugging Ruth was the most popular figure in baseball, and the Yankees outdrew the Giants at the Polo Grounds, which was home to both teams.

At the Giants' insistence, the Yankees built their own park across the Harlem River. Yankee Stadium opened in 1923 as both teams again won league championships. This time it was the Yankees who won the World Series as Ruth batted .368, scored eight runs and drove in three.

The Giants made it four pennants in a row in 1924 but lost to the Washington Senators in the World Series. It would be McGraw's last pennant. When the Giants won again in 1933, it was player-manager Bill Terry who led the way with a .322 BA. Rightfielder Mel Ott, another player destined for the Hall of Fame, topped the Giants with 23 HR and 103 RBI. King Carl Hubbell was the league's top pitcher with 23 wins and a league best 1.66 ERA on the road to baseball enshrinement. In the 1933 World Series, the Giants beat Washington four games to one; Hubbell won twice.

Terry, Hubbell and Ott were still

around in 1936 and 1937 when the Giants won two more pennants, although in 1937 Terry was only managing. They lost both years in the World Series to the New York Yankees.

The Giants won another pennant in 1951, and it took a dramatic home run by Bobby Thompson off Brooklyn's Ralph Branca in a one-game playoff to get them to the World Series. Sal Maglie and Larry Jansen tied for the league lead with 23 wins while future Hall of Famers Monte Irvin and rookie Willie Mays were offensive stars. Irvin led the league with 121 RBI while batting .312, fifth best in the league. Mays had 20 HR and drove in 68 runs in his first major league season. In the World Series, the Giants lost to the Yankees in six games.

Leo Durocher was managing the Giants when they won again in 1954, but they were decided underdogs against the Cleveland Indians in the World Series. Cleveland had set an American League record with 111 wins and were overwhelming favorites to crush the Giants.

New York's National Association (1871–1875) team was known as the Mutuals. Their 1883–1887 American Association team was nicknamed the Metropolitans.

However, in the eighth inning of a deadlocked first game, centerfielder Willie Mays made what has been described as the finest catch in World Series' history. Mays robbed Vic Wertz of at least a double that would have scored two runs to give Cleveland the win. Instead, pinch-hitter Dusty Rhodes slammed a three-run homer in the tenth-inning to win for the Giants, who went on to sweep the Indians in four straight.

Mays led the Giants during the regular season with a league-best .345 BA while hitting 41 home runs and driving in 110 runs.

The neighborhood around the Polo Grounds was in rapid decline and attendance fell off dramatically over the next few seasons. Hence, when Dodgers owner Walter O'Malley suggested to Giants owner Horace Stoneham that he join him in a move west, Stoneham moved to San Francisco following the 1957 season while the Dodgers took up residence in Los Angeles. Financially the deal made sense, but it broke the hearts of many loyal Giants fans who had the pleasure of watching some of the finest players in baseball history represent New York. In addition to those Hall of Famers already mentioned, the following also played at least part of their careers with the New York Giants: Travis Jackson, Fred Lindstrom, Johnny Mize, Amos Rusie and Hoyt Wilhelm.

Advertising Specialties

1886 New York League Baseball Club, Lorillard Team Card, 4″ × 5″ $1,500
1913 New York Nationals, T200 Fatima Team Card, 2⅝″ × 4¾″ $125
1934 R309-1 Goudey Premiums, New York Giants 1933 World Champs.....$350

Miscellaneous

1888 New York Ball Club with Tuxedos, Joseph Hall Cabinets Team Card, 6½″ × 4½″ $2,200

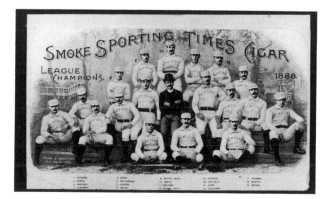

1888 Sporting Times Cigar label, black and white, 4½″ × 7″, National League champions, $1,500.

1950s Knickerbocker Beer coaster, 3¼″ × 3¼″, promoting Giants broadcasts over WMCA radio and telecasts over WPIX-TV, $15.

1929 sterling silver season pass to Giants home games at the Polo Grounds, $300.

1951 New York Giants Exhibit Supply
   Company Team Card $12
1954 New York Giants Exhibit Supply
   Company Team Card $12

Pennants

1900 through 1920   ....$750
1921 through 1930   ....$300
1931, 1932, 1933 Regular......................$200
1933 World Series $400
1934, 1935, 1936 Regular......................$200
1936 World Series $400
1936, 1937 New York Giants Felt Pen-
   nant-BF3, Type IV, Two Players on
   pennant $35
1936, 1937 New York Giants Felt Pen-
   nant-BF3, Type IV, Player standing
   by base on pennant $35
1937 Regular $200
1937 World Series $400
1938, 1939, 1940   ....$200
1941 through 1950   ....$100
1951 Regular......................................$50
1951 World Series $125
1952, 1953, 1954 Regular $50
1954 World Series $125
1955, 1956, 1957   ....$50

Pins

1930/1940s American Nut & Chocolate
   Co., 1⅛″ $15

Postcards

1903 PL, Photo by Falk, New York, N.Y....$750
1904 PL, The Rotograph Co., New York,
   N.Y..$500
1905 PL, Sepia, J.T. Dye, New York, N.Y.,
   6 Giant Players with large letters
   spelling Giants $200
1905 PL, Color, Copyright J.T. Dye, Pub.
   Souvenir Postcard Co., New York,
   N.Y..$150

1940s–1950s pennant, white lettering on blue background, player sliding, which was typical of pennants produced for all teams during this era, $100.

1950s generic pin, crossed bats above team name, produced for all Major League teams during this era (this style has been reproduced), $15.

1903 photographic postcard by Falk, 3½″ × 5½″, New York Giants, believed to be the earliest postcard showing a Major League team (taken on the grand staircase at the Waldorf Astoria Hotel in New York City), this was Manager John McGraw's first full season at the Giants helm, $750.

Publications

BOOKS

Dexter, Charles. *Thrilling True Story of the Baseball Giants.* Fawcett Publishing Co., 1952. ....$35.00
Graham, Frank. *The New York Giants.* G.P. Putnam's Sons, 1952. ....$50.00

Jennison, Christopher. *Wait Till Next Year: The Yankees, Dodgers, and Giants 1947–1957.* New York: W.W. Norton, 1974. ....$25.00
Kiernan, Thomas. *The Miracle at Coogan's Bluff.* New York: Crowell, 1975 ....$15.00
Stein, Fred. *Under Coogan's Bluff.* Glyndon, Md.: Chapter & Cash, 1981. ....$10.00
Stein, Fred & Nick Peters. *Day-By-Day in Giants History.* West Point, N.Y.: Leisure Press, 1984. ....$10.00

MEDIA GUIDES

1927 Roster Booklet.............................$150
1928 through 1932 Roster Booklet $100
1933 World Champs Roster Booklet $125
1954, 1935 Roster Booklet $100
1936, 1937 League Champs each Year $85
1938, 1939, 1940 ....$75
1941 through 1949 ....$60
1950 ....$50
1951 League Champs $55
1952, 1953 ....$50
1954 World Champs...............................$60
1955 ....$50
1956, 1957 ....$40

1927, roster guide for training season, 4″ × 9″, one of the first published in this form, $150.

PROGRAMS AND SCORECARDS

1900, 1901, 1902 ....$400
1903, 1904 ....$300
1905 World Champs $250
1906 through 1909 ....$200

1910	$150
1911, 1912, 1913 League Champs each Year	$160
1914	$150
1915, 1916	$125
1917 League Champs	$135
1918, 1919, 1920	$125
1921, 1922 World Champs each Year	$85
1923, 1924 League Champs each Year	$80
1925	$75
1926 through 1930	$50
1931, 1932	$35
1933 World Champs	$45
1934, 1935	$55
1936, 1937 League Champs each Year	$40
1938, 1939, 1940	$35
1941 through 1949	$20
1950	$15
1951 League Champs	$18
1952, 1953	$15
1954 World Champs	$18
1955, 1956, 1957	$15

YEARBOOKS

1887 *Sketches of the New York Baseball Club* by June Rankin	$2,500
1888 *Sketches of the New York & Brooklyn Baseball Clubs* by June Rankin	$2,500

1947, *The Giants of New York* by Gary Schumacher, considered the first modern Giants yearbook, includes a club history and profiles of the 1947 team, 9″ × 12″, 64 pages, $200.

1889 *Complimentary Testimonial to the Champions* by Digby Bell, DeWolff Hopper & J. Barton Key (player sketches of 1889 N.Y. Giants)	$2,500
1947 *The Giants of New York* by Gary Schumacher, "First Year"	$200
1948, 1949, 1950	None Issued
1951	$150
1952	$125
1953, 1954	$100
1955, 1956, 1957	$75

Schedules

1900 through 1909	$150
1910 through 1919	$100
1920 through 1929	$75
1930 through 1939	$45
1940 through 1949	$30
1950 through 1957	$25

Special Events

ALL-STAR GAME PRESS PINS

1934	None Issued
1942	None Issued

1889–1890 testimonial to the champion New York Giants on October 20, 1889, at the Broadway Theater, 6¾″ × 9½″, 28 pages, features photographs of the players and review of the championship season, $2,500.

ALL-STAR PROGRAMS

1934	$1,500
1942	$1,000

ALL-STAR GAME TICKETS

1934 Complete Ticket	$400
1934 Ticket Stub	$200
1942 Complete Ticket	$200
1942 Ticket Stub	$100

WORLD SERIES PRESS PINS

1905	None Issued
1911	None Issued
1912	$6,500
1913	$5,000
1917	$4,000
1921	$1,500
1922	$1,500
1923	$1,500
1924	$1,500
1933	$1,200
1936	$1,200
1937	$1,200
1951	$300
1954	$200

1917	$2,000
1921	$1,500
1922	$1,500
1923	$1,500
1924	$1,100
1933	$700
1936	$400
1937	$350
1951	$225
1954	$200

1912 World Series program, Brush Stadium-Polo Grounds, Giants vs. Red Sox, 9¼" × 11", 16 pages, $3,000.

1912 press pin, manufactured by Whitehead and Hoag for the games at Brush Stadium-Polo Grounds, 3½" in length, pendant shows a huge batter and the words New York Giants vs. Boston Red Sox (the Red Sox won the series in 7 games), $6,500.

WORLD SERIES PROGRAMS

1905	$7,000
1911	$3,000
1912	$3,000
1913	$2,000

WORLD SERIES GAME TICKETS

1905 Complete Ticket	$2,500
1905 Ticket Stub	$1,200
1911 Complete Ticket	$1,600
1911 Ticket Stub	$800
1912 Complete Ticket	$1,600
1912 Ticket Stub	$800
1913 Complete Ticket	$1,600
1913 Ticket Stub	$800
1917 Complete Ticket	$1,200
1917 Ticket Stub	$600
1921 Complete Ticket	$800
1921 Ticket Stub	$400
1922 Complete Ticket	$800
1922 Ticket Stub	$400
1923 Complete Ticket	$800
1923 Ticket Stub	$400
1924 Complete Ticket	$800
1924 Ticket Stub	$400
1933 Complete Ticket	$400
1933 Ticket Stub	$200

1936 Complete Ticket $400
1936 Ticket Stub $200
1937 Complete Ticket $400
1937 Ticket Stub $200
1951 Complete Ticket $150
1951 Ticket Stub $75
1954 Complete Ticket $150
1954 Ticket Stub $75

NEW YORK METS

National League 1962 to Present

In their first season as a National League expansion team, the 1962 New York Mets were arguably the worst team in modern baseball history, with a record of 40 wins and 120 losses. With Casey Stengel managing a collection of castoffs and "never will bes," the Mets somehow caught the fancy of fans who were starved for the return of National League baseball to New York. Despite the abysmal record, more than 922,000 fans turned out that first season to watch them play at the Polo Grounds, a park 40 years past its prime that was abandoned by the New York Giants when they moved to San Francisco in 1957.

Modern Shea Stadium was opened in 1964 and the Mets' fortunes slowly began to rise. A total of 1,732,597 fans turned out that first season at Shea despite another last-place finish.

The hapless Mets became the Amazing Mets in 1969 when Gil Hodges, in only his second season as Mets manager, led them to the National League pennant and World Series championship. Mets home attendance exceeded two million for the first time in 1969, and a club record 3,017,724 fans came to Shea Stadium in 1988.

Pitching has been the Mets' strong suit ever since Tom Seaver burst on the scene in 1967 to win 16 games in his rookie season. By 1969, when the Mets won their first championship, Seaver was the best pitcher in baseball and posted a 24–7 record. Lefthander Jerry Koosman, who also joined the Mets in 1967, won 17 games during the 1969 season and complimented Seaver exceptionally well. Koosman's 140 wins as a Met is second only to Seaver's 198. Many forget that Nolan Ryan, baseball's all-time strikeout king, began his career with the Mets and recorded a save in the third game of the 1969 World Series against the Orioles. Ryan struck out three in two-and-one-third innings.

Seaver and Koosman were still the pitching aces in 1973 when the Mets won their second pennant. Seaver captured his second Cy Young award as the league's best pitcher but the Mets lost to the Oakland A's in the World Series.

Continuing the Mets tradition of pitching excellence, righthander Dwight "Dr. K" Gooden joined the team in 1984 and was National League Rookie of the Year. In 1985, at 20 years of age, he became the youngest pitcher to win the Cy Young award. When the Mets won the pennant and World Series in 1986, Gooden became the first pitcher to record 200 or more strikeouts in his first three major league seasons.

Ballpark Giveaways

1978 Mets Photo Album $15
1980 Batting Helmet, Banner, Kids
     Jacket, Adult Jacket...........................$5
1981 Kahn's Stadium Cushion $5
1981 Team Picture, Major Memories
     Posters 1, 2, 3 ....$10
1982 Calendar, Thermal Mug, Photo Al-
     bum, Team Picture $10
1982 Seat Cushion $5
1983 Mets Calendar, Budweiser Tan-
     kard, Torn Apple Valley Team Pic-
     ture (N.L. champs) $10
1983 Yago Cushion $5
1984 Calendar $9

1990s Mets bumper sticker, produced by radio station WFAN to promote a Sports Sticker contest, 3¼″ × 11″, $5.

1984 Bat, Sports Watch $5
1985 Calendar $9
1985 Picnic Bag, Poncho...........................$5
1986 Calendar, Tankard $9
1986 Umbrella, Helmet, Windbreaker
      (world champs) $5
1987 Calendar $8
1987 Championship Ring $15
1987 Sports Bag, Watch, Cooler, Tote
      Bag, Batting Helmet $5
1988 Surf Book $15
1988 Calendar $7
1988 Ladies Tote Bag, Wallet, Sports
      Watch, Kids Jersey $5
1988 Thermos Mug, Relief Pitcher $6
1989 Armitron 1969 Yearbook, Gatorade
      Relief Pitcher, Pergament Poster,
      Snapper Calendar, Lincoln Mercury
      Magical Moment Post, Kahn's Base-
      ball Cards $7
1989 Smokey the Bear Helmet, Kahn's
      Jersey, Tropicana Glove, Met Life
      Beach Towel, Foot Locker Socks,
      Headstart Baseball Cap, Sharp Gar-
      ment Bag, RC Cola Sports Bag,
      Maybelline Cosmetic Bag $6
1989 Starter Wristband, Snapper Um-
      brella $6
1989 Ski Cap, Travel Bag $5
1990 Kahn Baseball Cards $7
1990 Sharpe Electronis Pins 1, 2, 3, 4 ....ea. $7
1990 N.Y. Lottery Calendar, Looney
      Tunes Visor, MHT Helmet, Starter
      Wrist Bank, Foot Locker Socks,
      Kahn Kids Jersey, Amaco Sun-
      glasses, R.C. Cola Sports Bag, Don-
      russ Card Book, Emerson Radio
      Banner $6
1991 Upper Deck Cards $7
1991 Wiz Commerative Cards 1, 2, 3 ....ea. $7
1991 Manchester Calendar, Tony the Ti-
      ger Dish, Kahn Kids T-shirt, R.C.
      Cola Sports Bag, MHT/Mastercard
      Wallet, Gatorade Relief, Pitcher,
      Foot Locker Socks, Sharp Travel
      Bag, Met Life Beach Towel,
      Emerson Radio Banner, Starter
      Head & Wrist Band, Tropicana
      Watch, Carvel Glove.........................$6
1992 Kahn's Baseball Cards, Upper Deck
      Heros of Baseball, Donruss Base-
      ball Book $7
1992 Wiz 30th Anniversary Team Picture
      Card Set $8
1992 Stroehmann Calendar, Coca-Cola
      Beach Towel, Sports Bottle, Carvel
      Glove, Kahn's T-shirt, Met Life
      Sports Bag, Sharpe Thermos,
      Emerson Radio Banner, Lincoln/
      Mercury Back Pack $8
1993 Chemical Bank Pin 1, 2 ....ea. $7
1993 Kahn's Baseball Cards, Upper Deck
      Heros of Baseball, Donruss Card
      Book $7
1993 Coca-Cola Calendar, Wiz Relief

1981 Mets Nostalgia Album, given away at Shea Stadium on April 18th and 19th, contains the history of the Mets, sponsored by Getty Oil, 32 pages, 8¼″ × 11″, $20.

Pitcher, Carvel Baseball, Chemical
Bank Beach Towel, Sharpe Adult
Jersey, Met Life Sports Ball, Wiz
Photo Album $6

Miscellaneous

BOBBIN' HEAD DOLLS

Category #II, 1962, White Square Base,
      Boy Head $275
Category #III, 1962, White Round
      Miniature, Boy Head $325
Category #IV, 1962, 1963, 1964, Green
      Round Base, Boy Head $60
Category #V, 1962, 1963, 1964, Green
      Round Base, Black Player $350
Category #VI, 1967 through 1972, Gold
      Round Base, Boy Head $60

Pennants

1962, 1963, 1964 Regular $30
1964 All-Star Game $75
1965 through 1969 Regular $50
1969 World Series................................$75
1970 ....$30
1971, 1972, 1973 Regular $20
1973 League Champs $50
1973 World Champs..............................$50
1974 through 1980 ....$20

1969 standard Major League pennant, produced under the auspices of Major League Baseball Properties, blue and orange Mets logo on a white field, 11″ × 28″, $30.

1981 through 1986 Regular $5
1986 World Series..................................$15
1987 through 1990 ....$5
1991, 1992, 1993 ....$3

Pins

1963, 1964, 1965 Crane Potato Chips, ⅞″,
   Round $5
1967, 1968, 1969 Crane Potato Chips, ⅞″,
   Round $5
1984 Crane Potato Chips, ⅞″, Round $3

1986 pin, 1¼″, orange, blue, and white, Mets logo inside a circle, National League Champions, $5.

Publications

BOOKS

Allen, Maury. *After the Miracle: The
   1969 Mets 20 Years Later.* New
   York: Watts, 1989. ....$10.00
Allen, Maury. *The Incredible Mets.*
   Paperback Library, 1969. ....$5.00
Allen, Maury. *Now Wait a Minute,
   Casey.* Doubleday & Co., 1965. ....$15.00
•Cohen, Stanley. *A Magic Summer:
   The '69 Mets.* New York: Harcourt
   Brace Jovanovich, 1988. ....$8.95

Cox, William R. *The Mets Will Win
   the Pennant.* G.P. Putnam's Sons,
   1964. ....$15.00
D'Agostino, Dennis. *This Date in New
   York Mets History.* New York:
   Stein and Day, 1981. ....$5.00
Fox, Larry. *Last To First: The Story of
   the Mets.* Harper & Row, 1970. ....$10.00
Getz, Mike. *The Mets Trivia Book.*
   West Point, N.Y.: Leisure Press,
   1984. ....$5.00
Getz, Mike. *New York Mets Trivia:
   The Silver Anniversary Book.* Boston: Quinlan Press, 1987. ....$5.00
Honig, Donald. *New York Mets—The
   First Quarter Century.* New York:
   Crown, 1986. ....$15.00
Koppett, Leonard. *The New York
   Mets: The Whole Story.* MacMillan
   Co., 1970. ....$30.00
Lang, Jack. *New York Mets: 25 Years
   of Baseball Magic.* New York:
   Henry Holt and Co., 1987. ....$10.00
Madden, Bill. *"Daily News"
   Scrapbook History of the New
   York Mets 1986 Season.* New York:
   Daily News, 1987. ....$15.00
Martin, Mollie. *The New York Mets.*
   Mankato, Mn.: Creative Education, 1982. ....$5.00
Mitchell, Jerry. *The Amazing Mets.*
   Grosset & Dunlap, 1964. Tempo
   Books, 1964, reissue. Grosset &
   Dunlap, 1970. ....$10.00
Nelson, Lindsey & Al Hirshberg.
   Backstage at the Mets. Viking
   Press, 1966. ....$10.00
Oppenheimer, Joel. *The Winning Season.* New York & Indianapolis:
   Bobbs-Merrill, 1973. ....$10.00
Parker, Kathryn. *We Won Today: My
   Season with the Mets.* Garden
   City, N.Y.: Doubleday, 1977. ....$10.00
Schecter, Leonard. *Once Upon a
   Time: The Early Years of the New
   York Mets.* Garden City, N.Y.,
   1983. ....$10.00
Schecter, Leonard. *Once Upon the
   Polo Grounds: The Mets That
   Were.* Dial Press, 1969. ....$10.00

Vecsey, George. *Joy In Mudville*. Mc-
Call Books, 1970. ....$10.00

MEDIA GUIDES

1962 First Year $100
1963, 1964 ....$50
1965, 1966 ....$25
1967, 1968 ....$22
1969 World Champs.............................$75
1970 ....$15
1971, 1972 ....$12
1973 League Champs $12
1974 ....$10
1975, 1976 ....$8
1977, 1978 ....$7
1979, 1980, 1981 ....$6
1982, 1983, 1984 ....$5
1985 ....$4
1986 World Champs $6
1987 through 1993 ....$4

1993 media guide, 4½″ × 9″, 264 pages, $4.

PROGRAMS AND SCORECARDS

1962 First Year $60
1963, 1964 ....$30
1965, 1966 ....$20
1967, 1968 ....$17
1969 World Champs.............................$20
1970 ....$15
1971, 1972 ....$12
1973 League Champs $12
1974 ....$10
1975, 1976 ....$8
1977, 1978 ....$7
1979, 1980, 1981 ....$6
1982, 1983, 1984 ....$5

1985 ....$4
1986 World Champs $6
1987 through 1993 ....$4

YEARBOOKS

1962 First Year $200
1963 ....$150
1964 ....$100
1965 ....$90
1966 ....$80
1967, 1968 ....$70
1969 World Champs $100
1970, 1971 ....$50
1972 ....$40
1973 League Champs $45
1974, 1975 ....$35
1976 ....$30
1977 through 1980 ....$15
1981 ....$12
1982 ....$10
1983, 1984, 1985 ....$8
1986 World Champs $7
1987 through 1993 ....$7

Schedules

1962 through 1969 ....$15
1970 through 1979 ....$10
1980 through 1985 ....$2
1986 through 1993 ....$1

1989 Metropolitan Life schedule, Mets Manager Dave
Johnson, 2½″ × 4⅛″, $1.

Special Events

ALL-STAR GAME PRESS PINS

1964 ....$200

1964 program, 48 pages, 8½″ × 11″, dedication of Shea Stadium on April 17, in a game against the Pittsburgh Pirates, $75.

ALL-STAR PROGRAMS

1964 ....$225

ALL-STAR GAME TICKETS

1964 Complete Ticket $70
1964 Ticket Stub....................................$35

LEAGUE CHAMPIONSHIP SERIES PROGRAMS

1969 ....$100
1973 ....$50
1986 ....$8
1988 ....$6

LEAGUE CHAMPIONSHIP SERIES TICKETS

1969 Complete Ticket $65
1969 Ticket Stub....................................$30
1973 Complete Ticket $35
1973 Ticket Stub....................................$15
1986 Complete Ticket $28
1986 Ticket Stub....................................$15
1988 Complete Ticket $28
1988 Ticket Stub....................................$15

WORLD SERIES PRESS PINS

1969 ....$200
1973 (not dated) $100
1986 ....$35

WORLD SERIES PROGRAMS

1969 ....$125
1973 ....$60
1986 ....$10

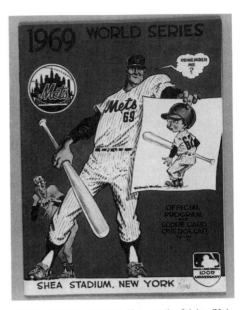

1969 World Series program, Mets vs. the Orioles (Mets won 4 to 1), 8½″ × 11″, 52 pages, $125.

WORLD SERIES GAME TICKETS

1969 Complete Ticket $70
1969 Ticket Stub....................................$35
1973 Complete Ticket $40
1973 Ticket Stub....................................$20
1986 Complete Ticket $30
1986 Ticket Stub....................................$15

NEW YORK YANKEES

American League 1903 to Present

The New York Yankees are the most successful team in baseball history—and they have 33 American League pennants and 22 World Series championships to prove it. Considering their first pennant did not occur until 1921 and their last was in 1981, they were American League champions more than half of the time during that 60-year span. From 1949 through 1953 they won five consecutive pennants and World Series championships, a record that will probably never be equaled.

Frank Farrell and Bill Devery purchased the Baltimore American League franchise for $18,000 in 1903 and moved it to New York. The team was nicknamed the Highlanders for two reasons. The club's first president was Joseph Gordon, and a famous Scottish military regiment was called the Gordon Highlanders. Second, the club's ballpark was named Hilltop Park because its location at Broadway between 165th and 168th Streets was elevated above its surroundings. The name Highlanders was a burden to headline writers; hence, beginning in 1913, the team officially became known as they Yankees.

Much of the Yankees' success was directly attributable to Babe Ruth, the greatest all-around player in baseball history. Ruth began his career as a pitcher with the Boston Red Sox in 1914. He won 23 games in 1916; 24 games in 1917; and was undefeated in World Series play, with the win in 1916 and two in 1918. Altogether he won 94 games as a pitcher, including five without a loss with the Yankees. Because of his remarkable power as a hitter, Babe was converted to a full-time outfielder by the Red Sox in 1919. When Boston owner Harry Frazee ran into cash flow problems that year, he sold Ruth to the Yankees before the 1920 season.

The Yankees won their first American League pennant in 1921 and followed with pennants in 1922 and 1923 and their first World Series win in 1923, the same year that Yankee Stadium opened. Yankee Stadium has been called "The House that Ruth Built" for good reason. Sharing the Polo Grounds with the National League Giants, Ruth and the Yankees outdrew the Giants by a large margin even though the Giants were world champions in 1921 and 1922. Asked to leave by the Giants, Yankee owner Colonel Jacob Ruppert built his own stadium across the Harlem River from the Polo Grounds and, with Ruth his principal attraction, drew larger crowds than ever.

Joined by another all-time great, first baseman Lou Gehrig, in 1923, Ruth and the Yankees continued to dominate the American League and won pennants in 1926, 1927, and 1928 and captured the World Series the last two years. Although the Yankees had many fine pitchers throughout the years, hitting was the Yankees' forte. When Babe Ruth's Yankee career was over in 1934, Joe DiMaggio arrived to carry on the superstar tradition, including a hitting streak of 56 consecutive games in 1941 and three American League Most Valuable Player awards. When Joe's career ended in 1951, Mickey Mantle was there to carry on as his splendid replacement. Mantle won three MVP awards and earned the Triple Crown in 1956. In recent years Don Mattingly has shown flashes of brilliance despite missing much of the 1990 and 1991 seasons with severe back spasms. Mattingly won the MVP award in 1985 and still carries a lifetime batting average well over .300.

More players, managers, and executives from the Yankees than any other team have been inducted into the Baseball Hall of Fame, which is not surprising considering the team's remarkable success over the years. In addition to Ruth, Gehrig, DiMaggio, and Mantle, other Hall of Fame Yankees are: Reggie Jackson, Willie Keeler, Clark Griffith, Frank Chance, Jack Chesbro, Herb Pennock, Paul Waner, Edward Barrow, Bill Dickey, Home Run Baker, Dazzy Vance, Joe McCarthy, Burleigh Grimes, Miller Huggins, Casey Stengel, Branch Rickey, Red Ruffing, Stan Coveleski, Waite Hoyt, Earle Combs, George Weiss, Yogi Berra, Lefty Gomez, Whitey Ford, Bucky Harris, Joe Sewell, Larry Mac Phail, Johnny Mize, Enos Slaughter, Catfish Hunter, Gaylord Perry, and Tony Lazzeri.

Advertising Specialties

1913 Fatima T200 Team Card, 2⅝″ × 4¾″ $100

Ballpark Giveaways

1966 Cap, Bat, Ball (if any of these items are dated, add $3) $5
1966 Ball (with facsimile autographs) $25
1967 Cap, Bat, Ball (if any of these items are dated, add $3) $5
1967 Ball (with facsimile autographs) $25
1968 Cap, Bat, Ball (see above) $5
1968 Ball (with facsimile autographs) $20
1969 Cap, Ball, Bat (see above) $5
1969 Ball (with facsimile autographs) $20
1970 Cap, Bat, Ball, T-shirt (if any of these items are dated, add $2) $5
1971 Cap, Bat, Ball, T-shirt (see above) $5
1972 Cap, Bat, Ball $5
1973 Cap, Bat, Ball, T-shirt $5
1974 Cap, Bat, Ball, T-shirt $5

1988 cardboard fold-over souvenir, 8½″ × 5½″, Beach Boys Concert at Yankee Stadium June 26. Cover shows Yankee logo on leisure shirt, color pictures inside of the 1988 Yankees and the Beach Boys. An ad for the sponsor Citicorp is on the back, $6.

1975 Cap, Bat, Ball, T-shirt, Pennant, Batting Gloves, Helmet $5
1975 Team Photo...................................$15
1977 Bat, Tote Bag, Shirt, Jacket $5
1978 Steak & Brew Burger Pennant, Dellwood Dairy Picture Album $15
1978 Dellwood Helmet, English Leather Jacket, Burger King Bat $6
1979 Chrysler/Plymouth Jacket, Burger King Bat, Tip Top Sports Bag.............$6
1979 Dellwood Dairy Picture Album, Burger King Bat $15
1980 Pepsi Pennant, Yankee Picture Album, Yankee Poster $12
1980 Tip Top Bread/Bit O'Honey School Bag, Dellwood Batting Helmet, Faberge Bat $6
1980 Stocking Cap, Cap, Jacket $5
1981 Sergio Valente/Martin Bros. Calendar, Lipton Tea Visor, McDonald's Cap, Frito Lays Jacket, Dellwood Jacket, City Bank Bat, Gulf Oil Tote Bag, N.Y. Air T-shirt $6
1981 Dellwood Picture Album $7
1982 Martin Bros/Adidas Calendar, Yankee Picture Album, Sports Phone Poster $13
1982 McDonald's Cap, Dellwood Jacket, Gulf Oil Tote Bag, CitiBank Bat, Tale Brand Jeans $6
1982 Yankee Gym Shorts $5
1983 Martin Bros. Adidas Calendar, N.Y. Bus Service Photo Album.................$12
1983 Yankee Poster $10
1983 CitiBank Jersey, Dellwood Dairy Jacket, CitiBank Cap $10
1984 Opening Issue Yankee Magazine, Dellwood Dairy Thermos $10
1984 Skoal Bandit Tote Bag, CitiBank Beach Towel, French's Bold & Spicy Helmet, CitiBank Digital Watch, CitiBank Cap, CitiBank Beach Towel $6

1984 American Enka Yankee Greats T-shirt, N.Y. Bus Service Calendar $10
1985 Ivory Soap Calendar.........................$9
1985 CitiBank Umbrella, Bic Pen, CitiBank Digital Watch, CitiBank Scarf, French's Mustard Visor $6
1986 Ivory Soap Calendar, Pepsi Umbrella, WABC Radio, M&M Sunglasses, Herr Cap, City Bank Bat, N.Y. Bus Service Mitt, Dellwood Thermos, American Enka Sports Bag, Kool-Aid Baseball, Chiquita Banana Watch, City Bank Scarf..........$6
1987 City Bank Radio, Herr Cap, BASF Beach Towel, WABC Radio Bat, Gatorade Glove, Dellwood Jacket, Chiquita Banana Watch, BASF Sports Bag, M&M School Clip Board, Pepsi Umbrella $6
1987 Mug $5
1988 Ivory Soap Calendar, Goodyear Cap, Pepsi Umbrella, BASF Beach Towel, Baskin Robins Helmet, Gatorade Glove, Thorn Apple Valley Bat, Dellwood Batting Glove, National Westminster Jacket, Kinney Shoes Socks, Chiquita Banana Watch $6
1988 Wiz Poster $7
1988 Beach Boys Concert Program $10
1988 Surf Card Book $15
1989 Ivory Soap Calendar, Texaco Cap, MSG Network Umbrella, BASF Beach Towel, Waldbrums Bat, Milk Duds Sunglasses, Dellwood Helmet, Modells Water Bottle, Kodak Yankee Pin, Chiquita Banana Watch, Coca-Cola Glove $6
1990 Ivory Soap Calendar, City Bank Cap, Dellwood Helmet, Thorn Apple Valley Fanny Pack, MSG Network Bat, Foot Locker Socks, Sunglasses, Coca-Cola Glove, Gatorade Sports Bag, Looney Tunes Visor, Chiquita Banana Watch, Modells Water Bottle $6
1990 City Bank Ring $10
1990 Wiz Poster #1, Wiz Poster #2 ....$9
1990 Wiz Poster #3 ....$8
1990 Wiz Poster #4, Donruss Card Folder $7
1991 Ivory Soap Calendar, City Bank Ring, Dellwood Helmet, Carvel Fanny Pack, Gatorade Neon Cap, Payday Sunglasses, WABC Sports Bag, Foot Locker Socks, Modells Water Bottle, Coca-Cola Lunch Bag....$6
1991 Wallet, Watch................................$5
1991 Donruss Card Folder $7
1991 Wiz Yankees 1950s Cards $10
1991 Wiz Yankees 1960s Cards..................$9
1991 Wiz Yankees 1970s Cards..................$8
1992 Universal Pictures Calendar, Dellwood Magnetic Schedule, City Bank Ring, Starter Baseball Glove,

Benjimen Moore Painter Cap, National West Bank Fanny Pack, Coca-Cola Bat, City Bank Sunglasses, Gatorade Cap, Good & Frutie Helmet, Modells Water Bottle, Foot Locker Socks, WABC Sports Bag $6

1992 Donruss Baseball Cards, Jolly Rancher Autographed Baseball, Wiz Yankees of the 1980s, Wiz Yankee Hall of Fame Cards, Wiz Award Winners Cards $7

1992 Watch $5

1993 Coca-Cola Calendar, Jolly Rancher Bat, Starter Baseball Glove, WABC Brief Case, Benjimen Neon Painter Cap, Dellwood Helmet, National West Bank, Deer Park Water Cooler, 64 oz. Cooler, Wiz Sunglasses, Foot Locker Socks, Gatorade Cap, City Bank Glove, Payday Wallet, Wiz Watch, WABC Sports Bag, Modells Water Bottle $6

1993 Donruss Card Book, Upper Deck Heros of Baseball $7

1993 Fleer Rookie League Magazine $5

Miscellaneous

1984 plastic Icee cup, 3½″ × 7″, Yankee and sponsor's logo on front and Yankee jacket on back. Icee produced these cups for other Major League teams where its product was sold, $6.

BOBBIN' HEAD DOLLS

Category #I, 1960, 1961, Orange Square Base, Boy Head $125
Category #II, 1961, 1962, White Square Base, Boy Head $145

Category #III, 1961, 1962, White Round Miniature, Boy Head $240
Category #IV, 1962, 1963, 1964, Green Round Base, Boy Head $100
Category #V, 1962, 1963, 1964, Green Round Base, Black Player $625
Category #VI, 1967 through 1972, Gold Round Base, Boy Head $70

EXHIBIT CARDS

1949, 1950, 1951 Exhibit Supply Co. Team Cards....................................$18
1952 Exhibit Supply Co. Team Card $16
1955, 1956 Exhibit Supply Co. Team Card $14

Pennants

1903 through 1920 ....$750
1921 through 1930 ....$300
1931, 1932 Regular $200
1932 World Series $400
1933, 1934, 1935, 1936 Regular $200
1936 World Series $400
1936, 1937 Felt Pennant BF3, Type IV, Batter on Pennant $35
1936, 1937 Felt Pennant BF3, Type IV, Player Fielding on Pennant $35
1936, 1937 Felt Pennant BF3, Type V, Champions on Pennant $35
1937 Regular $200
1937 World Series $400
1938 Regular $200
1938 World Series $400
1939 Regular $200
1939 All-Star Game $400
1939 World Series $400
1940 ....$200
1941 Regular $100
1941 World Series $200
1942 Regular $100
1942 World Series $200
1943 Regular $200
1943 World Series $200
1944, 1945, 1946, 1947 Regular $100
1947 World Series $200
1948, 1949 Regular $100
1949 World Series $200
1950 Regular $100
1950 World Series $200
1951, 1952, 1953 Regular $50
1951, 1952, 1953 World Series each Year..$125
1954 ....$50
1955, 1956, 1957, 1958 Regular $50
1955, 1956, 1957, 1958 World Series each Year..$125
1959, 1960 Regular $50
1960 All-Star Game $125
1960 World Series $125
1961, 1962, 1963, 1964 Regular $50
1961, 1962, 1963, 1964 World Series each Year $75

1950s pennant, 11½″ × 28″, Uncle Sam on a red field with yellow trim (also seen in different colors during this era), $50.

1980 polyester pennant, produced by Chrysler Corp. for American League Champion Series at Yankee Stadium against the Kansas City Royals, 12″ × 30″, $15.

1965 through 1970 ....$30
1971 through 1976 Regular $20
1976 League Champs $50
1976 World Series................................$50
1977 Regular $20
1977 All-Star Game $50
1977 League Champs $50
1977 World Series................................$50
1978 Regular $20
1978 League Champs $50
1978 World Series................................$50
1979, 1980 ....$20
1981 Regular $5
1981 League Champs $15
1981 World Series................................$15
1982 through 1990 ....$5
1991, 1992, 1993 ....$3

Pins

1930/1940s American Nut & Chocolate
  Co., 1⅛″, Round $15
1961 through 1965 Crane Potato Chips,
  ⅞″, Round $5
1967, 1968, 1969 Crane Potato Chips, ⅞″,
  Round $5
1984 Crane Potato Chips, ⅞″, Round $5
1964, 1965, 1966 Guy's Potato Chips, ⅞″,
  Round $5

Publications

BOOKS

Anderson, Dave. *The Yankees: The Four Fabulous Eras of Baseball's*

1960s–1970s pin, 1¾″, red, white, and blue, striped top hat on a baseball bat with Yankees in script lettering across the middle, $8.

Most Famous Team. New York:
  Random House, 1979. ....$15.00
Bizzelle, John. *I Hate the Yankees.*
  New York: Vantage Press, 1971. ......$10.00
Bove, Vincent. *And on the Eighth Day
  God Created the Yankees.*
  Plainfield, N.J.: Haven Books,
  1981. ....$10.00
Creamer, Robert W. *Search For
  Glory: The Amazing Saga of the
  1961 New York Yankees.* New
  York: G.P. Putnam, 1988. ....$10.00
Daniel, Dan. *The New York Yankees.*
  Packard Motor Car Co., 1952. ....$20.00

Durant, John. *The Yankees.* Hastings House, 1949, 1950. ....**$60.00**

•Falk, David, ed. *The Yankee Reader.* Thousand Oaks, Ca.: Ventura Ars, 1990. ....**$9.95**

Fleming, Gordon H. *Murderers Row: The 1927 New York Yankees.* New York: William Morrow, 1985. ....**$15.00**

•Forker, Dom. *The Men of Autumn: An Oral History of the 1949–1953 World Champion New York Yankees.* Dallas, Tex.: Taylor Pub. Co., 1990. ....**$8.98**

•Forker, Dom. *Sweet Seasons: An Oral History of the 1955–1964 New York Yankees.* Dallas, Tex.: Taylor Publishing Co., 1990. ....**$18.95**

Frommer, Harvey. *Baseball's Greatest Rivalries: The New York Yankees vs. Boston Red Sox.* New York: Athenium, 1984. Out of Print **$10.00**

Gallagher, Mark. *Day By Day In New York Yankees History.* West Point, N.Y.: Leisure Press, 1983 (paperback $5) **$15.00**

Gallagher, Mark. *The Yankee Encyclopedia.* West Point, N.Y.: Leisure Press, 1982. ....**$20.00**

Gallagher, Mark and Neil Gallagher. *Baseball's Greatest Dynasties: The New York Yankees.* New York: Gallery Books, 1990. ....**$5.00**

Getz, Mike. *New York Yankees Trivia.* Boston, Mass.: Quinlan Press, 1987 (paperback $5) **$10.00**

Golenboch, Peter. *Dynasty: The New York Yankees, 1949–1964.* Englewood Cliffs, N.J.: Prentice-Hall, 1975. ....**$10.00**

Graham, Frank. *The New York Yankees.* G.P. Putnam's Sons (1st print) 1943. Reissue, 1945, 1946, 1948, 1951, 1958. (Other editions $30) **$40.00**

Graham, Frank, Jr. *A Farewell To Heroes.* New York: Viking Press, 1981. ....**$10.00**

Gross, Milton. *The Yankee Doodle.* House of Kent: 1948. ....**$40.00**

•Henrich, Tommy with Bill Gilbert. *Five O'Clock Lightening: Ruth, Gehrig, Dimaggio and the Glory Days of the New York Yankees.* New York: Birch Lane Press, 1992. ....**$19.95**

•Honig, Donald. *New York Yankees: An Illustrated History.* New York: Crown, 1987. ....**$22.50**

Jacobson, Steve. *The Best Team Money Can Buy: The Turmoil and Triumph of the 1977 New York Yankees.* New York: Athenium, 1978. ....**$10.00**

Jennison, Christopher. *Wait Til Next Year: The Yankees, Dodgers, and Giants, 1947–1957.* New York: Athenium, 1978. ....**$25.00**

Jones, Harvey. *The Thrilling True Story of the Baseball Yankees.* Fawcett Publishing Co., 1952. ....**$40.00**

Kubec, Tony & Terry Pluto. *Sixty One: The Team, the Record, the Men.* New York: McMillan, 1987. .....**$10.00**

Lally, Dick. *Pinstriped Summers: Memories of Yankee Seasons Past.* New York: Arbor House, 1985. ....**$10.00**

•Linn, Ed. *Great Rivalries: The Yankees and the Red Sox.* New York: Tichnor & Fields, 1991. ....**$19.95**

Linn, Ed. *The Greening of the New York Yankees.* New York: Ballantine Books, 1978. ....**$10.00**

Linn, Ed. *Steinbrenner's Yankees: An Inside Account.* New York: Holt, Rinehart & Winston, 1982. ....**$10.00**

Mann, Jack. *The Decline and Fall of the New York Yankees.* Simon and Schuster, 1967. ....**$15.00**

Meany, Tom. *The Magnificent Yankees.* A. S. Barnes & Co., 1952. ....**$30.00**

Meany, Tom. *The Yankee Story.* E.P. Dutton & Co., 1960. ....**$20.00**

Mercurio, John. *A Chronology of New York Yankee Records.* New York: Perennial, 1989. ....**$10.00**

Mosedale, John. *The Greatest of All: The 1927 Yankees.* New York: Dial Press, 1974. ....**$15.00**

Rizzuto, Phil & Silverman, Al. *The Miracle New York Yankees.* Coward-McCann, 1962. ....**$20.00**

Rothaus, James R. *New York Yankees.* Mankato, Mn.: Creative Education, 1987. ....**$5.00**

Sahadi, Lou. *Year of the Yankees.* Chicago: Contemporary Books, 1979. ....**$10.00**

Salant, Nathan with Carl Wolfson. *This Date In New York Yankees History.* New York: Stein & Day, 1982. ....**$5.00**

Sullivan, George. *Baseball Backstage.* New York: Henry Holt and Co., 1986. ....**$10.00**

Sullivan, George & John Powers. *Yankees: An Illustrated History.* Englewood Cliffs, N.J.: Prentice-Hall, 1982. ....**$15.00**

Stokes, Geoffrey. *Pinstripe Pandemonium: A Season with the New York Yankees.* New York: Harper & Row, 1984. ....**$10.00**

•Tullius, John. *"I'd Rather Be a Yankee".* New York: McMillan, 1986. ....**$3.95**

United Press International. *The Bronx Bombers: A Celebration of the 1985 New York Yankees.* Chicago, Il.: Contemporary Books, 1985. ....**$10.00**

Ward, Don. *New York Yankees.* Man-

kato, Mn.: Creative Education,
1982. ....$5.00
Weil, Robert & James Fitzgerald.
Yankee Quizbook. Garden City,
N.Y.: Doubleday, 1981. ....$5.00
Weinberger, Miro, ed. *Yankees
Reader.* Boston, Mass.: Houghton-
Mifflin, 1991. ....$9.95

MEDIA GUIDES

1927 Roster Sheet (World Champs) $175
1928 Roster Sheet (World Champs) $160
1929, 1930, 1931 Roster Sheet $150
1932 Roster Booklet World Champs $200
1933 through 1939 Roster Booklet $100
1940 Roster Booklet $75
1941 Roster Booklet World Champs $65
1942 League Champs $65
1943 World Champs $65
1944, 1945, 1946 ....$60
1947 World Champs $65
1948 ....$60
1949 World Champs $65
1950, 1951, 1952, 1953 World Champs
    each Year $55
1954 ....$50
1955 League Champs $55
1956 World Champs $45
1957 League Champs $45
1958 World Champs $45
1959 ....$40
1960 League Champs $45
1961 World Champs $45
1962 World Champs $35
1963, 1964 League Champs each Year $35
1965, 1966 ....$20
1967, 1968 ....$17
1969, 1970 ....$15
1971, 1972 ....$12
1973, 1974 ....$10
1975 ....$8
1976 League Champs $10
1977 World Champs $9
1978 World Champs $9
1979, 1980 ....$6
1981 League Champs $8
1982, 1983, 1984 ....$5
1985 through 1993 ....$4

PROGRAMS AND SCORECARDS

1903 ....$600
1904 ....$300
1905 through 1909 ....$200
1910 through 1914 ....$150
1915 through 1920 ....$125
1921, 1922 American League Champs $75
1923 World Champs $80
1924, 1925 ....$50
1926 American League Champs $60
1927 World Champs $75
1928 World Champs $65
1929, 1930 ....$50

1931 ....$35
1932 World Champs $45
1933, 1934, 1935 ....$35
1936, 1937, 1938, 1939 World Champs
    each Year $45
1940 ....$35
1941 World Champs $25
1942 League Champs $25
1943 World Champs $25
1944, 1945, 1946 ....$20
1947 World Champs $25
1948 ....$20
1949 World Champs $25
1950, 1951, 1952, 1953 World Champs
    each Year $20
1954 ....$15
1955 League Champs $20
1956 World Champs $20
1957 League Champs $20
1958 World Champs $20
1959 ....$15
1960 League Champs $12
1961, 1962 World Champs each Year $12
1963, 1964 League Champs each Year $12
1965 through 1969 ....$10
1970 through 1975 ....$6
1976 League Champs $8
1977, 1978 World Champs each Year $8
1979 ....$6
1980 ....$4
1981 ....$6
1982 through 1989 ....$4
1990, 1991, 1992, 1993 ....$3

YEARBOOKS

1950 ....$300
1951 ....$250
1952 Big League Books $150
1952 Official $200
1953 Big League Books $100
1953 Official $125
1954 Big League Books $100
1954 Official $125
1955 Big League Books $100
1955 Official $125
1956 Big League Books $75
1956 Official $100
1957 Big League Books $75
1957 Official $100
1958 Big League Books $70
1958 Official $90
1959 Big League Books $65
1959 Official $80
1960 Big League Books $60
1960 Official $75
1961 Big League Books (Maris/Mantle
    year) $85
1961 Official $100
1962 Big League Books $55
1962 Official $65
1963 Big League Books $45
1963 Official $60
1964 Big League Books $35

1964 Official $60
1965 Big League Books $30
1965 Official $50
1966, 1967 ....$40
1968, 1969 ....$25
1970 ....$35
1971, 1972, 1973 ....$20
1974, 1975 ....$18
1976 League Champs $20
1977 World Champs $20
1978 ....$20
1979, 1980 ....$10
1981 League Champs $8
1982, 1983, 1984 ....$7
1985, 1986, 1987 ....$6
1988 through 1993 ....$5

Schedules

1903 through 1909 ....$150
1910 through 1919 ....$100
1920 through 1929 ....$75
1930 through 1939 ....$45
1940 through 1949 ....$30
1950 through 1959 ....$25
1960 through 1969 ....$15
1970 through 1979 ....$10
1980 through 1985 ....$2
1986 through 1993 ....$1

1987 official Yankee schedule, 2½″ × 4″, red, white,
and blue Yankees logo on white field with blue pin
stripes, $1.

Special Events

ALL-STAR GAME PRESS PINS

1939 ....None Issued
1960 ....$200
1977 ....$25

ALL-STAR PROGRAMS

1939 ....$800
1960 ....$75
1977 ....$20

ALL-STAR GAME TICKETS

1939 Complete Ticket $400
1939 Ticket Stub $200
1960 Complete Ticket $70
1960 Ticket Stub..................................$35
1977 Complete Ticket $40
1977 Ticket Stub..................................$20

LEAGUE CHAMPIONSHIP SERIES PROGRAMS

1976 ....$15
1977, 1978 each Year $12
1980, 1981 each Year $10

LEAGUE CHAMPIONSHIP SERIES TICKETS

1976 Complete Ticket $38
1976 Ticket Stub..................................$15
1977 Complete Ticket $38
1977 Ticket Stub..................................$15
1978 Complete Ticket $38
1978 Ticket Stub..................................$15
1980 Complete Ticket $28
1980 Ticket Stub..................................$15
1981 Complete Ticket $28
1981 Ticket Stub..................................$10

WORLD SERIES PRESS PINS

1921 ....$1,500
1922 ....$1,500
1923 ....$1,500
1926 ....$1,500
1927 ....$1,500
1928 ....$1,500
1932 ....$750
1936 ....$400
1937 ....$400
1938 ....$300
1939 ....$300
1941 ....$300
1942 ....$300
1943 ....$300
1947 ....$300
1949 ....$300
1950 ....$300
1951 ....$300
1952 ....$300
1953 ....$300
1955 ....$200
1956 ....$200
1957 ....$200
1958 ....$200
1960 ....$200
1961 ....$200
1962 ....$200
1963 ....$200

1964	(not dated)	$200
1976	(not dated)	$100
1977	(not dated)	$50
1978	(not dated)	$50
1981	(not dated)	$50

| 1978 | $35 |
| 1981 | $20 |

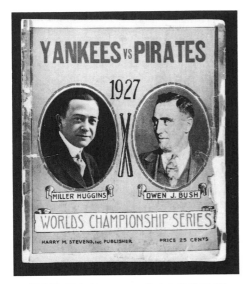

1927 World Series program, Yankee Stadium, 20 pages. The 1927 Yankees, reputed to be the greatest team of all time, swept the Pirates in four straight games, $2,500.

WORLD SERIES PROGRAMS

1921	$1,500
1922	$1,500
1923	$1,500
1926	$1,500
1927	$2,500
1928	$1,000
1932	$1,000
1936	$400
1937, 1938, 1939	$350
1941	$300
1942	$250
1943	$250
1947	$250
1949	$200
1950, 1951	$225
1952	$200
1953	$175
1955	$225
1956	$200
1957, 1958	$150
1960, 1961, 1962	$100
1963, 1964	$75
1976, 1977	$40

WORLD SERIES GAME TICKETS

1921 Complete Ticket	$800
1921 Ticket Stub	$400
1922 Complete Ticket	$800
1922 Ticket Stub	$400
1923 Complete Ticket	$800
1923 Ticket Stub	$400
1926 Complete Ticket	$600
1926 Ticket Stub	$300
1927 Complete Ticket	$600
1927 Ticket Stub	$300
1928 Complete Ticket	$600
1928 Ticket Stub	$300
1932 Complete Ticket	$400
1932 Ticket Stub	$200
1936 Complete Ticket	$400
1936 Ticket Stub	$200
1937 Complete Ticket	$400
1937 Ticket Stub	$200
1938 Complete Ticket	$400
1938 Ticket Stub	$200
1939 Complete Ticket	$400
1939 Ticket Stub	$200
1941 Complete Ticket	$200
1941 Ticket Stub	$100
1942 Complete Ticket	$200
1942 Ticket Stub	$100
1943 Complete Ticket	$200
1943 Ticket Stub	$100
1947 Complete Ticket	$200
1947 Ticket Stub	$100
1949 Complete Ticket	$200
1949 Ticket Stub	$100
1950 Complete Ticket	$150
1950 Ticket Stub	$75
1951 Complete Ticket	$150
1951 Ticket Stub	$75
1952 Complete Ticket	$150
1952 Ticket Stub	$75
1953 Complete Ticket	$150
1953 Ticket Stub	$75
1955 Complete Ticket	$150
1955 Ticket Stub	$75
1956 Complete Ticket	$150
1956 Ticket Stub	$75
1957 Complete Ticket	$150
1957 Ticket Stub	$75
1958 Complete Ticket	$150
1958 Ticket Stub	$75
1960 Complete Ticket	$70
1960 Ticket Stub	$35
1961 Complete Ticket	$70
1961 Ticket Stub	$35
1962 Complete Ticket	$70
1962 Ticket Stub	$35
1963 Complete Ticket	$70
1963 Ticket Stub	$35
1964 Complete Ticket	$70
1964 Ticket Stub	$35

1976 Complete Ticket	...........................$40		1978 Complete Ticket	...........................$40
1976 Ticket Stub	.................................$20		1978 Ticket Stub	.................................$20
1977 Complete Ticket	...........................$40		1981 Complete Ticket	...........................$30
1977 Ticket Stub	.................................$20		1981 Ticket Stub	.................................$15

Oakland, California

OAKLAND ATHLETICS

American League 1968 to Present

The Athletics came to Oakland by way of Philadelphia and Kansas City to establish themselves as one of the most successful franchises in baseball during the last 25 years. From 1971 through 1975 they won five consecutive Western Division titles. They won again in 1981; from 1988 through 1990 they won three more in a row. The A's were World Series champions in 1972, 1973, 1974, and 1989. Since American League play-offs began in 1969, the Athletics have captured nine division titles, more than any other team in the major leagues.

The Athletics' formula for the success has been a perfect blend of outstanding pitching and marvelous hitting. In the early 1970s pitchers Jim "Catfish" Hunter and Vida Blue were 20-game winners while Rollie Fingers was the best relief pitcher in baseball. Hunter and Fingers have been elected to baseball's hallowed Hall. Hall of Fame outfielder Reggie Jackson and third baseman Sal Bando were consistently among league leaders in home runs and RBIs, while shortstop Bert "Campy" Campaneris led the A's in stolen bases five consecutive years and won three American League titles during that span.

When the Athletics were winning three consecutive pennants in 1988, 1989 and 1990, Jose Canseco and Mark McGuire provided most of the power. In 1988 Canseco inaugurated baseball's 40/40 club, becoming the first player ever to hit 40 home runs (42) and steal 40 bases in a single season. As a result of Jose's magnificent season, he was an unanimous choice as the American League's Most Valuable Player. Rickey Henderson, who joined the A's from New York in 1989, won the MVP award in 1990 after batting .325 and leading the league in runs (119), on-base percentage (.439) and stolen bases (65). Righthander Dave Stewart emerged as baseball's premium pitcher by winning 20 or more games in four consecutive seasons. Righthander Bob Welch capped a brilliant 27 and 6 record by winning the Cy Young award in 1990. Throw in superb reliever Dennis Eckersley, who compiled 126 saves during the three pennant winning seasons, and it's easy to see why many were comparing the A's to the greatest team of all time. The one negative is that they lost in the World Series two of the three times they made it.

Ballpark Giveaways

1981 Cap, T-shirt, Socks, Shorts, Backpack, Ball (with facsimile autographs $15)	..................................$5
1981 J.C. Penney Visor, J.C. Penney Jacket	....$6
1981 Taco Bell Tankard	.........................$11
1982 KSFO Schedule Poster, Mother's Cookies Team Picture	....................$11
1982 Granny Goose Baseball Cards	..........$20
1982 J.C. Penney Visor	...........................$7
1982 7 Up Jacket, Atari T-shirt, Toyota Gym Bag, Chevrolet Wrist Bank	.........$6
1982 Cap, Socks, Helmet, Tank Top, Shorts, Ski Cap	...............................$5
1983 Oakland Hyatt Picture Pennant	........$12
1983 A's Bonus Book, Union Oil Sports Cup	....$10
1983 Granny Goose Cards	.......................$15
1983 Schedule Poster	............................$8
1983 Coca-Cola Gym Bag, Shell Gym Shorts, J.C. Penney Visor, 7-Up Watch, Hostess Jacket, Budweiser Cap, Chevrolet Seat Cushion	............$6

1983 Mother's Cookies Team Picture $11
1984 Budweiser Schedule Poster $9
1984 Mother's Cookies Cards $15
1984 Cap, Work-out Shorts, Work-out
     Shoes, Sweat Top, Work-out Run-
     ning Shoes $5
1985 Adidas Work-out Kit $7
1985 Mother's Cookies Cards $15
1985 PG & E Cap, Wells Fargo Mitt,
     Coca-Cola Bat, Pacific Bell Jersey,
     PG & E Radio, Union 76 Incredible
     Ball, Chevrolet Gym Bag $6
1985 Helmet $5
1986 Mother's Cookies Cards $15
1986 Chevrolet Bobbin' Head Doll $20
1986 Safeway Cap, Baby Ruth/But-
     terfinger Helmet, Coca-Cola Bat,
     PG & E Cooler Bag, Wells Fargo
     Mitt, Unocal Equipment Bag, Kool-
     Aid Watch $6
1987 Chevrolet Calendar $9
1987 Coca-Cola Bat, New Logo Cap $6
1987 Fuji Photo All-Star Cap, All-Star Kit $7
1988 Wells Fargo Activity Book, Nabisco
     Mitt, Gatorade Wallet, Gatorade
     Watch, Fuji Cap, J.C. Penney
     Warm-up Jacket, Leaf Binder,
     Smokey the Bear Helmet $6
1988 Mother's Cookies Cards $15
1988 Baskin-Robbins Autograph Ball $15
1988 World Champs Surf Baseball Book ...$12
1988 Lipton Tea Pitcher $7
1989 California Egg Commission Auto-
     graph Ball (world champs) $15
1989 Unocal Pins 1, 2, 3, 4, 5 ....ea. $8
1989 Mother's Cookies Baseball Cards......$12
1989 Leaf Wallet, Lipton Visor, Mr. Pea-
     nut Beach Towel, Gatorade Watch,
     Smokey the Bear Painter Cap,
     Coca-Cola Bat, Wells Fargo Activity
     Book $6
1989 Mitt $5
1990 Gatorade Replica World Champion-
     ship Ring..$15
1990 Kodak Photo Poster, Wells Fargo
     Activity Book, Looney Tunes Visor,
     Bank America Roll-up Cap, Mr.
     Peanut Beach Towel, PG & E
     Binder, Ortega Painter Cap, Sara
     Lee Lunch Bag, Sanwa Bank Mug $8
1990 Safeway/Unocal Pins ....ea. $7
1990 Leaf Card Album $7
1990 Mother's Cookies Cards $10
1991 Planter/Lifesavers Cap, Sunsense
     Sunglasses, Bank America Roll-up
     Car, Capri Sun Cooler Bag, Planter
     T-shirt, PG & E Binder.....................$6
1991 Unocal Pins ....ea. $7
1991 Mother's Cookies Cards $10
1991 Upper Deck Cards $7
1991 Kodak Poster..................................$7
1991 Gatorade American League Cham-
     pionship Ring $12
1992 Pacific Bell Magnet Schedule,
     Planters/Lifesavers Cap, Bank

America Roll-up Cap, Coca-Cola
     Duffle Bag, PG & E Binder $6
1992 Unocal Pins 1, 2, 3, 4 ....ea. $7
1992 Gatorade 25th Anniversary Poster,
     Wells Fargo 25th Anniversary Col-
     oring Book, Lipton Thermo Mug........$7
1992 Mother's Cookies Cards $10
1992 Jolly Rancher Autograph Baseball $10
1993 Pacific Bell Magnet Schedule,
     Planter/Lifesavers Cap, Chevron
     Football, Bank America Roll-up
     Cap, Nabisco Road Cap, Nabisco
     Home Cap, Jolly Rancher Jacket,
     Dyers Batting Helmet, Coca-Cola
     Elephant Bag, 93/94 Calendar $6
1993 Unocal Pins 1, 2, 3, 4, 5 ....ea. $7
1993 Gatorade Elephant Logo Ring $10
1993 Donruss Card Book $7
1993 Mother's Cookies Card Set $8
1993 Beach Towel, Ring $5

1990 A's activity book, 8½″ × 11″, 48 pages, presented by Wells Fargo Bank, $6.

Miscellaneous

BOBBIN' HEAD DOLLS

Category #VI, 1968 through 1972, Gold
     Round Base, Boy Head $22
Category #VI, 1968 through 1972, White
     Round Base, Boy Head $215

PENNANTS

1968, 1969, 1970 ....$30
1971, 1972 Regular $20

1972 League Champs	$50
1972 World Series	$50
1973 Regular	$20
1973 League Champs	$50
1973 World Series	$50
1974 Regular	$20
1974 League Champs	$50
1974 World Series	$50
1975 through 1980	$20
1981 through 1987 Regular	$5
1987 All-Star Game	$15
1988 Regular	$5
1988 League Champs	$15
1989 Regular	$5
1989 League Champs	$15
1989 World Champs	$15
1990 Regular	$5
1990 League Champs	$5
1991, 1992, 1993	$3

Pins

1968 Crane Potato Chips, 7/8", Round	$5
1984 Crane Potato Chips, 7/8", Round	$3

1970s pin, A's Fever Catch It, 3", Swingin' A's logo
leading a parade of 12 baseballs on a blue
background, $8.

Publications

BOOKS

Bergman, Ron. *The Moustache Gang: The Swaggering Saga of Oakland's A's.* New York: Dell, 1973. .....$10.00
Clark, Tom. *Champagne and Baloney, A History of Finley's A's.* New York: Harper & Row, 1976. ....$15.00
Darlington, Sandy. *The New Oakland A's.* Berkeley, Ca.: Arrowhead Press, 1981. ....$10.00
Heimerdinger, Debra. *Baseball Rhythms: Photography of the Oak-*

land *A's.* Richmond, Ca.: North Atlantic Books. $15.00
•Hickey, John. *Oakland A's.* San Francisco: Chronicle Books, 1991. ....$12.95
Martin, Mollie. *Oakland A's.* Mankato, Mn.: Creative Education, 1982. ....$5.00
Rothaus, James R. *Oakland A's.* Mankato, Mn.: Creative Education, 1987. ....$5.00
Shea, John & John Hickey. *Magic by the Bay.* Berkeley, Ca.: North Atlantic Books, 1990. ....$10.00

MEDIA GUIDES

1968 First Year	$50
1969, 1970	$15
1971	$12
1972 World Champs	$15
1973, 1974 World Champs each Year	$12
1975, 1976	$8
1977, 1978	$7
1979, 1980, 1981	$6
1982, 1983, 1984	$5
1985, 1986, 1987	$4
1988 League Champs	$6
1989 World Champs	$6
1990 League Champs	$6
1991, 1992, 1993	$4

PROGRAMS AND SCORECARDS

1968 First Year	$25
1969	$10
1970, 1971	$6
1972, 1973, 1974 World Champs each Year	$8
1975 through 1979	$6
1980 through 1987	$4
1988 League Champs	$6
1989 World Champs	$6
1990 League Champs	$6
1991, 1992, 1993	$3

YEARBOOKS

1968	$125
1969	$90
1970	$75
1971	$65
1972 World Champs	$50
1973 World Champs	$40
1974 World Champs	$30
1975	$25
1976	$20
1977, 1978, 1979	$18
1980	$15
1981	None Issued
1982, 1983	$8
1984 through 1993	None Issued

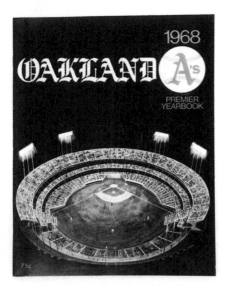

1968 A's Premier Yearbook, 8½" × 10¾", 72 pages,
new Oakland Coliseum on the cover, $125.

Schedules

1968 ....$20
1969 through 1974 ....$15
1975 through 1979 ....$10

The
OAKLAND A's
in 1970
Official Radio & TV Schedule

AtlanticRichfieldCompany ◆

1970 triple fold schedule, Atlantic Richfield Co.,
2¾" × 4", $20.

1980 through 1988 ....$2
1986 through 1993 ....$1

Special Events

ALL-STAR GAME PRESS PINS

1987 ....$40

ALL-STAR GAME TICKETS

1987 Complete Ticket $30
1987 Ticket Stub...................................$15

LEAGUE CHAMPIONSHIP SERIES PROGRAMS

1971, 1972, 1973 ....$50
1974 (this program is very rare)............$300
1975 ....$45
1981 Western Division Play-Off $15
1988, 1989, 1990 ....$10
1992 ....$10

1987 All-Star game program, 96 pages, 8½" × 11",
various pieces of baseball memorabilia, $12.

LEAGUE CHAMPIONSHIP SERIES TICKETS

1971 Complete Ticket $38
1971 Ticket Stub...................................$20
1972 Complete Ticket $38

1972 Ticket Stub $20
1973 Complete Ticket $58
1973 Ticket Stub $20
1974 Complete Ticket $58
1974 Ticket Stub $20
1975 Complete Ticket $58
1975 Ticket Stub $20
1988 Complete Ticket $28
1988 Ticket Stub $15
1989 Complete Ticket $28
1989 Ticket Stub $15
1990 Complete Ticket $18
1990 Ticket Stub $10
1992 Complete Ticket $18
1992 Ticket Stub $10

WORLD SERIES PRESS PINS

1972 ....$200
1973 ....$200
1974 ....$300
1988 ....$40
1989 ....$50
1990 ....$25

WORLD SERIES PROGRAMS

1972, 1973 ....$60
1974 ....$35
1988, 1989, 1990 ....$10

WORLD SERIES GAME TICKETS

1972 Complete Ticket $40
1972 Ticket Stub $20
1973 Complete Ticket $40
1973 Ticket Stub $20
1974 Complete Ticket $40
1974 Ticket Stub $20
1988 Complete Ticket $30
1988 Ticket Stub $15
1989 Complete Ticket $50
1989 Ticket Stub $15
1990 Complete Ticket $20
1990 Ticket Stub $10

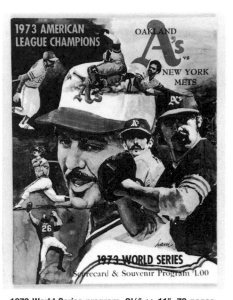

1973 World Series program, 8½″ × 11″, 73 pages, group of A's stars and Manager Dick Williams on the cover. This is the last World Series program produced by the competing team. Since then, Major League baseball has produced a generic program featuring all 4 teams participating in the league championship series, $60.

1972 ticket stub, World Series game 3 against the Cincinnati Reds, 4⅜″ × 2½″, $20.

Philadelphia, Pennsylvania

PHILADELPHIA ATHLETICS

National Association 1871–1875,
American Association 1884,
American League 1901–1954

Connie Mack and the Philadelphia Athletics are synonymous. Mack served as owner-manager for the club throughout its 54-year history as an American League franchise in Philadelphia. As a charter member of the American League in 1901, Mack and co-owner Ben Shibe put together an outstanding team from the beginning. The Athletics finished fourth in 1901 and won its first of nine pennants in 1902.

John McGraw, who jumped as manager of the American League Baltimore Orioles to manage the National League's New York Giants in midseason 1902, was asked to assess the champion Athletics. McGraw derisively referred to them as "White Elephants," but the clever Mack adopted the White Elephant as the team's symbol. The elephant remains the team's symbol to this day, even though the franchise now resides in Oakland, California.

Mack's initial star was second baseman Napoleon Lajoie, who won the American League's first Triple Crown in 1901 by batting .426, hitting 14 home runs, and driving in 125 runs. Because the Athletics had raided the National League Phillies to obtain Lajoie, the Phillies brought suit to prevent Lajoie from playing in Philadelphia with the Athletics. A lower court threw out the suit, but the Pennsylvania Supreme Court ruled against the Athletics on the second day of the 1902 season. Lajoie was promptly traded to Cleveland so the American League could retain the services of its first superstar.

Despite losing its best player, the Athletics won their first of nine championships in 1902 thanks largely to a pitching staff anchored by future Hall of Famers Rube Waddell (25–7) and Eddie Plank

(20–15), whom Mack had signed right off the campus of Gettysburg College. Since the two leagues were still at war, no World Series was played that year.

The Athletics won their second pennant in 1905 as Plank led the league with 26 wins (26 and 12) while the eccentric and colorful Waddell won 24 and lost 11. Andy Coakley had a 20 and 6 mark while future Hall of Famer Chief Bender won 16 and lost 10. But as brilliant as the A's pitching was in 1905, it was overshadowed by that of New York in the World Series as the Giants won four games to one. Every game ended in a shutout, the only time in Series history this occurred. Chief Bender won the second game 3 to 0 as two Giants errors accounted for the A's scoring. Giants pitchers Christy Mathewson, Joe McGinnity and Red Ames did not allow an earned run in the entire series.

A milestone occurred in 1909 when the Athletics moved into Shibe Park. Baseball's first all-steel-and-concrete stadium ushered in the era of the modern ballpark. More than 30,000 fans turned out for the park's grand opening on April 12, 1909. Shibe had nearly three times the capacity of antiquated Columbia Park, which had been hastily constructed of wood in 1901.

In 1910 and 1911 the Athletics won pennants and added the World Series championship both years by beating the Cubs and Giants respectively. Future Hall of Famer Jack Coombs (30–9) capped his sensational season with three more wins in the World Series. Chief Bender with a 22–5 regular season record, got the other Series victory. Future Hall of Famers second baseman Eddie Collins and third baseman Frank Baker, both of whom joined the Athletics in 1909, became hitting and fielding stars of the first magnitude. Baker became forever known as "Home Run" Baker by slamming two against the Giants in the 1911 World Series. Coombs (29–12), Plank (22–8), and

166

Bender (16–5) continued their amazing pitching in the World Series, with Bender winning two games and Coombs and Plank one each.

After finishing third to the Boston Red Sox and Washington Senators in 1912, the Athletics won another pennant and World Series championship in 1913. Bender's 21–10 record led the pitchers while "Home Run" Baker led the league in his specialty with 12 home runs, 117 RBI, and finished fifth in batting with a .337 mark. Collins was fourth in batting with a .345 average. In the four-games-to-one World Series triumph over the Giants, Bender won two while Plank and Joe Bush each won one.

In 1914 the Athletics won their sixth pennant in 14 seasons, but a turning point in the team's history occurred that year when a third major league, the Federal League, came into being. Salaries escalated tremendously during a bidding war for player talent. As champions, the Athletics players were enticed by wealthy Federal League owners to jump to the new league. The bidding war divided the Athletics into two camps—those loyal to Mack and those who wanted to jump. According to Mack, "even with this split we had won our sixth pennant. But during the World Series our team fell apart. The Boston Braves slaughtered us." The Braves captured the World Series in four straight games; immediately thereafter Mack broke up the team. After pitching aces Bender and Plank bolted to the Federal League, with Mack getting nothing, he decided to sell his remaining stars. Eddie Collins went to the Chicago White Sox for $50,000 and Home Run Baker was sold to the New York Yankees. Not a wealthy man, Mack relied solely on baseball income, so the sale of his stars enabled him to continue operating but necessitated building his team again from scratch.

It would be many years before the A's would again compete for the pennant. They finished last from 1915 through 1921, and began their slow climb upward in 1922 by finishing seventh. Eddie Rommel, who in 1921 led the league in losses with 23, was the league's leading pitcher with 27 victories in 1922. The A's finished sixth in 1923 and fifth in 1924 as future Hall of Famer Al Simmons took over center field and batted .308 and drove in 102 runs. The A's slugging star was Joe Hauser, who finished second to Babe Ruth's 47 home runs with 27 and fourth in the league in RBI with 115.

In 1925 Simmons slammed 29 home runs and drove in 129. Mickey Cochrane, one of baseball's all-time great catchers, joined the team and batted .331. Rommel led the team and league with 21 victories. The Athletics climbed to second place behind Washington.

They were third in 1926, and second in 1927 and 1928 to the world champion New York Yankees, considered by many the best team in baseball history. But the Athletics earned equal status to the all-time great Yankee teams by winning three consecutive pennants in 1929, 1930 and 1931. Another Hall of Famer, Jimmy Foxx, took over first base in 1929 and batted .354, hit 33 home runs, and drove in 118 runs. Al Simmons led the league with 157 RBI, batted .365, and blasted 34 home runs. George Earnshaw led the league with 24 wins and Lefty Grove, on his way to a Hall of Fame career, won 20 and lost only 6. One of the great moments in baseball history occurred in the opening game of the 1929 World Series against the Cubs when 35-year-old Howard Ehmke was selected as Mack's surprise starter and set a World Series strikeout record by fanning 13 Cubs. Earnshaw, Rommel and Rube Walberg got the other wins in Philadelphia's four-games-to-one triumph.

Philadelphia also had an 1884 Union Association team known as the Keystones and a team in the Players League of 1890.

The Athletics repeated as world champs in 1930 by beating St. Louis four games to two, with Earnshaw and Grove winning two each. During the regular season Grove led the league with 28 wins while Earnshaw won 22. The A's won their third consecutive pennant in 1931 but lost a thrilling World Series to the Cardinals four games to three.

Unfortunately, while the Philadelphia Athletics were enjoying unparalleled success on the field, the nation was mired in its worst depression in history. To survive, Mack again had to sell his finest players, and within a few years such Hall of Famers as Cochrane, Foxx, Simmons, Grove and Earnshaw were all playing elsewhere and the team never recovered. The A's finished last in 1935, 1936, 1938, 1940, 1941, 1942, 1943, 1945 and 1950. Third baseman George Kell, who broke in with the A's in 1944, is the only player from the 1940s and 1950s who ultimately made the Hall of Fame. In 1951 outfielder Gus Zernial led the league with 33 homers and 125 RBI, and in 1952 Bobby Shantz was the best pitcher in baseball with a 24–7 record. The Mack family sold the franchise after the 1954 season to Arnold Johnson, who moved the team to Kansas City. Connie Mack died in Philadelphia on February 9, 1957, at the age of 94.

1950s felt cereal round, 6″, Athletics elephant logo, $35.

Philadelphia Athletics (American Association)

1887 Kalamazoo Bats Team Card N690, 4½″ × 6½″, Cabinet Card issued by Charles Gross & Co. of Philadelphia as a promotion for its Kalamazoo Bats Cigarettes. The Philadelphia Athletic Club features a team photo with the caption in a white box at the bottom of the photo $2,700

1887 Kalamazoo Bats Team Card N690-1, 4½″ × 6½″, Cabinet Card issued by Charles Gross & Co. of Philadelphia as a promotion for its Kalamazoo Bats Cigarettes. The Philadelphia Athletic Club features a team photo with the caption in a white box at the bottom of the photo $2,000

1888 Joseph Hall Cabinet Team Card, 6½″ × 4½″ $1,800

Advertising Specialties

Philadelphia Athletics (American League)

1913 Fatima T200 Team Card, 2⅝″ × 4¾″, "World Champs" $125
1939 Schedule Matchbook, 1½″ × 4½″ $20
1950s Atlantic Refining Co. Ball Point Pen & Pencil $35

1939, schedule matchbook, 1½″ × 4½″, $20.

Pennants

1901 through 1905 Regular....................$750
1905 League Champs $1,500
1906 through 1909 ....$750
1910 Regular $750
1910 World Series..............................$1,500
1911 Regular $750
1911 World Series..............................$1,500
1912, 1913 Regular $750

1913 World Series..............................$1,500
1914 Regular $750
1914 League Champs $1,500
1915 through 1920 ....$750
1921 through 1930 Regular...................$300
1930 World Champs $600
1931 Regular $300
1931 League Champs $600
1932 through 1940 ....$200
1936, 1937 Felt Pennant-BF3, Type IV, Pitcher on Pennant $35
1936, 1937 Felt Pennant-BF3, Type V, Bat on Pennant $35

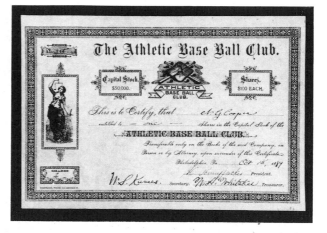

1889, 7½″ × 11″, stock certificate for one share of stock in The Athletic Baseball Club for 1889. The Athletics finished third in the American Association in 1889 with 75 wins and 58 losses under Bill Sharsig (a large supply of this stock was discovered several years ago), $500.

1936, 1937 Felt Pennant-BF3, Type V, Elephant on Pennant $35
1941, 1942, 1943 Regular......................$100
1943 All-Star Game $200
1944 through 1950 ....$100
1951 through 1954 ....$50

Pins

Philadelphia Athletics

1930/1940s American Nut & Chocolate
    Co., 1⅛″ $15

1950s pin, 1⅓″, white elephant with red A's blanket, $15.

Postcards

Philadelphia Athletics (American League)

1910 Individual player faces on elephant, Sporty Postcard Co., Newark, N.J. ...$500

Publications

BOOKS

"Baseball Padre" pseud. *Reflections on a Baseball Team.* Upper Darby, Pa.: Mackmen, 1979. ....$6.00
Lieb, Frederick. *Connie Mack.* G.P. Putnam's Sons, 1945. ....$40.00
Romanowski, Jerome. *The Mackmen.* Camden, N.J., 1979. ....$6.00
Standard Engraving Co. *Our Champions.* Philadelphia, Pa., 1902. ....$300.00
Tri-State Printers. *It All Started in 1908 and Ended In 1970.* 1970. ....$10.00

MEDIA GUIDES

Philadelphia Athletics (American League)

1928 Roster Sheet $125
1929, 1930, 1931 Roster Sheet $100
1932 Roster Booklet............................$125
1933, 1934, 1935 Roster Booklet $100
1936 through 1940 ....$75
1941 through 1949 ....$60
1950, 1951, 1952, 1953 ....$50
1954 Last Year $65

PROGRAMS AND SCORECARDS

Philadelphia Athletics (American League)

1901 ....$600
1902 American League Champs.............$400
1903, 1904 ....$300
1905 League Champs $225
1906 through 1909 ....$200
1910, 1911 World Champs each Year $175
1912 ....$150

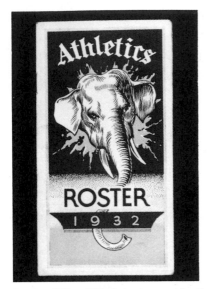

1932 roster, 3⅜″ × 6¼″, elephant cover, defending American League champion Athletics, $125.

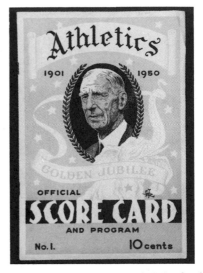

1950 Golden Jubilee year program featuring Connie Mack, owner-manager, on the gold cover, 6¾″ × 9⅞″, 12 pages, $20.

1913 World Champs	$175
1914 League Champs	$175
1915 through 1920	$125
1921 through 1925	$75
1926 through 1929	$50
1930 World Champs	$75
1931 League Champs	$75
1932 through 1940	$35
1941 through 1950	$20
1951 through 1953	$15
1954 Last Year	$25

YEARBOOKS

1902 *Our Champions* by Standard Engraving Co. (Photos & Sketches of Philadelphia Athletics)	$2,500
1905 *The Champion Athletics* by Charles Dryden	$2,500
1910 *Portraits of Chicago Cubs & Philadelphia Athletics* by Chicago Daily News	$2,500
1911 *Pennant Winning Plays and Players* by Philadelphia Evening Bulletin	$2,500
1911 *Philadelphia & New York* by Philadelphia Bulletin	$2,500
1929 *Connie Mack's Philadelphia Athletics,* American League Champion	$500
1949	$200
1950	$175
1951, 1952	$150
1953, 1954 (very common)	$100

1883, 3¾″ × 6″, official scorecard of the Philadelphia Athletics against the Cincinnati Red Stockings on August 22, 1883, at Athletic Park located at 25th and Jefferson Streets. This magenta on white scorecard includes a sketch of the park. The 1883 Athletics were champions of the American Association with 66 wins and only 32 losses under manager Lew Simmons, $500.

Schedules

1901 through 1909	$150
1910 through 1919	$100

1920 through 1929	...............................$75
1930 through 1939	...............................$45
1940 through 1949	...............................$30
1950 through 1954	...............................$25

Special Events

1909 dedication program from April 12, of Shibe Park, the first of the modern steel and concrete major league stadiums, 7¾″ × 10¾″, $750.

ALL-STAR GAME PRESS PINS

| 1943 | ....$350 |

ALL-STAR GAME TICKETS

| 1943 Complete Ticket | ....$200 |
| 1943 Ticket Stub | ....$100 |

WORLD SERIES PRESS PINS

1905	....None Issued
1910	....None Issued
1911	....$10,000
1913	....$6,500
1914	....$6,500
1915	....$6,000
1929 (not dated)	................................$1,500
1930 (not dated)	................................$1,500
1931 (not dated)	................................$1,500

WORLD SERIES PROGRAMS

1905	....$7,000
1910	....$5,000
1911	....$3,000

1943 program from All-Star game at Shibe Park with the Athletics elephant logo prominently displayed, 8″ × 10½″, 56 pages. In 1902 New York Giants manager John McGraw derisively referred to the Athletics as a "white elephant doomed to failure" and Owner-Manager Connie Mack adopted the white elephant as his team's symbol, $450.

1914 bar, ribbon, and pendant press pin from the World Series in which the heavily favored Athletics lost to the Boston Braves four games to none, 1¾″ × 5″, $6,500.

1913, 1914, 1915	$2,000
1929	$1,000
1930	$800
1931	$750

WORLD SERIES GAME TICKETS

1905 Complete Ticket	$2,500
1905 Ticket Stub	$1,200
1910 Complete Ticket	$1,600
1910 Ticket Stub	$800
1911 Complete Ticket	$1,600
1911 Ticket Stub	$800
1913 Complete Ticket	$1,600
1913 Ticket Stub	$800
1914 Complete Ticket	$1,600
1914 Ticket Stub	$800
1915 Complete Ticket	$1,200
1915 Ticket Stub	$600
1930 Complete Ticket	$400
1930 Ticket Stub	$200
1931 Complete Ticket	$400
1931 Ticket Stub	$200

PHILADELPHIA PHILLIES

National League 1876;
1883 to Present

Philadelphia was a charter member of the National League in 1876. In fact, Philadelphia hosted the first-ever National League game on April 22, 1876, but the franchise didn't last the season. Philadelphia was without National League baseball until 1883, when sporting goods magnate Albert J. Reach purchased the Worcester, Massachusetts, Brown Stockings and moved them to the City of Brotherly Love. Called the Phillies, the team's nickname remains the oldest in continuous use in the National League.

The Phillies' first game on May 1, 1883, was a 4 to 3 loss to the Providence Grays before 1000 fans at Recreation Park. The loss was a portent of things to come, because throughout the years the Phillies have been on the losing side a majority of the time.

It was not until 1915 that the Phillies won their first pennant. Led by right-hander Grover Cleveland Alexander's 31 and 10 record, the Phillies finished seven games in front of the defending world champion Boston Braves. In the World Series, however, Boston's American League champion Red Sox won four games to one. The lone Phillies' victory belonged to Alexander, who won the opening game by a 3 to 1 score. During the 1915 season

right fielder Gavvy Cravath, despite being a righthanded batter, supplied the power by slamming 24 home runs and driving in 115 to lead the league in both departments by a wide margin. It was only 280 seductive feet down the right field foul line at Baker Bowl (home of the Phillies since 1887)—an easy mark for Cravath's powerful bat.

Although the Phillies finished second in both 1916 and 1917, things took a turn for the worse in 1919 when they finished last to begin three consecutive years in the cellar. A fourth-place finish in 1932 was their best record until 1949, when they finished third. From 1919 through 1945, the Phillies finished in last place 16 times, the most abysmal record in baseball.

There were some bright spots during this span, however. In 1929 Lefty O'Doul won the National League batting title with a .398 average and right fielder Chuck Klein was league home run king with 43 and fourth in runs batted in with 145. The result was a fifth-place finish rather than the usual eighth spot. Klein toiled with the Phillies from 1928 through 1933 and again from 1936 through 1944 and finally received his deserved recognition in 1980 when he was inducted into the Hall of Fame.

Phillies' fortunes took a turn for the better when the Carpenter family purchased them in late 1943 and began to spend money to acquire good young players. It paid off in 1950 when the Phils took their first pennant since 1915. Known as the "Whiz Kids," the Phillies featured superb pitching by righthanders Robin Roberts and Curt Simmons and relief ace Jim Konstanty, who was named National League MVP. Right fielder Del Ennis led the club with a .311 batting average and topped the league in RBI with 126. Center fielder Richie Ashburn batted .303 and was brilliant defensively. However, in the World Series, they lost in four straight to the New York Yankees.

In 1976, 1977 and 1978, powerful young sluggers like outfielder Greg Luzinski and third baseman Mike Schmidt led a fearsome attack that enabled the Phillies to win division titles. Lefthander Steve Carlton was the league's top pitcher and Cy Young Award winner in 1972, 1977, 1980 and 1982.

However, it was not until 1980 that the

Phillies reached the World Series again. With 48 home runs and 121 RBI, Mike Schmidt won his first of three MVP awards. In the World Series Carlton won two games as the Phillies captured their first world championship by defeating Kansas City four games to two.

The Phillies made it to the World Series again in 1983, but lost to the Baltimore Orioles in five games. Cy Young Award winner John Denny got the Phillies' only win in the opener. In the 1993 World Series, the Phillies lost to the Toronto Blue Jays four games to two.

Advertising Specialties

1886 Lorillard Team card, 4″ × 5″ $1,200
1887 Kalamazoo Bats Team Card N690-1, 4½″ × 6½″ Cabinet Card issued by Charles Gross & Co. of Philadelphia as a promotion for its Kalamazoo Bats Cigarettes. The Philadelphia Baseball Club features a team photo on a black mount with the words "Smoke Kalamazoo Bats"...$2,700
1887 Kalamazoo Bats Team Card N690-1, 4½″ × 6½″ Cabinet Card issued by Charles Gross & Co. of Philadelphia as a promotion for its Kalamazoo Bats Cigarettes. The Philadelphia Baseball Club features a team photo on a black mount $2,000
1913 Fatima T200 Team Card, 2⅝″ × 4¾″ $100
1950 Ballpoint Pen and Pencil issued by Atlantic Refining Company $45
1959 Multicolored Felt Rounds $35

1980 poster of the world champion Phillies, 14″ × 22″, sold as a premium by the now defunct Philadelphia Bulletin newspaper, $25.

Ballbark Giveaways

1971 T-shirt, Bat, Batting Glove, Helmet, Cap, Ball $5
1971 Ball (if containing facsimile autographs) $15
1971 Poster $15
1972 Sweatshirt, T-shirt, Bat, Golf Cap, Cap, Batting Glove, Helmet, Ball $5
1972 Ball (if containing facsimile autographs) $15
1973 Sweatshirt, Warm-up Jacket, T-shirt, Bat, Helmet, Ball, Cap, Golf Cap, Batting Glove $5
1973 Ball (if containing facsimile autographs) $15
1974 Warm-up Jacket, Team Shirt, Helmet, T-shirt, Wrist Band, Bat, Cap, Ball $5
1974 Ball (if containing facsimile autographs) $15
1975 Warm-up Jacket, Team Shirt, Helmet, Bat, Wrist Band, Visor, Cap, Ball, Ski Cap $5
1975 AMC Sweatshirt (whenever sponsor appears on item add, $1) $6
1975 Ball (if containing facsimile autographs) $15
1976 Equipment Bag, Jacket $5
1976 Centennial Cap, Centennial Patch $7
1976 Old Tyme Bottle Bat $10

1970s clock, 16″ × 16″, Medford Meats, makers of Phillie Franks, yellow, blue, and red, for use in stores carrying the product, $30.

1977 Jacket, Team Jersey, Hat,
Pillowbag, Helmet, School Bag..........$5
1977 Red Bat $6
1978 Sweatshirt, Batting Glove, Gym
Shorts, Wrist Band, Tube Socks,
Cap, Poncho, Pennant, Shirt, Ski
Cap $5
1978 Tastycake Notebook, English Lea-
ther Jacket $6
1979 Poncho, Tote Bag, Cap, Roll-up Hat,
Ski Cap $5
1979 English Leather Jacket, Tasty Cake
Tank Top, Tastycake Back Pack.........$6
1979 Poster $10
1980 Ladies Sun Hat, Sweatshirt, T-shirt,
Cap, Gym Shorts, Tube Socks, Hel-
met $5
1980 Poster (world champions) $12
1981 World Series Ring $20
1981 Tote Bag, Sports Cap, T-shirt, Cap,
Team Jersey, Picnic Cup $5
1981 Poster..$8
1981 American Dairy Association Jacket.....$6
1982 Jacket, Bat, Tote Bag, Shirt, Roll-up
Hat, Batting Glove, Equipment Bag,
Tube Socks, Ski Cap $5
1982 Poster..$8
1983 Jacket, Sports Shorts, Wrist Band,
Dickie Turtle Neck $5
1983 100th Anniversary Poster.................$10
1983 Tastycake 100th Anniversary Patch,
Gulf 100th Anniversary Ball, Ther-
mos..$8
1983 MAB Paint Beach Towel, Tastycake
Flight Bag, Maxwell House
Sweatshirt, Roy Rogers Equipment
Bag, Thrift Drug Grey T-shirt $5
1984 Nylon Windbreaker, Warm-up
Shirt, Beach Towel, Painter Cap,
Sun Hat, Barbecue Apron, Cap,
Winter Scarf, Equipment Bag $5
1984 Wristwatch, Phanatic T-shirt $6
1984 Player Photo Cards (set) $10
1985 Phanatic T-shirt, Tastycake Travel
Bag, Mellon Bank Windbreaker,
MAB Beach Towel, MAB Family
Cooler, Wrist Watch, Ashburn Hat
Day $6
1985 Baseball Glove, Shirt, Cap, Wallet,
Back Pack $5
1986 Helmet, Women's Sunglasses,
Phanatic Beach Towel, Team Jersey Players Workout Jacket, Cap,
Backpack, Sports Socks, Radio $5
1986 Tastycake Glove, MAB Sportsbag $6
1987 Tastycake Photocards (set) $12
1987 MAB T-shirt, Mellon Baseball
Glove, Tastycake Travel Bag,
Watch $6
1987 Corduroy Cap, Jacket, Ball ($10
with facsimile autographs) $5
1988 Calendar, Signature Baseball $10
1988 Tastycake Photo Cards (set) $12
1988 Jacket, Glove, Corduroy Cap, Team
Shirt, Bat $5

1988 Phanatics 10th Anniversary
Sweatshirt, MAB Beach Towel,
Tastycake Flip Up Sunglasses,
Women's Watch, Tastycake Lunch
Bag, Phanatic Ski Cap.......................$6
1989 Jacket, Glove, Bat, Wristband,
Equipment Bag, Corduroy Cap,
Sports Bottle, Back Pack....................$5
1989 MAB Beach Towel, I. Goldberg
Warm-up Shirt, Mr. Goodbuy's
Baseball Cap, Tastycake Ladies
Nightshirt, Property of Phillies Grey
T-shirt, Tastycake Lunch Bag $6
1989 Tastycake Photo Card Set $12
1990 Women's Flight Bag, Team Road
Jersey, Warm-up Jacket $5
1990 Tastycake Corduroy Cap, Wawa/
Medford Women's Nightshirt, MAB
Caricature Towel, Breyers Neon
Sunglasses, US Healthcare Team
Equipment Bag, Texaco Men's
Sportsmens Hat, Gillette Property of
the Phillies T-shirt, Gatorade Sports
Beltbag, Campbell's Batting Helmet....$6
1990 Donruss Baseball Card Book $7
1992 Opening Day Poster $7
1992 Mellon PSFS Phillies Cap, Texaco
Oldtime Baseball Cap, Tastycake
Sunglasses, Gatorade Insulated
Sports Bottle, Campbell's Soup
Back Pack, MAB Women's Beach
Bag, IGA Team Jersey $6
1992 Donruss Baseball Cardbook, Upper
Deck Heros of Baseball $7
1992 T-shirt, Jacket $5
1993 Batting Helmet, Road Jersey $5
1993 Donruss Cardbook, Upper Deck........$7
1993 Tastycake Phanatic Cap, MAB Paint
Umbrella, Super Pretzel Equipment
Bag, Mellon PSFS Beach Towel,
Texaco Cap, Acme/Kraft Jacket,
Campbell Soup Back Pack $6
1993 Batting Helmet, Mesh Batting Prac-
tice Jersey...$5

Miscellaneous

BOBBIN' HEAD DOLLS

Category #II, 1961, 1962, White Square
Base, Boy Head $180
Category #III, 1961, 1962, White Round
Miniature, Boy Head $200
Category #IV, 1962, 1963, 1964, Green
Round Base, Boy Head $70
Category #V, 1962, 1963, 1964, Green
Round Base, Black Player $625
Category #VI, 1967 through 1972, Gold
Round Base, Boy Head $70

EXHIBIT CARD

1950 Exhibit Supply Co. Team Card $14

1983 League Champs $15
1984 through 1990 ....$5
1991, 1992, 1993 ....$3

Pins

1930/1940s American Nut & Chocolate
    Co., 1⅛" $15
1961 through 1965 Crane Potato Chips,
    ⅞", Round $5
1967 through 1969 Crane Potato Chips,
    ⅞", Round $5
1984 Crane Potato Chips, ⅞", Round $3
1964, 1965, 1966 Guy's Potato Chips, ⅞",
    Round $5

Publications

BOOKS

Allen, Lee. *Phillies Batting, Pitching,
    Fielding All-Time Records and
    Rosters.* Kirch Publishing Co.,
    1953. ....$30.00

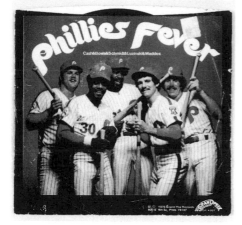

1976 *Phillies Fever* record in paper jacket, 7¼" ×
7¼", featuring five members of the 1976 Phillies (Greg
Luzinski, Dave Cash, Garry Maddox, Larry Bowa, and
Mike Schmidt) singing *Phillies Fever* written by Walt
Kahn, Lorenzo Wright, and Rich Wing, $10.

Pennants

1901 through 1915 Regular....................$750
1915 League Champs $1,500
1916 through 1920 ....$750
1921 through 1930 ....$300
1931 through 1940 ....$200
1936, 1937 Felt Pennant BF-3, Type IV,
    Pitcher on Pennant $35
1936, 1937 Felt Pennant BF-3, Type V,
    Liberty Bell on Pennant $35
1941 through 1950 Regular....................$100
1950 League Champs $200
1951, 1952 Regular $50
1952 All-Star Game $125
1953 through 1960 ....$50
1961 through 1970 ....$30
1971 through 1976 Regular $20
1976 All-Star Game $50
1977 through 1980 Regular $20
1980 League Champs $50
1980 World Champs.............................$50
1981, 1982, 1983 Regular $5

1950 picture pin showing black-and-white cameos of
14 members of the National League Champions, red
block letters and script, 3½". It was the Phillies first
N.L. pennant since 1915, but they lost to the Yankees
in the World Series in four straight games, $50.

1976 polyester pennant from the
All-Star game at Veterans Stadium
showing the stadium and names
of the American League stars
in red on a white field,
12" × 29½", $50.

1980 pin, 1½″, Phillies Phanatic mascot with Phillies pennant, produced by Harrison/Erickson. The Phillies defeated the Kansas City Royals in the 1980 World Series, giving the Phillies their only world championship in history, $15.

1953, *The Philadelphia Phillies* by Fred Lieb & Stan Baumgartner, Putnam, N.Y., 5¾″ × 8¼″, 246 pages, the complete history of the Philadelphia National League team through the 1950s, $100.

Ashburn, Rich & Allen Lewis. *Richie Ashburn's Phillies Trivia.* Philadelphia: Running Press, 1983. ....$10.00
Bilovsky, Frank & Richard Westcott. *The Phillies Encyclopedia.* West Point, N.Y.: Leisure Press, 1984. ......$20.00
Bodley, Hal. *The Team That Wouldn't Die: The Philadelphia Phillies, World Champion, 1980.* Wilmington, Del.: Serendipity Press, 1984. ....$15.00
Hinz, Bob. *Philadelphia Phillies.* Man-

kato, Mn.: Creative Education, 1982. ....$5.00
•Honig, Donald. *The Philadelphia Phillies: An Illustrated History.* New York: Prentice-Hall, 1992. ....$27.50
Lewis, Allen. *The Philadelphia Phillies.* New York: Simon & Schuster, 1982. ....$15.00
Lewis, Allen. *The Philadelphia Phillies: A Pictorial History.* Virginia Beach, Va.: J.C.P. Corp., 1981. ....$20.00
Lewis, Allen & Larry Shenk. *This Date In Philadelphia Phillies History.* New York: Stein & Day, 1979. ....$5.00
Lieb, Frederick & Stan Baumgartner. *The Philadelphia Phillies.* G.P. Putnam's Sons, 1953. ....$100.00
Philadelphia Phillies. *The World Champion Phillies & The Road To Victory.* Philadelphia, 1981. ....$10.00
Rothaus, James R. *Philadelphia Phillies.* Mankato, Mn.: Creative Education, 1987. ....$5.00
Tri-State Printers. *It All Started in 1908 and Ended In 1970.* 1970. ....$10.00

MEDIA GUIDES

1927 Roster Sheet $125
1928 through 1931 Roster Sheet $100
1932 Roster Booklet.............................$125
1933, 1934, 1935 Roster Booklet $100
1936 through 1940 Roster Booklet............$75
1941 through 1948 Roster Booklet............$60
1949 League Champs Roster Booklet........$70
1950 through 1955 ....$50
1956 through 1961 ....$40
1962, 1963, 1964 ....$200
1965, 1966 ....$20
1967, 1968 ....$17
1969, 1970 ....$15
1971, 1972 ....$12
1973, 1974 ....$10
1975, 1976 ....$8
1977, 1978 ....$7
1979 ....$6
1980 World Champs $8
1981 ....$6
1982, 1983, 1984 ....$5
1985 through 1993 ....$4

PROGRAMS AND SCORECARDS

1900 through 1902 ....$400
1903, 1904 ....$300
1905 through 1909 ....$200
1910 through 1914 ....$150
1915 League Champs $175
1916 through 1920 ....$125
1921 through 1925 ....$75
1926 through 1930 ....$50
1931 through 1940 ....$35

1941 through 1949	$20
1950 League Champs	$20
1951 through 1959	$15
1960 through 1969	$10
1970 through 1979	$6
1980 World Champs	$8
1981, 1982	$4
1983 League Champs	$6
1984 through 1989	$4
1990, 1991, 1992, 1993	$3

YEARBOOKS

1949	$200
1950 League Champs	$150
1951	$600
1952	$125

1953	$100
1954	$150
1955	$100
1956	$125
1957	$100
1958, 1959, 1960	$90
1961	$300
1962	$80
1963, 1964, 1965	$75
1966	$65
1967	$55
1968	$50
1969	$45
1970, 1971	$40
1972	$30
1973	$25
1974	$20
1975, 1976, 1977	$18
1978	$15
1979	$12
1980, 1981	$20
1982	$7
1983 League Champs	$10
1984, 1985, 1986	$5
1987	$8
1988 through 1993	$5

Schedules

1900 through 1909	$150
1910 through 1919	$100
1920 through 1929	$75
1930 through 1939	$45
1940 through 1949	$30
1950 through 1959	$25
1960 through 1969	$15
1970 through 1979	$10
1980 through 1985	$2
1986 through 1993	$1

Special Events

ALL-STAR GAME PRESS PINS

1952	$300
1976 Star Top	$75
1976 Bell Top	$75

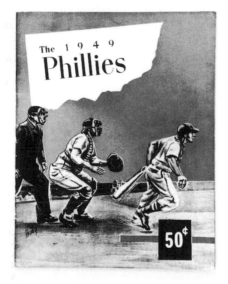

1949 yearbook, *The 1949 Phillies,* 8½″ × 11″, 40 pages, artist-drawn batter, catcher, and umpire in blue tone on a red-and-white background, $200.

1971 Arco schedule (unfolded), 3½″ × 6¾″, red, white, and blue, action scene of a player sliding into a base on the front and a diagram of Veterans Stadium seating arrangements on the back, $10.

ALL-STAR PROGRAMS

1952 ....$125
1976 ....$25

ALL-STAR GAME TICKETS

1952 Complete Ticket $150
1952 Ticket Stub..................................$75
1976 Complete Ticket $40
1976 Ticket Stub..................................$20

LEAGUE CHAMPIONSHIP SERIES PROGRAMS

1976, 1977 ....$15
1978 ....$12
1980 ....$10
1981 Eastern Division Play-Off $25
1983 ....$10

LEAGUE CHAMPIONSHIP SERIES TICKETS

1976 Complete Ticket $38
1976 Ticket Stub..................................$20
1977 Complete Ticket $38
1977 Ticket Stub..................................$20
1978 Complete Ticket $38
1978 Ticket Stub..................................$20
1980 Complete Ticket $28
1980 Ticket Stub..................................$15
1983 Complete Ticket $28
1983 Ticket Stub..................................$15

WORLD SERIES PRESS PINS

1915 ....$6,000
1950 ....$500
1980 ....$50
1983 ....$40

WORLD SERIES PROGRAMS

1915 ....$2,000
1950 ....$250
1980 ....$15
1983 ....$12

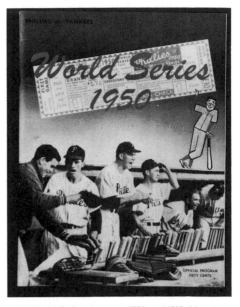

1950 World Series program, 8¾″ × 11¾″, 64 pages, showing a jubilant Phillies dugout, the Phillies cartoon mascot holding a green World Series ticket, and "World Series 1950" in red script lettering on a green background. The Phillies lost to the New York Yankees in four straight games, $250.

WORLD SERIES GAME TICKETS

1915 Complete Ticket $1,200
1915 Ticket Stub $600
1950 Complete Ticket $250
1950 Ticket Stub $125
1980 Complete Ticket $30
1980 Ticket Stub..................................$15
1983 Complete Ticket $30
1983 Ticket Stub..................................$15

Pittsburgh, Pennsylvania

PITTSBURGH ALLEGHENIES

American Association 1882–1886, Players League 1890

Pittsburgh's rich National League tradition dates back to 1887, when the Al-leghenies of the American Association switched leagues after the Kansas City franchise was expelled following the 1886 season.

In 1890 they lost many of their better players to the Players League, a one-season operation run by the players who lacked the finances or business acumen to compete any longer. The decimation of the Alleghenies, however, caused Pittsburgh to lose a club record 113 games.

When the Players League folded, it was expected that all players would return to their former teams. Louis Bierbauer, however, had other ideas. A second baseman with Brooklyn of the Players League, Bierbauer was expected to return to the Philadelphia Athletics of the American Association, where he had played the four previous seasons, but opted instead to play with Pittsburgh of the National League.

PITTSBURGH PIRATES

National League 1887 to Present

The Athletics and their American Association cohorts began calling the Pittsburgh team "pirates" for stealing their players. It's a nickname they have proudly worn ever since.

Mediocrity was the hallmark of Pittsburgh's 13 seasons at the close of the nineteenth century. A second place finish in 1893 was by far their best record. That changed dramatically after the 1899 season. The National League decided to reduce from 12 to 8 teams, with the Louisville Colonels one of the casualties. Louisville owner Barney Dreyfuss acquired controlling interest in the Pirates and brought 14 players from the Colonels along with him. And what great players they were—including future Hall of Famers Honus Wagner, Fred Clarke, and Rube Waddell plus outstanding stars like Deacon Phillipe, Tommy Leach, Chief Zimmer and Claude Ritchie. Like magic the Pirates became the best team in baseball and won pennants in 1901, 1902, and 1903 and a world championship in 1909.

Although the American League was formed in 1901 to complete with the National League as a second major league, no world championship was held until 1903. The Pirates were top-heavy favorites to beat the Boston Puritans, but lost the World Series five games to three with Phillipe recording all three Pirate victories. Bill Dinneen (with three wins) and Cy Young (with two) stymied the heavy-hitting Pirate batters. Young, of course,

went on to win 509 major league games, a record likely to remain forever.

Pittsburgh's greatest star was Honus Wagner. After joining the Pirates in 1900, the "Flying Dutchman" proceeded to win eight National League batting titles during his 21 seasons. The pinnacle of Wagner's fabulous career came in 1909 when he guided them to their first world championship after leading the league in batting at .339 and RBI with 100.

The 1909 Pirates also had outstanding pitching. Howie Camnitz won 25 games, Vic Willis recorded 22 victories, and Lefty Leifield notched 19. However, it was 12-game-winner Babe Adams who became the World Series hero against Detroit by winning three games while Camnitz, Willis, and Leifield failed to win a game.

Wagner performed brilliantly, getting 8 hits in 24 at bats (.333) while driving in 6 runs to clearly outplay Detroit's young superstar, Ty Cobb, who went on to become baseball's all-time leading batter with a .367 average. In the World Series Cobb matched Wagner with 6 RBI but only batted .231.

Another milestone occurred in 1909 when Forbes Field opened in June to rave reviews as only the second all-steel-and-concrete major league ballpark. Shibe Park in Philadelphia, which opened a few months earlier, was the first. Forbes Field served the Pirates faithfully until Three Rivers Stadium opened during the 1970 season. Three Rivers Stadium was built on almost the same site as Exposition Park, a 15,000-seat wooden structure, which had been the Pirates home from 1891 until Forbes Field opened.

After the 1909 championship, the Pirates languished in the second division much of the time until the early 1920s. Then, with another influx of future Hall of Famers such as Pie Traynor, Kiki Cuyler, Rabbit Maranville, and Max Carey, the Pirates finished third in 1922, 1923, and 1924 and then won the pennant in 1925. After falling behind three games to one in the 1925 World Series, the Pirates became the first team in history to rally from that deficit to capture the series with three straight wins over the defending world champion Washington Senators.

Two more future Hall of Famers, Paul "Big Poison" Waner in 1926 and Lloyd "Little Poison" Waner in 1927, joined the Pirates and immediately contributed to their success. The Pirates were National League champs again in 1927 as Paul led the league with a .380 batting average and 131 RBI while brother Lloyd batted .355. Carmen Hill led the team with 22 wins while Lee Meadows and Ray Kremer won 19 apiece with Kremer's 2.47 ERA, the best in the league. However, in the World Series the Pirates lost in four straight to the New York Yankees, considered by many to be the best team in baseball history.

Although the 1927 Pirates were the last Pittsburgh pennant winner for 33 years, the fans had much to cheer about. Paul Waner batted over .300 fourteen times, won three batting titles (1927, 1934 and 1936), finished with a .333 career batting average, and was league MVP in 1927. Lloyd batted above .300 ten times and had a lifetime .316 batting average. Another Hall of Famer, shortstop Arky Vaughn, hit .385 in 1935, the highest National League average in the twentieth century. Pie Traynor, who played with the Pirates from 1920 through 1937, compiled a .320 career batting average and was voted the best third baseman ever.

Another Pirate Hall of Famer, slugging outfielder Ralph Kiner, joined the team in 1946 and over the next seven seasons either won or shared the National League home run title, a record unmatched in baseball history. Despite Kiner's heroics, the Pirates finished last twice, seventh three times, sixth once and fourth once during his seven seasons in Pittsburgh.

In 1960 everything came together under manager Danny Murtaugh. Dick Groat led the league in batting at .325 and was league MVP while future Hall of Famer Roberto Clemente led the team with 94 RBI. Vernon Law (20–9) and Bob Friend (18–12) were the club's leading pitchers. In the World Series against the New York Yankees, the Pirates revenged their 1927 shellacking by beating the Bronx Bombers in seven thrill-packed games. In the seventh game, second baseman Bill Mazeroski broke a 9 to 9 tie in the bottom of the ninth with a home run off Bill Terry, the first time in history a home run ended the World Series.

Murtaugh was back at the helm in 1971 when the Pirates won another pennant and world championship. Willie Stargell was the National League's home run leader with 48 and paced the Pirates with

125 RBI. The World Series belonged to Roberto Clemente, who batted .404 and fielded brilliantly; and Steve Blass, who won two games (including the seventh and deciding game) as the Pirates beat the Baltimore Orioles four games to three. The Pirates were world champs again in 1979 after beating the Orioles by rallying from a three-games-to-one deficit. Stargell won both regular season and World Series MVP honors by batting .400 in the series with three homers and seven RBI. Like Clemente, Stargell was elected to baseball's Hall of Fame.

Clemente batted over .300 thirteen times and was league MVP in 1966. Tragically, he died on December 31, 1972, in a plane crash in his native Puerto Rico while on a mercy mission to earthquake-stricken Nicaragua.

Pittsburgh also had teams in the Union Association (1884) and the Federal League (1914–1915).

In the early 1980s, with attendance dipping below one million three times, it appeared Pittsburgh might lost its team. But local corporations purchased the ball club from the Galbreath family on October 2, 1985, and under manager Jim Leyland enjoyed a resurgence on the field and at the gate. Winning three consecutive Eastern Division championships (1990, 1991, 1992), the Pirates drew more than two million fans all three years.

Barry Bonds was league MVP in 1990 while Doug Drabek won the Cy Young Award after winning 22 games. Bonds was National League Player of the Year in 1991 and John Smiley became a 20-game winner for the first time. Smiley and All-Star outfielder Bobby Bonilla both left the team for free agency after the 1991 season, but in 1992 the Pirates won their third straight division title thanks to Andy Van Slyke and Bonds, who again was named league MVP. After the 1992 season, Bonds, as a free agent, signed with San Francisco.

In addition to Pirate Hall of Famers already mentioned, others honored are Bill McKechnie, who managed the team from 1922 through 1926, and Branch Rickey, who was general manager from 1951 through 1955. The following Hall of Famers spent a portion of their careers with the Pirates: Jake Beckley, Jack Chesbro,

Joe Cronin, Frankie Frisch, Pud Galvin, Hank Greenberg, Burleigh Grimes, Billy Herman, Waite Hoyt, Joseph Kelley, George Kelly, Chuck Klein, Fred Lindstrom, Al Lopez, Connie Mack, Heinie Manush, Casey Stengel, and Dazzy Vance.

Advertising Specialties

1887 Kalamazoo Bats Team Card N690-1, 4½" × 6½", Cabinet Card issued by Charles Gross & Co. of Philadelphia as a promotion for its Kalamazoo Bats Cigarettes. The Pittsburgh Baseball Club features a team photo with the caption in a white box at the bottom of the photo $2,700

1887 Kalamazoo Bats Team Card N690-1, Different Pose, 4½" × 6½", Cabinet Card issued by Charles Gross & Co. of Philadelphia as a promotion for its Kalamazoo Bats Cigarettes. The Pittsburgh Baseball Club features a team photo with the caption in a white box at the bottom of the photo $2,000

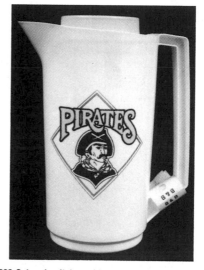

1992 Gatorade pitcher with yellow top, company logo on one side and Pirates logo on the other, 7½" × 9¼". These pitchers were used by numerous teams as ballpark giveaways, $7.

Ballpark Giveaways

1975 T-shirt, Wrist Band, Pennant (if dated $10) $5
1976 Jacket $5
1977 Helmet, Jacket $5
1979 Helmet, Visor, Batting Glove $5
1979 McDonald's Poncho, Tasty Cake Ski Cap $6
1980 Pirates World Championship Ring $25
1980 Color Team Photo $12
1980 Bat, Cap, Jersey, Ski Cap, Jacket $5
1981 Rolaids Color Team Photo, Folgers Tankard $10
1982 Pirates Calendar, Mug, Color Team Photo $10

1982 Visor, Ski Cap, Pennant (if dated $7) $5
1983 Atan Calendar, Budweiser Color Team Poster Budweiser Mug $10
1983 Budweiser Visor, Home Sports TV Cushion, Pirate Scarf $6
1984 Bucco Book, Bonanza Calendar, Foodland Thermos, Budweiser Mug..$10
1984 97 Bumper Sticker, Parrot's Birthday Wallet, 7-Up Cap, Gimbel's Wrist Watch, KDKA Beach Towel, Scarf $6
1985 Purina Dog Chow Calendar, Kahn's Color Team Photo $9
1985 Mellon Bank Umbrella, 7-Up Cap, Gulf Painter Cap $6

1913 Fatima Cigarettes photo card of Pirates who finished 4th in the National League, 1⅞" × 5". Included are Hall of Famers Honus Wagner, Fred Clarke and Max Carey, $100.

1986 Pirates Photo Album, Mug $8
1986 Seat Cushion, Umbrella, Picnic
       Cooler, Sports Bag, Sweatshirt, Cap $5
1987 Pirates Centennial Calendar, Old
       Timers Day Poster, Centennial
       Cups...$10
1988 Surf Book $10
1988 Mug $5
1988 Visor, Jacket, Cap, Corduroy Cap,
       Ski Cap, Glove, Helmet, Batting
       Glove $5
1991 Gatorade Pitcher............................$7
1993 Baseball Card Book, Great Mo-
       ments 1, 2, 3, 4, Pirate Picture
       Cards ....ea. $6
1993 Batting Helmet, Umbrella, Cooler
       Bag, Key Ring, Cap, Jersey, Sun-
       glasses, Pen & Pencil, Cap.................$5
1993 1925 Cap, Homestead Grays Cap,
       1994 All-Star Game Cap $6

Miscellaneous

Mug o' nuts stein with company label on one side and Pirates logo on the other, 4″ × 7″. These steins contained peanuts and were made for every major league city where the product was marketed, $10.

BOBBIN' HEAD DOLLS

Category #I, 1960, 1961, Gold Square
    Base, Mascot $175
Category #II, 1961, 1962, White Square
    Base, Mascot $400
Category #III, 1961, 1962, White Round
    Miniature, Mascot $275
Category #IV, 1962, 1963, 1964, Green
    Round Base, Mascot $140
Category #V, 1962, 1963, 1964, Green
    Round Base, Black Player $1,550
Category #VI, 1967 through 1972, Gold
    Round Base, Mascot $80

Pirates bank, 8″, produced by Stanford Pottery, Cleveland, Ohio, which also produced similar banks of Cleveland Indians and Boston Braves, $175.

Pennants

1901 through 1903 Regular $750
1903 League Champs $1,500
1904 through 1909 Regular $750
1909 World Champs $1,500
1910 through 1920 ....$750
1921 through 1925 Regular $300
1925 World Champs $600
1926, 1927 Regular $300
1927 League Champs $600
1928, 1929, 1930 ....$300
1931 through 1940 ....$200
1936, 1937 Felt Pennant-BF-3, Type V,
    Skull & Crossbones on Pennant $35
1941 through 1944 Regular $100
1944 All-Star Game $200
1945 through 1950 ....$100
1951 through 1959 Regular $50
1959 All-Star Game $200
1960 Regular $50
1960 World Champs $125
1961 through 1970 ....$30
1971 Regular $20
1971 League Champs $50
1971 World Champs $50
1972 through 1974 Regular $20
1974 All-Star Game $50
1975 through 1979 Regular $20
1979 League Champs $50
1979 World Champs $50
1980 ....$20
1981 through 1990 ....$5
1991, 1992, 1993 ....$3

1961 Bazooka pennant produced as a premium by the Topps Gum Co., 4½″ × 14½″, $35.

Pins

1930/1940s American Nut & Chocolate,
    1⅛″, Round $15
1961 through 1965 Crane Potato Chips,
    ⅞″, Round $5
1967, 1968, 1969 Crane Potato Chips, ⅞″,
    Round $5
1984 Crane Potato Chips, ⅞″, Round $3
1964 through 1966 Guy's Potato Chips,
    ⅞″, Round $5

1902 pin, 1¼″, red-and-blue Pittsburgh pennant. The Pirates walked away with the National League pennant, out-distancing 2nd place Brooklyn by 27½ games. Hall of Famers Honus Wagner and Fred Clarke had outstanding seasons and outfielder Ginger Beaumont led the league in batting with a .357 BA. The World Series between the American and National Leagues did not begin until 1903, $250.

Publications

BOOKS

Burtt, Richard L. *The Pittsburgh
    Pirates: A Pictorial History.* Vir-
    ginia Beach, Va.: Jordan, 1977. ....$15.00
Century Printing Co. *Forbes Field
    60th Birthday: Pittsburgh Pirates
    Album.* 1969. ....$20.00

Eckhouse, Morris & Carl Mastrocola.
    *This Date in Pittsburgh Pirates
    History.* New York: Stein & Day,
    1980. ....$5.00
Groat, Dick & Bill Surface. *The World
    Champions Pittsburgh Pirates.*
    New York: Coward-McCann, 1961. ..$30.00
Lieb, Frederick. *The Pittsburgh
    Pirates.* G.P. Putnam's Sons, 1948. ...$85.00
Martin, Mollie. *The Pittsburgh
    Pirates.* Mankato, Mn.: Creative
    Education, 1982. ....$5.00
•Richeal, Kip. *Pittsburgh Pirates: Still
    Walking Tall.* $19.95
Rothaus, James R. *Pittsburgh Pirates.*
    Mankato, Mn.: Creative Educa-
    tion, 1987. ....$5.00
Rowswell A. (Rowsy). *Pittsburgh
    Baseball Through the Years.* Fort
    Pitt Brewing Co., 1952. ....$35.00

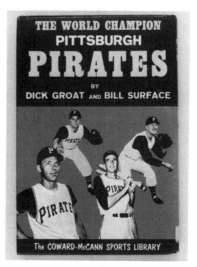

1961, *The World Champion Pittsburgh Pirates* by Dick Groat and Bill Surface, Coward-McCann, chronicles the Pirates 1960 season and the dramatic victory over the New York Yankees in the 7th game of the World Series, $30.

1909 scorecard postcard for World Series between Pirates and Detroit Tigers, sold at Pittsburgh to record details of the game and send to friends. This particular card reported Babe Adams' 6 hit shut-out victory in the 7th and deciding game as Adams won 3 of the 4 Pirate victories, $250.

Sahadi, Lou. *The Pirates.* New York: Times Books, 1988. ....$15.00
Smizik, Robert. *Pittsburgh Pirates: An Illustrated History.* New York: Walker, 1990. ....$15.00

Media Guides

1927 Roster Sheet League Champs $185
1928 through 1931 Roster Sheet $100
1932 Roster Booklet $125
1933, 1934, 1935 Roster Booklet $100
1936 through 1940 ....$75
1941 through 1949 ....$60
1950 through 1955 ....$50
1956 through 1959 ....$40
1960 World Champs $45
1961 ....$40
1962, 1963, 1964 ....$30
1965, 1966 ....$20
1967, 1968 ....$17
1969 ....$15
1970 Division Champs $17
1971 World Champs $15
1972 Division Champs $15
1973 ....$10
1974, 1975 Division Champs $12
1976 ....$8
1977, 1978 ....$7
1979 World Champs $8
1980, 1981 ....$6
1982, 1983, 1984 ....$5
1985 through 1993 ....$4

PROGRAMS AND SCORECARDS

1900, 1901, 1902 ....$400
1903 League Champs $300
1904 League Champs $315
1905 through 1908 ....$200
1909 World Champs $215
1910 through 1914 ....$150

1915 through 1920 ....$125
1921 through 1924 ....$75
1925 World Champs $85
1926 ....$50
1927 League Champs $55
1928, 1929, 1930 ....$50
1931 through 1940 ....$35
1941 through 1949 ....$20
1950 through 1959 ....$15
1960 World Champs $12
1961 through 1969 ....$10
1970 Division Champs $8
1971 League Champs $8
1972 Division Champs $8
1973 ....$6
1974, 1975 Division Champs each Year $8
1976, 1977, 1978 ....$6
1979 World Champs $8
1980 through 1989 ....$4
1990, 1991, 1992 Division Champs each Year $5
1993 ....$3

YEARBOOKS

1910 *Line Drives at the Pittsburgh Pirates,* Pittsburgh Press (Records, Sketches, and Photos of 1909 World Champions) $2,500
1951 ....$225
1952 ....$100
1953, 1954 ....$90
1955 ....$85
1956 ....$75
1957 ....$70
1958 ....$60
1959 ....$55
1959 *The 1959 Pittsburgh Pirates Story,* Phillie Cigars $25
1960 World Champs $75
1961, 1962 ....$45
1963, 1964 ....$35

1965	$30
1966 through 1969	$25
1969 *Pittsburgh Pirates Photo Album,* Foodland	$20
1970 Division Champs	$27
1971 World Champs	$22
1972	$20
1973	$15
1974, 1975 Division Champs each Year	$20
1976, 1977	$12
1978	$10
1979 World Champs	$15
1980, 1981	$8
1982, 1983, 1984	$7
1985 through 1993	$5

Schedules

1900 through 1909	$150
1910 through 1919	$100
1920 through 1929	$75
1930 through 1939	$45
1940 through 1949	$30
1950 through 1959	$25
1960 through 1969	$15
1970 through 1979	$10
1980 through 1985	$2
1986 through 1993	$1

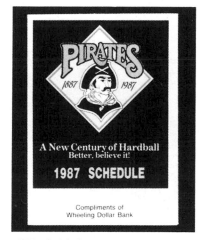

1987 schedule from Wheeling Dollar Bank, 2½" × 3½", $1.

Special Events

ALL-STAR GAME PRESS PINS

1944	None Issued
1959	$200
1974	$300

ALL-STAR PROGRAMS

1944	$500
1959	$150
1974	$45

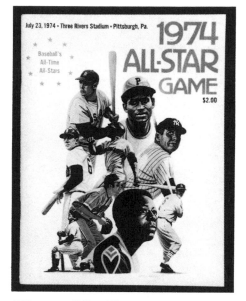

1974 program, 8½" × 11", 72 pages, All-Star game at Three Rivers Stadium (National League won by a score of 7 to 2), $45.

ALL-STAR GAME TICKETS

1944 Complete Ticket	$200
1944 Ticket Stub	$100
1959 Complete Ticket	$150
1959 Ticket Stub	$75
1974 Complete Ticket	$45
1974 Ticket Stub	$20

LEAGUE CHAMPIONSHIP SERIES PROGRAMS

1970, 1971	$30
1972	$25
1974, 1975	$15
1979	$12
1990, 1991, 1992	$5

LEAGUE CHAMPIONSHIP SERIES TICKETS

1970 Complete Ticket	$38
1970 Ticket Stub	$20
1971 Complete Ticket	$38
1971 Ticket Stub	$20
1972 Complete Ticket	$38
1972 Ticket Stub	$20

1970, ticket stub, opening game and official dedication at Three Rivers stadium, $50.

1974 Complete Ticket	$38	1925 Same as Regular Season Score-	
1974 Ticket Stub	$20	card	$1,000
1975 Complete Ticket	$38	1927 Same as Regular Season Score-	
1975 Ticket Stub	$20	card	$2,000
1979 Complete Ticket	$38	1960	$125
1979 Ticket Stub	$20	1971	$75
1990 Complete Ticket	$18	1979	$15
1990 Ticket Stub	$10		
1991 Complete Ticket	$18		

WORLD SERIES GAME TICKETS

1991 Ticket Stub	$10	
1992 Complete Ticket	$18	
1992 Ticket Stub	$10	
1903 Complete Ticket	$6,000
1903 Ticket Stub	$3,000
1909 Complete Ticket	$2,000

WORLD SERIES PRESS PINS

		1909 Ticket Stub	$1,000
1903	None Issued	1925 Complete Ticket	$800
1909	None Issued	1925 Ticket Stub	$400
1925	$500	1927 Complete Ticket	$600
1927	$500	1927 Ticket Stub	$300
1960	$200	1960 Complete Ticket	$70
1971 (not dated)	$100	1960 Ticket Stub	$35
1979 (not dated)	$50	1971 Complete Ticket	$40
		1971 Ticket Stub	$20
		1979 Complete Ticket	$40

WORLD SERIES PROGRAMS

1979 Ticket Stub	$20
1903	$15,000
1909	$6,000

Providence, Rhode Island

PROVIDENCE GRAYS

National League 1878–1885

Providence, Rhode Island's storied past as a major league baseball city is well documented. For two years, 1879 and 1884, the Grays were the best team in baseball. In fact, their fourth-place finish in 1885 was their poorest showing in eight major league seasons. The Grays finished sec-ond in 1880, 1881 and 1882. Their fabulous record is largely attributable to future Hall of Famers pitchers John Montgomery Ward and Charles Gardner "Old Hoss" Radbourn.

When the Grays won their first pennant in 1879, Ward led the league with 47 wins and only 19 losses. Their second championship, in 1884, came when Radbourn established a record that will never be equaled: 60 wins and 12 losses.

In the years they didn't win, these remarkable hurlers kept the Grays in the thick of the pennant race.

George Wright, another Hall of Famer, played a key role in the Grays' first championship as he managed and played shortstop. George and his brother, Harry, organized and starred on the 1869 Cincinnati Red Stockings, America's first professional team.

Providence first became a major league baseball city when Hartford relocated there following the 1877 season. Their first year in the Rhode Island capital was a big success. A new park seating 6000 spectators awaited the Grays, and it was filled to capacity for the first major league game in Providence history against Boston on May 1. The Grays lost a 1 to 0 heartbreaker, but theirs was an exciting season. Led by Monty Ward's 22 victories, the 1878 Grays finished third behind Boston and Cincinnati. Outfielder Paul Lines led the Grays and National League with a .358 BA, while Dick Higham (.320) and Lew Brown (.305) also batted above .300. With 18-year-old rookie Monty Ward proving to be one of the league's rising stars, the Grays were extremely optimistic approaching the 1879 season.

George Wright left Boston to become player-manager of the Grays and brought future Hall of Famer "Orator Jim" O'Rourke along with him to play right field. O'Rourke batted .348 and Hines won his second straight batting title with a .357 average. Ward had become the finest pitcher in baseball and led the league with 47 wins and 239 strikeouts. After clinching the pennant by beating Boston on September 28, the champion Grays were the toast of the town. They were escorted to Park Gardens where nearly 4000 saw the Grays treated to dinner and given gold badges from Mayor Doyle. A huge fireworks display to celebrate the championship followed.

Although Ward won 38 games in 1880, the Grays finished a distant second to Chicago. Hines again led the team in batting but his average dipped to .307. In 1881 Old Hoss Radbourn made his major league debut with the Grays and posted a 25–11 record. Monty Ward's record fell to 18–18 as the Grays finished second to Chicago once again. Joe Start led the Grays with a .328 average. In 1882 Harry Wright took over as manager and brother George returned as shortstop but batted only .162. Radbourn was second in the league with 33 victories and led in strikeouts with 201. Monty Ward, by now the change pitcher to Radbourn, won 19 and lost 12. Joe Start led the Grays in batting for the second consecutive year and was fourth in the league with a .329 average. For the third year in a row, the Grays were second to Cap Anson's White Stockings, but they were only three games back. The highlight of the season came on Memorial Day, when the Grays attracted their record attendance of 7,185. The 1882 season also marked the emergence of a second major league with the formation of the American Association.

In 1883 the Grays finished third behind Boston and Chicago, but Radbourn had now emerged as the finest pitcher in baseball by winning a league-high 48 games. Second baseman Jack Farrell was the Grays' only .300 hitter, with a career-high .305.

In 1884 Old Hoss Radbourn turned in the finest pitching performance in baseball history to lead the Grays to their second world championship. He pitched an astounding 679 innings over 75 games and won 60 games while losing only 12. He led the league in strikeouts with 441 and in ERA with 1.28. He also completed 73 of his 75 starts to establish records that will never again be equaled. With Frank Bancroft managing the team, Providence won 84 games and lost 28 to finish ten-and-one-half games in front of second-place Boston. Paul Hines, at .302, was the only Gray to bat above .300.

On July 17 Radbourn, a heavy drinker, was hauled before the Providence Board of Directors to answer charges of drunkenness and insubordination to Manager Bancroft. He was suspended until change pitcher Charley Sweeney, another imbiber, refused to be taken out of a game on July 22 and was expelled that evening, thereby necessitating Radbourn's reinstatement. From that point on, Old Hoss worked virtually every game for the remainder of the season. At the conclusion of the season the Grays met American Association champion New York Metropolitans in the first World Series, a best-of-three affair with all games in New York. Radbourn pitched a two-hit shutout in the opener as the Grays won 6 to 0, and gave up only three hits to win the second game the next day 3 to 1. Although the Grays clinched the Series with the two wins, a third game was played and Providence won 12 to 2. Because of cold, blustery weather, gate receipts for the three games were only $850 with the Grays, earning $100 apiece. The Grays attendance fell dramatically in 1885 as Radbourn's record dropped to 28 and 21 and the team finished in fourth place. The people of Providence seemed to lose interest in the team. Finally, on November 28, Boston President Arthur Soden personally bought the franchise and all its players for $6000, mainly to get Radbourn, who pitched for Boston in 1886.

While it lasted, the eight years of major league baseball in Providence were an overwhelming success, with two world championships and a host of future Hall of Famers proudly wearing the Providence gray.

1880 Providence Sunday Dispatch paper broadside, 13¾" × 19¾", dated May 9, 1880, featuring ten players including Hall of Fame pitcher John Montgomery Ward. The Grays were defending world champions, $2,500.

Richmond, Virginia

RICHMOND VIRGINIANS

American Association 1884

Richmond's tenure as a major league baseball city lasted less than two months. The Richmond Virginians were members of the Eastern League at the time with a record of 30 wins and 28 losses. However, when the opportunity to enjoy major league status presented itself, the Virginians resigned from the Eastern League and replaced Washington's disbanded team in the American Association in August.

Only one Washington player, reserve catcher John Hanna, joined the Virginians. Hanna started for the Virginians, and after batting just .066 with Washington, Hanna raised his average to .194. It was

hardly enough, however, to keep him in the major leagues.

The only Virginian to bat above .300 was rightfielder Mike Mansell, who hit .301 in 29 games.

The best player on the team was rookie center fielder Dick Johnston, who went on to play eight seasons of big league ball with a career batting average of .251 after making his major league debut with the Virginians.

Richmond's pitching was in the hands of Ed Dugan (5–14) and Pete Meegan (5–9). Dugan's season with Richmond was his only one in the majors, while Meegan pitched the following season with Pittsburgh's American Association team and then dropped out of the major leagues. Obviously with such statistics, the Virginians won only 12 games while losing 30. It was considerable improvement, however, over Washington's record of 12 wins and 51 defeats.

The biggest impact Richmond had on baseball was forcing Toledo's African-American brothers Fleetwood and Welday Walker out of the major leagues. A strongly worded letter threatening bloodshed should catcher Fleetwood Walker appear in a game at Richmond, and later against the Virginians at Toledo, prompted the Blue Stockings to release

Fleetwood on September 29. Welday was not on the roster at the time and played only five games earlier in the year. The Walkers were the last African-Americans to play in the majors until Jackie Robinson in 1947.

Richmond memorabilia would be scarce indeed. The most likely souvenirs would be scorecards, tickets, and possibly stock certificates from the last two months of the 1884 American Association season.

Rochester, New York

ROCHESTER HOP-BITTERS

American Association 1890

Rochester, New York, enjoyed one season in the major league spotlight represented by the Hop-Bitters as an 1890 member of the American Association. The nickname stemmed from team ownership by General Hans Brinker a German immigrant who rose from errand boy to a wealthy magnate and numbered breweries among his holdings.

The American Association was often called the Beer and Whiskey League because many team officials owned breweries and sold their products on club grounds during games.

Rochester had played in the minor league Atlantic Association in 1889 and moved up in class to the major leagues with virtually the same players. In 1890 talent at the major league level had dissipated considerably when many stars of the American Association and National League formed their own organization called the Players League.

Manager Pat Powers guided the Hop-Bitters to fifth place in the eight-team circuit with a record of 63 wins and 63 losses. Outfielder Sandy Griffin was the leading batter with a .307 average. Catcher Deacon McGuire batted .299 and enjoyed a 26-year career, which didn't end until 1912 when he played one game with the Detroit Tigers. McGuire's lifetime batting average was a solid .278.

Bob Barr won 28 games to lead the team, but his 24 losses was the worst rec-

1890 scorecard of Rochester Hop Bitters of the American Association hosting Brooklyn Gladiators, 5″ × 8½″, $750.

ord among league pitchers. He was a real workhorse for the Hop-Bitters pitching 493 innings (second best in the league) and recording 209 strikeouts (fourth best).

In the final analysis, Rochester was too small a market to sustain major league baseball. When the Players League disbanded after the 1890 season, the die was cast. The Association decided to go with larger cities in 1891.

Rockford, Illinois

ROCKFORD FOREST CITIES

National Association 1871

The Forest Cities was the Rockford, Illinois, in the National Association during its initial season of 1871. The Forest Cities fared poorly and finished last in the nine-team league with a record of 6 wins and 21 defeats.

Their chief claim to fame was future Hall of Famer Adrian Constantine "Cap" Anson who, in his first season of professional ball, batted a lofty .352 on his way to a 27-year career which lasted until 1898. Anson primarily played third base during his rookie season at Rockford, but he gained his principal fame as captain, manager and first baseman of the Chicago White Stockings. Anson's career batting average of .329 attests to his remarkable skills.

A July 4 game attracting 2,000 fans was the high-water mark of the season, but the Forest Cities bowed to Boston 21 to 12. Boston player Al Spalding, who was the dominant pitcher in the National Association during its five-year existence as the first professional league, was the game's principal attraction. Veteran second baseman Bobby Addy, who at 33 was in the twilight of his long playing career, was the only other Rockford player of note.

Although Rockford finished the season of 1871, they found it difficult to compete financially with the larger cities and lost their best players to other teams. When it came time to send in the $10 entry fee for the 1872 season, the Forest Cities declined without any fanfare. Rockford's status as a major league baseball city ended.

Any Rockford baseball memorabilia would be highly prized and extremely difficult to find because their one and only major league season lasted only 27 games.

Saint Louis, Missouri

SAINT LOUIS BROWNS

American Association 1882–1891, National League 1892–1899, American League 1902–1953

When baseball fans see or hear the name St. Louis Browns, they immediately think of ineptitude. As members of the American League from 1902 through 1953, the Browns won only one pennant (1944), finished last nine times, and wound up in the second division 39 times during their 52-year history.

But in a different era and a different league, the St. Louis Browns were champions of baseball. Chris Von Der Ahe's Browns were champions of the American Association for four consecutive years (1885 through 1888) and vanquished the National League champion Chicago White Stockings in post-season play in 1886 after the two teams tied at three wins each and a tie in 1885.

The Browns were built around captain and first baseman Charles A. Comiskey and slugging outfielder Tip O'Neill, and featured superb pitching by Bob Caruthers, Dave Foutz and Silver King.

Caruthers won 40 games in 1885, Foutz won 41 in 1886, and King won 45 in 1888.

The American Association of that era was called the Beer and Whiskey League because many of its owners not only owned breweries, but also sold beer and whiskey on Association grounds— something specifically prohibited at National League parks. Whereas the National League charged a 50 cent admission, the Association only charged 25 cents.

Comiskey, the only member of the champion Browns enshrined in the Hall of Fame, revolutionized first base play by being the first to position himself away from the bag. The rule requiring Hall of Famers to play at least ten seasons in the major leagues has undoubtedly kept Caruthers out since his winning percentage of .688 (218–99) in nine seasons is among the best in baseball history. For more fascinating reading on Chris Von Der Ahe's champion St. Louis Browns see *Baseball 1845–1891 from the Newspaper Accounts* by Preston D. Orem.

When St. Louis obtained the last-place Milwaukee Brewers franchise following the 1901 American League season, they adopted the most glamorous name in St. Louis baseball history and called their new team the Browns. After an auspicious second-place finish in 1902 under manager Jimmy McAleer, the Browns, who featured two future Hall of Famers in shortstop Bobby Wallace and outfielder Jesse Burkett, quickly faded into the second division.

The Browns finished sixth in 1903 and 1904 and reached the basement in 1905. It was one of nine last-place finishes in Browns history. In the Browns' 52 years in the American League, they finished in the second division a total of 39 times.

One of the years they didn't was 1922, when the Browns came within a game of winning their first American League pennant. The team was sparked by Hall of Famer George Sisler, who led baseball with a .420 BA—the highest mark in the twentieth century. The Browns won 93 games under manager Lee Fhol, but it left them one game back of the champion New York Yankees. In 1922 left fielder Ken Williams led the American League with 39 home runs and 155 RBI. That same season, Babe Ruth hit 35 home runs and drove in 96 runs in a much smaller ball-

park. If Williams, who played 14 seasons in the majors and compiled a .319 lifetime average, had played most of his career with any team but the Browns, he would be an almost certain Hall of Famer. Sisler, who batted .340 in 15 seasons (mostly with the Browns), received Hall of Fame recognition in 1939.

Sisler took over as player-manager in 1924 and the Browns finished fourth, third and seventh during his three years at the helm. In the meantime, the Cardinals, who were sharing Sportsman's Park with the Browns, won their first pennant in 1926 to capture the hearts and minds of St. Louis baseball fans forever.

Future Hall of Famer Heinie Manush joined the Browns in 1928 and promptly hit .378—only to lose the batting title to Washington's Goose Goslin by one percentage point. Goslin, another Hall of Famer, came to the Browns in 1930 in exchange for Manush and batted .326 with 30 home runs and 100 RBI. The Browns, however, finished sixth.

Hall of Famer Rogers Hornsby became player-manager late in 1933 and managed until he was replaced by fellow Hall of Famer Jim Bottomley midway during the 1937 season.

It was World War II before the Browns finally won a pennant. Major league playing talent was decimated by the war, with many stars in the service. In 1944, with youngsters and 4 Fs dominating the game, the Browns finally finished first. Shortstop Vern Stephens led the league with 109 RBI and was second with 20 HR. Nelson Potter was third in the league with 19 victories while Jack Kramer won 17 games. As fate would have it, the Browns met the Cardinals in the World Series and lost four games to two.

As an example of how baseball talent diminished during the war, the defending American League champion Browns brought up one-armed outfielder Pete Gray to play 77 games during the 1945 season. Gray batted .218 in his only major league season as the Browns finished third in 1945, six games back of Detroit.

The flamboyant Bill Veeck bought the Browns in 1950, but even this promotional genius couldn't bring consistently large crowds to see the Browns at Sportsman's Park. The Cardinals outdrew them by large numbers.

In 1951 Veeck signed a midget, Eddie

Gaedel, who made one plate appearance and walked on four pitches before his major league career was terminated. He also signed 45-year-old Hall of Famer Satchel Paige, the dominant pitcher in the Negro Leagues, who made his major league debut with Veeck's Indians in 1948. In three years with the Browns, Paige won 18 games, including 12 in 1952. The gimmicks worked for a while but not in the end, as the Browns didn't win and didn't draw.

Baltimore interests bought the club from the financially strapped Veeck following the 1953 season and moved the team to Maryland, where they were renamed the Orioles, resurrecting another hallowed name from the past.

The name Browns, made famous by Chris Von Der Ahe's American Association champions in the 1880s remains only a memory. If the American League team had achieved the success of their famous predecessors, St. Louis might still be a two-team baseball city.

SAINT LOUIS MAROONS

Union Association 1884, National League 1885–1886

St. Louis businessman Henry Lucas was the first to test baseball's reserve clause by signing players not under specific contract to major league teams, and thus formed the Union Association in 1884.

The St. Louis Brown Stockings played in the National Association in 1875 and in the National League from 1876 to 1877. The Terriers represented St. Louis in the Federal League in 1914 and 1915.

His own St. Louis Maroons, which he also managed, ran away with the Union Association pennant that season and did well financially. However, keeping the Union Association afloat cost Lucas his $17,000 profit. In exchange for not operating the Union Association in 1885, Lucas and the Maroons were allowed to join the National League, where they finished last. Although they improved to sixth in 1886, Lucas, now heavily in debt, relinquished his ownership on August 18 and dropped out of baseball. Although others kept the

franchise going for the remainder of the season, it was the end of National League ball in St. Louis until 1892.

For further reading on the St. Louis Maroons see *Baseball 1845–1891 from the Newspaper Accounts* by Preston D. Orem.

Advertising Specialties

St. Louis Browns (American Association and American League)

1888 Joseph Hall Cabinet Card, 4½″ × 6½″ $2,200
1937 Booklet issued by Kellogg Co. featuring photos of the 1937 Browns....$500
1913 Fatima T200 Team Card, 2⅜″ × 4¾″ $100

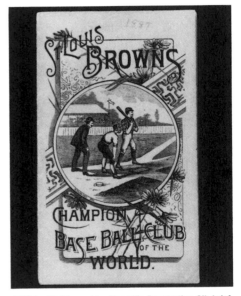

1887 booklet issued by Merrell's Penetrating Oil, brief history of the 1886 world champions, sketches of the prominent players and testimonials for using the product, 3½″ × 6″, 12 pages, $2,500.

Ballpark Giveaway

1945 St. Louis Browns Introduction Ball Park Giveaway, Flag Shaped Program, First Known Ballpark Giveaway $300

Pennants

1936, 1937 Felt Pennant—BF3, Type IV, Catcher on Pennant $35

1880s multicolor diecut figure of St. Louis player, 3″ × 6″. Issuer is unknown, but figures in various poses from ten different American Association and National League teams have been discovered, $400.

1936, 1937 Felt Pennant—BF3, Type V,
Bat on Pennant $35

Pins

1930/1940s American Nut & Chocolate
Co., 1⅛″, Round $5

Postcards

1908 PL, Triple Fold, 3½″ × 16½″, Star
Photo Co., St. Louis $750
1914 PL, Spring Training at St. Peters-
burg, Fla., Pub Unknown $350

Publications

BOOKS

•Godin, Roger A. *The 1922 St. Louis
Browns: Best of the American
League's Worst.* Jefferson, N.C.:
McFarland & Co., 1991. ....$24.95
Hawkins, John C. *This Date In Balti-
more Orioles-St. Louis Browns
History.* New York: Stein & Day,
1982. ....$5.00
Mead, William B. *Even the Browns.*
Chicago: Contemporary Books,
1978. ....$10.00
Sullivan, John. *A Study In Brown.*
1966. ....$15.00

Tracy, David Dr. *The Psychologist At
Bat.* Sterling Publishing Co., 1951. ...$30.00

MEDIA GUIDES

1927 Roster Booklet.............................$150
1928 through 1931 Roster Booklet $125
1932 through 1935 Roster Booklet $100
1936 through 1940 Roster Booklet...........$75
1941, 1942, 1943 Roster Booklet..............$60
1944 Roster Booklet League Champs........$70
1945 through 1949 ....$60
1950 through 1953 ....$50

PROGRAMS AND SCORECARDS

1902 ....$600
1903, 1904 ....$300
1905 through 1909 ....$200
1910 through 1914 ....$150
1915 through 1920 ....$125
1921 through 1925 ....$75
1926 through 1930 ....$50
1931 through 1940 ....$35
1941 through 1943 ....$20
1944 League Champs $25
1945 through 1949 ....$20
1950 through 1953 ....$15

YEARBOOKS

1950 ....$325
1951 ....$300
1952, 1953 ....$275

Schedules

1902 through 1909 ....$150
1910 through 1919 ....$100
1920 through 1929 ....$75
1930 through 1939 ....$45
1940 through 1949 ....$30
1950, 1951, 1952 ....$25
1953 ....$30

Special Events

ALL-STAR PROGRAMS

1948 ....$300

ALL-STAR GAME TICKETS

1948 Complete Ticket $200
1948 Ticket Stub $100

WORLD SERIES PRESS PINS

1944 ....$500

WORLD SERIES PROGRAMS

1944 ....$325

1953 schedule issued by Falstaff Brewing Co. for the Browns final season in St. Louis, 3″ × 5″. The team moved to Baltimore to become the Orioles after the 1953 season, $30.

WORLD SERIES GAME TICKETS

1944 Complete Ticket $200
1944 Ticket Stub $100

SAINT LOUIS CARDINALS

National League 1899 to Present

With the breakup of the American Association following the 1891 season, Chris Von Der Ahe's Browns became members of the National League. The stronger teams of the Association, of which the Browns were one, were absorbed into what became a 12-team circuit.

Whereas the last Browns team in the Association finished second under manager Charles Comiskey, Von Der Ahe decided to take over the managerial reins himself when Comiskey signed to manage Cincinnati. It proved to be a disaster: The Browns finished in eleventh place. Without the astute Comiskey in charge, everything became chaotic.

Realizing he was no manager, Von Der Ahe had the sense to step down from the post and hired Bill Watkins to manage the 1893 team. They moved up a notch to tenth place.

The Browns' troubles continued. After

finishing eleventh in 1895 and 1896, they were twelfth in 1897 and 1898. In addition, a fire which destroyed much of Sportsman's Park on April 16, 1898, resulted in injuries and subsequent lawsuits against Von Der Ahe, forcing him into bankruptcy.

Although Von Der Ahe received much criticism for his flamboyant ways, he was baseball's first great innovator. He turned Sportsman's Park into the "Coney Island of the West" by installing chute-the-chutes beyond centerfield, night horse racing, an all-girl cornet band, boating, a Wild West Show, and boxing.

In 1899 the Browns had a new owner, Frank Robinson, a trolley magnate who also owned the Cleveland Spiders (dual ownership was allowed in those days). Robison promptly brought his best Cleveland players to St. Louis and changed the color of the stockings from brown to vivid red. As a result, Willie McHale, a writer for the *St. Louis Republic* began referring to the team as the "Cardinals," and the name caught on.

In 1899 the Cardinals finished fifth as Hall of Fame immortal Cy Young won 26 of his all-time record 509 major league victories. The Cardinals were hardly a success under the new regime, as a fourth place finish in 1901 was their highest standing until 1914, when they finished third. In the meantime the Cardinals were seventh in 1906, 1909 and 1910 and last in 1903, 1907, 1908 and 1913.

Hall of Fame second baseman Rogers Hornsby joined the club in 1915 and became one of the outstanding hitters in baseball history. His .358 career batting average is second only to Ty Cobb's .367. In mid-season 1925, Hornsby was given the added responsibility of managing, replacing Branch Rickey in that post. In 1926 he took the team all the way to the top as the Cardinals won their first pennant. St. Louis went wild and the delirium reached fever pitch when the Cardinals upset the New York Yankees in the World Series, four games to three. Hornsby had an outstanding season, batting .317, hitting 11 home runs, and driving in 93 runs. Another Hall of Famer, Sunny Jim Bottomley led the league with 120 RBI and paced the Cardinals with 19 home runs. Third baseman Les Bell was the Cardinals' leading batter with a .325 average. He also slammed 11 home runs and drove in 100 runs. Right-handed pitching hero Grover Cleveland Alexander beat the Yankees twice and saved the seventh and deciding game for fellow Hall of Famer Jess Haines, who also won two World Series Games.

Two years later the Cardinals were champions again. Jim Bottomley led the league in homers (31) and RBI (136). Hall of Famer Chick Hafey was close behind with 27 HR and 111 RBI. The infield had two other future Hall of Famers in second baseman Frankie Frisch and shortstop Rabbit Maranville. Billy Sherdel led the pitching staff with 21 wins, followed by Jesse Haines with 20, and Grover Cleveland Alexander with 16. However, in the World Series the Yankees got revenge for their setback in 1926 by sweeping the Cardinals in four straight.

The Cardinals won two more National League pennants in 1930 and 1931 under manager Gabby Street and subsequently lost to Philadelphia in the 1930 World Series but defeated the Athletics in 1931. In 1930 every regular batted .300 or better, with rightfielder George Watkins leading the way with a .373 BA. Frisch led in RBI with 114 while Hafey had 107. In 1931 Hafey led the league with a .349 average and topped the Cardinals with 95 RBI.

Now known as the "Gashouse Gang," the Cardinals got superb pitching from the colorful Dean brothers, Dizzy and Paul, on route to the 1934 National League title. Dizzy led the league with 30 wins while Paul, also known as Daffy, had 19. In the World Series the Deans won two games each as the Cardinals beat Detroit in seven games.

Although the Cardinals finished second in 1935, 1936, 1939 and 1941, their next pennant was not until 1942. Two future Hall of Famers, outfielders Enos "Country" Slaughter and Stan "The Man" Musial, who batted .311 and .315 respectively, were the top Redbird batters. Mort Cooper led the league with 22 wins, followed by 20-game-winner Johnny Beasley. Avenging their 1928 defeat, the 1942 Cards beat the Yankees four games to one as Beasley chalked up two wins.

In 1943 the Cards and Yanks met again in the Series with New York avenging the four-game-to-one margin. Stan Musial led the league in batting (.357) while Cooper led the league for the second straight year with 21 victories.

The Cardinals won their third consecutive pennant in 1944 as Musial batted .347 and center fielder Johnny Hopp batted .336. Mort Cooper led the league in wins for the third straight season with 22. It was an all St. Louis World Series as the Cardinals beat the Browns in six games.

After finishing second in 1945, the Cardinals were National League champs again in 1946 as Musial batted .365 to lead the league while Slaughter won the RBI title with 130. Howie Pollet topped the league with 21 wins. In the World Series the Cardinals won a thriller from the Red Sox in seven games as Slaughter scored from first on Harry Walker's double in the eighth inning of the deciding game. The year 1946 was also the first time in club history the Cardinals drew more than a million fans.

In 1964 Johnny Keane guided the Cardinals to their tenth National League pennant and seventh world championship. Third baseman Ken Boyer led the National League in RBI with 119, and right-handers Ray Sadecki (with 20 wins) and Bob Gibson (with 19) paced the Cardinal pitchers. In the World Series against the Yankees the Cardinals won in seven games. In his first season of a Hall of Fame career, Lou Brock led the Cardinals with a .348 batting average.

In 1967 first baseman Orlando Cepeda led the offense by batting .325, hit 25 HR, and had a league-leading 111 RBI in another championship season. Righthander Dick Hughes had the league's best win percentage with a 16–6 record. Future Hall of Famer Bob Gibson was the pitching star in the World Series. He won three games and led the Cardinals to victory over the Boston Red Sox in seven games. Former Cardinal second baseman and Hall of Famer Red Schoendienst managed the team adroitly.

The Cardinals repeated as National League champs in 1968 as Gibson led the league with 22 wins and Nelson Briles won 19. In the World Series they lost to the Detroit Tigers in seven games. Mickey Lolich won 3 and 31-game-winner Denny McLain won one for the Tigers. Bob Gibson won twice for the Cardinals.

With Whitey Herzog at the helm in 1982, the Cards won the National League East and vanquished the Atlanta Braves three straight in the playoffs. They then beat the Milwaukee Brewers four games to three in the World Series. It was the last world championship for the Cardinals. Although they won National League pennants in 1985 and 1987, they bowed to the Kansas City Royals and the Minnesota Twins respectively. In 1985 Joaquin Andujar and John Tudor each won 21 games, the last time the Cardinals have had a 20-game winner. Willie McGee was National League batting champ (.353) as well as MVP in 1985 and won the batting title again in 1990 (.335), the last Cardinal to do so.

Always a fine baseball town, St. Louis' Cardinals exceeded 3 million in attendance for the first time in 1987 and then set their all-time record in 1989 as 3,080,980 passed through the turnstiles at Busch Stadium in downtown St. Louis.

A Cardinal since 1982, shortstop Ozzie Smith ranks as one of the best defensive players of all time and has been chosen thirteen times to the National League All-Star team, including selection in 1993. When his career finally ends, he is almost certain to be elected to the Baseball Hall of Fame and join an illustrious group of St. Louis Cardinals who preceded him. Those Hall of Famers not already mentioned include: Walter Alston, Jake Beckley, Roger Bresnehan, Roger Connor, Miller Huggins, John McGraw, Ducky Medwich, Johnny Mize, Wilbert Vance, Hoyt Wilhelm; and managers Roger Connor, Bill McKechnie, and Branch Rickey.

Ballpark Giveaways

1971 Cap, Bat, T-shirt	$5
1972 Bat, T-shirt, Helmet	$5
1973 Souvenir Tumbler	$15
1973 Bat, Team Shirt	$5
1974 Maxwell House Coffee Mug	$6
1975 Batting Glove, Ball (with facsimile autographs $25)	$5
1975 Poster	$15
1976 Cushion, Jacket	$5
1977 Jacket, Batting Helmet, Ball (with facsimile autographs $25)	$5
1977 Iron-on Emblem	$10
1978 Batting Helmet, Cap, Banner, Pennant (if dated $10)	$5
1979 Helmet, Cap, T-shirt (if dated $10), Pennant (if dated $10)	$5
1980 Cap, T-shirt (if dated $10), Gym Bag	$5
1981 Jacket, Wrist Band, Visor, Back Pack	$5
1981 Fred Bird Poster (first), Bird Watchers Kit	$10
1982 Helmet, T-shirt	$5
1982 Fred Bird Poster	$8
1983 Visor, Jacket, Bat	$5
1984 Jacket, Sports Bag	$5
1985 Batting Glove, Sports Bag	$5
1986 Seat Cushion, Jacket, Wallet, Helmet, Cooler Bag, Visor, Sports Bag, T-shirt	$5
1986 Bud Light Mug	$7
1986 Budweiser Can Wrap	$6
1987 Calendar (first)	$8
1987 K-Mart Seat Cushion, Gatorade Watch, Post Dispatch Cooler, Budweiser Can Wrap	$6
1987 Sporting News Coffee Mug	$7
1988 Hardees Calendar	$8

Advertising Specialties

1913 Fatima T200 Team Card, 2⅝″ × 4¾″ $150

1950s felt round, $35.

1974 plastic coffee mug, issued by Maxwell House Coffee at a Cardinals game, 3¼″ × 4″, Cardinals logo on one side and Maxwell House logo on the other, $6.

1988 Championship Pin, Bud Light Mug,
 Sporting News Mug $7
1988 Busch Rally Towel, Gatorade
 Watch, Pasta House Pennant, Texas
 Gold Batting Glove $6
1988 Surf Baseball Book $10
1988 Glove $5
1989 Hardees Calendar, Domino Pizza
 Mug, Levi/J.C. Penney Pin, Sporting
 News Travel Mug $7
1989 Pepsi Bat, Gatorade Watch, Chevro-
 let/KMOX Jacket, Pasta House Pen-
 nant, Amoco/KMOX Beach Towel,
 Eagle Snack/Coca-Cola Jersey, Mis-
 souri Lottery Umbrella, Magnet
 Schedule $6
1990 Busch Magnet Schedule, Hardees
 Calendar, Hunter Helmet, Chevro-
 let/KMOX Travel Kit, Bud Light
 Mug, Pasta House Pennant, Amoco/
 KMOX Beach Towel $6
1991 Busch Magnet Schedule, Hardees
 Autograph Team Poster, Jolly
 Rancher Sunglasses, Busch Lite
 Mug, Olive Garden Travel Mug,
 Post Dispatch Card Album, Mis-
 souri Lottery Cooler, Pasta House
 Co. Pennant, Busch Neon Cap $6
1991 Upper Deck Cards $7
1992 Busch Magnet Schedule, Hardees
 Calendar, Busch Lite Mug, Pay Day
 Wallet $6
1992 KC Life Baseball Card Set, Upper
 Deck Cards, Post Dispatch Card Al-
 bum $7
1992 Coca-Cola Pin Series ....ea. $7
1993 Busch Magnet Schedule, Pasta
 House Co. Pennant, Amoco/KMOX
 Beach Towel, GM Parts Helmet,
 Busch Cap $5
1993 Post Dispatch Card Album, Upper
 Deck Cards $7
1993 Feid Weiners Autograph Ball $10
1993 KC Life Baseball Card Set $7

Miscellaneous

BOBBIN' HEAD DOLLS

Category #II, 1961, 1962, White Square
 Base, Mascot $325
Category #III, 1961, 1962, White Round
 Miniature, Mascot $245
Category #IV, 1962, 1963, 1964, Green
 Round Base, Mascot $140
Category #V, 1962, 1963, 1964, Green
 Round Base, Black Player $450
Category #VI, 1967 through 1972, Gold
 Round Base, Mascot $80

Pennants

1900 through 1920 ....$750
1921 through 1926 Regular...................$300
1926 World Series $600
1927, 1928 Regular $300

1928 League Champs $600
1929, 1930 Regular $300
1930 League Champs $600
1931 Regular $200
1931 World Series $400
1932, 1933, 1934 Regular....................$200
1934 World Series $400
1936, 1937 Felt Pennant-BF3, Type V, Bat
 on Pennant $35
1936, 1937 Felt Pennant-BF3, Type V,
 Cardinal on Pennant $35
1936, 1937 Felt Pennant-BF3, Type V,
 Four Birds Flying on Pennant $35
1935 through 1940 Regular..................$200
1940 All-Star Game $400
1941, 1942 Regular $100
1942 World Series $200
1943 Regular $100
1943 League Champs $200
1944 Regular $100
1944 World Series $200
1945, 1946 Regular $100
1946 World Series $200
1947 through 1950 ....$100
1951 through 1957 Regular $50
1957 All-Star Game $125
1958, 1959, 1960 ....$50
1961 through 1964 Regular $30
1964 World Series $75
1965, 1966 Regular $30
1966 All-Star Game $75
1967 Regular...$30
1967 World Series $75
1968 Regular...$30
1968 League Champs $75
1969, 1970 ....$30
1971 through 1980 ....$20
1981, 1982 Regular $5
1982 League Champs $15
1982 World Series..................................$15
1983, 1984, 1985 Regular $5
1985 League Champs $15
1986, 1987 Regular $5
1987 League Champs $15
1988, 1989, 1990 ....$5
1991, 1992, 1993 ....$3

Pins

1930/1940s American Nut & Chocolate
 Co., 1⅛″, Round $15
1961 through 1965 Crane Potato Chips,
 ⅞″, Round $5
1968 through 1969 Crane Potato Chips,
 ⅞″, Round $5
1984 Crane Potato Chips, ⅞″, Round $3
1964, 1965, 1966 Guy's Potato Chips, ⅞″,
 Round $5

Publications

BOOKS

Borst, Bill. *Baseball Through a Knot-
 hole: A St. Louis History.* St. Louis:
 Krank Press, 1980. ....$15.00

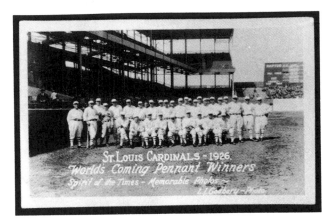

1926 photographic postcard of 1926 National League Champions who defeated the New York Yankees in the World Series, 3½″ × 5″, $350.

Broeg, Bob. *Baseball's Redbirds, A Century of Cardinals' Baseball In St. Louis.* St. Louis: River City Publishers, 1981. ....$15.00

Broeg, Bob. *The Pilot Light and the Gashouse Gang.* St. Louis: Bethany Press, 1980. ....$15.00

Craft, David. *Red Birds Revisited.* Chicago: Bonus Books, 1990. ....$10.00

Fleming, Gordon. *The Dizziest Season: The Gashouse Gang Chase the Pennant.* New York: William Morrow, 1984. ....$15.00

Honig, Donald. *St. Louis Cardinals: An Illustrated History.* New York: Prentice-Hall, 1991. ....$20.00

Hood, Robert E. *The Gashouse Gang.* New York: William Morrow, 1976. ...$15.00

Leptich, John & Dave Barauowski. *This Date In St. Louis Cardinals History.* New York: Stein & Day, 1982. ....$5.00

Lieb, Frederick. *The St. Louis Cardinals.* G.P. Putnam's Sons, 1944, 1945, 1947. ....$30.00

Neuman, Jeffrey. *The Cardinals.* New York: Collier-McMillan, 1985. ....$10.00

•Rains, Bob. *The St. Louis Cardinals: The Official 100th Anniversary History.* New York: St. Martin's Press, 1992. (paperback $12.95) $24.95

Rothaus, James R. *St. Louis Cardinals.* Mankato, Mn.: Creative Education, 1987. ....$5.00

St. Louis Dispatch. *Celebration.* St. Louis, 1982. ....$10.00

Stockton, Ray J. *The Gashouse Gang and a Couple of Other Guys.* A.S. Barnes & Co., 1945. Bantam Books, 1948, reissue. $30.00

Tiemann, Robert L. *Cardinal Classics.* St. Louis: Baseball Histories, Inc., 1982. ....$15.00

Tully, Mike & Fred Lies. *Racin' Redbirds—A Celebration of the 1985

St. Louis Cardinals. Chicago: Contemporary Books, 1985. ....$15.00

Media Guides

1926 First Known Roster Sheet World Champs	$200
1927 Roster Sheet	$125
1928 Roster Sheet League Champs	$115
1929 Roster Sheet	$100
1930 Roster Sheet League Champs	$115
1931 World Champs	$115
1932, 1933 Roster Booklet	$125
1934 Roster Booklet World Champs	$115
1935 Roster Booklet	$100
1936 through 1940 Roster Booklet	$75
1941 Roster Booklet	$60
1942 Roster Booklet World Champs	$65
1943 Roster Booklet League Champs	$70
1944 Roster Booklet World Champs	$70
1945 Roster Booklet	$60
1946 Roster Booklet World Champs	$70
1947, 1948, 1949 Roster Booklet	$60
1950 through 1955	$50
1956 through 1961	$40
1962, 1963	$30
1964 World Champs	$55
1965, 1966	$20
1967 World Champs	$25
1968 League Champs	$25
1969, 1970	$15
1971, 1972	$12
1973, 1974	$10
1975, 1976	$8
1977, 1978	$7
1979, 1980, 1981	$6
1982 World Champs	$7
1983, 1984	$5
1985 through 1993	$4

PROGRAMS AND SCORECARDS

1900, 1901, 1902	$400
1903, 1904	$300
1905 through 1909	$200

1910 through 1914	$150
1915 through 1920	$125
1921 through 1925	$75
1926 World Champs	$55
1927	$50
1928 League Champs	$55
1929	$50
1930 League Champs	$55
1931 World Champs	$40
1932, 1933	$35
1934 World Champs	$40
1935 through 1940	$35
1941	$20
1942 World Champs	$25
1943 League Champs	$25
1944 World Champs	$25
1945	$20
1946 World Champs	$25
1947, 1948, 1949	$20
1950 through 1959	$15
1960 through 1963	$10
1964 World Champs	$15
1965, 1966	$10
1967 World Champs	$15
1968 League Champs	$12
1969	$10
1970 through 1979	$6
1980, 1981	$4
1982 World Champs	$6
1983, 1984	$4
1985 League Champs	$6
1986	$4
1987 League Champs	$6
1988, 1989	$4
1990, 1991, 1992, 1993	$3

YEARBOOKS

1951 First Year	$200
1952	$150
1953, 1954	$100
1955, 1956	$75
1957	$65
1958	$60
1959	$55
1960	$50
1961	$45

1962	$40
1963	$35
1964 World Champs	$50
1965, 1966	$30
1967 World Champs	$50
1968 League Champs	$40
1969	$25
1970	$20
1971, 1972	$18
1973, 1974	$15
1975, 1976, 1977	$12
1978 through 1987	None Issued
1988	$8
1989 through 1993	$5

Schedules

1900 through 1909	$150
1910 through 1919	$100
1920 through 1929	$75
1930 through 1939	$45
1940 through 1949	$30
1950 through 1959	$25
1960 through 1969	$15
1970 through 1979	$10
1980 through 1985	$2
1986 through 1993	$1

Special Events

ALL-STAR GAME PRESS PINS

1940	None Issued
1957	$200
1966	$50

ALL-STAR PROGRAMS

1940	$450
1957	$150
1966	$100

ALL-STAR GAME TICKETS

1940 Complete Ticket	$200
1940 Ticket Stub	$100

1989, 4-fold schedule, Budweiser,
2⅜″ × 4″, $1.

1957 Complete Ticket $150
1957 Ticket Stub $75
1966 Complete Ticket $70
1966 Ticket Stub $35

LEAGUE CHAMPIONSHIP SERIES PROGRAMS

1982 ....$10
1985 ....$8
1987 ....$6

LEAGUE CHAMPIONSHIP SERIES TICKETS

1982 Complete Ticket $28
1982 Ticket Stub $15
1985 Complete Ticket $28
1985 Ticket Stub $15
1987 Complete Ticket $28
1987 Ticket Stub $15

WORLD SERIES PRESS PINS

1926 ....$500
1928 ....$500
1930 ....$500
1931 ....$500
1934 ....$500
1942 ....$500
1943 ....$500
1944 ....$500
1946 ....$500
1964 ....$200
1967 ....$75
1968 ....$75
1982 (not dated) $50
1985 (not dated) $45
1987 ....$30

WORLD SERIES PROGRAMS

1926 ....$2,000
1928 ....$1,000
1930 ....$800

1931 ....$750
1934 ....$500
1942 ....$250
1943, 1944 ....$250
1946 ....$200
1964 ....$100
1967, 1968 ....$100
1982 ....$15
1985 ....$12
1987 ....$10

WORLD SERIES GAME TICKETS

1926 Complete Ticket $600
1926 Ticket Stub $300
1928 Complete Ticket $600
1928 Ticket Stub $300
1930 Complete Ticket $400
1930 Ticket Stub $200
1931 Complete Ticket $400
1931 Ticket Stub $200
1934 Complete Ticket $400
1934 Ticket Stub $200
1942 Complete Ticket $200
1942 Ticket Stub $100
1943 Complete Ticket $200
1943 Ticket Stub $100
1944 Complete Ticket $200
1944 Ticket Stub $100
1946 Complete Ticket $200
1946 Ticket Stub $100
1964 Complete Ticket $70
1964 Ticket Stub $35
1967 Complete Ticket $70
1967 Ticket Stub $35
1968 Complete Ticket $70
1968 Ticket Stub $35
1982 Complete Ticket $30
1982 Ticket Stub $15
1985 Complete Ticket $30
1985 Ticket Stub $15
1987 Complete Ticket $30
1987 Ticket Stub $15

Saint Paul, Minnesota

SAINT PAUL SAINTS

Union Association 1884

Saint Paul, Minnesota, had a long and distinguished minor league history, but their status as a major league city lasted only a few weeks. When Wilmington's Union Association team disbanded in September 1884, the Saint Paul Saints took their place.

The Saints were officially admitted to the league on September 24 but played only eight games, winning two and losing six before the Union Association faded into oblivion.

Although he batted only .217 in seven games with the Saints, catcher Charley

Ganzel's excellent 14-year big league career was launched with St. Paul. Ganzel compiled a .259 lifetime batting average and played on the National League champion Detroit Wolverines in 1887 and was an integral part of the Boston Beaneaters, who won National League championships in 1891, 1892, 1893 and 1897.

Batting averages compiled over eight games mean very little, but pitcher Jim Brown led Saints' batters with a .313 average, and posted a 1–4 record while appearing in six of the eight games.

Pat Dealey, who shared catching duties with Ganzel, played five years in the majors and batted .251. Shortstop Joe Werrick, a St. Paul native who batted only .074 with the Saints, compiled a .250 BA over four major league seasons. Right fielder

Scrappy Carroll improved his .097 St. Paul BA to .171 over three seasons in the majors.

Although the Saints had no future Hall of Famers, Ganzel ranked among the best catchers in baseball during his 14 big league seasons. Lou Galvin, who was 0 and 2 as a Saints pitcher, was the brother of Hall of Famer Pud Galvin, who won 359 games during his 14 years in the majors.

If any Saints memorabilia exists from their eight game major league tenure, it would be extremely scarce. It gives baseball buffs, particularly those in the twin cities of Minneapolis–St. Paul, something to search for. The chances of locating anything are extremely remote, but nonetheless possible. That's what makes the hobby so enjoyable.

San Diego, California

SAN DIEGO PADRES

National League 1969 to Present

During their 25-year history, the San Diego Padres have had their share of disappointments. As an expansion team entering the National League in 1969, the Padres finished last in the Western Division for six consecutive years. It was not until that sixth season, in 1974, that the Padres first drew more than a million fans (1,075,399).

Despite the disappointments, Padres fans have had numerous memorable moments, including a National League championship in 1984. They also have had their share of outstanding players. The first Padre to bat above .300 was Cito Gaston (.318) in 1970. The remarkable Tony Gwynn, who first joined the team in 1982, won a batting championship his first full season in 1984 (.351) and has won three other National league batting titles by hitting .370 in 1987, .313 in 1988, and .336 in 1989. Gwynn led the league in hits four times, including a career-high 218 in 1987, when he established his career-high batting average of .370. The Padres' powerful outfielder is almost certain to be in-

ducted into the Hall of Fame five years after his illustrious career ends.

The year 1974 was a critical one in franchise history as Ray Kroc bought the team to prevent it from moving to Washington, D.C. Prior to this, the Padres' highest attendance mark had been 644,272. Kroc's fresh infusion of cash enabled the Padres to slowly work their way up the division ladder and eventually take the 1984 pennant. 1974 was also the first full season for Dave Winfield, who had been the Padres' first selection in the June 1973 draft. Winfield led the Padres in RBI with 75. In 1979 Winfield set the all-time Padres RBI standard by knocking in 118. It broke Nate Colbert's previous record of 111 RBI set back in 1972. Former Dodger star and league MVP Steve Garvey joined the Padres in 1983 and his team-high 86 RBI was instrumental in their 1984 pennant. In the National League Championship Series against the Cubs, Garvey was named MVP as he batted .400 and drove in seven runs as the Padres came from a two-game deficit to win three games to two. In the World Series the Padres bowed to the Detroit Tigers four games to one.

Although batting has dominated Padres history, they have had some excellent pitching throughout the years. Clay Kirby's 231 strikeouts in 1971 is still the club record, while Randy Jones became the first 20-game winner in 1975 and established the club-record 22 in 1976. Hall of Fame reliever Rollie Fingers was outstanding for the Padres during his four seasons (1977–1980). In addition to Jones (1976), Hall of Famer Gaylord Perry (1978) and reliever Mark Davis (1989) won Cy Young Awards as the leagues best pitcher. Eric Show, a Padre from 1981 through 1990, holds the career record for wins with 100.

The Padres all-time attendance mark for Jack Murphy Stadium is 2,210,352 in 1985. In 1992 newcomer Gary Sheffield won the NL batting title with a .330 BA and was named Player of the Year by *The Sporting News*, while Fred McGriff was league home run king with 35. Now in their second quarter century, the San Diego Padres hope the best is yet to come.

In addition to Hall of Famers Fingers and Perry, other past or present Padres who loom as Hall of Fame possibilities are Garvey, Winfield and Ozzie Smith. When Gwynn's illustrious career ends, he is almost certain to be inducted.

1969 cloth patch issued by Fleer Gum Co. for the Padres first season in the National League, 2½″ × 3¼″, $10.

1986	Union Tribune Team Photo	$8
1987	Arby's Calendar, Tony the Tiger Team Poster, Union Tribune Team Photo, Great America Savings Commemorative Pin	$8
1987	U.S. Forest Service Flip Book	$7
1987	Smokey the Bear Baseball Cards	$10
1987	Coca-Cola Beach Towel, Pepsi Sports Bag	$6

Ballpark Giveaways

1982	San Diego Trust & Savings Bank Cap, Dow T-shirt, Pepsi Wrist Band, 7-Up Bat	$6
1982	Union Tribune Team Photo, 7-Up Tankard	$10
1983	San Diego Trust & Savings Bank Cap, Pepsi Helmet, Dow Jersey	$6
1983	Union Tribune Team Picture	$10
1984	Calendar, National League Champs Union Tribune Team Photo	$12
1984	Smokey the Bear Baseball Cards	$12
1984	Mother's Cookies Baseball Cards	$15
1984	7-Up Beach Towel, Servomation Watch, Pepsi Sports Bag	$6
1985	Miller Lite 1984 Highlights Record Album, Miller Lite Calendar, Union Tribune Team Photo	$10
1985	U.S. Forest Service Batting Tips, Pepsi All-Star Bag, Franzee Painter Cap, S.D. Trust & Savings Bank Cap	$6
1985	Beach Towel	$5
1986	San Diego Trust & Savings Bank Cap, Coca-Cola Beach Towel, Pepsi Sports Bag, Coca-Cola Glove, U.S. Forest Service Baseball Tips Book, Pepsi Baseball (with facsimile autographs $10)	$6

1974 plastic baseball, McDonald's logo on black base, given away with circular cards of Padres players. Fans could obtain the cards at McDonald's locations in San Diego area throughout the season, $50.

1988 S.D. Trust & Savings Cap, Coca-
Cola Beach Towel, Pepsi Sports Bag ...$6
1988 Coca-Cola Poster, Union Tribune
Team Photo $8
1989 S.D. Trust & Savings Cap, Coca-
Cola Beach Towel, Smokey the
Bear Notebook $6
1989 Coca-Cola Pitcher & Cups, Union
Tribune Team Photo $7
1990 KFMB Magnet Schedule, Jack in
the Box Bumper Sticker, S.D. Trust
& Savings Cap, Coca-Cola Beach
Towel, Gatorade Notebook $6
1990 Donruss Baseball Card Book $7
1990 Smokey the Bear Wall Calendar,
Gatorade Poster $7
1991 K-Mart Magnet Schedule, Tony the
Tiger Helmet, S.D. Trust & Bank
Cap, Jack in the Box Bumper
Sticker, American Raisin Binocu-
lars, B-100 F.M. Fanny Pack, Coca-
Cola Beach Towel, Coor 3D
Glasses, Blue Cross Sunglasses, Se-
curity Pacific Bank T-shirt, 1992
All-Star Game Cap $6
1991 Upper Deck Cards, Gatorade Poster ...$7

Miscellaneous

BOBBIN' HEAD DOLLS

Category #VI, 1969 through 1972, Gold
Round Base, Boy Head $70

Pennants

1969, 1970 ....$30
1971 through 1978 Regular $20
1978 All-Star Game $50
1979, 1980 ....$20
1981, 1982 Regular $5
1982 All-Star Game $15
1983, 1984 Regular $5
1984 League Champs $15
1984 World Series..................................$15
1985 through 1990 ....$5
1991, 1992, 1993 ....$3

Pins

1968, 1969 Crane Potato Chips, ⁷⁄₈″,
Round $5
1984 Crane Potato Chips, ⁷⁄₈″, Round $3

Publications

BOOKS

Rothaus, James. *San Diego Padres.*
Mankato, Mn.: Creative Educa-
tion, 1987. ....$5.00

1992 pin issued for the All-Star game at San Diego,
July 14, 3″, $2.

MEDIA GUIDES

1969 First Year $30
1970 ....$15
1971, 1972 ....$12
1973, 1974 ....$10
1975, 1976 ....$8
1977, 1978 ....$7
1979, 1980 ....$6
1981, 1982, 1983 ....$5
1984 League Champs $7
1985 through 1993 ....$4

PROGRAMS AND SCORECARDS

1969 First Year $25
1970 through 1979 ....$6

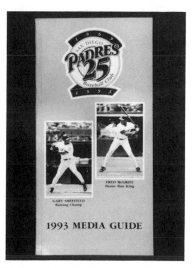

1993 Padres media guide, measuring 4½″ × 9″ with
194 pages, $4.

1980 through 1983 ....$4
1984 League Champs $6
1985 through 1989 ....$4
1990, 1991, 1992, 1993 ....$3

YEARBOOKS

1969 ....$75
1970 through 1978 ....None Issued
1979 ....$12
1980 ....$10
1981 ....None Issued
1982, 1983 ....$9
1984 League Champs $12
1985, 1986 ....$6
1987 through 1992 ....None Issued

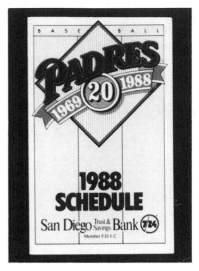

1988 schedule issued by San Diego Trust and Savings
Bank, 2¼″ × 3½″, $1.

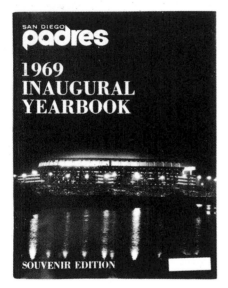

1969 yearbook from Padres first season, 8½″ × 11″,
64 pages, night view of San Diego stadium
on cover, $75.

Schedules

1969 First Year $20
1970 through 1979 ....$10
1980 through 1985 ....$2
1986 through 1993 ....$1

1969 scorecard from first Padres National League
home game on April 12, vs. the Los Angeles
Dodgers, $50.

ALL-STAR PROGRAMS

1978 ....$50
1992 ....$10

Special Events

ALL-STAR GAME TICKETS

1978 Complete Ticket $40
1978 Ticket Stub....................................$20
1992 Complete Ticket $20
1992 Ticket Stub....................................$10

ALL-STAR GAME PRESS PINS

1978 ....$75
1992 ....$20

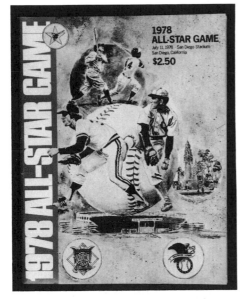

1978 program, 8½″ × 11″, 44 pages, All-Star game, $50.

1984 program, 8½″ × 11″, 60 pages, NLCS vs. the Chicago Cubs, $20.

LEAGUE CHAMPIONSHIP SERIES TICKETS

1984 Complete Ticket $28
1984 Ticket Stub..................................$15

WORLD SERIES PRESS PINS

1984 (not dated) $50

WORLD SERIES PROGRAMS

1984 ....$15

WORLD SERIES GAME TICKETS

1984 Complete Ticket $30
1984 Ticket Stub..................................$15

San Francisco, California

SAN FRANCISCO GIANTS

National League 1958 to Present

Giants owner Horace Stoneham saw attendance in New York dwindle as the neighborhood around the Polo Grounds declined, so he welcomed the suggestion of Brooklyn Dodger owner Walter O'Malley that he move to San Francisco. O'Malley had decided to move the Dodgers to Los Angeles, and it was imperative he get another club owner to move to the West Coast with him for scheduling purposes. After the City of San Francisco agreed to construct a new ballpark for the Giants, Stoneham made the move in time for the 1958 season.

While Candlestick Park was being built, the Giants played their first two seasons in Seals Stadium, former home of the San Francisco Seals of the Pacific Coast League. Despite a seating capacity of less than 24,000, the Giants drew 1,272,625 their first season in San Francisco—more than doubling their final season's attendance in New York.

Willie Mays, who came with the Giants

from New York, made an immediate impact on Bay Area fans by batting .347 and leading the league in runs (129) and stolen bases (31). The Giants finished third their initial season in San Francisco, 12 games behind the pennant-winning Milwaukee Braves. First baseman Willie McCovey, a future Hall of Famer like Mays, joined the team in 1959 and promptly batted .354 with 13 home runs and 38 RBI. In his first major league game on July 30, he gave graphic evidence of his future greatness by going 4 for 4 against the Phillies. McCovey proceeded to win the Rookie of the Year Award.

In 1962, under manager Al Dark, the Giants won their first pennant in San Francisco by edging the Dodgers by one game. Mays led the league with 49 home runs and was second with 141 RBI. Jack Sanford was second in wins with 24 while Billy O'Dell was fifth with 19 victories. Future Hall of Famer Juan Marichal, who joined the Giants in 1960, won 18 of his 243 career victories in 1962; Billy Pierce won 16 and lost only 6. Another future Hall of Famer, Gaylord Perry, joined the team late in the season and posted a 3–1 record. The Giants lost a thrilling World Series to the New York Yankees four games to three, including a heartbreaking 1 to 0 loss in the final game.

When baseball went to divisional playoffs, the Giants won Western Division titles in 1971 and 1987 but lost to Pittsburgh and St. Louis in those championship series. However, in 1989, the Giants beat Chicago in the NLCS to win the pennant but were defeated by Bay Area rival Oakland in the World Series. Much success in recent years is directly attributable to first baseman Will Clark, who joined the team in 1986 and has been a standout ever since. In 1993 All-Star outfielder Barry Bonds joined the Giants as a free agent from Pittsburgh, so the future remains bright as the Giants carry on an outstanding tradition that has roots in 1883 New York.

Ballpark Giveaways

1970 Bat (if dated $10), Cap, T-shirt, Helmet, Ball (with facsimile autographs $25) $5
1971 Bat (if dated $10), Cap, T-shirt, Helmet $5
1972 Bat (if dated $10), Cap, T-shirt, Helmet $5

1959 Bazooka-Bloney felt round premium, available from the Topps Gum Co. by sending wrappers from Bazooka-Bloney Gum, 6", $35.

1973 Bat (if dated $10), Cap, T-shirt, Helmet $5
1974 Bat (if dated $10), Cap, T-shirt, Helmet, Jacket................................$5
1975 Bat, Cap, T-shirt, Tote Bag, Jacket $5
1976 Bat, Cap, T-shirt, Tote Bag, Jacket $5
1977 Bat, Cap, T-shirt, Jacket, Helmet, Back Pack $5
1978 Bat, Cap $5
1978 English Leather Jacket, Let's Dine Out Helmet, Straw Hat Pizza Jersey, Let's Dine Out Backpack $6
1978 Team Picture (with sponsor's name $15)...$14
1979 Cap, Backpack $5
1979 Dubuque Jacket, Kirkpatrick Tote Bag, Straw Hat Pizza Helmet, Patrick & Co. School Kit $6

1969, cloth patch, Fleer Gum Co., 2½" × 3¼", $5.

1979 Dubuque Photo Album....................$15
1979 Krazy Don's Autograph Ball.............$20
1980 Cap..$5
1980 Photo Album (with sponsor $15)......$14
1980 Dubuque Jacket, Kirkpatrick Tote
Bag, J.C. Penney T-shirt, KTTV
Banner, Patrick & Co. Binder.............$6
1981 Coca-Cola/Dubuque Jacket,
Kirkpatrick Sports Cap, J.C.
Penney's T-shirt, Wheaties Helmet,
KTTV Banner, Patrick & Co.
Binder, Wishbone Sun Visor..............$6
1981 Lowenbrau Team Picture................$14
1982 Coca-Cola Cap, J.C. Penney's Jersey, KTTV Banner, Shell Travel Kit,
Atari Bat, Wheaties Helmet, Oakland Tribune T-shirt, Wishbone
Cushion, Maxwell House Tote Bag.....$6
1982 Yago Pennant $10
1982 Lowenbrau Poster, Safeway/Hills
Brothers Coffee Mug, Mother's
Cookies Team Photo........................$14
1983 Coca-Cola Cap, J.C. Penney's Jersey, Shell Jersey, Wishbone Sun Vi-
sor...$6
1983 Mother's Cookies Cards $18
1983 Lowenbrau Team Photo.................$13
1984 Chevrolet Calendar, Lowenbrau
Poster, Lowenbrau Team Photo........$13
1984 Budweiser Candlestick Beverage
Warmer, Coca-Cola Cap, PG & E
Ski Cap, J.C. Penney's Tote Bag,
Macho Croix T-shirt $6
1984 Shell All-Star T-shirt $7
1984 Mother's Cookies Cards $15
1987 United Air Lines Sports Cap,
Safeway Cooler Bag, Sunkist BBQ
Apron, Coca-Cola Mitt, Humm Baby
T-shirt..$6
1987 Mother's Cookies Cards $12
1987 Topps Baseball Card Book $7
1987 Miller Lite Team Picture $11
1988 Miller Calendar $11
1988 California Egg Commission Auto-
graph Baseball $12
1988 United Airlines Cap, Coca-Cola Bat,
Baskin Robins Batting Helmet, Ortho Sunglasses, Safeway Tote Bag,
Purina Dog Chow Batting Gloves,
Sunkist Sun Visor, Smokey the Bear
Painter Cap $6
1988 Surf Baseball Card Book $9
1988 Mother's Cookies Cards $10
1989 Budweiser Calendar, Autograph
Baseball $11
1989 Autograph Baseball $12
1989 Sunkist Cap, Coca-Cola Bat $6
1989 Roll-up Cap, Sports Cap, Flip-up
Sunglasses $5
1989 Back to School Thermos $9
1989 Team Picture................................$10
1989 Mother's Cookies Cards $8
1990 Budweiser Calendar $10
1990 Chevron Commemorative Pins
1, 2 ....ea. $7

1990 AT & T Relief Pitcher, Budweiser
Championship Pennant, Team Pic-
ture..$8
1990 Mother's Cookies Trade Cards..........$8
1990 Donruss Card Album........................$7
1990 Cherry 7-Up Magnet Schedule,
Bank America Cap, AT & T Photo
Badge, United Airlines Lunch Bag,
Ortho Fanny Pack, Coca-Cola
Squeeze Bottle, Sunkist Neon Cap,
United Airlines Roll-up Cap $6
1991 O'Doul's Calendar, San Francisco
Chronicle Mug, Giants Raisins
Poster...$8
1991 Donruss Card Album, Upper Deck
Cards $7
1991 Mother's Cookies Cards $8
1991 Yellow Pages Magnet Schedule, Or-
tho Fanny Pack, Sunkist Neon Cap,
AT & T Cap, Coca-Cola Sports Bag.....$6
1991 Wrist Band, Flashlight $5
1992 O'Doul's Calendar, Cellular One
Schedule Mug, San Francisco
Chronicle Mug $7
1992 Coca-Cola Commemorative Pin,
Donruss Card Album, Upper Deck
Cards $7
1992 AT & T Family Pack, Ortho Picnic
Cooler, Pacific Bell Magnet Sched-
ule, AT & T Cap...............................$6
1992 Wrist Watch $5
1993 O'Doul Calendar, 7-Up Autograph
Beverage Pitcher, Team Poster $7
1993 Upper Deck Cards, Donruss Album,
Coca-Cola Commemorative Pin $7
1993 Mother's Cookies Cards $8
1993 Pacific Bell Magnet Schedule,
Chevron Football, Jolly Rancher
Lunch Bag, Coca-Cola Ruck Sack,
Welcome the Marlins Pin, Welcome
the Rockies Pin, Wells Fargo Cap $6
1993 Sunglasses, Helmet, BBQ Apron.........$5

Miscellaneous

BOBBIN' HEAD DOLLS

Category #I, 1960, 1961, Orange Square
Base, Boy Head $175
Category #II, 1961, 1962, White Square
Base, Boy Head $240
Category #III, 1961, 1962, White Round
Miniature, Boy Head $180
Category #IV, 1962, 1963, 1964, Green
Round Base, Boy Head $60
Category #V, 1962, 1963, 1964, Green
Round Base, Black Player $1,550
Category #VI, 1967 through 1972, Gold
Round Base, Boy Head $70

Pennants

1958 First Year $55
1959, 1960 ....$50
1961 Regular..$35

1961 All-Star Game	$75
1962 Regular	$30
1962 League Champs	$75
1963	$30
1964 Regular	$30
1964 All-Star Game	$75
1965 through 1970	$30
1971 Regular	$20
1971 League Champs	$50
1972 through 1980	$20
1981 through 1987 Regular	$5
1987 League Champs	$15
1988	$5
1989 Regular	$5
1989 League Champs	$15
1990 through 1993	$3

Pins

1961 through 1965 Crane Potato Chips, ⅞", Round	$5
1967 through 1969 Crane Potato Chips, ⅞", Round	$5
1984 Crane Potato Chips, ⅞", Round	$3
1964, 1965, 1966 Guy's Potato Chips, ⅞", Round	$5

Publications

BOOKS

Brannon, Jody. *San Francisco Giants.* Mankato, Mn.: Creative Education, 1982. ....$5.00

Einstein, Charles. *A Flag for San Francisco.* Simon & Schuster, 1962, 1963. J. Lowell Pratt, 1963, reissue. $10.00

Hodges, Russ & Al Hirshbert. *My Giants.* Doubleday & Co., 1963. ....$10.00

King, Joe. *The San Francisco Giants.* Prentice Hall, 1958. ....$15.00

Manel, Mike. *The San Francisco Giants: An Oral History.* Santa Cruz, Ca.: Clatworthy, 1979. ....$15.00

Orseth, Ed. *Giant Orange & Dodger Blue: Where Were You In '62?* San Francisco: Dungeon Printing, 1987. ....$15.00

•Peters, Nick. *San Francisco Giants Almanac: 30 Years of Baseball By the Bay.* Berkeley, Ca.: North Atlantic Books, 1988. ....$8.95

Rosenbaum, Art & Robert Stevens. *The Giants of San Francisco.* Coward-McMann, 1963. ....$20.00

Rothaus, James R. *San Francisco Giants.* Mankato, Mn.: Creative Education, 1987. ....$5.00

•Shea, John & John Hickey. *Magic by the Bay.* Berkeley, Ca.: North Atlantic Books, 1990. ....$12.95

•Stein, Fred. *Giants Diary: A Century of Baseball in New York & San*

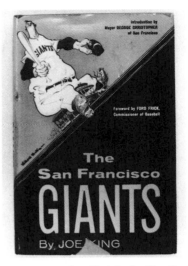

1958, *The San Francisco Giants* by Joe King, Prentice Hall, the story of the giants move to San Francisco and their previous history in New York, 5¾" × 8¼", 177 pages, $15.

Francisco. Berkeley, Ca.: North Atlantic Books, 1987. ....$14.95

Stein, Fred & Nick Peters. *Day By Day In Giants History.* West Point, N.Y.: Leisure Press, 1984. ....$15.00

MEDIA GUIDES

1958 First Year	$50
1959, 1960, 1961	$40

1993 media guide with letters SF on the cover, 4½" × 9", 280 pages, $4.

1962 League Champs	$35
1963, 1964	$30
1965, 1966	$20
1967, 1968	$17
1969, 1970	$15
1971 League Champs	$15
1972	$12
1973, 1974	$10
1975, 1976	$8
1977, 1978	$7
1979, 1980, 1981	$6
1982, 1983, 1984	$5
1985, 1986	$4
1987 League Champs	$6
1988	$4
1989 League Champs	$6
1990 through 1993	$4

PROGRAMS AND SCORECARDS

1958 First Year	$35
1959	$15
1960, 1961	$10
1962 League Champs	$12
1963 through 1969	$10
1970	$6
1971 League Champs	$8
1972 through 1979	$6
1980 through 1986	$4
1987 League Champs	$6
1988	$4
1989 League Champs	$6
1990 through 1993	$5

YEARBOOKS

1958 First Year	$250
1959	$75
1960	$40
1961	$35
1962 League Champs	$40
1963, 1964, 1965	$30
1966, 1967, 1968, 1969	$25
1970	$20
1971 Division Champs	$30
1972	$18
1973, 1974, 1975	$15
1976	$12
1977, 1978, 1979	None Issued
1980, 1981, 1982, 1983	$8
1984, 1985	$7
1986 through 1993	None Issued

Schedules

1958 First Year	$40
1959	$25
1960 through 1969	$15
1970 through 1979	$10
1980 through 1989	$2
1990 through 1993	$1

1958 yearbook, the Giants' first in San Francisco, 8½" × 10¼", 48 pages, showing a Willard Mullin cartoon Giant loaded down with books recounting past triumph of the Giants and their players, $250.

1964 schedule, 2½" × 4", Hamm's Beer Giants, $15.

Special Events

ALL-STAR GAME PRESS PINS

1961	$200
1984	$40

ALL-STAR PROGRAMS

1961	$400
1984	$15

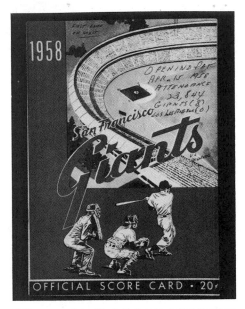

1958 program from Giants first game in San Francisco against the Los Angeles Dodgers (won by the Giants 8 to 0 before a capacity crowd of 23,844 fans at Seals Stadium), 7″ × 10¼″, $200.

1962 World Series program vs. the New York Yankees, 9″ × 12″, 54 pages. This frequently rain-delayed series was won by New York in 7 games (very scarce), $225.

ALL-STAR GAME TICKETS

1961 Complete Ticket $70
1961 Ticket Stub..................................$35
1984 Complete Ticket $30
1984 Ticket Stub..................................$15

LEAGUE CHAMPIONSHIP SERIES PROGRAMS

1971 (very rare) $400
1987 ....$12
1989 ....$10

LEAGUE CHAMPIONSHIP SERIES TICKETS

1971 Complete Ticket $38
1971 Ticket Stub..................................$15
1987 Complete Ticket $28
1987 Ticket Stub..................................$15
1989 Complete Ticket $28
1989 Ticket Stub..................................$15

WORLD SERIES PRESS PINS

1962 ....$200
1989 ....$50

1961 program, All-Star game, 8¾″ × 11¾″, 44 pages (one of the more difficult programs to obtain), $400.

WORLD SERIES PROGRAMS

1962	$225
1989	$10

WORLD SERIES GAME TICKETS

1962 Complete Ticket	$70
1962 Ticket Stub	$35
1989 Complete Ticket	$30
1989 Ticket Stub	$15

Seattle, Washington

SEATTLE PILOTS

American League 1969

Although the Seattle Pilots introduced major league baseball to the Pacific Northwest in 1969, they lasted only one season as an American League expansion team. Underfinanced from the beginning, the team moved to Milwaukee during spring training prior to the 1970 season.

During their lone season the Pilots finished sixth in the American League Western Division with a record of 64 wins and 98 defeats. Steve Hovley was the leading batter with a .277 BA while Tommy Davis led the Pilots with 80 RBI. First baseman Don Mincher socked a team-leading 30 home runs and drove in 78 runs. Righthanders Gene Brabender and Diego Segui were the leading pitchers, with records of 13–14 and 12–6 respectively.

A new stadium was planned for the future, but the Pilots played their games in Sicks Stadium, a renovated minor league ballpark previously used by the Seattle Raniers of the Pacific Coast League. Although expanded to seat approximately 25,000, it was seldom filled.

Seattle was in the midst of a tremendous economic slump. Lack of employment played a big role in the Pilots' lack of success at the gate. The Pilots did draw 677,944 fans, which was higher than attendance in Chicago and Cleveland.

Much like the Boston Braves' move to Milwaukee during spring training of 1953, the Pilots moved to Milwaukee during spring training of 1970 to become the Brewers.

Under threat of a lawsuit against major league baseball, Seattle interests were assured that when the leagues expanded again they would be one of the cities to get a team. That became a reality in 1977 when the Seattle Mariners were formed as an American League expansion team. The Mariners play their home games in a brand-new indoor facility known as the Kingdome.

Because of the brief lifespan of the Seattle Pilots their memorabilia is quite collectible and commands higher prices than other team items from 1969. No Seattle Pilots are in the Baseball Hall of Fame. For further reading on the Pilots see *The Seattle Pilots Story* by Carson Van Lindt, 1993.

Miscellaneous

BOBBIN' HEAD DOLLS

Category #VI, 1969 Gold Round Base,
   Boy Head $225

1969 cloth patch issued by Fleer's Gum Co., Pilots
logo, 2½″ × 3¼″, $10.

1969 pennant, 12″ × 29½″, Pilots
logo on red material, $50.

Pins

1969 Crane Potato Chips, ⅞″, Round $20

Publications

BOOKS

• Van Lindt, Carson. *Seattle Pilots
   Story.* 1993. ....$12.95

MEDIA GUIDES

1969 ....$45

PROGRAMS AND SCORECARDS

1969 ....$55

1969 program, 6¾″ × 7″, 62 pages, Pilots first game
against the Chicago White Sox on April 11th, $100.

YEARBOOKS

1969 ....$200

Schedules

1969 ....$40

SEATTLE MARINERS

American League 1977 to Present

Founded in 1977 as an American League
expansion franchise for the Pacific Northwest, the Seattle Mariners struggled for 14
seasons before earning their first winning
record in 1991. Even with a record of 83
wins and 79 losses, the Mariners finished
fifth in the Western Division.

The year 1991 also marked the first
time the Mariners exceeded two million
in attendance (2,147,905). In fact, the
57,762 fans that saw the team's inaugural
game in the Kingdome on April 6, 1977,
continues as the single-game record.

Beleaguered by financial problems
over the years, the Mariners received an
infusion of cash by Japanese investors in
1992, although Americans continued to
make the operating decisions.

Brighter days appear on the horizon
with the emergence of Ken Griffey, Jr. as a
superstar. Griffey was the Mariners' first
draft choice in 1987 and was their starting
outfielder two years later. In 1989 he
played with his father, Ken Griffey, mark-
ing the first time in major league history a
father and son combination played at the
same time. Griffey Jr.'s .327 batting average in 1991 is the best in club history.

Since 1977 Leon Roberts (1978); Bruce
Bochte (1979, 1980); Al Paciorek (1981);

Phil Bradley (1985, 1986); Alvin Davis (1989); Edgar Martinez (1990, 1991); and Griffey (1990, 1991) all have batted .300 or better. Gorman Thomas holds the club home run record with 32 (in 1985) and Alvin Davis holds the record for RBI with 116 in 1984.

In Randy Johnson, a flame-throwing lefthander who joined the team in 1989, the Mariners have an outstanding talent and the tallest player in major league history (six feet, ten inches). He was second in the American League in strikeouts in 1991 with 228. Although the Mariners have not yet had a 20-game winner, Mark Langston (with 19 in 1987) and Eric Hanson (with 18 in 1990), have come closest.

Although the Mariners have not enjoyed much success in their brief history, an abundance of young talent spearheaded by Ken Griffey, Jr., bodes well for the future.

1977 ceramic mug bearing Mariners original logo, 3¼″ × 3¼″, $10.

Ballpark Giveaways

1981 Ball $5 (with facsimile autographs) ..$15
1982 Photo Album, Tankard $10
1982 Seat Cushion, Tote Bag....................$5
1983 Color Photo Mug $8
1983 Ball $5 (with facsimile autographs) ..$15
1984 T-shirt, Beach Towel, Sports Watch....$5
1984 Ball $5 (with facsimile autographs) ..$15
1984 Baseball Cards $10
1985 Calendar, Yearbook (only one in
    team history) $10

1992 Donruss Mariners album, complete with eight cards of Mariners players, 6½″ × 8″, $7.

1985 Gym Socks, Wallet, Seat Cushion $5
1985 Pitcher $6
1986 Calendar, Schedule Poster, Ther-
    mos, Team Poster $7
1986 Autograph Baseball $10
1986 Seat Cushion, Sports Watch, Roll-
    up Cap, Umbrella, T-shirt, Jacket,
    Batting Glove $5
1987 Calendar, Schedule Poster, Picture
    Pennant $7
1987 Seat Cushion, Radio, Cap, Sports
    Bag, Cooler, Jacket $5
1988 Rainier Bank Calendar $8
1988 Mother's Cookies Trading Cards $12
1988 Washington Natural Gas Seat Cush-
    ion, Rainer Bank Glove, Coors Pic-
    nic Cooler, Oscar Mayer T-shirt,
    Ortho Barbecue Apron, Smokey the
    Bear Helmet, Holland America/
    Westover Beach Towel $6
1988 Surf Baseball Book $10

Pennants

1977 First Year $30
1978, 1979 Regular $20
1979 All-Star Game $50
1980 ....$20
1981 through 1990 ....$5
1991, 1992, 1993 ....$3

Pins

1984 Crane Potato Chips, ⅞″, Round $3

Publications

MEDIA GUIDES

1977 First Year $20
1978 ....$7

1993 Mariners media guide, 4¼″ × 9″, 256 pages, $4.

1979 press pin, All-Star game, Mariners original Trident logo, 1″ × 1¼″, $50.

1977 complete ticket, Mariners' first home game at Kingdome, April 6, vs. the California Angels, $50.

1979 program, 64 pages, 8½″ × 11″, All-Star Game, $25.

1979, 1980, 1981 ....$6
1982, 1983, 1984 ....$5
1985 through 1993 ....$4

PROGRAMS AND SCORECARDS

1977 First Year $15
1978, 1979 ....$6

1980 through 1989 ....$4
1990 through 1993 ....$3

YEARBOOKS

1977 through 1984 ....None Issued
1985 ....$10
1986 through 1993 ....None Issued

Schedules

1977 First Year $15
1978, 1979 ....$10
1980 through 1985 ....$2
1986 through 1993 ....$1

Special Events

ALL-STAR GAME TICKETS

1979 Complete Ticket $40
1979 Ticket Stub..................................$20

Syracuse, New York

SYRACUSE STARS

National League 1879; American Association 1890

Syracuse, New York, enjoyed two years as a major league city as the Syracuse Stars played in the National League in 1879 and then had a franchise in the American Association in 1890.

The National League Stars of 1879 were basically the same team that finished second to Buffalo in the International League the year before. The step up in class was too much to handle as the Stars finished seventh in the eight-team league. Second baseman Jack Farrell was the team's leading batter with a .303 BA. Righthander Harry McCormick was third in the league with five shutouts but finished with a record of 18 wins and 33 losses despite an ERA of 2.99. Lack of batting support was obviously very costly.

On June 18 the Stars attracted 1000 fans, their largest home crowd of the season. By the end of the season their crowds had dwindled to 200 per game. On September 12 the Stars disbanded due to poor attendance which they blamed on the National League-standard 50 cents admission fee. The club did well financially in previous years, when admission was only 25 cents. The Stars' final record in 1879 was 22 wins and 48 defeats.

In 1890 Syracuse joined the American Association and finished sixth in the eight-team league with a record of 55 wins and 72 losses. Second baseman Cupid Childs was the batting star with a .345 BA, fifth best in the league. In only his second year in the majors, Childs went on to play 13 more seasons in the big leagues and compile a .306 BA. Three other Stars, first baseman Mox McQuery (.308), outfielder Rusty Wright (.305) and outfielder Henry Simon (.301), all batted above .300. Sub-par pitching doomed the Stars. John Keefe led the league in losses with 24 in his only major league season.

George Frazier not only owned the Stars who wore blood red uniforms but also served as manager. After an August western swing which saw the Stars win 9 of 16 games, 10,000 fans turned out for a victory procession. Frazier was hailed as the second Napoleon as a wire across the parade route carried pictures of Frazier and the French emperor. In their homecoming game after the successful road trip, the Stars drew a standing-room-only crowd of 3,000, their largest of the season. It was the highlight of the season for the Stars, who dropped out of the American Association when the season ended and thus finished Syracuse's tenure in the major leagues.

Toledo, Ohio

TOLEDO BLUE STOCKINGS

American Association 1884

Toledo, Ohio, had two major league teams, both members of the American Association. Their 1884 American Association team, known as the Blue Stockings, finished eighth in the 12-team league under player-manager Charley Morton. The Blue Stockings had the unique distinction of signing the Walker brothers, Fleetwood and Welday. They were the first African-American players in history to reach the major leagues.

Fleetwood, the better of the two, was a catcher and appeared in 42 games before suffering a broken collarbone that sidelined him much of the year. Welday was an outfielder who appeared in only five games and batted .222.

Their careers came to an end when the owners of the Richmond, Virginia, Virginians sent the following letter to Manager Morton on September 5: "We the undersigned, do hereby warn you not to put up Walker, the Negro catcher, the days you play in Richmond, as we could mention the names of 75 determined men who have sworn to mob Walker if he comes on the grounds in a suit. We hope you will listen to our words of warning so there will be no trouble, and if you do not, there certainly will be. We only write this to prevent much bloodshed, as you alone can prevent."

When Toledo played at Richmond on September 13, Walker did not catch; when Richmond appeared at Toledo on September 21, Walker was not used. He was released on September 29. The Walker brothers were the last African-Americans to play in the majors until Jackie Robinson played with the Brooklyn Dodgers in 1947.

Toledo's star attraction in 1884 was pitcher Tony Mullane, who was second in the league with 37 wins and third in strikeouts with 329. The Blue Stockings lacked batting punch, with only second baseman Sam Barkley (.306) batting over .300.

Despite a home crowd of 10,000 on September 22, which helped the club treasury immensely, the team still lost money and dropped out of the league at the end of the season.

TOLEDO MAUMEES

American Association 1890

Toledo's final fling in the majors came in 1890 when the Maumees represented the city in the American Association. Morton was back at the helm as manager and the team finished fourth with a record of 68 wins and 64 losses. Outfielder Ed Swartwood (.327) was the lone .300 hitter while righthander Egyptian Healy won 22 games and was fourth in the league in strikeouts (225) and fifth in the league in ERA (2.89).

Toronto, Ontario, Canada

TORONTO BLUE JAYS

American League 1977 to Present

The Toronto Blue Jays, Canada's second major league team, has been highly successful during its brief 15-year history. The team's greatest desire—an American League pennant and World Series championship—finally became a reality in 1992. In 1985, just nine years after the franchise was founded, the Blue Jays were champions of the American League Eastern Division, but they bowed to the eventual world champion Kansas City Royals in the League Championship Series. The Jays won division titles in 1989 and 1991 but lost in the play-offs to Oakland and Minnesota. Finally, in 1992, they beat Oakland in the play-offs and Atlanta in the World Series.

Despite freezing temperatures 44,649 jammed Exhibition Stadium on April 7, 1977, as the fledgling franchise made its major league debut by beating the Chicago White Sox 9 to 5. Although the team ended with a record of 54 wins and 107 losses, an expansion-club-record 1,701,052 fans saw the Jays in Toronto. It was a premonition of things to come, as home attendance reached an all-time major league record of 4,001,526 in 1991. This broke the previous attendance mark of 3,885,284 set in 1990, the team's first full season in the new all-purpose stadium known as the Skydome.

Under the skillful guidance of Pat Gillick, who has been in charge of baseball operations since the beginning, the Jays have blended power hitting and solid pitching. Slugging outfielder George Bell turned in the best single season performance for the Jays in 1987 on his way to the American League's Most Valuable Player Award. Bell set club records with 47 home runs and 134 RBI and batted .308. Infielder-outfielder Bob Bailor, the Jays' first pick in the expansion draft in 1976,

proved them correct by batting .310—the highest mark ever for a player on a first-year expansion club. Thus far 16 Jays have batted .300 or better, with Rance Mulliniks setting the pace with a .324 average in 1984, closely followed by Tony Fernandez who batted .322 in 1987. Perhaps the most popular Jay in history is catcher Ernie Whitt, who played from 1977 through the 1989 season and contributed much to the club's success.

Pitcher Dave Steib, another long time Jay, hurled for the club from 1979 through 1992 and holds club records with 174 wins and 1631 strikeouts. Jack Morris set the single-season win record with 21 victories after joining the Blue Jays in 1992. Relief pitcher Tom Henke, a Blue Jay from 1985 to 1993, saved a club record 217 games for Toronto.

Because of the short duration of the franchise, no Blue Jays thus far have been elected to the Hall of Fame, although former Boston Red Sox star Bobby Doerr was a Blue Jay's coach from 1977 through 1981.

Ballpark Giveaways

1981	Shoppers Drug Mart Calendar, Belvue General Bakeries Poster, Mountain Blend Coffee Mug $12
1981	Shopsy Jacket, Laura Second T-shirt, Dominion Helmet, Coca-Cola Cap, Mr. Submarine Sports Bag, Quaker Oats Toque, Thrifty Seat Cushion $6
1981	Sun Visor $5
1982	Shoppers Drug Mart Calendar, Mountain Blend Coffee Mug, Gillette Photo Album, General Bakery Poster $12
1982	Sport Catelli Bat, Dominion Helmet, Shopsy Jacket, Thrifty Seat Cushion, Earl Warren Banner, Coca-Cola Cap, Mr. Submarine Sports Bag, Hewpex Radio, Quaker Oats Toque $6
1982	Sun Visor $5

1983 Shoppers Drug Mart Calendar, General Bakeries Poster $11
1983 Dominion Helmet, Sport Catelli Bat, Coca-Cola Cap, Earl Warren Travel Banner, Mr. Submarine Sports Bag, Dominion Watch, Quaker Oats Toque, Jello Pops T-shirt $6
1984 Shoppers Drug Mart Calendar, General Bakeries Poster $11
1984 Coca-Cola Cap, Shopsy Rag Ball, Sport Catelli Bat, P. Lawson Travel Banner, Dominion Watch, Quaker Oats Toque, Mr. Submarine Sports Bag $6
1984 Seat Cushion $5
1985 Shoppers Drug Mart Calendar, General Bakeries Poster $10
1985 Quaker Oats Toque, Shopsy Rag Ball, Hostess Seat Cushion, P. Lawson Travel Banner, Sport Catelli Bat, Dominion Watch, Mr. Submarine Sports Bag $6
1986 Shoppers Drug Mart Calendar $10
1986 Poster $9
1986 Kentucky Fried Chicken Wrist Band, Mr. Submarine Sports Bag, Sport Catelli Bat, Bittner's Rag Ball, Hostess Seat Cushion, Quaker Oats Toque, Coca-Cola Cap $6
1986 Watch $5
1987 Shoppers Drug Mart Calendar, Ault Food Poster $10
1987 Coca-Cola Cap, Chiquita Bat, Mr. Submarine Sports Bag, Hostess Seat Cushion, Kentucky Fried Chicken Wrist Band, Commerce Bank $6
1987 Sports Wallet, Dominion/A&P Watch, Bittner's Scarf, Quaker Oats Toque $6
1988 Shoppers Drug Mart Calendar, CIBC Poster $10
1988 Coca-Cola Cap, Mr. Submarine Sports Bag, CIBC Wallet, Toronto Sun Visor, Crayola Fun Book, Chef Boyardee Bat, Kentucky Fried Chicken Thermal Bag, Hostess Seat Cushion, A&P/Dominion Watch, Quaker Oats Toque $6
1989 Shoppers Drug Mart Calendar, CIBC Poster, Esso/Imperial Oil Travel Mug $10
1989 A&P/Dominion Watch, Chef Boyardee Bat, Mr. Submarine Sports Bag, Mr. Freeze Visor, Kentucky Fried Chicken Thermal Bag, Hostess/Frito Lay Seat Cushion, CIBC Wallet $6
1989 Honda Autographed Baseball $7
1989 Quaker Oats Toque, Scarf $5
1990 Shoppers Drug Mart Calendar, Esso/Imperial Oil Travel Mug $9
1990 Honda Autographed Baseball, CIBC Pennant $7
1990 Maxwell House Coffee Mug $8

1990 A&P/Dominion Watch, Coca-Cola Cap, Wintario Visor, Chef Boyardee T-shirt, Mr. Submarine Sports Bag, Frito Lay/Hostess Seat Cushion, Sunkist Scarf $6
1991 Shoppers Drug Mart Calendar $9
1991 Maxwell House Coffee Mug $8
1991 Coca-Cola Away Cap, Kentucky fried Chicken Wrist Pack, Nabisco Activity Book, CIBC Knap Sack, Esso Towel, Mac's Banner, Sunkist Scarf, Mr. Submarine Sports Bag $6
1991 Honda Autographed Ball, Upper Deck Cards $7
1992 Shoppers Drug Mart Calendar World Champs $10
1992 Upper Deck Card Set, Nabisco Card Set $7
1992 Coca-Cola Away Cap, Telemedia Radio, Nabisco Activity Book, CIBC Knap Sack, Mac's Squeeze Bottle $6
1992 Loblaw's Lunch Box, Maxwell House Mug $7
1992 Honda Autograph Baseball World Champs $15
1993 Shoppers Drug Mart Calendar, Loblaw's Lunch Box, Esso Thermo Mug $8
1993 Dominos World Champion Pin $10
1993 CIBC Knap Sack, Coca-Cola Cap $6
1993 Honda Autographed Ball, Upper Deck Cards $7
1993 Maxwell House Mug $7

Pennants

1977 First Year $30
1978, 1979, 1980 ....$20
1981 through 1990 ....$5
1991 Regular $3
1991 All-Star Game $10
1992 Regular $3
1992 League Champs $10
1992 World Champs $10
1993 ....$3

Pins

1984 Crane Potato Chips $3

Postcards

1990 CH 4¾" × 6¾", The Postcard Factory, Markham, Ontario $5

Publications

BOOKS

• Bjarkman, Peter C. *The Toronto Blue Jays.* New York & Toronto: Bison Books, 1990. ....$7.98
Cary, Louis E. *Baseball's Back In Town.* Toronto, Ont.: Controlled Media Corp., 1977. ....$25.00

1992 picture pin, world champions, 6″, $8.

Caulfield, Jon. *Jays: A Fan's Diary.* Toronto: McClelland Steward, 1985. ....$15.00

Driscoll, David. *Blue Jays Jazz.* London, Ont.: Troy Communications, 1988. ....$15.00

Fidlin, Ken & Fred Thornhill. *The Official Blue Jays Album: A Dozen Years of Baseball Memories.* Toronto: Seal Books, 1989. ....$15.00

Humber, William. *Cheering for the Home Team: The Story of Baseball In Canada.* Ernin, Ont.: Boston Mills Press, 1983. ....$20.00

Martinze, Buck. *From Worst to First: The Toronto Blue Jays of 1985.* Toronto: Fitzhenry & Whiteside, 1985. ....$10.00

Millison, Lawrence. *Ballpark Figures: The Blue Jays and the Business of*

Baseball. Toronto: McClelland & Stewart, 1987. ....$15.00

Robertson, John. *Blue Jays 1985: How the East Was Won.* Toronto: Key Porter Books, 1985. ....$10.00

Robertson, John. *"Oh, Oh, Blue Jays."* Toronto: Key Porter Books, 1983. ....$10.00

Robertson, John. *O.K., O.K. Blue Jays: The Story of the Amazing Jays 1983 Season.* Toronto: Toronto Sun, 1983. ....$10.00

Robertson, John. *Those Amazing Jays.* Toronto: Key Porter Books, 1984. ....$10.00

Van Rindt, Phillippe & Patrick Blednick. *Fungo Blues: An Uncontrolled Look at the Toronto Blue Jays.* Toronto: McClelland and Steward, 1985. ....$10.00

MEDIA GUIDES

1977 First Year $22
1978 ....$7
1979, 1980, 1981 ....$6
1982, 1983, 1984 ....$5
1985 Division Champs $6
1986, 1987 ....$4
1988 ....$4
1989 Division Champs $6
1990 ....$4
1991 Division Champs $6
1992 World Champs $6
1993 World Champs $5

PROGRAMS AND SCORECARDS

1977 First Year $12
1978, 1979 ....$6
1980 through 1984 ....$4
1985 Division Champs $6
1986, 1987, 1988 ....$4
1989 Division Champs $6

1992 postcard, 4″ × 6″, world champions, $2.

1993 media guide, world champion Blue Jays, 4¼″ × 9″, 372 pages, $4.

1987 Labatt's schedule, 1½″ × 3¾″, $1.

1990	....$3
1991 Division Champs	...........................$5
1992 World Champs	...............................$5
1993	....$3

YEARBOOKS

1977 First Year	.....................................$45
1978	....$20
1979	....$15
1980	....$10
1981	....$8
1982, 1983, 1984	.................................$7
1985 through 1993	...............................$6

Schedules

1977 First Year	.....................................$20
1978, 1979	....$10
1980 through 1985	...............................$2
1986 through 1993	...............................$1

Special Events

ALL-STAR GAME PRESS PINS

1991	....$25

1977 complete ticket, Blue Jays first Major League game at Exhibition Stadium on April 7, vs. Chicago White Sox, 2⅛″ × 7″, $100.

1989 scorebook, opening game at the Skydome, June 5, vs. Milwaukee Brewers, 8″ × 10¾″, 210 pages, $25.

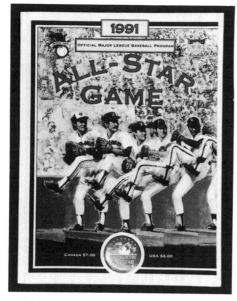

1991 program, All-Star, Skydome, 8⅛″ × 10⅞″, 52 pages, $10.

1985 program, American League championship series vs. Kansas City Royals, 8″ × 11″, 32 pages, $10.

ALL-STAR GAME TICKETS

1991 Complete Ticket $20
1991 Ticket Stub..................................$10

LEAGUE CHAMPIONSHIP SERIES PROGRAMS

1985 ....$8
1989 ....$5
1991, 1992 ....$5

LEAGUE CHAMPIONSHIP SERIES TICKETS

1985 Complete Ticket $28
1985 Ticket Stub..................................$15
1989 Complete Ticket $28
1989 Ticket Stub..................................$15

1991 Complete Ticket $18
1991 Ticket Stub..................................$10
1992 Complete Ticket $18
1992 Ticket Stub..................................$10

WORLD SERIES PRESS PINS

1992 ....$25

WORLD SERIES PROGRAMS

1992 ....$12

WORLD SERIES GAME TICKETS

1992 Complete Ticket $30
1992 Ticket Stub..................................$15

Troy, New York

TROY HAYMAKERS

National Association 1871–1872

Troy, New York, was a hotbed of early baseball with the Haymakers, original members of the National Association. The Haymakers played in the National Association in both 1871 and 1872 and after a lapse of seven years returned to the majors when they joined the National League in 1879 for a four-year run. During their four seasons in the National League, they were known as the Trojans although some old-timers still referred to them as Haymakers. In the end, the farming community in upstate New York was simply too small to support major league baseball. In 1883 the franchise was moved to New York City.

During their first season in 1871, the Haymakers had a record of 15 wins and 15 losses and finished seven-and-one-half games behind the champion Philadelphia Athletics. In 1872 their record was 15 and 10, but they wound up 13 games behind the league champion Boston Red Stockings. J. W. Scofield owned the team and served as treasurer of the National Association. Left fielder Steve King was the team's batting star and compiled a .396 BA in 1871. Player-manager Lipman Pike played right field and batted a solid .351 during their first season.

In 1872 many of the Haymakers' better players had been signed by other teams, who would offer them more money. Player-manager Lip Pike joined the Lord Baltimores. Batting star Steve King was back, but his average dipped to .296. Although the team played well attendance in Troy was sparse and the team dropped out the Association in late July. The Haymakers had no players who ultimately made the Hall of Fame, but major league baseball in Troy was far from over.

TROY TROJANS

National League 1879–1882

The Trojans entered the National League in 1879 but were overmatched by the other clubs in the league and finished last with a record of only 19 wins and 56 losses. Future Hall of Famer Dan Brouth-

ers led the team in batting with a .274 average and was third in the league in home runs with four. Troy attendance averaged approximately 400 per game.

In 1880, the team improved considerably and climbed to fourth place in the standings with a record of 41 wins and 42 losses. Four future Hall of Famers made their major league debuts that season with Troy. Third baseman Roger Connor, catcher Buck Ewing, and pitchers Mickey Welch and Tim Keefe graced the Trojans lineup and accounted for the dramatic improvement. Connor was third in the league with a .332 BA while Welch won 34 games. Keefe, as the backup to Welch, won six and lost six in his rookie season. Ewing, called up late in the year, saw limited action in 13 games on his way to an 18-year major league career and a lifetime .303 BA. Connor batted .317 over 18 seasons while Keefe recorded 336 wins in 14 seasons and Welch won 309 games in 13 years. This is the only time in baseball history that four future Hall of Famers debuted with the same team in the same year, and it is unlikely to ever occur again.

In 1881 the Trojans dropped to fifth place in the eight-team National League. Connor again led the Trojans in batting but his average fell to .292. Welch won 21 and lost 18 and Keefe posted a record of 18 wins and 27 defeats.

The Trojans' final season in the major leagues was 1882 as they finished seventh with 35 wins and 48 losses. Connor was third in the league in batting with a .330 BA but both Welch (14–16) and Keefe (17–26) had sub-par years.

In the end, Troy was simply too small to support major league baseball, but the city that spawned four future Hall of Famers in a single season will always hold a lofty niche in the annals of baseball history.

Washington, D.C.

WASHINGTON SENATORS (NATIONALS)

National Association 1871–1872, 1875;
Union Association 1884;
American Association 1884, 1891;
National League 1886–1889, 1892–1899;
American League 1901–1971

"First in war, first in peace and last in the American League" was a prophetic statement that epitomized the Washington Senators during much of their 70 seasons as charter members of the American League. There were ten last-place finishes, and most of the other years the Senators were hopelessly mired in the second division.

Only three American League pennants graced the Griffith Stadium flagpole (in 1924, 1925, and 1933) and only once (in 1924) were the Senators world champions. In that memorable World Series the immortal Walter Johnson, the finest pitcher of the twentieth century, won the seventh and deciding game in relief against the New York Giants. Walter was only a month shy of his thirty-seventh birthday—well past his career peak—when he registered the World Series victory. Johnson's record of 413 wins (all with Washington) against 277 losses is truly remarkable considering the ineptitude of the Senators during most of his 21 seasons.

Although Johnson forever remains the Senators' all-time brightest star, other outstanding players wore Senators uniforms. As a 24-year-old player-manager, second baseman Bucky Harris led them to their only world championship in 1924 and directed them to another pennant in 1925. Another fellow Hall of Famer and player-manager, shortstop Joe Cronin, led them to their only other pennant (in 1933)

was another outstanding Senator. Clark Griffith came to Washington in 1912 to manage the team and ultimately became its owner. At the twilight of his career as an outstanding pitcher (236–145), he appeared in three games over three seasons with no wins or losses and a perfect 0.00 ERA.

Outfielders Sam Rice (18 seasons), Goose Goslin (11 seasons) and Heinie Manush (6 seasons) played together for numerous years and all ultimately were elected to the Baseball Hall of Fame. Other Hall of Famers who played at least one season with the Senators are Stan Coveleski, Ed Delahanty, Harmon Killebrew, Al Simmons, George Sisler and Tris Speaker. Former Boston Red Sox star Ted Williams managed the Senators in their final three seasons (1969, 1970 and 1971).

Senators' history is divided into two phases: The original Senators played from 1901 through the 1960 season, moved to Minnesota, and became the Twins, the expansion Senators who replaced them in Washington for the 1961 season stayed through 1971 and then moved to Texas. Perennial American League home run leader Frank Howard was the team's outstanding star while pitcher Dick Bosman and reliever Darold Knowles were among the league's top pitchers several years. While people castigate Washington as being a poor baseball town, they should be aware the team had neither won a pennant since 1933 nor finished in the first division since 1946. Considering these facts, overall support for the team was remarkable.

Advertising Specialties

1888 Joseph Hall Cabinet Team Card,
    4½" × 6½" $2,200
1913 Fatima T200 Team Card, 2⅛" ×
    4¾" $100
1959 Bazooka Gum Felt Round $35

1938 pencil with Nationals' home
schedule, ¼″ × 7½″, $10.

1948 matchbook schedule for home games, red,
white, and blue, 1½″ × 4½″, $15.

1970 scarf with facsimile autographs of the Senators
surrounding the red, white, and blue Senators logo,
13¾″ × 13¾″, $20.

Miscellaneous

BOBBIN' HEAD DOLLS

Category #II, 1961, 1962, White Square
   Base, Boy Head $215
Category #III, 1961, 1962, White Round
   Miniature, Boy Head $230
Category #IV, 1962, 1963, 1964, Green
   Round Base, Boy Head $165
Category #V, 1962, 1963, 1964, Green
   Round Base, Black Player $650
Category #VI, 1967 through 1972, Gold
   Round Base, Boy Head $80

Pennants

1901 through 1920 ....$750
1921 through 1924 Regular...................$300
1924 World Champs $750
1925 Regular $300
1925 League Champs $750
1926 through 1930 ....$300
1931 through 1937 Regular..................$200
1936, 1937 Felt Pennant-BF3, Type V, Bat
   on Pennant $35
1936, 1937 Felt Pennant-BF3, Type V,
   Capitol Building on Pennant $35
1938, 1939, 1940 ....$200
1941 through 1950 ....$100
1951 through 1956 Regular $50
1956 All-Star Game $125
1957, 1958, 1959 ....$50
1960, 1961, 1962 Regular $30
1962 All-Star Game $75
1963 through 1969 Regular $30
1969 All-Star Game $75
1970 ....$30
1971 ....$20

Pins

1930/1940s American Nut & Chocolate
   Co., 1⅛″, Round $15
1961 through 1965 Crane Potato Chips,
   ⅞″, Round $5
1967 through 1969 Crane Potato Chips,
   ⅞″, Round $5
1964 through 1966 Guy's Potato Chips,
   ⅞″, Round $5

Postcards

1951 CH, Eastern Air Advertising, Washington, D.C. $150

1925 Senators pennant for the defending world champions, who repeated as American League champions but lost to the Pittsburgh Pirates in a seven game World Series, 11″ × 27¼″, $750.

THE 1951 WASHINGTON SENATORS

1951 black-and-white postcard of the Senators who finished 7th in the American League, 3½″ × 4″, $150.

1964 pin, ⅞″, red, white, and blue, issued by Guy's Potato Chips, who did pins for all 16 Major League teams. When a complete set was acquired, it could be traded to the company for a regulation baseball, $5.

Publications

BOOKS

Bealle, Morris. *The Washington Senators.* Columbia Publishing Co., 1947. ....$100.00

Povich, Shirley. *The Washington Senators.* G.P. Putnam's Sons, 1948. ....$100.00
Price, Brian. *Rounding Third: Professional Baseball In Washington.* Walnut Creek, Ca.: Preservation Press, 1979. ....$25.00

MEDIA GUIDES

1928 Roster Sheet	$125
1929, 1930, 1931 Roster Sheet	$100
1932 Roster Booklet	$125
1933 Roster Booklet League Champs	$115
1934, 1935 Roster Booklet	$100
1936 through 1940	$75
1941 through 1949	$60
1950 through 1955	$50
1956 through 1961	$40
1962, 1963, 1964	$30
1965, 1966	$20
1967, 1968	$17
1969, 1970	$15
1971	$12

PROGRAMS AND SCORECARDS

1901	$600
1902	$400
1903, 1904	$300
1905 through 1909	$200

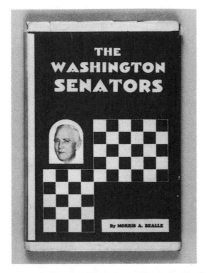

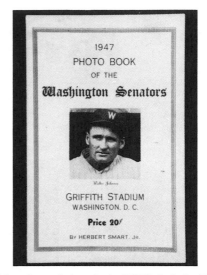

1947, *The Washington Senators* by Morris Bealle, Columbia Publishing Co., 1947, 196 pages, 6½″ × 9¼″, history of Washington baseball from 1867 through 1946, $100.

Extremely rare first yearbook, *1947 Photo Book of the Washington Senators,* Senator immortal Walter Johnson on the cover, photos and sketches of all the players and coaches, 5½″ × 8¾″, 14 pages, $400.

1910 through 1914	$150
1915 through 1920	$125
1921 through 1923	$75
1924 World Champs	$85
1925 League Champs	$85
1926 through 1930	$50
1931, 1932	$35
1933 League Champs	$40
1934 through 1940	$35
1941 through 1949	$20
1950 through 1959	$15
1960 through 1969	$10
1970, 1971	$6

Schedules

1901 through 1909	$150
1910 through J19	$100
1920 through 1929	$75
1930 through 1939	$45
1940 through 1949	$30

YEARBOOKS

1947	$400
1949	$350
1950	$300
1952	$100
1953 (very easy to obtain)	$40
1954	$70
1955	$65
1956, 1957, 1958	$60
1959, 1960	$55
1961 Expansion	$100
1962	$50
1963	$40
1964	$35
1965	$30
1966, 1967	$25
1968	$20
1969, 1970, 1971	None Issued

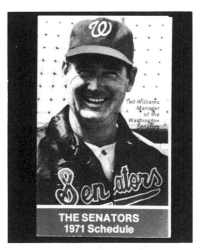

1971 Senators schedule, Ted Williams on the front, their final season in the American League, 2½″ × 4″, $20.

1950 through 1959	$25
1960	$15
1961	$35
1962 through 1968	$15
1969 Ted Williams 1st Year as Manager	$20
1970	$10
1971 Last Year	$15

Special Events

ALL-STAR GAME PRESS PINS

1937	None Issued
1956	$200
1962	$200
1969	$75

1956 press pin, ¾″ × 1″, All-Star game at Griffith Stadium honoring long-time Senators' owner Clark Griffith the previous year. Griffith's likeness is on the pin in bas relief, $200.

ALL-STAR PROGRAMS

1937	$600
1956	$150
1962	$100
1969	$75

ALL-STAR GAME TICKETS

1937 Complete Ticket	$400
1937 Ticket Stub	$200
1956 Complete Ticket	$150
1956 Ticket Stub	$75
1962 Complete Ticket	$75

1962 Ticket Stub	$35
1969 Complete Ticket	$75
1969 Ticket Stub	$35

WORLD SERIES PRESS PINS

1924	$500
1925	$500
1933	$500

WORLD SERIES PROGRAMS

1924	$1,000
1925	$750
1933	$600

1925 World Series program vs. the Pittsburgh Pirates with Senators Manager Bucky Harris and Pirates Manager Bill McKechnie on the cover, 8″ × 10½″, 64 pages, $750.

WORLD SERIES GAME TICKETS

1924 Complete Ticket	$800
1924 Ticket Stub	$400
1925 Complete Ticket	$800
1925 Ticket Stub	$400
1933 Complete Ticket	$400
1933 Ticket Stub	$200

Wilmington, Delaware

WILMINGTON QUICKSTEPS

Union Association 1884

The debut of Wilmington, Delaware, as a major league city began late and ended early. After dominating the Eastern League with a record of 49 wins and only 12 losses, the Wilmington Quicksteps jumped to the Union Association in late August 1884. The Quicksteps replaced the Philadelphia Keystones, who dropped out of the league after compiling a record of 21 wins and 46 losses. The Quicksteps fared even worse, winning only two games and losing 16 before disbanding. Wilmington's franchise was transferred to St. Paul, Minnesota, which finished the first and only season of the Union Association.

Obviously a woeful ball club, the Quicksteps did not have one player hit .300 during their 18 games. Outfielder Tom Lynch, who batted .313 in 13 games with the Keystones, compiled a team-leading .276 average with the Quicksteps. Lynch played in 13 games with the Philadelphia National League club in 1885, where his major league career ended.

The Quicksteps' second leading batter was pitcher Edward Sylvester "The Only" Nolan, who batted .273 and won one game while losing four. He played five seasons in the majors, and his win-loss record (23–52) was far outshone by his .240 batting average.

Second baseman Charley Bastian, who batted only .200 for Wilmington, had the longest major league tenure of any Quickstep player but batted only .189 during his eight-year career. Catcher Tony Cusick played four years in the majors with a career .193 batting average, and shortstop Henry Myers batted .174 over three major league seasons.

The Quicksteps were a losing venture from the start. Even while dominating the Eastern League with their 49–12 record, they averaged crowds of only 400 at home and lost $3,000. Their ill-fated Union Association venture cost them an additional $1500 before they decided enough was enough.

Because of the team's brief lifespan, any collectibles, such as scorecards or ticket stubs, would be extremely scarce. Anyone acquiring memorabilia from the 1884 Quicksteps must bear in mind that they were in the Eastern League most of the year, so any material from that portion of the season would be considerably less rare than that from their time in the Union Association.

Obviously no Wilmington Quicksteps are in the Hall of Fame and for further reading on Wilmington's short lived major league tenure see *Baseball 1845–1891 from the Newspaper Accounts* by Preston D. Orem.

Worcester, Massachusetts

WORCESTER RUBY LEGS

National League 1880–1882

Worcester, Massachusetts, had a National League team from 1880 through 1882 known as the Ruby Legs. After a fifth-place finish in 1880, the Ruby Legs finished last in the eight-team league in both 1881 and 1882 and faded into oblivion. An example of the team's futility: Only two players, Buttercup Dickerson (.316) and Pete Hotaling (.309), ever batted above .300, and both did it in 1881. The largest attendance for a Ruby Legs game was on Memorial Day 1881, when 3,652 fans turned out.

Entering the 1882 season Worcester proudly announced that the franchise was solvent, with a cash balance of $1,581.92 and all bills paid. However, their record on the field was abysmal. At the end of July they had won only 11 games against 40 losses. To further emphasize the futility of the Ruby Legs, seventh-place Troy had won 24 and lost 27 through July.

Worcester's most consistent player during their final major league season was first baseman Harry Stovey, who batted .289. He went on to play 14 seasons in the big leagues and wound up with a .288 BA. In 1890 with the Boston Reds of the Players League, he led the league in stolen bases. Ruby Legs catcher Doc Bushong, although never a robust hitter (.214 in 12 seasons), stayed in the big leagues because of his excellent defensive abilities.

In 1882, Worcester went through three managers—Freeman Brown, Tommy Bond, and Jack Chapman—hoping to find the right combination. Nothing worked, and the team finished the season with only 18 wins and 66 defeats. Thirty-three of those losses were pinned on lefthander Lee Richmond, who had pitched a perfect game against Cleveland in 1880 while winning 32 games and losing 32.

Worcester was averaging only 200 spectators per game in 1882, and visiting clubs were not making expenses when they played there. The National League long coveted franchises in New York and Philadelphia, and on September 22 a special meeting was held in Philadelphia to force Worcester and Troy officials to resign the league. The final indignity came in the final game of the season at Worcester, when the Ruby Legs lost to Troy 4 to 1. Gross receipts from the game totaled only $3, lowest in major league history.

Publications

YEARBOOKS

1880 Ups & Downs of the Worcester Baseball Club by F.E. Pollard (Review of 1880 Season) **$2,500**

Index